Oracle9i
XML Handbook

ORACLE® *Oracle Press*™

Oracle9*i*
XML Handbook

Ben Chang,
Mark Scardina,
Stefan Kiritzov

Osborne/**McGraw-Hill**

New York   Chicago   San Francisco
Lisbon   London   Madrid   Mexico City   Milan
New Delhi   San Juan   Seoul   Singapore   Sydney   Toronto

Osborne/**McGraw-Hill**
2600 Tenth Street
Berkeley, California 94710
U.S.A.

To arrange bulk purchase discounts for sales promotions, premiums, or fund-raisers, please
contact Osborne/**McGraw-Hill** at the above address. For information on translations or book
distributors outside the U.S.A., please see the International Contact Information page immediately
following the index of this book.

Oracle9*i* XML Handbook

234567890 CUS CUS 0198765432
Book p/n 0-07-213496-8 and CD p/n 0-07-213497-6
parts of
ISBN 0-07-213495-X

Publisher
Brandon A. Nordin

Vice President & Associate Publisher
Scott Rogers

Acquisitions Editor
Jeremy Judson

Project Editor
Jennifer Malnick

Acquisitions Coordinator
Jessica Wilson and Athena Honore

Technical Editors
Jinyu Wang and Bernd Rintelmann

Copy Editor
Robert Campbell

Proofreader
Susie Elkind

Indexer
Jack Lewis

Computer Designers
Roberta Steele, George Charbak, Tabitha Cagan

Illustrators
Lyssa Wald, Michael Mueller

Series Design
Damore Johnson Design, Inc.

Cover Designer
Sarah Hinks

This book was composed with Corel VENTURA™ Publisher.

To our families for their support

About the Authors

Ben Chang is a 12-year veteran at Oracle Corporation, where he heads the CORE and XML Development Group in the Server Technologies Division as Director. In addition to working on Oracle6 to Oracle9i releases, he served the longest tenure as Development Release Manager for Oracle 8.0, spanning five releases. He also served three years as Chair of the Oracle C Coding Standards Committee, has given XML presentations at a number of conferences on five continents, and is a W3C DOM Working Group Committee member. He previously worked at IBM Corp., Pacific Bell, Bellcore, and GE R&D. He holds an M.S. in Electrical Engineering (Computer Systems) from Stanford University and a B.S. in Electrical Engineering and Computer Science from U.C. Berkeley.

Mark Scardina is Oracle's XML Evangelist for Server products. He is also the Group Product Manager for the CORE and XML Development Group, which is tasked with providing the XML infrastructure components used throughout the Oracle product stack, including the XML Developer's Kits. Mark represents Oracle on the W3C XSL Working Group. He has worked for Socket Communications and ACE Technologies and holds a B.S. in Information Systems Management from the University of San Francisco.

Stefan Kiritzov is a Development Manager in the CRM Technology &Architecture group at Oracle, and has 19 years' experience in developing system software. Before joining Oracle, he worked for AT&T, NCR, SHL Systemhouse, and ICT. He holds an M.S. and B.S. in Mathematics from Kliment Ohridsky University in Bulgaria.

Contents at a Glance

Contents

Acknowledgments

The authors would like to thank Philip Greenspun, the inspiration for the first edition of this book; supportive Oracle management in Roger Choplin, Juan Loaiza, Chuck Rozwat, and, ultimately, Larry Ellison; the hard-working Oracle Press editorial team of Jeremy Judson, Jenny Malnick, Jessica Wilson, and Athena Honore, without whom the book would not have been possible; Jeremy Burton, for his unwavering enthusiasm; Jinyu Wang and Bernd Rintelmann, for their incisive comments; members of the CORE and XML Development, and other helpful Oracle employees; and, finally, our families, for their understanding and support.

Introduction

n March 1999, Philip Greenspun gave a talk at Oracle Corporation headquarters that inspired us to write the first edition of this book. His class covered the Internet, XML, how to create database-backed Web sites, why the usage of Oracle databases was so pervasive in the industry, and why he thought the people in Oracle's development groups should author more Oracle Press books. He especially harped on this last point in his joking and pointed manner.

We took it as a challenge and came up with a book outline about the XML work they were doing at Oracle; contacted Jeremy Judson at Oracle Press about writing such a book; signed the necessary contracts; committed to a schedule; e-mailed Philip about writing the foreword, to which he graciously agreed, stating enthusiastically, "Count me in!"; and started writing the chapters. We also tried to heed Philip's advice about organizing the book around problem areas, rather than technologies or bureaucracies.

Fast forward a year to mid 2000: We, having survived a truly adventurous experience in trying to keep to the book's schedule while putting in long hours at work at Oracle, finally put to bed the first edition of the Oracle XML Handbook. Truly an experience that none of us, our families, and the Oracle Press editors will forget! The fruits of this labor resulted in thousands of copies sold in countries across the world, translation into a number of languages, and the book being acclaimed with the "Best Book" XML-Journal award in 2000 by a vote of some 5,000 of its readers in the XML industry. In addition, more than $2000 was donated to the ArsDigita Foundation and America's Promise.

Fast forward another year to late 2001: We, having survived a less tumultuous experience in keeping to the second edition's book schedule, finally put to bed the industry updates and Oracle9i additions to this version. Our hope is that readers can benefit from the straightforward examples and learn about some of the latest Oracle XML features.

Long Live XML!

NOTE
*A portion of the book's sales will go to the ArsDigita Foundation and America's Promise to help support their worthy causes in trying to improve education. Their Web sites are **http://arsdigita.org** and **http:// www.americaspromise.org**, respectively.*

XML at Work

You are probably reading this book because you plan to use XML in a real-world application. This is good because XML is not an application but an enabling technology. To assist you in building XML-enabled applications, we have included many different application scenarios and specific code samples along with sample XML and XSL files where appropriate. You may use this code freely, and we hope it leads you to use XML effectively to significantly enhance your applications.

NOTE
*If you have comments about or any find mistakes with the book or CD, feel free to e-mail us at **oraclexmlhandbook@yahoo.com**.*

Intended Audience

This book is designed to be a user's guide to the Oracle XML components. It is not a complete reference as all of the component API documentation is available electronically and, if included, would easily double the size. The reference documentation is available on the Oracle Technology Network. This book is written for the programmer who either needs to begin using XML with Oracle for application development or for those readers interested in learning how XML is being used within Oracle products. While many of the examples use Java, much of the XML functionality can be experimented with using the component command-line interfaces and a simple text editor for XML, XSL, and XSQL files.

How to Use This Book

This book is not intended to be read in sequence. Chapters 1 and 2 are introductory material to XML and Oracle's XML technologies, so if you are already familiar with these, you can skip these chapters. For those interested in building XML-enabled Oracle9i database applications, Chapters 3, 7, 8, and 9 are recommended, along with Chapter 10, for in-depth explanations of the OTN applications. Chapters 4, 5, and 6 should be read if you plan on also using the Oracle Application Server, Internet File System, or Oracle Text. Chapter 11 gives our perspective on the future of XML. Finally, Appendix A goes over some of the basic W3C specifications, Appendix B covers the W3C XML specification, and Appendix C goes over additional W3C XML specifications. An overview of each of the chapters follows.

Chapter 1: Oracle and XML   Chapter 1 updates and introduces Oracle's efforts in the XML industry, explains XML basic concepts and terminology, XML's reason for existence, and Oracle's XML strategy in the industry. It also presents the Oracle Technology Network and its XML link, overviews of Oracle's XML-enabled products and XML components, and finally an example book-selling XML-enabled application.

Chapter 2: Oracle's XML CORE Technologies   This chapter updates and introduces the components of the Oracle XML Developer's Kit (XDK), reviews the Java/C/C++/PLSQL XML parsers and XSLT processors, the Java/C++ XML Schema Processors, the Java/C++ Class Generators, and the Java Transviewer Beans. Working sample code for accessing and manipulating XML/XSL files is also included.

Chapter 3: Developing for the Oracle9i Database   Chapter 3 updates and covers Oracle9i's built-in Java Virtual Machine and Oracle's Java XML components. It also focuses on how XML data can be saved in and retrieved from the database using the XDK's XSQL Servlet, and finally, the design and implementation of a book-selling XML-enabled application.

Chapter 4: Developing for Oracle Application Servers   This chapter updates and covers the Oracle Application Server architectures and its link to XML and the XDK components. It also includes the creation of a bookstore application as an Application Servlet.

Chapter 5: The Oracle Internet File System (iFS)   Chapter 5 updates and introduces Oracle's next generation file system (iFS). It covers its architecture, how it can act as an XML file system, and also how it uses XML internally for mapping a file's data to a relational schema. It also includes several Java code examples of common file operations.

Chapter 6: Searching XML Documents with Oracle Text   This chapter updates and covers Oracle 9i's text search engine, Oracle Text, reviewing its architecture, and its ability to search stored XML documents. The bookstore example is extended through sample code to create indexes and perform XML-based searches.

Chapter 7: Oracle E-Business XML Services   This new chapter explains an XML-based Services and Events framework that is used to develop, deploy, manage, and execute Web-based services for B2B application integration. It goes over the SOAP-based technology and explains how this framework is used by the Oracle e-Business Applications technology.

Chapter 8: Oracle and XML in Action   Chapter 8 updates and covers how the XML components can be assembled in end-to-end solutions. The design of an XML-enabled database application is presented, including an XML-powered Web site and a business-to-client messaging system. XML and XSL example files and sample code are all included.

Chapter 9: A Case Study Using Oracle's XML-Enabled Technology Stack   This new chapter explains in-depth how a powerful XML application, an FAQ application, could be built using Oracle's products, along with the code listings. The important capabilities of the XSLT processor, the XML Class Generator, the XSQL Servlet, the XML SQL Utility, Oracle Text, and the new XML datatypes and operators introduced in Oracle 9i are all illustrated with this application.

Chapter 10: XML-Based Applications Offered on OTN   This chapter updates and introduces the Oracle Technology Network's (OTN) XML Web site and its XML demos. It covers how these demos can be installed and run, including details on the specific XML features and capabilities each demonstrates.

Chapter 11: Future Trends   Chapter 11 updates and reviews the XML standards efforts of the W3C and OASIS and the future directions for XML based on the work of these organizations. It also looks at how XML and its related technologies are being used in several of the major companies in the XML industry.

Appendix A: W3C XML, DOM, SAX, and XSLT Specifications   Appendix A updates and covers the major XML specifications. It includes a discussion of the two W3C standards of XML document interfaces, DOM and SAX. It also covers the other associated XML technology standards of namespaces, XPath, and XSL Transformation.

Appendix B: W3C XML Schema Specifications   This new appendix gives a high-level overview of the new W3C XML Schema specifications and illustrates its usage in a number of examples.

Appendix C: Other W3C Specifications   Appendix C gives high-level overviews of the new W3C XML Query, XML Protocol and SOAP specifications, and illustrates their usage in a number of examples.

Glossary   The glossary contains a list of common XML terms and their definitions used throughout the book.

The Accompanying CD and Web Site

On the accompanying CD, you will find Oracle9i production versions of Oracle's XDK for Java, C, C++, and PL/SQL components, including the XML parser, XSL processor, TransViewer Java beans, and XSQL Servlet along with many illustrative demos. More recent versions of the Oracle XDK can also be downloaded for free from the OTN site.

The source code used in this book is also available for download from the Oracle Press Web site at **http://www.osborne.com/oracle**. You may also download the latest XML components and Oracle9i the Oracle Technology Network Web site at **http://technet.oracle.com/tech/xml**.

CHAPTER
1

Oracle and XML

xtensible Markup Language (XML) is a meta-markup language, meaning the language, as specified by the *World Wide Web Consortium's (W3C)* XML 1.0 specification, enables users to define their own markup languages to describe and encapsulate data into XML files. These files can then be displayed within browsers such as Netscape Navigator and Microsoft Internet Explorer, exchanged across the Internet between applications and businesses, or stored in and retrieved from databases. The power of XML comes from its simplicity, its being part of an open standard, and the incorporation of user-defined markup tags that lend semantics to the embedded data.

XML's origins come from the *Standard Generalized Markup Language (SGML)*— ratified by the *International Standards Organization (ISO)* in 1986—on which *Hypertext Markup Language (HTML)*, created in 1990, is based. While SGML is still a widely used standard in the document world, and HTML is still widely used as the basis of millions of Web pages on the World Wide Web, XML is rapidly gaining widespread acceptance because of its advantages in data exchange, storage, and description over the existing markup languages. Since the publication of its v1.0 specifications by the W3C in February 1998, XML has been widely seen as the language and data interchange of choice for e-commerce.

XML Basic Concepts and Terminology

As with any standard, numerous concepts and technical terms need to be explained. Because XML was developed to convey data, a relevant example is a data record of a book listing from a standard database. A complex SQL query would typically return data in this format:

```
History of Interviews, Juan, Smith, 99999-99999, Oracle Press, 2000.
```

If XML is used as the output form, however, this record now has additional context for each piece of data, as evidenced in the following:

```
<book>
    <title>History of Interviews</title>
    <author>
        <firstname>Juan</firstname>
        <lastname>Smith</lastname>
    </author>
    <ISBN>99999-99999</ISBN>
    <publisher>Oracle Press</publisher>
    <publishyear>2000</publishyear>
    <price type="US">1.00</price>
</book>
```

Certain items of note in this example are explored in detail later. Notice that the file has symmetry, and each piece of data has its context enclosing it in the form **<context> ... </context>**. The angle brackets and text inside are called *tags,* and each set of tags and its enclosed data is called an *element.* This relationship can be thought of as similar to a column in a database table in which the text of the tag is the column heading and the text between the tags is the data from a row in that column. In the preceding example, "title" could be the name of the column and "History of Interviews" could be the data in a row.

Notice, too, that several tags contain tags instead of data. This is a significant feature of XML, which permits nesting of data to define relationships better. Returning to the database metaphor, the **<author>** tag could be modeled as a table whose columns were **<firstname>** and **<lastname>**. In XML terminology, these column tags are referred to as *children* of the *parent* **author** tag.

Now look at the **<price>** tag and you see it includes text of the form name="value". These name-value pairs are called *attributes,* and one or more of these can be included in the start tag. Attributes are not legal in end tags (for example, **</tag name="foo">**).

One final terminology note: the entire XML example is enclosed by **<book>... </book>**. These tags are defined as the *root* of the document, and only one may exist. XML documents that follow these rules of only having one root and all open tags properly closed are considered *well-formed.*

XML's basic concepts and terminology are straightforward and are formalized in an open Internet standard. As the W3C XML 1.0 specification states, "XML documents are made up of storage units called *entities,* which contain either parsed data or unparsed data. *Parsed data* is made up of characters, some of which form character data and some form markup. *Markup* encodes a description of the document's storage layout and logical structure." XML documents have both physical and logical structure. The *physical structure* of the XML document simply refers to the XML file and the other files which it may import, whereas the *logical structure* of an XML document refers to the prolog and the body of the document.

The XML of the **book** example represents the body of an XML document, but it is missing important information that helps identify its nature. This information is in the prolog, defined in the following section.

Prolog

The *prolog* consists of the XML declaration, that is, the version number; a possible language encoding; other attributes (name="value" pairs); and an optional *document type definition (DTD),* which may be an internal one contained in the XML document or an external DTD referred to in a separate file. For example:

```
<?xml version="1.0" encoding="UTF-8" standalone="no" ?>
<!DOCTYPE book SYSTEM "book.dtd">
```

Note that a line that has **<? ... ?>** is an example of an XML *processing instruction (PI)*, which is discussed later in the chapter. In this example, xml is the name of the XML PI. In addition, the character set encoding supported in the example is a compressed version of Unicode called UTF-8. Finally, the stand-alone attribute refers to whether the processor needs to include or import other external files.

The second line of the prolog refers to a *DOCTYPE*. This is where the declaration of the data model for this XML document is done. Why is this important? Remember, an XML file has both physical and logical representations. In some applications, it may be sufficient to process the XML without knowing whether information is missing, but most of the time, an application wants to validate the XML document it receives. To do this, the application must know what elements are required, which ones can have children, which ones can have attributes, and so forth. In XML terms, the data model is referred to as the *document type definition (DTD)*. This DTD can be contained within the XML file itself or simply referred to in order, so the processor can locate it.

Document Type Definition (DTD)

DTDs come to XML by way of SGML; they are not in XML syntax. The work done by the W3C Working Group XML Schema defines a new type of model definition using XML syntax and extends the functionality of the DTD to support data types. In the preceding example, the DTD is contained in an external file. It could have also been indicated through a *uniform resource locator (URL)* of the form **http:// www .foobar.com/book.dtd**. Or, it could have been declared internally in the XML file. For example, within the XML file itself, the declaration could have looked like the following:

```
<!-- DTD bookcatalog may have a number of book entries -->
<!DOCTYPE bookcatalog [
<!ELEMENT bookcatalog (book)*>
<!-- Each book element has a title, 1 or more authors, etc. -->
<!ELEMENT book (title, author+, ISBN, publisher, publishyear, price)>
<!ELEMENT title (#PCDATA)>
<!ELEMENT author (firstname, lastname)>
<!ELEMENT firstname (#PCDATA)>
<!ELEMENT lastname (#PCDATA)>
<!ELEMENT ISBN (#PCDATA)>
<!ELEMENT publisher (#PCDATA)>
<!ELEMENT publishyear (#PCDATA)>
<!ELEMENT price (#PCDATA)>
<!ATTLIST price type (US|CAN|UK|EURO) #REQUIRED>
]>
```

Following the **DOCTYPE** declaration of the DTD is the root element declaration, **<!ELEMENT>** of **bookcatalog**. An element simply consists of a start tag, for example, **<foo>**; all of the text in between; and the corresponding end tag, for example, **</foo>**. Only one root element, however, may exist within an XML document. The root element marks the beginning of the document and is considered the parent of all the other elements, which are nested within its start tag and end tag. For XML documents to be considered "valid" with respect to this DTD, the root element **bookcatalog** must be the first element to start off the body of the XML document.

Following this is the *element declaration*, which stipulates the child elements that must be nested within the root element **bookcatalog**, the content model for the root element. Note that all the child elements of **bookcatalog** are explicitly called out in its element declaration, and **author** has a **+** as a suffix. This is an example of the *Extended Backus-Naur Format (EBNF)* that can be used for describing the content model. The allowed suffixes are

- **?**   For 0 or 1 occurrence
- *****   For 0 or more occurrences
- **+**   For 1 or more occurrences

Note also the use of **#PCDATA** to declare that the element text must be non-marked-up text, and the price's required attribute values are explicitly declared. The difference between **CDATA** and **PCDATA** is that **CDATA** sections are simply skipped by the parser and aren't checked for well-formedness; hence, they can be viewed as "non-Parsed Character DATA."

Thus, a validating XML parser, by parsing the XML document according to the rules specified in the DTD, tries to determine whether the document conforms to the DTD (valid), in that the structural relationships and sequences are the same.

Body of Document

The prolog precedes the root element, which contains the remainder of the XML document. The remainder of the XML document is composed of elements, processing instructions, content, attributes, comments, entity references, and so forth. As previously mentioned, elements must have start tags and corresponding end tags nested in the correct order; otherwise, the XML document is not *well-formed,* and XML parsers may signal errors because of this. Elements can also have attributes, or name-value pairs, such as **<author firstname="Juan" lastname="Smith">**. Built-in attributes defined by the XML 1.0 specification also exist, such as **xml:space="preserve"** to indicate that the data between the elements be represented preserving white space.

Entity references are similar to macros in that entities are defined once, and references to them, such as **&*nameofentity*,** can be used in place of their entire definitions. For example, **<!ENTITY Copyright "Copyright 2000 by Smith, Jones, and Doe – All rights reserved">** could be declared; thus, **&Copyright;** could be used as a shortcut throughout the XML document. An XML parser must recognize entities defined in DTDs, even though the validity check may be turned off. Again, built-in entities also exist as defined by the XML 1.0 specifications, such as those for the ampersand, **&amp**; apostrophe, **&apos**; less than, **<** and so forth. Comments are recognized when they are enclosed in the **<!-- -->** construct.

Some additional basic terminology associated with XML parser *application programming interfaces (APIs)* can be categorized as belonging to the following areas:

- Document Object Model (DOM)

- Simple API for XML (SAX)

- Namespaces

- Parser

- Extensible Stylesheet Language Transformation (XSLT)

- XML Schema

For the most part, these APIs are stipulated by the W3C specifications, so application developers can use standard programming interfaces. Note that if some functionality is not specified, vendors may decide to implement their own enhancements to the specifications.

Document Object Model (DOM) APIs

The XML document is structured in the sense that start tags have corresponding end tags, and these tags are nested in an ordered fashion. Because of this structure, the XML document can be viewed as a tree whose nodes consist of these tags, as well as information between and corresponding to these tags. Indeed, when the XML parser parses the XML document, a parse tree representation of the XML document can be formed in memory, which is referred to as a *Document Object Model (DOM)*.

The W3C has created a set of DOM APIs for accessing and navigating this tree. The components of this tree are the root element of the document, child and sibling nodes, elements, attributes, and text nodes that represent the textual content of an element or attribute. Other components include character data (CDATA) sections to mark off blocks of text that would otherwise be regarded as markup, comments, entity references, processing instructions, and so forth. XML parsers that provide all the DOM APIs are said to be compliant with the W3C DOM recommendation.

The following Java code sample demonstrates a simple use of the parser and DOM APIs. The XML file given to the application is parsed, and the element nodes and attribute values in the document are printed. Finally, the use of setting the parser options is demonstrated.

```java
import java.io.*;
import java.net.*;
import org.w3c.dom.*;
import org.w3c.dom.Node;

import oracle.xml.parser.v2.*;

public class DOMSample
{
    static public void main(String[] argv)
    {
        try
        {
            if (argv.length != 1)
            {
                // Must pass in the name of the XML file.
                System.err.println("Usage: java DOMSample filename");
                System.exit(1);
            }

            // Get an instance of the parser
            DOMParser parser = new DOMParser();

            // Generate a URL from the filename.
            URL url = createURL(argv[0]);

            // Set various parser options: validation on,
            // warnings shown, error stream set to stderr.
            parser.setErrorStream(System.err);
            parser.setValidationMode(true);
            parser.showWarnings(true);

            // Parse the document.
            parser.parse(url);

            // Obtain the document.
            XMLDocument doc = parser.getDocument();
```

```java
      // Print document elements
      System.out.print("The elements are: ");
      printElements(doc);

      // Print document element attributes
      System.out.println("The attributes of each element are: ");
      printElementAttributes(doc);
   }
   catch (Exception e)
   {
      System.out.println(e.toString());
   }
}

static void printElements(Document doc)
{
   NodeList nl = doc.getElementsByTagName("*");
   Node n;

   for (int i=0; i<nl.getLength(); i++)
   {
      n = nl.item(i);
      System.out.print(n.getNodeName() + " ");
   }

   System.out.println();
}

static void printElementAttributes(Document doc)
{
   NodeList nl = doc.getElementsByTagName("*");
   Element e;
   Node n;
   NamedNodeMap nnm;

   String attrname;
   String attrval;
   int i, len;

   len = nl.getLength();

   for (int j=0; j < len; j++)
   {
```

```
            e = (Element)nl.item(j);
            System.out.println(e.getTagName() + ":");
            nnm = e.getAttributes();

            if (nnm != null)
            {
                for (i=0; i<nnm.getLength(); i++)
                {
                    n = nnm.item(i);
                    attrname = n.getNodeName();
                    attrval = n.getNodeValue();
                    System.out.print(" " + attrname + " = " + attrval);
                }
            }
            System.out.println();
        }
    }

    static URL createURL(String fileName)
    {
        URL url = null;
        try
        {
            url = new URL(fileName);
        }
        catch (MalformedURLException ex)
        {
            try
            {

                File f = new File(filename);

                url = f.toURL();
            }
            catch (MalformedURLException e)
            {
                System.out.println("Cannot create url for: " + fileName);
                System.exit(0);
            }
        }
        return url;
    }
}
```

Simple API for XML (SAX) APIs

Simple API for XML (SAX) is a standard interface for event-based XML parsing. This means that notification of certain events and data encountered during the parsing of the XML document can be reported by callback functions to the application program. On notification of these events, the application program then must deal with them. For example, the application program can have data structures using *callback event handlers.* Finally, the types of information and notifications passed back by these callback functions are in the vein of such things as the start and end of elements and information related to an element's content, such as CDATA, processing instructions, and/or sub-elements.

SAX, initially developed by David Megginson, has become a W3C XML standard. One advantage of using SAX parsing over using the DOM is that an in-memory representation of the parse tree doesn't have to be built, thus saving memory and resulting in better performance for certain types of operations, such as searching. On the other hand, modifying, updating, and performing other structural operations may be made more efficient by using a DOM Parser.

The following code sample demonstrates a simple use of the parser and SAX API. The XML file given to the application is parsed and prints some information about the contents of this file. Sample code of various useful interfaces is also provided.

```java
import org.xml.sax.*;
import java.io.*;
import java.net.*;
import oracle.xml.parser.v2.*;

public class SAXSample extends HandlerBase
{
    // Store the locator
    Locator locator;

    static public void main(String[] argv)
    {
        try
        {
            if (argv.length != 1)
            {
                // Must pass in the name of the XML file.
                System.err.println("Usage: SAXSample filename");
                System.exit(1);
```

```
        }
        // Create a new handler for the parser
        SAXSample sample = new SAXSample();

        // Get an instance of the parser
        Parser parser = new SAXParser();

        // Set Handlers in the parser
        parser.setDocumentHandler(sample);
        parser.setEntityResolver(sample);
        parser.setDTDHandler(sample);
        parser.setErrorHandler(sample);

        // Convert file to URL and parse
        try
        {
            parser.parse(fileToURL(new File(argv[0])).toString());
        }
        catch (SAXParseException e)
        {
            System.out.println(e.getMessage());
        }
        catch (SAXException e)
        {
            System.out.println(e.getMessage());
        }
    }
    catch (Exception e)
    {
        System.out.println(e.toString());
    }
}

static URL fileToURL(File file)
{
    String path = file.getAbsolutePath();
    String fSep = System.getProperty("file.separator");
    if (fSep != null && fSep.length() == 1)
        path = path.replace(fSep.charAt(0), '/');
    if (path.length() > 0 && path.charAt(0) != '/')
        path = '/' + path;
```

```
s       try
        {
            return new URL("file", null, path);
        }
        catch (java.net.MalformedURLException e)
        {
            throw new Error("unexpected MalformedURLException");
        }
    }
//////////////////////////////////////////////////////////////////
// Sample implementation of DocumentHandler interface.
//////////////////////////////////////////////////////////////////

    public void setDocumentLocator (Locator locator)
    {
        System.out.println("SetDocumentLocator:");
        this.locator = locator;
    }

    public void startDocument()
    {
        System.out.println("StartDocument");
    }

    public void endDocument() throws SAXException
    {
        System.out.println("EndDocument");
    }

    public void startElement(String name, AttributeList atts)
                                                    throws SAXException
    {
        System.out.println("StartElement:"+name);
        for (int i=0;i<atts.getLength();i++)
        {
            String aname = atts.getName(i);
            String type = atts.getType(i);
            String value = atts.getValue(i);

            System.out.println("   "+aname+"("+type+")"+"="+value);
```

```java
    }

}

public void endElement(String name) throws SAXException
{
    System.out.println("EndElement:"+name);
}

public void characters(char[] cbuf, int start, int len)
{
    System.out.print("Characters:");
    System.out.println(new String(cbuf,start,len));
}

public void ignorableWhitespace(char[] cbuf, int start, int len)
{
    System.out.println("IgnorableWhiteSpace");
}


public void processingInstruction(String target, String data)
        throws SAXException
{
    System.out.println("ProcessingInstruction:"+target+" "+data);
}

//////////////////////////////////////////////////////////////////////
// Sample implementation of the EntityResolver interface.
//////////////////////////////////////////////////////////////////////

public InputSource resolveEntity (String publicId, String systemId)
        throws SAXException
{
    System.out.println("ResolveEntity:"+publicId+" "+systemId);
    System.out.println("Locator:"+locator.getPublicId()+" "+
                        locator.getSystemId()+
                        " "+locator.getLineNumber()+" "
                        +locator.getColumnNumber());
    return null;
}
```

```
//////////////////////////////////////////////////////////////////
// Sample implementation of the DTDHandler interface.
//////////////////////////////////////////////////////////////////

    public void notationDecl (String name, String publicId,
                              String systemId)
    {
    System.out.println("NotationDecl:"+name+" "+publicId+" "+systemId);
    }

    public void unparsedEntityDecl (String name, String publicId,
                                    String systemId, String notationName)
    {
    System.out.println("UnparsedEntityDecl:"+name + " "+publicId+" "+
                    systemId+" "+notationName);
    }

//////////////////////////////////////////////////////////////////
// Sample implementation of the ErrorHandler interface.
//////////////////////////////////////////////////////////////////

    public void warning (SAXParseException e)
            throws SAXException
    {
       System.out.println("Warning:"+e.getMessage());
    }

    public void error (SAXParseException e)
            throws SAXException
    {
       throw new SAXException(e.getMessage());
    }

    public void fatalError (SAXParseException e)
            throws SAXException
    {
       System.out.println("Fatal error");
       throw new SAXException(e.getMessage());
    }
}
```

Namespace APIs

These interfaces give information relating to the XML document namespaces identified by *Uniform Resource Identifier (URI)* references that qualify element and attribute names and locate resources that could be on different machines or XML documents, and so forth. Namespaces can allow for identical names for elements and attributes if the latter are qualified with URIs to differentiate the names. For example, **foo:hello** is called a qualified name, with the namespace prefix **foo** mapped to the URI, **www.oracle.com**, and the local part being **hello**. Note that URI references can contain characters not allowed in names; that is why **foo** serves as a substitute for the URI.

The following code sample demonstrates a simple use of the parser and namespace extensions to the DOM API. The XML file given to the application, along with the elements and attributes, is printed.

```java
import java.io.*;
import java.net.*;
import oracle.xml.parser.v2.DOMParser;
import org.w3c.dom.*;
import org.w3c.dom.Node;

// Extensions to DOM Interfaces for Namespace support.
import oracle.xml.parser.v2.XMLElement;
import oracle.xml.parser.v2.XMLAttr;

public class DOMNamespace
{
    static public void main(String[] argv)
    {
        try
        {
            if (argv.length != 1)
            {
                // Must pass in the name of the XML file.
                System.err.println("Usage: DOMNamespace filename");
                System.exit(1);
            }

            // Get an instance of the parser
            Class cls = Class.forName("oracle.xml.parser.v2.DOMParser");
            DOMParser parser = (DOMParser)cls.newInstance();
```

```
        // Generate a URL from the filename.
        URL url = createURL(argv[0]);

        // Parse the document.
        parser.parse(url);

        // Obtain the document.
        Document doc = parser.getDocument();

        // Print document elements
        printElements(doc);

        // Print document element attributes
        System.out.println("The attributes of each element are: ");
        printElementAttributes(doc);
    }
    catch (Exception e)
    {
        System.out.println(e.toString());
    }
}

static void printElements(Document doc)
{
    NodeList nl = doc.getElementsByTagName("*");
    XMLElement nsElement;

    String qName;
    String localName;
    String nsName;
    String expName;

    System.out.println("The elements are: ");
    for (int i=0; i < nl.getLength(); i++)
    {
        nsElement = (XMLElement)nl.item(i);

    // Use the methods getQualifiedName(), getLocalName(), getNamespace()
        // and getExpandedName() in NSName interface to get Namespace
        // information.
        qName = nsElement.getQualifiedName();
        System.out.println("  ELEMENT Qualified Name:" + qName);
```

```
        localName = nsElement.getLocalName();
        System.out.println("  ELEMENT Local Name    :" + localName);

        nsName = nsElement.getNamespace();
        System.out.println("  ELEMENT Namespace     :" + nsName);

        expName = nsElement.getExpandedName();
        System.out.println("  ELEMENT Expanded Name :" + expName);
    }

    System.out.println();
}

static void printElementAttributes(Document doc)
{
    NodeList nl = doc.getElementsByTagName("*");
    Element e;

    XMLAttr nsAttr;

    String attrname;
    String attrval;
    String attrqname;

    NamedNodeMap nnm;
    int i, len;

    len = nl.getLength();

    for (int j=0; j < len; j++)
    {
        e = (Element) nl.item(j);
        System.out.println(e.getTagName() + ":");

        nnm = e.getAttributes();

        if (nnm != null)
        {
            for (i=0; i < nnm.getLength(); i++)
            {
                nsAttr = (XMLAttr) nnm.item(i);

                // Use the methods getQualifiedName(), getLocalName(),
```

```
                    // getNamespace() and getExpandedName() in NSName
                    // interface to get Namespace information.

                    attrname = nsAttr.getExpandedName();
                    attrqname = nsAttr.getQualifiedName();
                    attrval = nsAttr.getNodeValue();

                    System.out.println(" " + attrqname + "(" + attrname +
                                        ")" + " = "+attrval);
                }
            }
            System.out.println();
        }
    }

    static URL createURL(String fileName)
    {
        URL url = null;
        try
        {
            url = new URL(fileName);
        }
        catch (MalformedURLException ex)
        {

            try {
                File f = new File(fileName);
                url = f.toURL();
            }
            catch (MalformedURLException e)
            {
                System.out.println("Cannot create url for: " + fileName);
                System.exit(0);
            }
        }
        return url;
    }
}
```

Parser APIs

Application programs invoke the parse API to read an XML document and provide access to its content and structure by DOM or SAX APIs. Usually, initialization and termination functions must also be invoked in association with the parse function. Note that various flags, such as to discard white space and to turn on validation, can be set with some initialization functions before the parse function is invoked by the application program. For example, while some XML parsers are only nonvalidating, meaning they cannot check to see whether the XML document conforms to the DTD, other parsers (such as those from Oracle) have optional validation, meaning users can specify validation or nonvalidation before invoking the parse function. In addition, the parse routine must be able to accept different language encodings as specified in the XML document.

Extensible Stylesheet Language Transformation (XSLT) APIs

If transformation or formatting of XML documents is required, the W3C has the *Extensible Stylesheet Language Transformation (XSLT)* recommendation that allows for the application of stylesheets, written in user-defined XML and XSLT tags/ functions, to XML documents by an XSLT processor. Essentially, what this XSLT processor does is correlate patterns in the stylesheet within the XML document, and then apply commands—for example, HTML tags to surround data found—and output the results as a separate XML document. To continue the preceding example, using an XSLT processor, the book's **<title>** tag can be "matched" through a stylesheet function and then have bold HTML tags, for example, **<B>** and **</B>**, applied to the data, resulting in another XML document that will have the HTML bold tags surrounding the book title data. The APIs for the application of stylesheets to XML files are relatively straightforward, and some XML parsers, such as Oracle's, incorporate an XSLT processor—the transformation APIs are relatively few.

XML Schema APIs

The W3C now has the XML Schema Recommendation, which allows simple and complex datatypes to be specified for constructs such as document elements and nodes. Previously, with just a DTD, only string datatypes were allowed to describe elements that were plainly of a real or integer datatype value, as an example. Now *long, short, int,* and other traditional datatypes are allowed to be embedded in the content model for a document, along with *facets* such as maximum and minimum values, to restrict the data. To validate a document against an XML Schema, only an extra API or two need be added to the application program, along with the necessary changes to the XML document that will conform to the XML Schema.

Why XML?

Created correctly, an XML document is easy to read and understand. The tags associated with the data, for example, **<author><first name>Juan</first name></author>**, lend meaning to the data so that it can easily be understood. One consequence of this is that searches can be done more efficiently on the Internet if Web pages are in XML format. Not only can data be searched for, but the context associated with the data can also be added to the search, thereby enabling a more precise mechanism for searching. In addition, if the tags associated with the data have sufficient semantics associated with them, an end user ten years from now could probably understand the XML document without much of a problem, unlike with some other document formats.

Another big advantage of XML is based on the open standards created by the W3C. Thus, no company can hijack the standards and hold other companies captive to what it has created. If other companies want certain functionality, the W3C working group committees, composed of member representatives of companies in the industry, meet and discuss the relevance and add functionality as needed. If companies do not want to wait until the W3C takes action, then they may proceed to try implementing functionality not currently specified. Such companies take the risk that end consumers of this functionality may not adopt such extensions, however, because they have not been introduced by the W3C. Eventually, these companies need to make modifications to this functionality, and in the end, formally introducing these extensions to the W3C so that everyone can benefit works to their advantage.

Because XML documents are simple to create, easy to understand, and based on open standards, you can imagine the wide variety of XML-based applications that are being built currently. These applications deal with XML-based e-books or e-magazines, or any documents that need to be stored and interchanged with other applications. They deal with online businesses that need to extract data and forward data to other online businesses in a common format—for example, *business-to-business (B2B),* which deals with converting data stored in traditional relational databases to XML—and so forth. In essence, both the document-centric and data-centric worlds benefit extremely well from XML, and the current applications reflect this.

The developers of these applications also benefit from the willingness of companies in the industry to allow free downloads and use of common XML functionality, such as XML parsers and XSLT processors. Because such functionality is freely available on the Internet and can also be written in a short time if company internal releases are needed, the developers of these applications can quickly complete writing of their programs in Internet time. In addition, because these components are based on open standards, developers could conceivably go from one vendor to another, switch out functionality, and have it work. Naturally, considerations such as performance, memory use, full functionality, support, and so forth are other features these developers must consider before using such freeware. Nonetheless, given that the number of implementations is growing and many are becoming widely available, application developers should be able to develop XML-based products quickly.

Finally, given all the previously mentioned advantages, industry-specific DTDs for health, finance, and a number of other industries have been created to govern the format of XML files exchanged among businesses over the Internet. The clear benefit of this is that B2B can be facilitated over the Internet with XML as the data format for exchange and storage. No longer do businesses in a specific industry have to worry about converting files from one format to another, as long as that specific industry can agree on a specified XML format for auto parts, for example. In the end, consumers and businesses that have transactions over the Internet will be the direct beneficiaries from the conversion of both data and documents to XML.

Oracle's XML Strategy

Back in 1997 and 1998, when the original work was done to create the XML 1.0 recommendation, Oracle was not involved. In fact, a search of Oracle's global intranet at the time resulted in no hits for "XML." Less than 24 months later, the same search produced thousands of hits. This rapid adoption of XML technology started with Oracle's Architectural Review Board (ARB) handing down the charter to the CORE Development Group to develop the XML infrastructure components that would be made available to development groups across Oracle.

Along with the charter, the ARB articulated Oracle's XML strategy in a single succinct sentence: "Deliver the best platform for developers to productively build and cost-effectively deploy reliable and scalable Internet applications exploiting XML." Important to note is that this statement has a development, rather than a product, focus. This is totally consistent because XML, unlike its other markup cousins, is not an application. XML is an enabling technology and, thus, draws its significance in the context of developed solutions.

Once this XML development strategy began to be circulated and implemented, widespread interest in using this technology in some way spread to virtually every Oracle software product. A recent count in 2001 yielded more than 60 development groups using XML in some way within their products.

Interest was not confined to internal groups. Mergers and acquisitions across Oracle's customer base brought the requirement to integrate disparate systems, many of which were proprietary. XML, along with its companion technology, XSL, is well suited to provide the foundation to link these systems.

The Internet and its requirement of distributed access to a wide range of systems through firewalls and across a variety of wired and wireless mediums is an environment ideal for transporting XML documents and data because of the low technology agreement that must be made between XML-enabled applications and servers. XML has quickly become the integration point for all data, whether it's data warehousing, self-service and B2B electronic commerce, content management, or back-office integration. Therefore, it is natural for Oracle's object-relational databases to become XML enabled in support of this requirement.

Oracle's Efforts in the XML Industry

Oracle is heavily involved in XML, not only as a core technology to be made available for application development, but also as a driver of the standards and its related technologies. The following is an overview of Oracle's XML development and standards efforts with such groups as the Worldwide Web Consortium, the Sun Java Community Process, and the Open Applications Group.

Oracle on the W3C Working Group Committees

Even though Oracle was not involved in the initial W3C XML working group, the huge corporate adoption has forced Oracle not only to become involved in all the XML standards bodies, but also to help drive them. Oracle is a member of the following W3C XML Working Groups in the XML Technology area:

- **XML CORE Working Group**   Responsible for specifying the underlying XML technologies that serve all the other XML working groups. Examples of these include XBase, which specifies the format and behavior of XML-based URIs, and XInclude, which specifies the syntax and manner in which other XML files may be included in an XML document.

- **XSL Working Group**   Responsible for defining the Extensible Stylesheet Language in its two implementations. XSLT defines the stylesheet syntax and functionality used to transform one XML document into another one, while XSLFO defines the stylesheet syntax to render an XML document into a variety of electronic publishing formats.

- **XML Schema Working Group**   Responsible for defining the syntax and use of simple data types and complex structures within an XML document. It also provides a schema definition XML file format to replace DTDs and adds support for data and structure-type validation.

- **XML Linking Working Group**   Responsible for defining how XML resources are referenced from within XML documents. Encompassing the functionality of HTML links, XLinks are also permitted to reference multiple documents, be they in-line or out-of-line, and also to define behaviors.

- **DOM Working Group**   Responsible for the DOM APIs for accessing XML documents. These APIs provide programmatic access and manipulation of the actual in-memory structure of the elements and nodes of an XML document.

- **XML Query Working Group**   Responsible for the specification of a grammar and syntax for querying XML documents. Because of an XML document's hierarchical tree structure, it can be navigated and query result data sets returned.

Oracle's XML Developer's Kit

As previously mentioned, the CORE and XML Development group within the Database division produces all the basic infrastructure XML components that development groups across Oracle use. Any product that deals with XML must be able to determine whether the XML document is valid, which means it conforms to the specified DTD or XML Schema, and well formed, which means start tags must have corresponding end tags in correct nesting order. This is accomplished with an XML parser. Because Oracle's development groups have different requirements and different customers, the XML parser, along with the incorporated XSLT processor, were coded in four different languages: C, C++, Java, and PL/SQL. In addition, different implementations of the XML parser are available, including command-line executables, libraries, and jars. To facilitate visual application development, several Java beans are available to view, edit, and transform XML. Support for W3C XML Schema, DOM Level 2, SAX Level 2, and so forth have also been added to the Oracle XDK.

The Oracle XML Parser for Java is written in Java and can run in the Java VM of Oracle8i and Oracle9i. It has optional validation, with DTD caching, full international character-set support, full DOM and SAX support, and an integrated XSLT processor. It is also quite fast compared to other Java XML parsers. The XML Parsers for C and C++ are available on Solaris, Linux, HP-UX, and Windows NT; have full support for DOM and SAX interfaces, full international character set support, and an integrated XSLT processor; are also quite fast compared to other C and C++ XML parsers; and are available with Oracle server releases. The XML Parser for PL/SQL is based on the Java XML parser and allows PL/SQL APIs to the XML parser interfaces; it is also available from Oracle server releases.

Additionally, XML Schema Processors in Java, C, and C++ have been added to take advantage of the W3C XML Schema Recommendation to enhance XML documents with richer datatype information. Instead of DTDs with only string datatypes to describe elements and attributes, we now have a much more extensive set of datatypes to describe these in documents, along with namespaces and other constructs as stipulated in the Recommendation to describe parts of the XML document. Hence, these processors validate XML documents against this new form of content model and issue warnings or errors if the documents are nonconformant.

The XML TransViewer beans are bean encapsulations of some of the XML/XSLT classes—specifically, a XSLT Transformer bean, an XML DOM Parser bean, an XML Source Viewer/Editor bean, and an XML Tree Viewer bean, all of which are installed as an XML Palette starting with JDeveloper 3.1. DBView and DBAccess beans were added to exploit the power of Oracle databases so that extensive code didn't need to be written by the application programmer to connect to the database, execute the SQL query, format the result set as XML and apply a stylesheet to it, and store and retrieve XML from Character Large Object (CLOB) tables in the database and file system.

In addition, Java and C++ Class Generators also exist, which take a DTD or XML Schema now, and generate code that can be called programmatically to create XML documents conformant to that DTD or XML Schema.

Finally, the XSQL Servlet is a Java servlet that can run in the Web server to produce dynamic XML documents based upon one or more SQL queries. It can also optionally transform the resulting XML document in the server or client using XSLT. It uses a declarative **.xsql** XML file for instructions and transformations. Essentially, the XSQL Servlet establishes a connection to the database, strips off any tags before passing the SQL statement to the database, retrieves the row-set data and embeds it in XML with tags corresponding to the applicable database columns and tables, and applies an optional stylesheet to the XML.

Oracle's Technology Network

The XML component releases are available through Oracle's Technology Network (OTN), located at **http://otn.oracle.com/tech/xml**. Internal Oracle development groups use a mirror server of this OTN site without having to register, and also Oracle Japan has one in Japanese on **http://www.oracle.co.jp/download/rdbms/index .html**. The OTN Web page looks like the ones shown here.

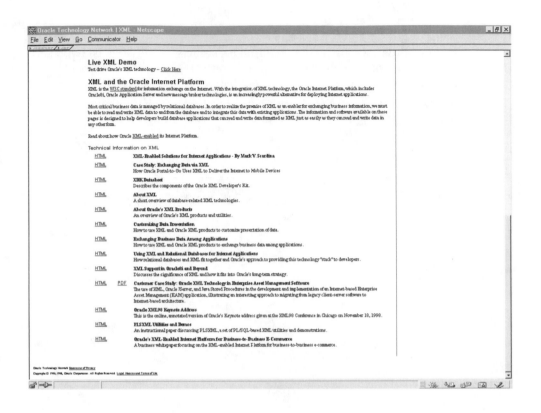

Each of the XML component releases has a staging area, including libraries/
DLLs, executables, documentation, and samples—which can be downloaded, used,
and incorporated in other applications for free! For example, the Java XML Parser
V2 Web page looks like Figure 1-1.

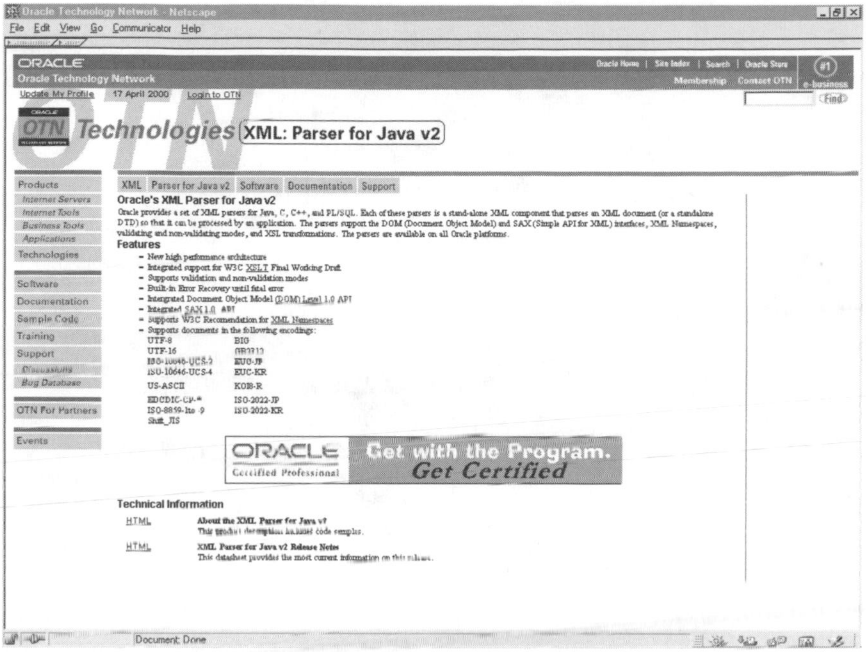

FIGURE 1-1.   *OTN's XML Parser for Java v2 Web page*

Finally, along with the white papers and other collateral, an XML discussion forum exists for the user community to post information, bugs, and so forth. The XML discussion forum Web page looks like the page shown in the three following screens.

Topic	Topic Starter	Replies	Last Post
Error while running xsql-vtg.bat	pkd1234 (Prasanta De, pde@ctronsoft.com)	0	April 17, 2000 01:48 PM
XML schema	Anu()	3	April 17, 2000 11:57 AM
XMLCreate XML from DB table...	andrey zinatullin (andrey@tg².tc.faa.gov)	3	April 17, 2000 11:26 AM
Validate with a DTD	Guy (guy.merose@edf.fr)	0	April 17, 2000 11:01 AM
Where are classes for oracle.xml.parser.v2?	GMurphy	2	April 17, 2000 09:21 AM
OAS4.0.8.1 + JSP Patch for XSQL Servlet	mmorley	0	April 17, 2000 08:42 AM
public identifier	Sander	0	April 17, 2000 08:11 AM
XSQL Pages & XSQL Servlet	Mirko Schulze ()	1	April 17, 2000 05:15 AM
XSQL servlet with OAS	Kumar Tambyraja (c.tambyraja@bham.ac.uk)	0	April 17, 2000 05:03 AM
Retrieving data from a relational table and CLOB as a whole XML file	Maciej Marczukajtis (mmarczuk@elka.pw.edu.pl)	0	April 17, 2000 02:15 AM
XSQL vs JSP	Kathy Bradford	0	April 17, 2000 12:40 AM
XDK License vs. OTN Licence	Kathy Bradford ()	0	April 17, 2000 12:30 AM
Customizing BC4J, extending classes	inazio (siae1104@gc.ehu.es)	2	April 17, 2000 12:20 AM

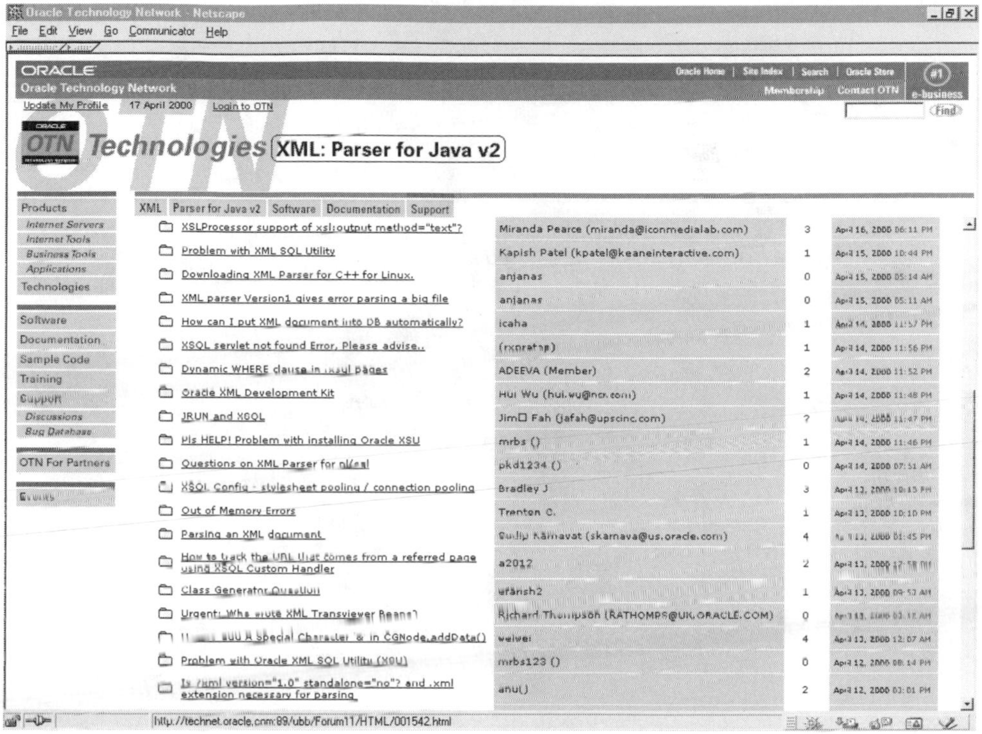

In addition, the parsers are packaged with other Internet products within the Internet Platform ISV kit. Finally, Oracle products such as Oracle8i and Oracle9i, JDeveloper 3.1, Applications11i, and Oracle9iAS (Oracle's new Application Server) preload the XML parser in their Java VMs or libraries, so application developers can access the parser APIs through these products.

Overviews of Oracle's XML-Enabled Products

Over 60 internal Oracle development groups across the server, tools, and applications divisions make use of the XML components in the products they develop. They make use of the C, C++, Java, and PLSQL XML/XSLT Parsers and Schema Processors to parse and transform XML documents, the Class Generators in Java and C++ to aid in application development, and the XSQL Servlet to provide document publishing and rendering services. These Oracle development groups and products include Oracle products providing XML APIs, products using XML for data interchange, products using XML for configuration, and products using XML for content management and publishing.

Oracle Products Providing XML APIs

Oracle has enhanced a number of its server products and tools to provide external XML APIs that can be used by applications. These APIs are principally provided by the XML components mentioned previously as running in the various Oracle servers.

Oracle 8i/9i JServer

Since Oracle 8i, developers have been able to use an internal Java Virtual Machine that runs within the database. JServer loads Java classes as stored procedures in the same manner as is done for PL/SQl These Java classes can make use of an in-memory JDBC connection when performing SQL queries. The initial release of JServer was JDK 1.1 compliant, while the version in Oracle 9i is JDK 1.2 compliant. The XDK's Java components can be loaded into JServer when the application would benefit from high-performance database access.

JDeveloper

JDeveloper is Oracle's premier IDE and, since version 3.0, has been incorporating XML capabilities for both internal use and application development. All of the XDK's Java components can be used with JDeveloper, and the XML TransViewer beans can be installed on a toolbar palette. Starting with version 3.1, JDeveloper has made significant XML enhancements. Along with the previously mentioned TransViewer Beans palette, additional data beans can generate XML-formatted data. The editor now understands **.xml** and **.xsl** type files and provides color-syntax highlighting, along with syntax checking. Finally, JDeveloper's Business Components for Java uses an XML format for its business rules and data.

Oracle9i Application Server

Oracle9i Application Server (Oracle9iAS) is Oracle's middle-tier server product. Providing both Web and application servers, Oracle9iAS has the XDK components integrated. The Java XDK components can be run in Oracle9iAS' JVM to provide XML interfaces to Web and Java applications. The PL/SQL components can be run in Oracle9iAS' PL/SQL run-time environment as well. This middle-tier capability is especially important for those applications that have extensive XSL processing or need to support thousands of users.

XML SQL Utility

Written in Java with an available PL/SQL package, the XML SQL Utility enables developers to submit SQL queries through JDBC and to receive the results wrapped in the XML format of the schema. In addition to providing a text stream output, the XML SQL Utility can output a DOM result set object, as well as the DTD or Schema definition corresponding to the queried database schema. As with the XDK's Java components, the XML SQL Utility can be loaded as a stored procedure in Oracle 8i/9i and used with any JDBC-enabled relational database.

Oracle Products Using XML for Data Interchange

Many of Oracle's applications have used database tables to exchange data. With the advent of the XML standard, these applications have adopted XML as their data messaging and reporting formats.

Oracle Integration Server

Oracle Integration Server uses XML as the format of the messages it sends and receives between applications. The Oracle Message Broker packages these XML messages in Java Messaging Service envelopes for delivery to connected applications.

Oracle Reports 6*i*

Oracle Reports adds support for XML-formatted reports, as well as catalog publishing for B2B data interchange. It also supports applying XSL stylesheets to the reports, so they can be displayed in Internet browsers.

Oracle Applications Release 11*i*

Oracle's enterprise suite of business applications includes Customer Relationship Management, Manufacturing/Supply Chain, Financials, Internet Procurement, Human Resources, and Projects. These applications use XML as the format for exchanging data and messages to achieve integration.

Self-Service Purchasing

Self-service purchasing uses XML documents as the "shopping cart" data exchanged between consumers and vendors. It also uses XML to format and provide catalog information to the consumer online.

Oracle Products Using XML for Configuration

Application configuration files have historically been formatted as flat files with custom parsers required to retrieve data. By using an XML format instead, these applications can leverage XML's easily extensible structure and build in open standards–based parsers to retrieve data.

Oracle Designer 6*i*

This rapid application-development tool uses a component repository to aid development. This repository uses *Extensible Metadata Interchange (XMI)* format to describe stored component behaviors and attributes. XMI is a standard subset of XML, enabling the open exchange of components over the Web.

Internal Release Application

Internal Release Application is an internal Oracle application designed in Java that uses XML-formatted files for its configuration and product status.

Oracle Configurator Developer

This product provides a configuration modeling environment for the Oracle Applications Release 11i products, which provide a drag-and-drop interface to develop sales models. XML is used in the formatting of configuration rules that constrain the model In the areas of object state, quantitative modeling parameters, product compatibility and dependencies, and design chart rules.

Oracle Products Using XML for Content Management and Publishing

Content management and publishing is a principal application area in which XML technology is producing its greatest impact. Oracle has a number of products supporting this application area and has XML-enabled them to read, write, and search XML documents, and render them using XSL.

Oracle Internet File System (*i*FS)

Oracle Internet File System (iFS), a set of Java APIs, provides file-level interfaces to application developers who want to store documents in Oracle 8i/9i in a flexible manner. Not only can a wide range of document types, including XML, be stored intact in LOBs, but also they can be parsed and taken apart to be stored in a distributed manner in a schema. The mapping for this is specified in a **.typ** file.

Oracle Text

Oracle Text is the text search engine available in Oracle 8i. Its support for XML includes the capability to index XML documents stored in *CLOBs* and to find occurrences of elements and attributes through SQL queries.

Oracle9*i* Application Server Wireless Edition (Oracle9*i*AS WE)

Oracle9iAS WE is a platform designed to provide information services to a wide range of wired and wireless devices, including cell phones, PDAs, pagers, and palmtops. Using XML for both information feeds and outputs, Portal-to-Go includes device-specific gateways that transmit XSL-transformed XML to the appropriate receiving device format.

Oracle Discoverer 3*i*

This product has been totally redesigned to use XML not only for data transfer, but also for component behavior and attribute encapsulation. Together with XSL, Discoverer provides easily customizable Web reports and user interfaces.

Overviews of Use of Oracle's XML Components

Oracle's XML components are being used not only internally, as previously mentioned, but also in many applications that require a high degree of data portability between applications and enterprises. Following is a listing and brief descriptions of a number of these applications; keep them in mind as you read through the book.

Document Creation and Publishing

A company has one or more document repositories of marked-up text fragments in XML or SGML and is interested in publishing composite documents dynamically. It can do this by using XSL stylesheets to assemble the fragments and electronically deliver the composite document to users.

Personalized Information Delivery Service

A company receives data feeds from a variety of information sources and uses XSL to normalize and store in a database. This information store is then used to back one or more Web sites or portals, which receive http requests from a variety of wired and wireless clients. XSL stylesheets, in conjunction with the XSQL Servlet, deliver dynamically the appropriate rendering to the requesting device.

Easily Customized Data-Driven Applications

An application is built to deliver data and interactivity to a thin client. Data is queried from a database, along with the UI components, and together rendered dynamically through one or more XSL stylesheets to the client application. Storage is relational data materialized in XML, as well as XML stored in LOBs.

E-Commerce Using an XML Shopping Cart

An e-commerce Web site compiles customer orders into XML and delivers the content to one or more vendor databases for processing. XSL is used to transform and divide the cart for compliant transfers. Data is stored relationally and materialized in XML.

Business-to-Business Internet Messaging

A multiple client-to-server or servers-to-server application stores a data resource or inventory in a repository that is shared across enterprises. A resource release triggers an availability XML message, which then transforms that resource using XSL into multiple client-compliant formats. Conversely, a resource acquisition by one client sends an XML message to the other clients signaling removal. Messages are stored in LOBs, and data is stored relationally and materialized in XML.

Application Integration Through XML Messaging

A number of applications are required to communicate and share data to integrate businesses or business processes. XML is used as the message payload transformed by XSL, enveloped and routed. These XML messages are stored in LOBs.

An Example and an Application

Application programs that take advantage of XML to facilitate e-commerce can be written much faster when they make use of the Oracle *XML Developer's Kit (XDK)*. Instead of coming up with code to parse XML files, transform XML files according to stylesheets, and retrieve data from database tables and convert them to XML, the application developers can simply code against the open-standard APIs provided in the XDK, use the functionality already provided, and quickly come up with application programs to do what is wanted. Thus, if customer-input data from Web sites needs to be encapsulated in XML form and relayed to some other site, then developers using the XDK can quickly come up with a useful application program to do so. One such example, an application program that allows the sale of books over the Internet, is described in this section.

The owner of the Amazingly Enjoyable Books Web site has a need for an application program to capture data entered on her Web site by customers, store such data in XML and have the XML stored in the database, and retrieve such data in a presentable form. As Ms. PowerTooler Programmer, you need to write this application program in one day because the Web site owner has promised to triple her payments to you if you can get things up and running by tomorrow. Remembering that the Oracle Technology Network XML Web site has a number of useful XML components and utilities, you go to **http://technet.oracle.com/tech/xml** and begin downloading components such as the Java XML/XSLT Parser and the XSQL Servlet. You begin with the sample programs provided and start seeing how quickly you can finish the application program for the owner of the Web site.

From conversing with the owner, you realize the data provided by customers from the Web site is minimal, making your job easier, and you immediately come up with a DTD that governs the structure of the XML document that stores the customer data:

```
<!-- DTD book customer list may have a number of book customers -->
<!ELEMENT bookcustomerlist (bookcustomer)*>
<!-- Each book customer has a name, address,
     1 or more book orders, etc.-->
<!ELEMENT bookcustomer (customer*, book+, totalsales)>
<!ELEMENT customer (firstname, lastname, address, city, state,
                    country, zip)>
<!ELEMENT firstname (#PCDATA)>
<!ELEMENT lastname (#PCDATA)>
<!ELEMENT address (#PCDATA)>
<!ELEMENT city (#PCDATA)>
<!ELEMENT state (#PCDATA)>
<!ELEMENT country (#PCDATA)>
<!ELEMENT zip (#PCDATA)>
<!ELEMENT book (title, author+, ISBN, publisher, publishyear, price,
                purchasedate, totalsales)>
<!ELEMENT title (#PCDATA)>
<!ELEMENT author (firstname, lastname)>
<!ELEMENT firstname (#PCDATA)>
<!ELEMENT lastname (#PCDATA)>
<!ELEMENT ISBN (#PCDATA)>
<!ELEMENT publisher (#PCDATA)>
<!ELEMENT publishyear (#PCDATA)>
<!ELEMENT price (#PCDATA)>
<!ELEMENT purchasedate(#PCDATA)>
<!ELEMENT totalsales (#PCDATA)>
```

You start writing your application program, capturing the data entered by customers, and storing it in an XML structure in memory (or in an external file) that is conformant to the DTD you just specified. For example, the UI may resemble the form shown in Figure 1-2.

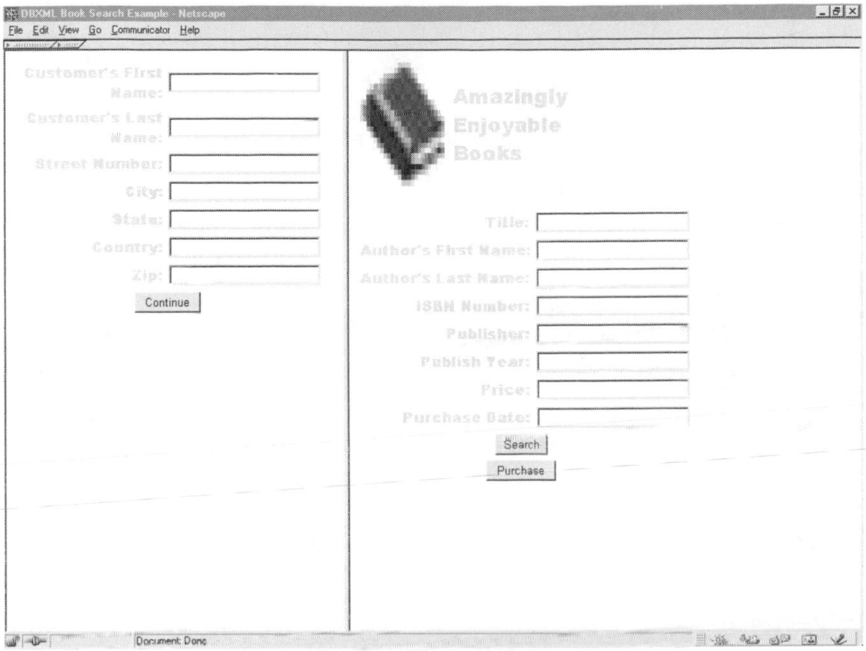

FIGURE 1-2.   *Book Search Form example*

For storage and retrieval of information to the database on the server, a SQL statement can also be made, thus allowing the Oracle XSQL Servlet to operate on the XML file, an optional XSL file, and the constructed SQL statement. The XSQL Servlet, running from the Web server, then establishes a connection to the database and executes the SQL statement, along with the associated data, from the back-end server. Row-set data from the database tables is then retrieved, converted into XML, has the XSL stylesheet applied to it, and is served from the Web server to the browser client if retrieval of information is wanted. If the DML operation is only to insert data, no retrieval operation is necessary.

The following XML file could be an entry that results from retrieving information from the database tables, converting it into XML, and passing it to some other application/Web site:

```
<?xml version="1.0"?>
<!DOCTYPE bookcustomerlist SYSTEM "bookcustomer.dtd">
<bookcustomerlist>
  <bookcustomer>
```

```
<customer>
  <firstname>Juan</firstname>
  <lastname>Smith</lastname>
  <address>1 Oracle Parkway</address>
  <city>Redwood Shores</city>
  <state>California</state>
  <country>USA</country>
  <zip>94065</zip>
</customer>
  <book>
      <title>Men are from Mars</title>
      <author>
          <firstname>James</firstname>
          <lastname>Collins</lastname>
      </author>
      <ISBN>9999</ISBN>
      <publisher>Oracle Press</publisher>
      <publishyear>2000</publishyear>
      <price>1.00</price>
      <purchasedate>January 1, 2000</purchasedate>
    </book>
  <totalsales>1000.00</totalsales>
  </bookcustomer>
</bookcustomerlist>
```

This type of application will be expanded in greater detail and extended throughout the book. It represents the area in which XML will have its greatest impact on application development.

CHAPTER
2

Oracle's XML CORE Technologies

he importance of XML and its related technologies being an open standard is that components, libraries, and applications built to these standards have the potential for a high level of interoperability and reuse. This was fundamental in Oracle's decision to build its own infrastructure components and libraries. This XML functionality has been encapsulated into *XML Developer's Kits (XDKs)* for the four supported languages —Java, C, C++, and PL/SQL.

To effectively work with XML documents, you must call upon a number of components and utilities. A developer needs to parse XML, validate XML against a DTD or an XML Schema, transform XML by applying a stylesheet, generate XML documents from data, and so forth. The following sections will discuss the parsers, processors, generators, viewers, and utilities that make up this XDKs, while providing examples of how to put them to use.

XML Parser for Java V2

The Oracle XML parser for Java makes it easy for Java programmers to extend their existing Java applications seamlessly to support XML. It processes XML documents and provides access to the information contained in them through a variety of user-friendly APIs. The parser fully supports both the tree-based *Document Object Model (DOM)* and event-based *Simple API for XML (SAX)* standards. It also has a built-in XSLT processor that makes transforming XML documents from one format to another extremely simple. The parser can be used in any environment that supports JDK 1.1.x or higher, and it can also be run inside the Oracle8i and Oracle9i JServer. The parser is completely internationalized and supports every character set supported by Java, in addition to numerous others. This support means that the parser provides error messages in nearly every language supported by Oracle8i and Oracle9i, making it an invaluable tool if you're writing XML applications for non-English-speaking users.

SAX Support

Quite often, applications that require only SAX (Level 1 and Level 2) support do not want to be burdened with a parser that always builds a full-blown DOM tree in memory. The Oracle XML SAX parser's high-performance, event-based run-time engine addresses this requirement. Using the SAX parser, applications can leverage the full power of the SAX model to parse extremely large documents without incurring prohibitive memory costs.

The following code demonstrates how the SAX APIs can be used to extract useful information from an XML document:

```
// This example demonstrates a simple use of the SAXParser.
// An XML file is parsed and some information is printed out.
```

```java
import org.xml.sax.*;
import java.io.*;
import java.net.*;
import oracle.xml.parser.v2.*;

public class SAXHandler extends HandlerBase
{
   public static void main(String[] argv)
   {
      try
      {
         // Get an instance of the parser
         Parser parser = new SAXParser();

         // Create a SAX event handler and register it with the parser
         SAXHandler handler = new SAXHandler();
         parser.setDocumentHandler(handler);

         // Convert file to InputSource and parse
         InputSource xmldoc =
             new InputSource(new FileInputStream(argv[0]));
         parser.parse(xmldoc);
      }
      catch (Exception e)
      {
         System.out.println(e.toString());
      }
   }

   ////////////////////////////////////////////////////////////////////
   // Sample implementation of DocumentHandler interface.
   ////////////////////////////////////////////////////////////////////

   public void startElement(String name, AttributeList atts)
         throws SAXException
   {
      System.out.println("StartElement:"+name);
      for (int i=0;i<atts.getLength();i++)
      {
         String aname = atts.getName(i);
         String type = atts.getType(i);
         String value = atts.getValue(i);

         System.out.println("   "+aname+"("+type+")"+"="+value);
      }
   }

   public void characters(char[] cbuf, int start, int len)
```

```
    {
        System.out.print("Characters:");
        System.out.println(new String(cbuf,start,len));
    }
}
```

To use the XML parser's SAX support, you need to use the **SAXParser** class to parse your XML document. The first thing to do, therefore, is to get an instance of this class:

```
Parser parser = new SAXParser();
```

You then need to register your SAX event handler with the parser, so it would know what methods to invoke when a particular event occurs. Because not all events may be of interest to you, make sure the handler you register extends the **org.xml.sax.HandlerBase** class. This class provides some default behavior for handling events (typically these do nothing). You can then override the methods for those events of interest to you. In the preceding example, the assumption is that the only events of interest are a subset of those specified by the **org.xml.sax .DocumentHandler** interface, namely, **startElement** and **characters**. Arguably, these are the most important SAX events generated because XML documents typically consist of markup and text. This handler can be registered with the **SAXParser** with a simple API call:

```
parser.setDocumentHandler(handler);
```

The **startElement** event is triggered every time a new element is encountered within the XML document by the **SAXParser**. When this event occurs, you can print the element name and its attributes:

```
public void startElement(String name, AttributeList atts)
            throws SAXException
{
        . . .
}
```

The **characters** event is triggered every time unmarked-up text is encountered by the **SAXParser**. This text is often the "value" of an element and can be retrieved by listening for this event:

```
public void characters(char[] cbuf, int start, int len)
{
        . . .
}
```

Once the handler has been registered, all that remains is to parse an XML document using the **SAXParser**:

```
parser.parse(xmldoc);
```

The input XML document could contain a list of book data, such as the following:

```
<booklist>
    <book isbn="1234-123456-1234">
      <title>C Programming Language</title>
      <author>Kernighan and Ritchie</author>
      <publisher>IEEE</publisher>
      <price>7.99</price>
    </book>
    <book isbn="1230-23498-2349879">
      <title>Emperor's New Mind</title>
      <author>Roger Penrose</author>
      <publisher>Oxford Publishing Company</publisher>
      <price>15.99</price>
    </book>
</booklist>
```

The following output would be generated:

```
StartElement:booklist
StartElement:book
    isbn(CDATA)=1234-123456-1234
StartElement:title
Characters:C Programming Language
StartElement:author
Characters:Kernighan and Ritchie
StartElement:publisher
Characters:IEEE
StartElement:price
Characters:7.99
StartElement:book
    isbn(CDATA)=1230-23498-2349879
StartElement:title
Characters:Emperor's New Mind
StartElement:author
Characters:Roger Penrose
StartElement:publisher
Characters:Oxford Publishing Company
StartElement:price
Characters:15.99
```

Implementation of SAX Level 2 comes mainly in the form of support of Namespaces, and querying or setting features or properties in the parser. With Namespace support, element and attribute names may now return an optional Namespace URI followed by a local name, e.g., **<foo:bar xmlns:foo="http://www.oracle.com/"/>**, where **http://www.oracle.com/** is the Namespace URI and **bar** is the local name. In addition, the qualified name or **qName**, **foo:bar**, may also be returned. Without Namespace support, element and attribute names simply return a local name. The SAX Level 2 interfaces affected by Namespace support are **XMLReader**, **Attributes**, and **ContentHandler**. An example of SAX 2 Namespace support, followed by code for the **startElement** and **endElement** callback methods in the **ContentHandler** interface, might look like the following:

```java
// This example demonstrates how SAX Level 2 Namespace

// support, followed by how the callback
// methods startElement and endElement can be used.

import java.io.*;
import java.net.URL;
import java.net.MalformedURLException;
import org.xml.sax.*;
import org.xml.sax.helpers.*;
import oracle.xml.parser.v2.SAXParser;

public class SAX2Namespace {
  static public void main(String[] args) {
    String fileName;
    //Get the file name
    fileName = args[0];
    try {
      // Create handlers for the parser
      // For all the other interface use the default provided by
      // Handler base
      DefaultHandler defHandler = new XMLDefaultHandler();
      SAXParser parser = new SAXParser();
      parser.setContentHandler(defHandler);
      parser.setErrorHandler(defHandler);
      parser.setEntityResolver(defHandler);
      parser.setDTDHandler(defHandler);
      try
      {
        parser.parse(createURL(fileName));
      }
      catch (SAXParseException e)
      {
        System.err.println(args[0] + ": " + e.getMessage());
      }
      catch (SAXException e)
```

```
            {
                System.err.println(args[0] + ": " + e.getMessage());
            }
        }
        catch (Exception e)
        {
            System.err.println(e.toString());
        }
    }
    static URL createURL(String fileName) {
        URL url = null;
        try {
            url = new URL(fileName);
        } catch (MalformedURLException ex) {
            try {
                File f = new File(fileName);
                url = f.toURL();
            } catch (MalformedURLException e) {
                System.out.println("Cannot create url for: " + fileName);
                System.exit(0);
            }
        }
        return url;
}
private SAX2Namespace() throws IOException
{
}
}
class XMLDefaultHandler extends DefaultHandler
{
    public void XMLDefaultHandler()
    {
    }
    public void startElement(String uri, String localName,
                             String qName, Attributes atts)
    throws SAXException
    {
        System.out.println("ELEMENT Qualified Name:" + qName);
        System.out.println("ELEMENT Local Name     :" + localName);
        System.out.println("ELEMENT Namespace      :" + uri);

        for (int i=0; i<atts.getLength(); i++)
        {
            qName = atts.getQName(i);
            localName = atts.getLocalName(i);
            uri = atts.getURI(i);

            System.out.println(" ATTRIBUTE Qualified Name    :" + qName);
            System.out.println(" ATTRIBUTE Local Name        :" + localName);
            System.out.println(" ATTRIBUTE Namespace         :" + uri);
```

```
            // You can get the type and value of the attributes either
            // by index or by the Qualified Name.

            String type = atts.getType(qName);
            String value = atts.getValue(qName);

            System.out.println(" ATTRIBUTE Type           :" + type);
            System.out.println(" ATTRIBUTE Value          :" + value);

            System.out.println();
        }
    }

    public void endElement(String uri, String localName,
                           String qName) throws SAXException
    {
        System.out.println("ELEMENT Qualified Name:" + qName);
        System.out.println("ELEMENT Local Name    :" + localName);
        System.out.println("ELEMENT Namespace     :" + uri);
    }
}
```

For SAX Level 2, the additional parameters being passed in are the Namespace URI, the local name, and the **qName**. Other SAX Level 2 include the querying and setting of features and properties in the parser, e.g., getter/setter methods such as **getFeature, setFeature, getProperty, setProperty,** as in the following:

```
void process(String filename) throws SAXException, IOException
{
    URL url = createURL(filename);

    // Validating, Namespace = true, NamespacePrefix = true
    parser.setFeature("http://xml.org/sax/features/validation", true);
    parser.setFeature("http://xml.org/sax/features/namespaces", true);
    parser.setFeature("http://xml.org/sax/features/namespace-prefix", true);

    try
    {
        parser.parse(url.toString());
    }

    catch (XMLParseException e)
    {
        System.out.println();
        System.out.println(e);
    }

    // Non-validating, NamespacePrefix = false
    parser.setFeature("http://xml.org/sax/features/validation", true);
```

```
parser.setFeature("http://xml.org/sax/features/namespace-prefix", true);

try
{
    parser.parse(url.toString());
}

catch (XMLParseException e)
{
    System.out.println();
    System.out.println(e);
}
}
```

For this code example, note that one can control Namespace support in SAX Level 2 processing. In default processing, namespace-prefix is false, meaning that **qNames** are optionally reported and Namespace declarations (xmlns attributes) are not reported. In our example, however, in the code stub that sets validation, namespaces, and namespace-prefixes to be true, given

<foo:bar xmlns:foo="http://www.oracle.com/" foo1="bar1" foo:stock="wayout.com"/>,

an element will have the Namespace URI of "**http://www.oracle.com/**", a local name of "**bar**", and a **qName** of "**foo:bar**"; the first attribute will have no Namespace URI, no local name, and a qName of "**xmlns:foo**"; another attribute will have no Namespace URI, a local name, and a qName of "**foo1**"; and the last attribute will have the Namespace URI "**http://www.oracle.com/**" and a local name of "**stock**".

DOM Support

The Oracle XML parser also supports the DOM (Level 1, and Level 2 CORE/Events/ Traversal/Range) specification. The power of the DOM lies in its capability to provide access to an in-memory tree representation of the entire XML document. Using the DOM, applications can perform tasks such as searching for specific data in an XML document, adding or deleting elements and attributes in the XML document, and transforming the DOM to an entirely different document. The Oracle DOM parser uses the high-performance SAX parser internally to build the DOM tree in memory. It provides a handle to the root of the DOM tree—the document node—from which the rest of the tree can be accessed. The XML parser comes with a set of classes that implement the DOM APIs and extend them to provide other useful features, such as printing a document fragment, retrieving Namespace information, and selecting nodes from a tree specified by an XPath pattern.

The following code demonstrates some of the DOM functionality in the XML Parser:

```
// This example demonstrates a simple use of the DOMParser
// An XML file is parsed and some information is printed out.

import java.io.*;
import java.net.*;
import oracle.xml.parser.v2.DOMParser;
import org.w3c.dom.*;
import org.w3c.dom.Node;
// Extensions to DOM Interfaces for Namespace support.
import oracle.xml.parser.v2.XMLElement;
import oracle.xml.parser.v2.XMLAttr;

public class DOMExample
{
    public static void main(String[] argv)
    {
        try
        {
            // Generate a new input stream from given file
             FileInputStream xmldoc = new FileInputStream(argv[0]);

            // Parse the document using DOMParser
            DOMParser parser = new DOMParser();
            parser.parse(xmldoc);

            // Obtain the document.
            Document doc = parser.getDocument();

            // Print some information regarding attributes of elements
            // in the document
            printElementAttributes(doc);
        }
        catch (Exception e)
        {
            System.out.println(e.toString());
        }
    }
    static void printElementAttributes(Document doc)
    {
        NodeList nl = doc.getElementsByTagName("*");
        Element e;
        XMLAttr nsAttr;
        String attrname, attrval, attrqname;
        NamedNodeMap nnm;
```

```
for (int j=0; j < nl.getLength(); j++)
{
   e = (Element) nl.item(j);
   System.out.println(e.getTagName() + ":");

   nnm = e.getAttributes();

   if (nnm != null)
   {
      for (int i=0; i < nnm.getLength(); i++)
      {
         nsAttr = (XMLAttr) nnm.item(i);

         // Use the methods getQualifiedName(), getLocalName(),
         // getNamespace() and getExpandedName() in NSName
         // interface to get Namespace information.

         attrname = nsAttr.getExpandedName();
         attrqname = nsAttr.getQualifiedName();
         attrval = nsAttr.getNodeValue();

         System.out.println(" " + attrqname + "(" + attrname +
            ")" + " = " +attrval);
      }
   }
   System.out.println();
}
}
}
```

The DOM APIs, unlike the SAX ones, can be used only after the XML document is completely parsed. The downside of this is that large XML documents can occupy a lot of memory, which could ultimately affect the performance of your application. In pure functionality terms, however, the DOM is definitely the more powerful API to use. The first thing to be done before you begin using any of the DOM APIs is to parse your document using a new instance of the **DOMParser**:

```
// Parse the document using DOMParser
DOMParser parser = new DOMParser();
parser.parse(xmldoc);
```

Then you need to request the parser to return a handle to the root of the Document Object Model, which it has constructed in memory:

```
// Obtain the document.
Document doc = parser.getDocument();
```

Using the preceding handle, you can access every part of the XML document you just parsed. The **DOMExample** class assumes you want to access the elements in the document and their attributes. To do this, you first need to obtain a list of all the elements in the document. A DOM method called **setElementsByTagName** enables you to retrieve, recursively, all elements that match a given tag name under a certain level. It also supports a special tag name "*", which matches any tag. Given this information, you need to invoke this method at the top level of the document via the handle to the root you obtained earlier in this section:

```
NodeList nl = doc.getElementsByTagName("*");
```

The preceding call generates a list of all the elements in the document. Each of these elements contains the information regarding its attributes. To access this information, you need to traverse this list:

```
len = nl.getLength();
for (int j=0; j < len; j++)
{
   e = (Element) nl.item(j);
   ...
}
```

To obtain the attributes of each element in the loop, you can use a DOM method called **getAttributes**. This method generates a special kind of DOM list called the **NamedNodeMap**. Once you obtain this list, traversing it to obtain information about the attributes themselves is straightforward:

```
for (int i=0; i < nnm.getLength(); i++)
{
   nsAttr = (XMLAttr) nnm.item(i);

// Use the methods getQualifiedName() and getExpandedName() in NSName
// interface to get Namespace information.

   attrname = nsAttr.getExpandedName();
   attrqname = nsAttr.getQualifiedName();
   attrval = nsAttr.getNodeValue();

   System.out.println(" " + attrqname + "(" + attrname +
                      ")" + " = " + attrval);
}
```

The preceding snippet makes use of the XML Parser's Namespace support to retrieve additional information regarding the attributes of each element. This kind of code would be useful if the XML document you had to parse had elements with many attributes that belonged to different namespaces. For example, imagine that the **book** XML document you saw in the preceding section looked like this:

```
<booklist xmlns:osborne="http://www.osborne.com"
          xmlns:bookguild="http://www.bookguild.com"
          xmlns:dollars="http://www.currency.org/dollars">
   <book osborne:isbn="1234-123456-1234" title="C Programming Language"
         author="Kernighan and Ritchie" bookguild:publisher="IEEE"
         dollars:price="7.99"/>
   <book osborne:isbn="1230-23498-2349879" title="Emperor's New Mind"
         author="Roger Penrose" bookguild:publisher="Oxford Publishing
                 Company"
         dollars:price="15.99"/>
</booklist>
```

The generated output would look like this:

```
xmlns:osborne(http://www.w3.org/2000/xmlns/;osborne)=http://www.osborne.com
xmlns:bookguild(http://www.w3.org/2000/xmlns/:bookguild) =http://www.bookguild.com
xmlns:dollars(http://www.w3.org/2000/xmlns/:dollars) =
http://www.currency.org/dollars

book:
osborne:isbn(http://www.osborne.com:isbn) = 1234-123456-1234
title(title) = C Programming Language
author(author) = Kernighan and Ritchie
bookguild:publisher(http://www.bookguild.com:publisher) = IEEE
dollars:price(http://www.currency.org/dollars:price) = 7.99

book:
osborne:isbn(http://www.osborne.com:isbn) = 1230-23498-2349879
title(title) = Emperor's New Mind
author(author) = Roger Penrose
bookguild:publisher(http://www.bookguild.com:publisher) =
        Oxford Publishing Company
dollars:price(http://www.currency.org/dollars:price) = 15.99
```

Some of the DOM Level 2 functionality includes methods that create iterators and tree-walkers to traverse a node and its children in document order (depth-first, pre-order traversal, equivalent to the order in which the start tags occur in the text representation of the document), objects used to navigate a document tree or subtree using the view of the document defined by their **whatToShow** flags and filter (if any) so that any method that performs navigation using a **TreeWalker** will automatically support any view defined by a **TreeWalker,** iterator methods used to step through a set of nodes or the document subtree governed by a particular **Node** or the results of a query or any other set of nodes, and objects to "filter out" nodes.

An example of such stub code would be the following:

```
// This filter accepts everything
NodeFilter n1 = new nf1();
// Node iterator doesn't allow expansion of entity references
NodeIterator ni =
            doc.createNodeIterator(elems[0],NodeFilter.SHOW_ALL,n1,false);
// Move forward
XMLNode nn =(XMLNode) ni.nextNode();
while (nn != null)
{
    System.out.println(nn.getNodeName() + " " + nn.getNodeValue());
    nn = (XMLNode)ni.nextNode();
}
// Move backward
nn = (XMLNode)ni.previousNode();
while (nn != null)
{
    System.out.println(nn.getNodeName() + " " + nn.getNodeValue());
    nn = (XMLNode)ni.previousNode();
}

// Node iterator allows expansion of entity references
ni = doc.createNodeIterator(elems[0],NodeFilter.SHOW_ALL,n1,true);
// Move forward
nn =(XMLNode) ni.nextNode();
while (nn != null)
{
    System.out.println(nn.getNodeName() + " " + nn.getNodeValue());
    nn = (XMLNode)ni.nextNode();
}
// Move backward
nn = (XMLNode)ni.previousNode();
while (nn != null)
{
    System.out.println(nn.getNodeName() + " " + nn.getNodeValue());
    nn = (XMLNode)ni.previousNode();
}

// This filter doesn't accept expansion of entity references
NodeFilter n2 = new nf2();

// Node iterator allows expansion of entity references
ni = doc.createNodeIterator(elems[0],NodeFilter.SHOW_ALL,n2,true);
// Move forward
nn =(XMLNode) ni.nextNode();
while (nn != null)
{
```

```
      System.out.println(nn.getNodeName() + " " + nn.getNodeValue());
      nn = (XMLNode)ni.nextNode();
}
// Move backward
nn = (XMLNode)ni.previousNode();
while (nn != null)
{
      System.out.println(nn.getNodeName() + " " + nn.getNodeValue());
      nn = (XMLNode)ni.previousNode();
}

// After detaching, all node iterator methods throw an exception
ni.detach();
try
{
      nn = (XMLNode)ni.nextNode();
}
catch(DOMException e)
{
      System.out.println(e.getMessage());
}
try
{
      nn = (XMLNode)ni.previousNode();
}
catch(DOMException e)
{
      System.out.println(e.getMessage());
}
// Treewalker allows expansion of entity references
TreeWalker tw =
            doc.createTreeWalker(elems[0],NodeFilter.SHOW_ALL,n1,true);
nn = (XMLNode)tw.getRoot();
// Traverse in document order
while (nn != null)
{
      System.out.println(nn.getNodeName() + " " + nn.getNodeValue());
      nn = (XMLNode)tw.nextNode();
}

tw = doc.createTreeWalker(elems[0],NodeFilter.SHOW_ALL,n1,true);
nn = (XMLNode) tw.getRoot();
// Traverse the depth left
while (nn != null)
{
      System.out.println(nn.getNodeName() + " " + nn.getNodeValue());
      nn = (XMLNode)tw.firstChild();
}
tw = doc.createTreeWalker(elems[0],NodeFilter.SHOW_ALL,n2,true);
nn = (XMLNode)tw.getRoot();
// Traverse in document order
while (nn != null)
{
      System.out.println(nn.getNodeName() + " " + nn.getNodeValue());
      nn = (XMLNode)tw.nextNode();
}
tw = doc.createTreeWalker(elems[0],NodeFilter.SHOW_ALL,n2,true);
nn = (XMLNode) tw.getRoot();
```

```
    // Traverse the depth right
    while (nn != null)
    {
        System.out.println(nn.getNodeName() + " " + nn.getNodeValue());
        nn = (XMLNode)tw.lastChild();
    }
```

`...`

```
    class nf1 implements NodeFilter
    {
      public short acceptNode(Node node)
      {
        return FILTER_ACCEPT;
      }
    }
    class nf2 implements NodeFilter
    {
      public short acceptNode(Node node)
      {
        short type = node.getNodeType();

        if ((type == Node.ELEMENT_NODE) || (type == Node.ATTRIBUTE_NODE))
          return FILTER_ACCEPT;
        if ((type == Node.ENTITY_REFERENCE_NODE))
          return FILTER_REJECT;
        return FILTER_SKIP;
      }
    }
```

XSLT Support

Using the built-in XSLT processor, you can transform an XML document into another
XML document, an HTML document, or a variety of other text formats. The processor
can be invoked either programmatically (using the given APIs) or from the command
line (using the **oraxsl** utility) and takes, as input, the XML document (to be transformed)
and the XSLT stylesheet that operates on it. It performs the transformation specified
by the XSLT stylesheet and generates either a result DOM tree or a text output stream.
The diagram shown in Figure 2-1 represents the architecture of the XSLT processor.

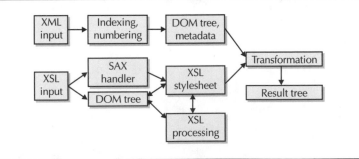

FIGURE 2-1. *The Java XSLT processor architecture*

The XSLT processor operates on two inputs: the XML document to transform and the XSLT stylesheet to use. It calls out to an XPath engine whenever it needs to match patterns. The XPath engine often needs to traverse the XML DOM tree to retrieve nodes; it passes these back to the XSLT processor. Whenever the XSLT processor needs to generate a result node, it generates a special XSLT event. This event is handled by an XSLT event handler, serving as a midtier caching agent, which waits for subsequent events that affect the same result node. A simple example of this is when the result node to be built is an **XMLElement**. Multiple XSLT events, such as one to create the element simply followed by several that depict its attributes, may be generated by the XSLT processor. Once the XSLT event handler gets complete information about a node, it generates an appropriate SAX event, which can then be processed by a registered SAX handler.

Currently, two output mechanisms are supported by the XSLT Processor for Java: a DOM tree and a text output stream. Either of these can be invoked through appropriate API calls made using the **XSLProcessor** class. If the API to build a result DOM tree is invoked, a DOM tree builder is registered as the SAX event handler for XSLT. Similarly, if the API to output to a text stream is invoked, an **OutputWriter** is registered as the SAX event handler. The advantage of this architecture is that a DOM tree Is not built as the result tree unless you require it. If your XSLT application simply needs a text output (such as HTML), you can use the less memory-intensive **OutputWriter** mechanism to do the processing. Remember, if your XSLT stylesheet contains **xsl:output** instructions, you must use the **OutputWriter** mechanism for these to be interpreted correctly.

Programmatic Invocation of the XSLT Processor

The XSLT processor exposes two Java classes: **XSLProcessor** and **XSLStylesheet**, which you need to use to perform an XSL transformation. An **XSLStylesheet** object holds all information about an XSLT stylesheet, such as its templates, keys, variables, and attribute sets. This object, once constructed, can be used multiple times to apply the same transformation to a variety of XML documents. It can also be "tweaked" periodically by setting suitable stylesheet parameter values from the outside.

The following code demonstrates how the XSLT APIs could be used:

```
import java.util.*;
import java.io.*;
import java.net.*;
import org.w3c.dom.*;
import oracle.xml.parser.v2.*;

/**
 * This is a simple example of how to use the XSL processing
 * capabilities of the Oracle XML Parser V2.0. An input XML document
 * is transformed using a given input stylesheet
 */
```

```
public class XSLExample
{
    public static void main (String args[]) throws Exception
    {
        DOMParser parser;
        XMLDocument xmldoc, xsldoc, out;
        FileInputStream xmlstream, xslstream;

        try
        {
            // Create an instance of the DOMParser
            parser = new DOMParser();
            parser.setPreserveWhitespace(true);

            // parse input XML file
            xmlstream = new FileInputStream(args[0]);
            parser.parse(xmlstream);
            xmldoc = parser.getDocument();

            // parse input XSL file
            xslstream = new FileInputStream(args[1]);
            parser.parse(xslstream);
            xsldoc = parser.getDocument();

            // instantiate a stylesheet
            XSLStylesheet xsl = new XSLStylesheet(xsldoc, null);

            // Apply stylesheet
            XSLProcessor processor = new XSLProcessor();
            XMLDocumentFragment result =
                    processor.processXSL(xsl, xmldoc);

            // print the transformed document
            result.print(System.out);
        }
        catch (Exception e)
        {
            e.printStackTrace();
        }
    }
}
```

The preceding example is fairly straightforward. It accepts, as input, the XML input file, and the XSL stylesheet to apply to it. The first thing you need to do is to parse these using the **DOMParser** and to retrieve the roots of their respective DOM trees:

```
// Create an instance of the DOMParser
parser = new DOMParser();
parser.setPreserveWhitespace(true);

    // parse input XML file
    xmlstream = new FileInputStream(args[0]);
    parser.parse(xmlstream);
    xmldoc = parser.getDocument();

    // parse input XSL file
    xslstream = new FileInpurStream(args[1]);
    parser.parse(xslstream);
    xsldoc = parser.getDocument();
```

The important thing to note is the parser is explicitly made white space preserving (by default, it is not). This is crucial, as it allows XSLT white space rules to determine how white space should be dealt with. The next step is to construct a stylesheet object:

```
    // instantiate a stylesheet
    XSLStylesheet xsl = new XSLStylesheet(xsldoc, null);
```

This example, being extremely simple, assumes the input stylesheet does not reference anything external, such as included stylesheets, external entities, and so forth. Only in such a case can you get away with passing a null as the second argument to the **XSLStylesheet** constructor. Otherwise, you need to create a URL to serve as a reference point for resolving external references within the stylesheet.

The next step is to create a new **XSLProcessor** and to use it to apply the stylesheet on the input XML document:

```
    // Apply stylesheet
    XSLProcessor processor = new XSLProcessor();
    DocumentFragment result = processor.processXSL(xsl, xml);
```

The transformed output is now available to you as a document fragment, which can be further manipulated using the regular DOM APIs. For the sake of simplicity, this example prints the results:

```
    // print the transformed document
    result.print(System.out);
```

A simple, yet powerful, stylesheet is the identity stylesheet:

```
<?xml version="1.0"?>
<!-- Identity transformation -->
<xsl:stylesheet version="1.0" xmlns:xsl="http://www.w3.org/1999/XSL/Transform">
  <xsl:template match="*|@*|comment()|processing-instruction()|text()">
     <xsl:copy>
         <xsl:apply-templates select="*|@*|comment()|processing-
         instruction()|text()"/>
     </xsl:copy>
  </xsl:template>
</xsl:stylesheet>
```

If you apply this stylesheet to any XML document, you get the same document back. You can test the preceding example by passing it a reference to a file containing the identity stylesheet and (say) the **booklist** example. The output generated would be as expected:

```
<booklist>
   <book isbn="1234-123456-1234">
    <title>C Programming Language</title>
    <author>Kernighan and Ritchie</author>
    <publisher>IEEE</publisher>
    <price>7.99</price>
   </book>
   <book isbn="1230-23498-2349879">
    <title>Emperor's New Mind</title>
    <author>Roger Penrose</author>
    <publisher>Oxford Publishing Company</publisher>
    <price>15.99</price>
   </book>
</booklist>
```

Command-Line Invocation of the **XSLT** Processor

The XSLT processor comes with a command-line utility, **oraxsl**. This can be invoked from your shell (or MS-DOS command prompt) and can be used to transform multiple XML documents using a single stylesheet. The CLASSPATH environment variable needs to point to the **xmlparserv2.jar** file; and the PATH environment needs to point to the Java interpreter that comes with the JDK. It uses multiple threads to achieve a level of parallelization while performing the transformations. The following is its invocation syntax:

oraxsl options* source? stylesheet? result?

NOTE
* indicates 0 or more, while ? indicates 0 or 1.

The **oraxsl** tool expects to be given a stylesheet; an XML file to transform; and, optionally, a result file. If no result file is specified, it outputs the transformed document to the standard output device (usually just your screen). If multiple XML documents need to be transformed by a single stylesheet, the **-l** or **-d** options in conjunction with the **-s** and **-r** options should be used instead. These (and other) options are described in Table 2-1.

Option	Purpose
-h	Help mode (prints oraxsl invocation syntax).
-v	Verbose mode (some debugging information is printed and could help in tracing any problems that are encountered during processing).
-w	Show warnings (by default, warnings are turned off).
-e <error log>	A file to write errors to (specify a log file to write errors and warnings).
-t <# of threads>	Number of threads to use for processing (using multiple threads could provide performance improvements when processing multiple documents).
-l <xml file list>	List of files to transform (allows you to explicitly list the files to be processed).
-d <directory>	Directory with files to transform (the default behavior is to process all files in the directory). If only a certain subset of the files in that directory, e.g., one file, need to be processed, this behavior must be changed by using -l and specifying just the files that need to be processed. You could also change the behavior by using the '-x' or '-i' option to select files based on their extension.

TABLE 2-1. *Command-line options for **oraxsl***

Option	Purpose
-x <source extension>	Extensions to exclude (used in conjunction with -d. All files with the specified extension will not be selected).
-i <source extension>	Extensions to include (used in conjunction with -d. Only files with the specified extension will be selected).
-s <stylesheet>	Stylesheet to use (if -d or -l is specified, this option needs to be specified to specify the stylesheet to be used. The complete path must be specified).
-r <result extension>	Extension to use for results (if -d or -l is specified, this option must be specified to specify the extension to be used for the results of the transformation. So, if one specifies the extension "out", an input document "foo" would get transformed to "foo.out". By default, the results are placed in the current directory. This can be changed by using the -o option which allows you to specify a directory to hold the results).
-o <result directory>	Directory to place results (this must be used in conjunction with the -r option).

TABLE 2-1. *Command-line options for **oraxsl** (continued)*

Examples of Using oraxsl

Consider the following directory structure:

C:\xml, C:\xml\input, C:\xml\output

Assume **C:\xml\input** contains a set of XML documents (**doc1.xml**, **doc2.xml**, and so forth) you want to transform with the stylesheet **C:\Stylesheet.xsl**. You can do this by using **oraxsl** in a variety of ways.

If you want to transform each document in turn, you can type

oraxsl C:\xml\input\document1.xml C:\xml\Stylesheet.xsl document1.out

and repeat this for each document you want to transform.

To transform all XML documents (having the extension **xml**) in the **C:\xml\input** directory using the stylesheet **C:\xml\Stylesheet.xsl** and to place the results in **C:\xml\output** with the extension **.out** appended to them, type

oraxsl -s C:\xml\Stylesheet.xsl -d C:\xml\input -i xml -o C:\xml\output -o C:\xml\results -r out

Note that **doc1.xml** would be transformed to **doc1.xml.out**, **doc2.xml** would be transformed to **doc2.xml.out**, and so on. If many documents need to be transformed, it would improve performance to start several parallel transformations. To do this, you can use the **-t** flag to specify a number of threads. The larger the number of threads being used, the greater the memory consumption, so choose this number wisely. If, for example, you decide to use five simultaneous threads to do the transformations, you can add **-t 5** to the command-line argument list.

Suppose you want to transform only a subset of the documents in a directory. You need to list these out separately, using the **-l** option:

oraxsl -s C:\xml\Stylesheet.xsl -d C:\xml\input -l doc1.xml doc2.xml -o C:\xml\output -o C:\xml\results -r out

This would transform only the documents **doc1.xml** and **doc2.xml** to **doc1.xml.out** and **doc2.xml.out**, respectively.

XML Schema Support

By importing the XML Schema package and invoking the **setValidationMode** method with the **SCHEMA_VALIDATION** argument, one can also now validate XML documents against XML Schemas, the successors to DTDs. The Oracle XML Schema processor is compliant to the latest W3C Candidate Recommendation: Part 0 – Primer, Part 1 – Structures, Part 2 – Datatypes. The major advantages of XML Schemas are the support of simple and complex datatypes, and the constraints of the XML document structures, including Namespace support that was also lacking with DTDs. With datatypes support, this makes the conversion of XML document data into database data and vice versa even more straightforward. With the XML Schema processor, both a command-line version and APIs from a library are available for invocation.

An example of a driver Java code follows:

```
import oracle.xml.parser.schema.*;
import oracle.xml.parser.v2.*;

import java.net.*;
import java.io.*;
import org.w3c.dom.*;
import java.util.*;

public class XSDSetSchema
{
   public static void main(String[] args) throws Exception
   {
      if (args.length != 2)
      {
         System.out.println("Usage: java XSDSample <schema_file> <xml_file>");
```

```
      return;
   }

   XSDBuilder builder = new XSDBuilder();
   URL    url = createURL(args[0]);

   // Build XML Schema Object
   XMLSchema schemadoc = (XMLSchema)builder.build(url);
   process(args[1], schemadoc);
}

public static void process(String xmlURI, XMLSchema schemadoc)
throws Exception
{

   DOMParser dp  = new DOMParser();
   URL       url = createURL (xmlURI);

   // Set Schema Object for Validation
   dp.setXMLSchema(schemadoc);
   dp.setValidationMode(XMLParser.SCHEMA_VALIDATION);
   dp.setPreserveWhitespace (true);

   dp.setErrorStream (System.out);

   try
   {
      System.out.println("Parsing "+xmlURI);
      dp.parse (url);
      System.out.println("The input file <"+xmlURI+">
                        parsed without errors");
   }
   catch (XMLParseException pe)
   {
      System.out.println("Parser Exception: " + pe.getMessage());
   }
   catch (Exception e)
   {
      System.out.println ("NonParserException: " + e.getMessage());
   }

}

// Helper method to create a URL from a filename BCC
static URL createURL(String fileName)
{
   URL url = null;
   try
   {
      url = new URL(fileName);
   }
   catch (MalformedURLException ex)
   {
      File f = new File(fileName);
      try
      {
         String path = f.getAbsolutePath();
         // This is a bunch of weird code that is required to
```

```java
            // make a valid URL on the Windows platform, due
            // to inconsistencies in what getAbsolutePath returns.
            String fs = System.getProperty("file.separator");
            if (fs.length() == 1)
            {
                char sep = fs.charAt(0);
                if (sep != '/')
                    path = path.replace(sep, '/');
                if (path.charAt(0) != '/')
                    path = '/' + path;
            }
            path = "file://" + path;
            url = new URL(path);
        }
        catch (MalformedURLException e)
        {
            System.out.println("Cannot create url for: " + fileName);
            System.exit(0);
        }
    }
    return url;
}

}
```

Examples of an XML Schema, **catalogue.xsd**, and the XML file, **catalogue.xml**, that references it follow:

```xml
<?xml version="1.0"?>
<schema xmlns="http://www.w3.org/2000/10/XMLSchema"
        targetNamespace="http://www.publishing.org/namespaces/Catalogue"
        elementFormDefault="qualified"
        xmlns:xsi="http://www.w3.org/1999/XMLSchema-instance"
        xmlns:cat="http://www.publishing.org/namespaces/Catalogue">

    <complexType name="PublicationType">
        <sequence>
            <element name="Title" type="string" minOccurs="1"
             maxOccurs="unbounded"/>
            <element name="Author" type="string" minOccurs="1"
             maxOccurs="unbounded"/>
            <element name="Date" type="year" minOccurs="1" maxOccurs="1"/>
        </sequence>
    </complexType>
    <element name="Publication" type="cat:PublicationType" abstract="true"/>
    <element name="Book" substitutionGroup="cat:Publication">
        <complexType>
          <complexContent>
            <extension base="cat:PublicationType">
                <sequence>
                  <element name="ISBN" type="string" minOccurs="1"
                   maxOccurs="1"/>
                  <element name="Publisher" type="string" minOccurs="1"
                   maxOccurs="1"/>
                </sequence>
            </extension>
          </complexContent>
```

```
            </complexContent>
          </complexType>
      </element>
      <element name="Magazine" substitutionGroup="cat:Publication">
          <complexType>
            <complexContent>
              <restriction base="cat:PublicationType">
                <sequence>
                  <element name="Title" type="string" minOccurs="1"
                   maxOccurs="unbounded"/>
                  <element name="Author" type="string" minOccurs="0"
                   maxOccurs="0"/>
                  <element name="Date" type="year" minOccurs="1" maxOccurs="1"/>
                </sequence>
              </restriction>
            </complexContent>
          </complexType>
      </element>
      <element name="Catalogue">
          <complexType>
            <sequence>
              <element ref="cat:Publication" minOccurs="0"
               maxOccurs="unbounded"/>
            </sequence>
          </complexType>
      </element>
</schema>
```

Note that in this XML Schema, a "year" datatype now exists, along with limits on the value, i.e., facets, along with Namespaces support. The XML document follows:

```
<?xml version="1.0"?>
<Catalogue xmlns="http://www.publishing.org/namespaces/Catalogue"
           xmlns:xsi="http://www.w3.org/1999/XMLSchema-instance"
           xsi:schemaLocation=
                     "http://www.publishing.org/namespaces/Catalogue
                      catalogue.xsd">
        <Magazine>
              <Title>Natural Health</Title>
              <Date>1999</Date>
        </Magazine>
        <Book>
              <Title>Illusions The Adventures of a Reluctant Messiah</Title>
              <Author>Richard Bach</Author>
              <Date>1977</Date>
              <ISBN>0-440-34319-4</ISBN>
              <Publisher>Dell Publishing Co.</Publisher>
        </Book>
        <Book>
              <Title>The First and Last Freedom</Title>
              <Author>J. Krishnamurti</Author>
              <Date>1954</Date>
              <ISBN>0-06-064831-7</ISBN>
              <Publisher>Harper &amp; Row</Publisher>
        </Book>
</Catalogue>
```

The Java Class Generator

The XML Class Generator for Java creates Java source files from an XML DTD or an XML Schema to assist in programmatically creating valid document instances from dynamic data. This is useful when you want an application to send an XML message to another application according to an agreed-upon DTD or XML Schema, or you want a Web form to construct an XML document. You can construct, optionally validate, and print XML documents that comply with the input DTD or XML Schema in your Java applications using the generated classes. The Class Generator works in conjunction with the Oracle XML Parser for Java, which parses the DTD or XML Schema and passes the parsed DTD or XML Schema to the class generator, as shown in Figure 2-2.

The Class Generator then queries the DTD or XML Schema for all the elements. A Java class is generated for each of these elements. These classes have methods to set the attributes and add child nodes by the corresponding content model. The Java class corresponding to the root element also has methods to validate and print the constructed XML document. In the following subsections, we use an example to show how the XML Class Generator for Java can be used to process a DTD or XML Schema and generate classes for the DTD's or XML Schema's elements. It then shows how to use the methods of the element classes to programmatically construct a valid XML document.

The Input DTD

The following DTD file for book data, **bookcatalog.dtd**, is used as the input to the class generator. Here, the DTD specifies the XML document root is BOOKCATALOG. BOOKCATALOG consists of one or more BOOKs. Each BOOK contains a required ISBN attribute as an unique identifier, as well as several optional attributes and child elements, such as TITLE for book title, AUTHORNAME for author's name, PUBLISHER

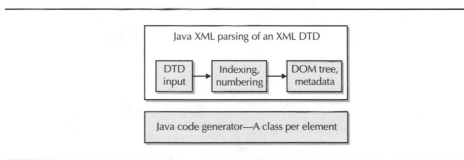

FIGURE 2-2. *Architecture of the XML Class Generator*

for publisher, and so on. Optional attributes and children are followed by a **?** in the element definition:

```
<!-- DTD for Book Data -->
<!ELEMENT BOOKCATALOG (BOOK)*>
<!ELEMENT BOOK (TITLE, AUTHORNAME, PUBLISHER?, PUBLISHYEAR?, PRICE?)>
<!ATTLIST BOOK ISBN CDATA #REQUIRED>
<!ATTLIST BOOK BOOKTYPE (Fiction|SciFi|Fantasy) #IMPLIED>
<!ELEMENT TITLE (#PCDATA)>
<!ELEMENT AUTHORNAME (#PCDATA)>
<!ELEMENT PUBLISHER (#PCDATA)>
<!ELEMENT PUBLISHYEAR (#PCDATA)>
<!ELEMENT PRICE (#PCDATA)>
```

Processing the DTD to Generate Java Classes

The following code sample processes a DTD and generates the corresponding classes for elements in the DTD. The sample uses an external DTD file along with the name of the root element. The class generator can also parse an XML document and use the DTD defined in the document. Running the class generator on the preceding DTD creates Java classes for each element (BOOKCATALOG, BOOK, TITLE, and so on). A Java application can then use the methods defined on these classes to create a valid XML document containing employee data.

```java
public class SampleMain
{
    public static void main (String args[])
    {
        // validate arguments
        if (args.length != 1)
        {
            System.out.println("Usage: java SampleMain "+
                               "-root <rootName> <fileName>");
            return ;
        }
        try // to open the External DTD File
        {
            // instantiate the parser
            XMLParser parser    = new XMLParser();
            String doctype_name = null;
            parser.parseDTD(fileToURL(args[2]), args[1]);
            DTD dtd = (DTD)parser.getDoctype();
            doctype_name = args[1];
            // generate the Java files...
            ClassGenerator generator = new ClassGenerator();
```

```
          // set generate comments to true
          generator.setGenerateComments(true);
          // set output directory
          generator.setOutputDirectory(".");
          // set validating mode to true
          generator.setValidationMode(true);
          // generate Java src
          generator.generate(dtd, doctype_name);
      }
      catch (Exception e)
      {
          System.out.println ("XML Class Generator: Error " +
                              e.toString());
          e.printStackTrace();
      }
   }
}
```

Creating a Valid XML Document from Java Classes

The following Java code shows how generated methods might be used. Here, two BOOK records are created: book1 and book2. The required attributes are enforced by adding them as parameters to the constructor. In this case, ISBN is a required attribute for the BOOK element. Elements for each column are also created (title1, authorname1, and so on). If an element has an enumerated attribute, a static constant is defined in the class for each value in the enumeration. To build an XML document tree, the various data elements are grouped by assigning them to each row element as tree nodes. Each BOOK element is then added as a node to the document root element BOOKCATALOG. In this example, classes generated by the class generator are in uppercase:

```
public class CreateBooks
{
   public static void main (String args[])
   {
      try
      {
         BOOKCATALOG bookList = new BOOKCATALOG();
         // New book book1
         BOOK book1 = new BOOK("7654"); // create book1 and set ISBN
         TITLE title1 = new TITLE("The Adventures of Don Quixote");
         book1.setBOOKTYPE(BOOK.BOOKTYPE_FICTION);
         AUTHORNAME authorname1 = new AUTHORNAME("Miguel Cervantes");
         PUBLISHER publisher1 = new PUBLISHER("Oracle Press");
```

```
PUBLISHYEAR publishyear1= new PUBLISHYEAR("2000");
PRICE price1= new PRICE("1.00");

// New book book2
BOOK book2 = new BOOK("7788"); // create book2 and set ISBN
TITLE title2 = new TITLE("The Iliad");
book2.setBOOKTYPE(BOOK.BOOKTYPE_FICTION);
AUTHORNAME authorname2 = new AUTHORNAME("Homer");
PUBLISHER publisher2 = new PUBLISHER("Oracle Press");
PUBLISHYEAR publishyear2= new PUBLISHYEAR("1000");
PRICE price1= new PRICE("");



book1.addnode(isbn1); // Add data as tree nodes to book1
book1.addnode(title1);
...

book2.addnode(isbn2); // Add data as tree nodes to book2
book2.addnode(title2);
...

bookList.addNode(book1); // Add book1 as tree node to
                         // bookList doc root
bookList.addNode(book2); // Add book2 as tree node to
                         // bookList doc root

bookList.validateContent();
bookList.print(System.out);
}
catch (Exception e)
{
System.out.println(e.toString());
e.printStackTrace();
}
}
}
```

XML Document Created by Java Application

The input for the preceding Java application can be received from various sources, such as a Web form, SAX parser, or JDBC result set. The preceding Java application creates an XML document that can then be transformed as HTML output using the

XSLT processor or stored in the database using the XSQL Servlet. The XML document created is similar to the following:

```
<?xml version="1.0"?>
<!DOCTYPE BOOKCATALOG SYSTEM "bookcatalog.dtd">
<BOOKCATALOG>
  <BOOK ISBN = "7654" BOOKTYPE="Fiction">
    <TITLE>The Adventures of Don Quixote</TITLE>
    <AUTHORNAME>Miguel Cervantes</AUTHORNAME>
    <PUBLISHER>Oracle Press</PUBLISHER>
    <PUBLISHYEAR>2000</PUBLISHYEAR>
    <PRICE>1.00</PRICE>
  </BOOK>
  <BOOK ISBN = "7788" BOOKTYPE="FICTION">
    <TITLE>The Iliad</TITLE>
    <AUTHORNAME>Homer</AUTHORNAME>
    <PUBLISHER>Oracle Press</PUBLISHER>
    <PUBLISHYEAR>1000</PUBLISHYEAR>
    <PRICE></PRICE>
  </BOOK>
</BOOKCATALOG>
```

The Input XML Schema

As mentioned previously, the input could be from an XML Schema instead of a DTD, and the mechanisms are similar for the Java driver program and the input content model. Examples of an XML Schema and the Java program that calls the necessary class generator methods follow, respectively:

```
<xsd:schema xmlns:xsd="http://www.w3.org/1999/XMLSchema">

<xsd:element name="comment" type="xsd:string"/>

<xsd:element name = "PurchaseOrder">
  <xsd:complexType>
      <xsd:element name="shipTo" type="Address"/>
      <xsd:element name="billTo" type="Address"/>
      <xsd:element ref="comment" minOccurs="0"/>
      <xsd:element name="items" type="Items"/>
      <xsd:attribute name="orderDate" type="xsd:date"/>
      <xsd:attribute name="shipDate" type="xsd:date"/>
      <xsd:attribute name="receiveDate" type="xsd:date"/>
  </xsd:complexType>
</xsd:element>

<xsd:complexType name="Address">
  <xsd:element name="name" type="xsd:string"/>
```

```
    <xsd:element name="street" type="xsd:string"/>
    <xsd:element name="city" type="xsd:string"/>
    <xsd:element name="zip" type="xsd:decimal"/>
    <xsd:attribute name="country" type="xsd:NMTOKEN"
        use="fixed" value="US"/>
</xsd:complexType>

<xsd:complexType name="Items">
    <xsd:element name="item" minOccurs="0" maxOccurs="unbounded">
        <xsd:complexType>
          <xsd:element name="productName" type="xsd:string"/>
          <xsd:element name="quantity" type="xsd:int"/>
          <xsd:element name="price" type="xsd:decimal"/>
          <xsd:element name="shipDate" type="xsd:date" minOccurs='0'/>
          <xsd:element ref="comment" minOccurs="0"/>
          <xsd:attribute name="partNum" type="xsd:string"/>
        </xsd:complexType>
    </xsd:element>
</xsd:complexType>

</xsd:schema>

import oracle.xml.classgen.*;
import oracle.xml.parser.v2.*;
import oracle.xml.parser.schema.*;
import java.io.*;
import java.util.*;

public class TestPo
{
    public static void main (String args[])
    {
        TestPo testpo = new TestPo();
        try
        {
            PurchaseOrder po = new PurchaseOrder();
            Address address = new Address();
            Items items = new Items();

            // Create shipTo address
            address.addName("Mary Smith");
            address.addStreet("Laurie Meadows");
            address.addCity("San Mateo");
            address.addZip(new Float(98806));

            // Add shipTo address to the PurchaseOrderType
            po.addShipTo(address);

            // Create billTo address
            address.addName("John Smith");
```

```
address.addStreet(" 1 North Broadway");
address.addCity("New York");
address.addZip(new Float(11208));

// Add billTo address to the PurchaseOrderType
po.addBillTo(address);

// Add comment to the PurchaseOrderType
po.addComment(new Comment("Happy Birthday"));

// Create the items
items.addProductName("Perfume");
items.addQuantity(1);
items.addPrice(new Float(75));
items.addComment(new Comment("Have a nice day!"));
items.addShipDate(new String("Nov 14, 2000"));
items.setPartNum("1TMZ411");

// Add items to PurchaseOrderType
po.addItems(items);

// Set purchase order date
po.setOrderDate("December 17, 2000");
po.setShipDate("December 19, 2000");
po.setReceiveDate("December 21, 2000");


//po.print(System.out);

// Get Elements of Purchase Order
Vector elements = po.getElements();

System.out.print("The child element node types of PurchaseOrder is:");
for (int i = 0; i < elements.size(); i++)
{
    System.out.print(elements.elementAt(i));
    System.out.print("   ");
}

System.out.println();
System.out.println("The attributes of PurchaseOrder is: ");
System.out.print("Order Date = " );
System.out.print(po.getOrderDate());
System.out.println();
System.out.print("Ship Date = " );
System.out.print(po.getShipDate());
System.out.println();
System.out.print("Receive Date = " );
System.out.print(po.getReceiveDate());
System.out.println();
```

```
      }
      catch (InvalidContentException e)
      {
         System.out.println(e.getMessage());
         e.printStackTrace();
      }
      catch (Exception e)
      {
         System.out.println(e.toString());
         e.printStackTrace();
      }
   }
}
```

Viewing and Transforming XML with Java

Many XML developers today use Oracle JDeveloper as an *integrated development environment (IDE)* to speed their development cycle and take advantage of the component approach in building applications based on numerous prebuilt components. The JavaBeans component model is fully supported in Oracle JDeveloper. In JDeveloper, you can build Java beans that can later be reused in other projects, or install and use Java beans that are built by Oracle or third-party vendors. The beans in JDeveloper can be installed on the JDeveloper Tools palette and later be customized and included in your application. Once the beans are installed, you can use drag-and-drop to add beans from the Tools palette to your application. When you add a bean to your application design surface, JDeveloper automatically generates the code needed to instantiate and customize the bean. This usually includes creating an instance of the bean, setting the bean properties to customize the bean, and adding Action Listeners to the bean to enable the application to handle the events generated by the bean. Because this technology is so powerful and easy to use, it is natural to encapsulate key XML functionality into Java beans.

The XML TransViewer beans are a set of XML components for Java applications or applets that make adding a visual interface to an XML application easy. These visual and nonvisual Java components can be integrated into Oracle JDeveloper to enable developers to create and deploy XML-based database applications quickly. The following beans are provided:

- **DOMBuilder** bean

- **XSLTransformer** bean

- **XMLSourceView** bean

- **XMLTreeView** bean

- **XMLTransformPanel** bean

- **DBView** bean

- **DBAccess** bean

If you install these beans into your JDeveloper environment, you benefit by the automatic code generation that JDeveloper performs when you include the beans in your application. If you do not use JDeveloper and work In a command-line JDK environment, you can also use the beans to visualize and transform XML. In this case, you simply use the beans as you would any other classes. The examples in this chapter were developed using JDeveloper. Three of the beans—the **DOMBuilder** bean, the **XSLTransformer** bean, and the **DBAccess** bean—are nonvisual beans. The rest are visual beans that extend JPanel and can be included in your application anywhere you can use JPanel. Let's review the beans one by one, highlighting what they do and how you can use them.

DOMBuilder Bean

The **DOMBuilder** bean encapsulates the Java XML Parser with a bean interface and extends its functionality to permit asynchronous parsing. By registering a listener, Java applications can parse large or successive documents by having control return immediately to the caller. The following sample code shows a program that takes a list of XML files as parameters and parses all of these files concurrently:

```
package sample;

import java.awt.event.*;
import oracle.xml.async.*;
import oracle.xml.parser.v2.*;
import org.w3c.dom.*;
import java.net.*;
import java.io.*;
```

```java
public class MParse extends Object
  implements DOMBuilderListener, DOMBuilderErrorListener{
  int numArgs,i;
  String Args[];
  DOMBuilder tParser;

  public MParse(String[] args) {
    Args=args;
  }
  public void parse() {
    for (i=0;i<Args.length;i++) {
      // new instance of the asynchronous parser
      tParser=new DOMBuilder(i);
      // add this object as Listener so we will be notified
      // when parsing is complete
      tParser.addDOMBuilderListener(this);
      // or when an error occurs
      tParser.addDOMBuilderErrorListener(this);
      System.out.println("Start parsing "+Args[i]);
      try {
        tParser.parse(new URL("file:"+(String)Args[i]));
      } catch (Exception e) {
        System.out.println(e.toString());
      }
    }
    System.out.println("Multiple files parsed in background threads");
  }

  public static void main(String[] args) {
    MParse mParse = new MParse(args);
    mParse.parse();
  }

  // Implementing DOMBuilderListener Interface

  // This method is called by the DOMBuilder object when
  // the parsing of the document starts.
  public void domBuilderStarted(DOMBuilderEvent p0) {

  }
  // This method is called by the DOMBuilder object when
  // the parsing of the document produces an error.
  public void domBuilderError(DOMBuilderEvent p0) {

  }
  // This method is called by the DOMBuilder object when
  // the parsing of the document is completed.
  public void domBuilderOver(DOMBuilderEvent p0) {
```

```
    DOMBuilder parser;
    XMLDocument xmlDoc;
    int id;
    // Get a reference to the parser instance that
    // finished parsing.
    parser=(DOMBuilder)p0.getSource();
    // Get the parser id to identify the file being parsed
    id=parser.getId();
    System.out.println("Parse completed for file "+Args[id]);
    // get the dom tree
    xmlDoc=parser.getDocument();
    // Here we do whatever we would like to do with the
    // parsed document.
  }

  // Implementing DOMBuilderErrorListener Interface

  // This method is called when parsing error occurs.
  public void domBuilderErrorCalled(DOMBuilderErrorEvent p0) {
    int id=((DOMBuilder)p0.getSource()).getId();
    System.out.println("Parse error for "+Args[id]+": "+
    p0.getException().getMessage());
  }
}
```

If you run this program using the command

java Sample.mParse booklist1.xml booklist2.xml booklist3.xml

you get output such as that shown in Figure 2-3.

Start parsing booklist1.xml
Start parsing booklist2.xml
Start parsing booklist3.xml
Multiple files parsed in background threads
Parse completed for file booklist2.xml
Parse completed for file booklist1.xml
Parse completed for file booklist3.xml

FIGURE 2-3. *Example output in JDeveloper that uses the DOMBuilder bean*

If you have to parse a large number of files, you can use the **DOMBuilder** bean to deliver significant time savings. Depending on the system and the number of concurrent threads (instances of DOMBuilder), we have achieved up to 40 percent faster times compared to parsing the files one after another.

The asynchronous parsing in a background thread implemented in DOM Builder can also be used in interactive visual applications. If the application parses a large file using the normal parser, the user interface will freeze until the document is parsed completely. This can easily be avoided if the DOMBuilder is used instead. After calling the parse method of DOMBuilder, the application receives control back immediately. The application can then display a window with the message *Parsing, please wait.* The window can also show a Cancel button, so the user can abort the operation if he or she decides to do so. If no user action is taken, the program resumes when the domBuilderOver method is called by the **DOMBuilder** bean upon completion of the parsing task in the background.

XSLTransformer Bean

The **XSLTransformer** bean encapsulates the Java XML Parser XSLT processing engine with a bean interface and extends its functionality to permit asynchronous transformation. By registering a listener, Java applications can transform large or successive documents by having control returned immediately to the caller. Because the XSL transformations are time-consuming, you may consider using this asynchronous interface for XSL transformations. The **XSLTransformer** bean can benefit applications that transform large numbers of files by transforming multiple files concurrently. It also can be used for visual applications for achieving responsive user interfaces. The considerations here are the same as with the **DOMBuilder** bean. From a programming standpoint, the preceding sample demonstrates the general approach that can also be applied to XSLTransformerListener interface, the calling application is notified when the transformation is over. Therefore, the calling application can do something else between requesting the transformation and getting the result.

XMLSourceView Bean

The **XMLSourceView** bean improves the viewing of XML and XSL files by color-highlighting XML/XSL syntax. The bean also supports Edit mode. Easily integrated with the **DOMBuilder** bean, it allows for pre- or postparsing visualization and validation against a specified DTD. The following code illustrates a simple application that shows an XML file with the XML syntax highlighted. Figure 2-4 shows a screen shot of this program.

FIGURE 2-4. *Sample program using the XML DOMBuilder bean in JDeveloper*

```java
import java.awt.*;
import oracle.xml.srcviewer.*;
import oracle.xml.treeviewer.*;
import oracle.xml.parser.v2.XMLDocument;
import oracle.xml.parser.v2.*;
import org.w3c.dom.*;
import java.net.*;
import java.io.*;
import java.util.*;
import java.awt.event.*;
import javax.swing.*;
import javax.swing.event.*;

public class ViewSample
{
```

```
public static void main(String[] args)
{
   String fileName = new String ("booklist.xml");
   if (args.length > 0) {
      fileName = args[0];
   }
   JFrame         frame         = setFrame ("XMLViewer");
   XMLDocument    xmlDocument    = getXMLDocumentFromFile (fileName);
   XMLSourceView  xmlSourceView = setXMLSourceView (xmlDocument);
   XMLTreeView    xmlTreeView    = setXMLTreeView (xmlDocument);
   JTabbedPane    jtbPane        = new JTabbedPane ();

   jtbPane.addTab ("Source", null, xmlSourceView,
                   "XML document source view");
   jtbPane.addTab ("Tree", null, xmlTreeView,
                   "XML document tree view");
   jtbPane.setPreferredSize (new Dimension(400,300));
   frame.getContentPane().add (jtbPane);
   frame.setTitle    (fileName);
   frame.setJMenuBar (setMenuBar());
   frame.setVisible  (true);
}

static JFrame setFrame (String title)
{
  JFrame frame = new JFrame (title);
  //Center the window
  Dimension screenSize =
            Toolkit.getDefaultToolkit().getScreenSize();
  Dimension frameSize  = frame.getSize();
  if (frameSize.height > screenSize.height) {
     frameSize.height = screenSize.height;
  }
  if (frameSize.width > screenSize.width) {
    frameSize.width = screenSize.width;
  }
  frame.setLocation ((screenSize.width - frameSize.width)/2,
                     (screenSize.height - frameSize.height)/2);
  frame.addWindowListener(new WindowAdapter() {
    public void windowClosing(WindowEvent e) {
       System.exit(0);
    }
```

```
      });
      frame.getContentPane().setLayout (new BorderLayout());
      frame.setSize(new Dimension(400, 300));
      frame.setVisible (false);
      frame.setTitle (title);
      return frame;
}

static JMenuBar setMenuBar ()
{
   JMenuBar menuBar = new JMenuBar();
   JMenu    menu    = new JMenu ("Exit");
   menu.addMenuListener (new MenuListener () {
      public void menuSelected (MenuEvent ev) { System.exit(0); }
      public void menuDeselected (MenuEvent ev) {}
      public void menuCanceled (MenuEvent ev) {}
   });
   menuBar.add (menu);
   return menuBar;
}


/**
 * creates   XMLSourceView object
 */
static XMLSourceView setXMLSourceView(XMLDocument xmlDocument)
{
   XMLSourceView xmlView = new XMLSourceView();
   xmlView.setXMLDocument(xmlDocument);
   xmlView.setEditable(true);
   xmlView.setBackground(Color.yellow);
   return xmlView;
}
/**
 * creates   XMLTreeView object
 */
static XMLTreeView setXMLTreeView(XMLDocument xmlDocument)
{
   XMLTreeView xmlView = new XMLTreeView();
   xmlView.setXMLDocument(xmlDocument);
   xmlView.setBackground(Color.yellow);
   return xmlView;
}
```

```
static XMLDocument getXMLDocumentFromFile (String fileName)
{
  XMLDocument doc = null;

  try {
    DOMParser parser = new DOMParser();
    try {
      FileInputStream in = new FileInputStream(fileName);
      parser.setPreserveWhitespace(false);
      parser.setBaseURL(new URL("file://"));
      parser.parse(in);
      in.close();
    } catch (Exception ex) {
      ex.printStackTrace();
      System.exit(0);
    }

    doc = (XMLDocument)parser.getDocument();

    try {
      doc.print(System.out);
    } catch (Exception ie) {
      ie.printStackTrace();
      System.exit(0);
    }

  }
  catch (Exception e) {
    e.printStackTrace();
  }
  return doc;
}
}
```

XMLTreeView *Bean*

The **XMLTreeView** bean displays a visual view of an XML document, enabling users to manipulate the tree easily with a mouse to hide or view selected branches. The code sample previously shown uses the bean together with the **XMLSourceView** bean. Figure 2-5 shows a screen shot from this sample application with the **XMLTreeView** bean window selected.

XMLTransformPanel Bean

The **XMLTransformPanel** bean enables users to transform an XML document to almost any text-based format, such as XML and HTML, by applying an XSL

```
Exit

┌─────────┬──────┐
│ Source  │ Tree │
├─────────┴──────┴──────────────────────────────┐
│  ☐ [DOCUMENT]                                   │
│     ▢ version = '1.0'                           │
│  ◉ ☐ booklist                                   │
│     ◉ ☐ book                                    │
│           ▢ isbn="1234-123456-1234"             │
│        ◉ ☐ title                                │
│              ▢ "C Programming Language"         │
│        ◉ ☐ author                               │
│              ▢ "Kernighan and Ritchie"          │
│        ◉ ☐ publisher                            │
│              ▢ "ECC"                            │
│        ◉ ☐ price                                │
│              ▢ "7.99"                           │
│     ☐─ ☐ book                                   │
│     ☐─ ☐ book                                   │
│     ☐─ ☐ book                                   │
│     ☐─ ☐ book                                   │
└─────────────────────────────────────────────────┘
```

FIGURE 2-5.   *An example of using the XML TreeView bean to visualize XML as a tree*

stylesheet. The bean can be included as part of the application that manages XML and XSL data, and it has the following list of features:

- Imports and exports XML and XSL files from the file system.

- Supports multiple database connections.

- Imports and exports XML, XSL, and HTML/text files from Oracle8i databases. The bean maintains its own *Character Large Object (CLOB)* tables in the database. Each CLOB table has two columns. The first column is a string type and is used to store the data name for the data stored in the second column. The second column is a CLOB type and is used to store the actual text data. In other words, the first column contains the filename and the second column contains the file data itself. Once you log in, the bean lists all CLOB tables in the user schema. If you click a particular table name, the bean lists the filenames in the table. You can create and delete tables; and retrieve, replace, and add files to the tables. These tables can be used as a "file system" in the database to organize your file information.

■ Creates XML from database result sets. This feature enables you to submit any SQL query to the database you are currently connected to. The bean converts the result set into XML and automatically loads this XML data into the beans XML buffer for further processing. Figures 2-6 and 2-7 show the bean database interface and the query we use to create the XML data from the EMP table in the database.

■ Edits the XML and XSL data loaded into the bean.

■ Applies the XSL transformation to the XML buffer and shows the result. The bean also enables you to export the result to the file system or to a CLOB table in the database. Figure 2-8 shows the resulting page after the bean applies an XSL stylesheet to the data shown in Figure 2-7.

The CLOB tables created by the bean can be used by trigger-based stored procedures to mirror tables or views in the database into HTML data that are held in these CLOB tables. For example, using the bean, you can create a SQL query that selects the information you need and stores the resulting XML data in a CLOB table. Then, using the bean, you can develop an XSL stylesheet and interactively apply the stylesheet to this XML data until you are satisfied by the data presentation (the HTML output

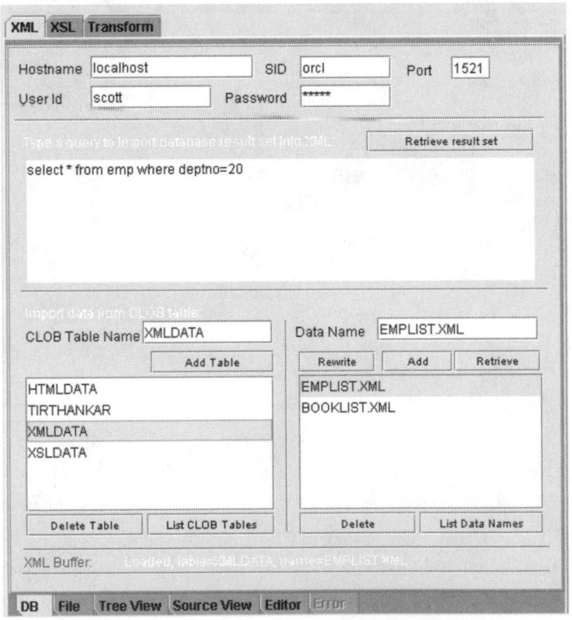

FIGURE 2-6. *Retrieving a query result set as an XML file*

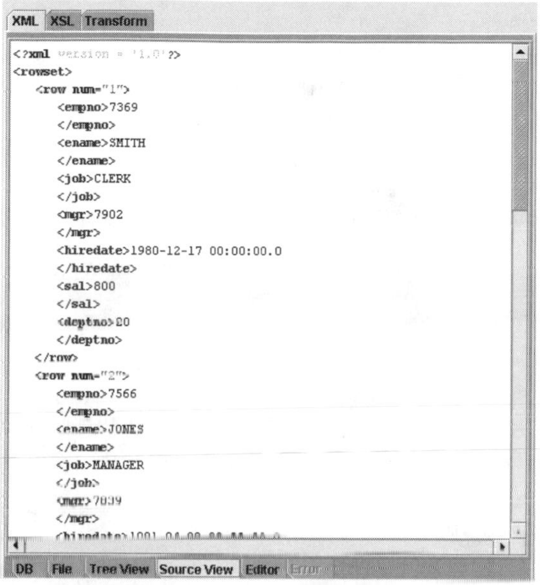

FIGURE 2-7. *The XML generated by the TransViewer bean*

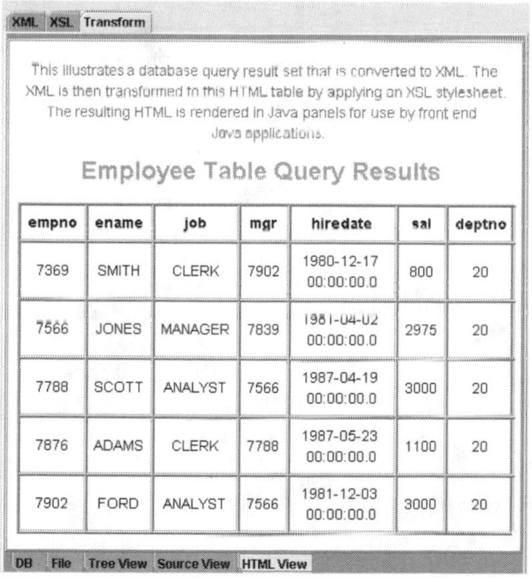

FIGURE 2-8. *The XML TransViewer bean shows the result in an HTML view window*

produced by the XSL transformation). Once you have the SQL (the data selection layer) and the XSL (the data presentation) layer ready, you can create a trigger on the original table or view used by your SQL query. This trigger runs a stored procedure that runs the query, applies the stylesheet, and stores the resulting HTML in a CLOB table. This process repeats any time the source data table is updated. Therefore, the HTML stored in the CLOB table always mirrors the last data stored in the tables being queried. A simple JSP page can then be used to display this HTML. In this scenario, multiple end users do not produce multiple data queries that contribute to bigger loads to the database. The HTML is regenerated only when the underlying data changes.

DBView Bean

The **DBView** bean is a visual bean that can be used to display database information using XML and XSL transformations. It allows views into database tables and column data of these tables, as shown in the **XMLTransformPanel** bean example.

DBAccess Bean

The **DBAccess** bean is a nonvisual bean that allows access to CLOB tables managed by the XMLTransformPanel bean. This access is through JDBC to the CLOB tables that may store the XMLand XSL files, or even the files resulting from applying the XSL stylesheet to the XML file. It is used in the **XMLTransformPanel** bean example.

XML Parser for PL/SQL

The Oracle XML parser for PL/SQL provides you with a convenient way of extending your existing PL/SQL applications to support XML. The parser is built on the Oracle XML parser for Java V2 and needs the latter to be installed inside the Oracle8i/9i JVM to run. It uses the Oracle8i/9i Java Stored Procedures mechanism to invoke the Java parser to do the actual parsing and manipulation of the XML document. Because of this, the parser cannot run in a release earlier than Oracle8i/9i. The parser fully supports the XML, DOM, Namespaces, and XSLT specifications. Support for SAX is planned in a future release of the parser.

Three PL/SQL packages encompass the functionality of the parser, namely, **xmlparser**, **xmldom**, and **xslprocessor**. The **xmlparser** package contains methods to parse an XML document from a string, a file, or a CLOB. It also contains methods to parse an XML DTD and to set it prior to parsing the actual XML document. The parser, like its Java counterpart, is optionally validating, and you can also instruct it to preserve white space (for XSLT processing), if required. The **xmldom** package implements the DOM interfaces. In addition, it provides methods to write an XML document or *document type definition (DTD)* that is stored in memory to a string, a file, or a CLOB. The **xslprocessor** package provides support for doing XSLT processing through methods that wrap the XSLT APIs in the Oracle XML Parser for Java.

Examples

Quite often, a DTD may be stored within the database as a CLOB. Referring to such a DTD directly from the XML document is not currently possible. To validate an XML document using this DTD, you need to parse the DTD beforehand and register it with the parser before it begins parsing the actual XML document. The following code demonstrates how this can be done:

```
create or replace procedure dtdexample(dtd clob, root varchar2,
            inpfile varchar2, errfile varchar2) is
p xmlparser.Parser;
doc xmldom.DOMDocument;
dt xmldom.DOMDocumentType;
nl xmldom.DOMNodeList;

begin
-- new parser
    p := xmlparser.newParser;

-- set error log
    xmlparser.setErrorLog(p, dir || '/' || errfile);

-- parse dtd clob and register it
    xmlparser.parseDTDClob(p, dtd, root);
    dt := xmlparser.getDoctype(p);
    xmlparser.setDoctype(p, dt);

-- parse input file
    xmlparser.setValidationMode(p, true);
    xmlparser.parse(p, inpfile);

exception when others then
raise;
end dtdexample;
/
show errors;
```

The first thing the preceding example does is to create a new instance of the parser. Remember, for the purpose of recording any errors that may occur during parsing, you need to specify a file to which the parser should output error messages:

```
-- new parser
    p := xmlparser.newParser;
```

```
-- set some characteristics
   xmlparser.setErrorLog(p, dir || '/' || errfile);
```

The next step is to parse the DTD, get a handle to it, and register it with the parser:

```
-- parse dtd clob and register it
   xmlparser.parseDTDClob(p, dtd, root);
   dt := xmlparser.getDoctype(p);
   xmlparser.setDoctype(p, dt);
```

Note that you need to specify the root element of the XML document while parsing the DTD. Before parsing the XML document, make sure you set it up to be validating. Once you do this, you can invoke the parse method, which then uses the DTD you just registered to validate the XML document:

```
-- parse input file
   xmlparser.setValidationMode(p, true);
   xmlparser.parse(p, dir || '/' || inpfile);
```

The preceding example does not generate any output. It would, however, write any errors (validation or otherwise) that occur to the error file you specified.

Using the XML Parser for Java, you saw how the XSLT support in the parser can be leveraged using the **XSLStylesheet** and **XSLProcessor** classes. In the XML Parser for PL/SQL, this functionality is provided by **xslprocessor.Stylesheet** and **xslprocessor .Processor**. In addition to these interfaces, the parser also provides you with methods to use XPath expressions to extract data from a DOM tree. The following code shows how this can be done:

```
create or replace procedure xslexample is

p xmlparser.Parser;
xmlbuf varchar2(512);
xslpat varchar2(512);
xmldoc xmldom.DOMDocument;
xmldocnode xmldom.DOMNode;
n xmldom.DOMNode;
begin
   xmlbuf := '<timegram><time>12:00</time></timegram>';
   xslpat := 'timegram/time/text()';

-- new parser
   p := xmlparser.newParser;

-- parse xml buffer
   xmlparser.parseBuffer(p, xmlbuf);
```

```
-- get document
   xmldoc := xmlparser.getDocument(p);

-- select a single node matching the XPath expression and
-- print its value
   xmldocnode := xmldom.makeNode(xmldoc);
   n := xslprocessor.selectSingleNode(xmldocnode, xslpat);
   dbms_output.put_line('Value of the first selected node is: ' ||
                        xslprocessor.valueOf(n, '.'));
exception when others then
   raise;
end xslexample;
/
show errors;
```

The purpose of the preceding example was to show how easy it is to use XPath, almost as a query language, with a DOM tree built by the Oracle XML parser. To illustrate, we define a small XML document to contain the time and an XPath expression that can retrieve that value:

```
xmlbuf := '<timegram><time>12:00</time></timegram>';
xslpat := 'timegram/time/text()';
```

As usual, you need to parse the XML document and get a handle to the root of the DOM tree:

```
-- new parser
   p := xmlparser.newParser;
-- parse xml buffer
   xmlparser.parseBuffer(p, xmlbuf);
-- get document
   xmldoc := xmlparser.getDocument(p);
```

You can now use the methods provided by the **xslprocessor** package to search the DOM tree using the given Xpath expression. The example uses the method **selectSingleNode** to retrieve the first node that matches a pattern. If you expect multiple nodes to match your pattern and are interested in all of them, you can choose to use the **selectNodes** method instead. After obtaining the node, the method obtains its value:

```
-- select a single node matching the Xpath expression and
-- print its value
   xmldocnode := xmldom.makeNode(xmldoc);
   n := xslprocessor.selectSingleNode(xmldocnode, xslpat);
   dbms_output.put_line('Value of the first selected node is: ' ||
                        xslprocessor.valueOf(n, '.'));
```

NOTE
*The **valueOf** method is being used with an XPath expression '.'. This is equivalent to the XSLT statement '<xsl:value-of select=".">'.*

The preceding example generates the output you would expect:

```
Value of the first selected node is: 12:00
```

The XML Parser and XSLT Processor for C

Oracle's XML Parser and its integrated XSLT Processor for C are provided in two forms: as a stand-alone, command-line executable, and as a library for linking with applications. Most users will write their own applications and use the XML library. The executable is provided as a quick way to familiarize new users with XML by parsing and validating their own test documents, and it will also be used to apply stylesheets to the XML document.

Parser and XSLT processor messages are kept in an external file (for internationalization), so your environment must tell the parser / XSLT processor where to find it. If you have an **ORACLE_HOME** directory defined, it will look in **$ORACLE_HOME/mesg** for the file. Otherwise, **ORA_XML_MESG** should be set to the *absolute* path of the directory containing the message file. Note that the file ending in **.msb** contains the actual messages. The matching **.msg** file exists so that you can look up the Cause/Action information for errors.

The Stand-Alone Parser and Integrated XSLT Processor

The stand-alone command-line parser / XSLT processor (named **xml**) is provided in the C distribution in the **bin/** subdirectory. Note that, on Windows NT, the XML shared libraries (DLLs) must be in the same directory as the executable or installed in a location that is in the search path. The XML DLLs are installed by default in the **bin/** directory, so no extra step is necessary when executing **xml** from this directory.

The command-line syntax for use of the stand-alone parser is

```
xml [switches] document
```

where *document* is the required XML input document and *switches* are optional
controls that change the parser's behavior. If no document is given or if the switches
are invalid (or **-h** for Help), a brief usage message is printed:

```
% xml
No document specified.
Usage: xml [switches] [document]
    -c              Conformance check only, no validation
    -e <encoding>   Specify default input file encoding
    -f              File - Interpret <document> as filespec, not URI
    -h              Help - show this usage help
    -l <language>   Language for error reporting
    -p              Print document/DTD structures after parse
    -s <stylesheet> Stylesheet - specifies the stylesheet
    -r              Exercise the stream interface for XSLT
    -v              Version - show parser version and exit
    -w              Whitespace - preserve ALL whitespace
    -W              Warning - stop parsing after a warning
    -x              Exercise SAX interface for parser (prints document)
```

If a document is specified but nothing else, that document is parsed and
validated, and the parser exits with a zero return code (indicating success). If an
error occurred, the error message is printed to standard error and the (nonzero)
error code is returned.

Parser switches are described in detail in Table 2-2.

Switch	Description
-c	**C**onformance check only. By default, the XML parser validates the document against its DTD (if there is one). When -c is specified, the document is parsed and tested for well-formedness, but not validated.

TABLE 2-2. *Command-line switches for **xml***

Switch	Description
-e *encoding*	**E**ncoding. Sets the *default* input file encoding. Input encoding can be automatically determined for some types of files (UCS-4, UTF-16, EBCDIC, etc) based on a Byte Order Mark which starts the file. For other files, the assumed encoding type may be specified with **-e**. If not given, the default encoding is UTF-8. Since ASCII parsing is about twice as fast as UTF-8, it is recommended that you specify **-e ASCII** if you *know* your input is ASCII. See the XML 1.0 specification, Appendix F (Autodetection of Character Encodings) for more information. Supported encodings are US-ASCII, ASCII, UTF-8, UTF-16, ISO-10646-UCS-2, ISO-8859-1, ISO-8859-2, ISO-8859-3, ISO-8859-4, ISO-8859-5, ISO-8859-6, ISO-8859-7, ISO-8859-8, ISO-8859-9, ISO-8859-10, EUC-JP, SHIFT_JIS, BIG5, GB2312, KOI8-R, EBCDIC, EBCDIC-CP-{US,CA,NL,WT,DK,NO,FI,SE,IT, ES,GB,FR,HE,BE,CH,ROECE,YU,IS}.
-h	**H**elp. Prints out the brief list of options shown above.
-l *language*	**L**anguage. Sets the language used for parser messages. By default, U.S. English is used.
-p	**P**rint. After successfully parsing (and perhaps validating) an input document, prints to standard out a tree-structured version of the document starting at the root *element*. If two **-p**'s are given (as -p -p or -pp) then the printout starts at the root *node*.
-s *stylesheet*	**S**tylesheet. Runs the document through the XSL processor after a successful parse, using the given stylesheet.
-v	**V**ersion. Prints out the version number of the parser then exits.
-w	**W**hitespace. Tells the parser to retain *all* whitespace. This parser differs from the 1.0 standard in that by default it omits whitespace used for formatting only. That is, text between element markup that is composed of *only* whitespace is suppressed unless **-w** is specified. Such whitespace commonly occurs at the end of each line, and at the front of lines for indenting (formatting) of documents.

TABLE 2-2. *Command-line switches for **xml*** (continued)

The Parser / XSLT Processor Library

The XML parser / XSLT processor is provided as a library named **libxml8.a** (or **libxml8.dll** on Windows NT), and for Oracle9i, it is named **libxml9.a** or **libxml9.dll**. This is the same library used by the stand-alone parser / XSLT processor. The library is intended to run against an Oracle 8.1.6 or later environment. For use with Oracle 8.1.5, a compatibility library named **libxmlc8.a** (or **libxmlc8.dll**) is provided and must be linked with the executable.

The library contains an API for initializing, parsing a file or buffer, resetting, and shutting down, plus full DOM, SAX, and XSLT implementations. Typical use would be *initialize, parse, terminate*. If multiple documents are to be parsed, the sequence would be *initialize, parse, parse, ..., terminate*. All data presented by a parse remains valid until termination or cleanup. If only the results on each parse are needed without retaining older data, the sequence would be *initialize, parse, clean, parse, clean, ..., terminate*. For applying stylesheets to the XML documents, an additional call to *xslprocess* before *terminate* or *clean* would be necessary.

Initialize

The parser must be initialized with **xmlinit** before it can be used. Each call to the initialization function returns a context pointer of type **(xmlctx *)**, which must be passed to all subsequent calls. Multiple initialize calls may be made, which return independent contexts. The prototype is as follows:

```
xmlctx *xmlinit(uword *err, const oratext *encoding,
                void (*msghdlr)(void *msgctx, const oratext *msg,
                                uword errcode),
                void *msgctx, const xmlsaxcb *saxcb,
                void *saxcbctx, const xmlmemcb *memcb,
                void *memcbctx, const oratext *lang);
```

The arguments to **xmlinit** are detailed in Table 2-3.

Parameter	I/O	Description
err	Out	Returned error code. On success, a context pointer is returned; on error, a NULL pointer is returned and err is set to the numeric error code indicating the problem. Required.

TABLE 2-3.   *Callback arguments for* **xmlinit**

encoding	In	Default encoding of XML files or buffers, if the encoding cannot be automatically determined. This is equivalent to the -e standalone parser switch (see the -e documentation for a list of supported encodings). May be NULL, in which case the default is UTF-8.
msghdlr	In	Pointer to message handler function. If NULL, error messages are written to standard error. If supplied, error messages are formatted and handed to the msghdlr function along with the numeric error code.
msgctx	In	Context pointer to be passed to msghdlr calls. This is an optional pointer; whatever value is supplied is simply passed to the message handler calls. It has no meaning to the parser itself, only to the user.
saxcb	In	SAX callback structure. If provided, the SAX interface will be used to return information on the parsed document. If NULL, the DOM interface is used. Note that all SAX callback functions within the structure are optional. See the SAX section following.
saxcbctx	In	SAX callback context pointer. Like the message context pointer, this is an optional user-defined pointer which if supplied is simply passed to all SAX callback functions. It has no meaning to the parser itself, only to the user.
memcb	In	Memory callback structure. If not provided, the parser does its own memory allocation and freeing. However, the user may opt to provide hooks for its own allocation, reallocation, and freeing functions which will be used instead.
memcbctx	In	Memory callback context. Like the message and SAX callbacks, you may specify a context pointer which is to be passed to all memory callback functions.
lang	In	Language for error messages. Language for error messages. Currently ignored, and U.S. English is assumed.

TABLE 2-3. *Callback arguments for* **xmlinit** *(continued)*

Parse

Two functions are provided to do the actual parsing of XML documents: **xmlparse** and **xmlparsebuf**. The **xmlparse** function parses a document stored in an external file; **xmlparsebuf** parses a document in a memory buffer. A third function, **xmlparsedtd**, parses an external DTD only and is used by the Class Generator (more on this later in the chapter). All three functions return a numeric error code: zero on success, nonzero on error. The prototype is as follows:

```
uword xmlparse(xmlctx *ctx, const oratext *filename,
               const oratext *encoding, ub4 flags);
```

The arguments to xmlparse are detailed in Table 2-4.

Parser flag bits are shown in Table 2-5.

The **xmlparsebuf** function is similar to **xmlparse** but takes a pointer to a buffer (**buffer**) and the length of that buffer (**len**) as arguments instead of a filename. The other arguments are the same as for **xmlparse**:

```
uword xmlparsebuf(xmlctx *ctx, const oratext *buffer, size t len,
                  const oratext *encoding, ub4 flags);
```

Cleanup

After a document has been parsed, pointers to data returned through DOM or SAX calls remain valid until an explicit cleanup or terminate call (that is, allocated memory is not released). Note that the DOM interface can only peruse and modify

Argument	I/O	Description
ctx	In	Context pointer returned by `xmlinit`.
filename	In	Path of XML document to parse.
encoding	In	Default encoding of document, if encoding cannot be automatically determined. Overrides the default passed to `xmlinit`.
flags	In	Mask of flag bits which modify the parser's behavior. See the following table.

TABLE 2-4. *Arguments for Xmlparse*

Flag name	Function (when set)
XML_FLAG_VALIDATE	Validates the parsed document against its DTD (if there is one).
XML_FLAG_DISCARD_WHITESPACE	Discards whitespace used only for formatting (at ends of lines, and indenting at beginnings of lines).
XML_FLAG_DTD_ONLY	Parses an external DTD only; setting this flag is like calling xmlparsedtd.

TABLE 2-5. *Flags for xmlparse*

the *current* (last parsed) document. If you are parsing multiple documents between the initialize and terminate calls, and you don't need the old data from previous parses, call **xmlclean** after each parse. This frees all allocated memory, but, remember, pointers to old data are invalid at this point. The prototype is as follows:

```
void xmlclean(xmlctx *ctx);
```

The **ctx** argument is the same context pointer returned by **xmlinit**.

Terminate

The terminate function, **xmlterm**, shuts down the parser and frees all allocated memory. The parser may not be used until another **xmlinit** call is made. If you want to parse multiple files in a single session, use **xmlclean** between files to release memory, instead of doing **xmlinit/xmlterm** each time. The prototype is as follows:

```
uword xmlterm(xmlctx *ctx);
```

This function returns an error code, which is zero on success or nonzero on error.

Example

The following shows the simplest possible skeleton program to demonstrate the use of the top-level parser functions.

```
main()
{
    xmlctx *ctx;
    uword   ecode;

    if (!(ctx = xmlinit(&ecode, NULL, NULL, NULL, NULL,
```

```
                                    NULL, NULL, NULL, NULL)))
    {
        /* An error occurred, ecode holds the error code */
        return 1;
    }
    if (ecode = xmlparse(ctx, "testdoc.xml", NULL, XML_FLAG_VALIDATE))
    {
        /* Parse or validation failed, error code in ecode */
        return 1;
    }
    /* Manipulate parsed data with DOM interface here */
    (void) xmlterm(ctx);
    return 0;
}
```

If you wanted to parse additional files in the preceding example while retaining the data from previous parses, just make more **xmlparse** calls before terminating. Remember, only the *latest* (current) document is accessible through the DOM interface, but any pointers to data for previous documents will still be valid. If you want to parse multiple files, but don't need to retain old data, call **xmlclean** each time. For example (omitting return code checks):

```
for (i = 1; i <= 9; i++)
{
    sprintf(filename, "file%d.xml", i);
    (void) xmlparse(ctx, filename, NULL, XML_FLAG_VALIDATE);
    xmlclean(ctx);
}
```

Document Object Model (DOM) API

The DOM API is used to query and manipulate a parsed document or to create a new document from scratch. The DOM interface is selected unless a SAX callback structure is passed to **xmlinit** (which turns off DOM and enables SAX). DOM is simply a set of functions composing an API. After a document has been successfully parsed (and perhaps validated), you can call the DOM functions to retrieve data, search, edit, and so forth.

DOM is a complicated API with many calls. We cannot describe them here; instead, you should read the W3C's DOM Level 1 specification for full details. This specification is located at **http://www.w3.org/TR/REC-DOM-Level-1/**.

Because DOM is an object-oriented specification and the C language is *not* object oriented, some changes had to made. In particular, the C function namespace is flat, so the names of DOM methods that are the same in several different classes have been changed to make them unique, as detailed in Table 2-6.

DOM Name	C Name
Attr::getName, ...	getAttrName, ...
CharacterData::getData, ...	getCharData, ...
DocumentType::getName, ...	getDocTypeName, ...
Entity::getPublicId, ...	getEntityPublicID, ...
NamedNodeMap::item	getChildNode
NamedNodeMap::getLength	getNodeMapLength
NodeList::item	getChildNode
NodeList::getLength	getNodeMapLength
Notation::getPublicId, ...	getNotationPubID, ...

TABLE 2-6. *DOM APIs*

Consult the parser header file **oraxml.h** for documentation of all DOM functions.

Simple API for XML (SAX)

Simple API for XML (SAX) is the alternative API for accessing a parsed document.
To use SAX, a set of callback functions is passed to **xmlinit**. The parser then invokes
these functions as the matching parts of a document are encountered. Compare this
to DOM, in which the document is parsed and a node tree is constructed in memory,
which can then be queried and modified through the DOM API. SAX functions are
invoked as the document is parsed. Each SAX function returns a **(sword)** error code.
If the code is nonzero, an error is indicated and parsing stops immediately.

The SAX callback structure (**xmlsaxcb**) is defined as follows:

```
struct xmlsaxcb
{
    sword (*startDocument)(void *ctx);
    sword (*endDocument)(void *ctx);
    sword (*startElement)(void *ctx, const oratext *name,
                          const struct xmlnodes *attrs);
    sword (*endElement)(void *ctx, const oratext *name);
    sword (*characters)(void *ctx, const oratext *ch, size_t len);
    sword (*ignorableWhitespace)(void *ctx, const oratext *ch,
                                 size_t len);
    sword (*processingInstruction)(void *ctx, const oratext *target,
                                   const oratext *data);
```

```
sword (*notationDecl)(void *ctx, const oratext *name,
                      const oratext *publicId,
                      const oratext *systemId);
sword (*unparsedEntityDecl)(void *ctx, const oratext *name,
                            const oratext *publidId,
                            const oratext *systemId,
                            const oratext *notationName);
sword (*nsStartElement)(void *ctx, const oratext *qname,
                        const oratext *local,
                        const oratext *nsp,
                        const struct xmlnodes *attrs);
}
```

Any or all callback functions may be specified; none are required. An optional context pointer may be provided and it will be passed to each callback function. Its use is entirely up to the user.

The callback functions are described in detail in Table 2-7.

Callback function	Description
startDocument	Invoked immediately before the parse begins.
endDocument	Invoked immediately after a successful parse ends.
startElement	Invoked when an element start-tag is found. If the namespace version of this callback is also supplied, it is called instead.
endElement	Invoked when an element end-tag is found.
characters	Invoked for each CDATA or #PCDATA.
ignorableWhitespace	Invoked for each run of ignorable whitespace, unless all whitespace is being retained (in which case characters is invoked).
processingInstruction	Invoked for each processing instruction.
notationDecl	Invoked for each NOTATION declaration in the DTD.
unparsedEntityDecl	Invoked for each unparsed entity (those with NDATA defined).
nsStartElement	The namespace version of startElement which provides the element's name broken down into namespace, local part, etc.

TABLE 2-7. *SAX Callback Functions*

The following program fragments show how to declare, register, and use the SAX callbacks:

```
/* declare SAX callback functions */
sword startdocument(void *ctx);
sword enddocument(void *ctx);
sword startelement(void *ctx, const oratext *name,
                   const xmlnodes *attrs);
sword endelement(void *ctx, const oratext *name);
sword characters(void *ctx, const oratext *ch, size_t len);
sword whitespace(void *ctx, const oratext *ch, size_t len);
sword pi(void *ctx, const oratext *target,
         const oratext *data);
sword notation(void *ctx, const oratext *name,
               const oratext *publicId,
               const oratext *systemId);
sword entity(void *ctx, const oratext *name,
             const oratext *publidId,
             const oratext *systemId,
             const oratext *notationName);
/* declare SAX callback context */
typedef struct
    uword    depth;  /* nested element level, for indenting */
} sax_context;

/* declare SAX callback structure */
xmlsaxcb sax_callback = {
    startdocument, enddocument, startelement, endelement,
    characters, whitespace, pi, notation, entity
};
/* declare SAX context and initialize */
sax_context saxctx = { 0 };   /* depth = 0 */
/* initialize parser specifying SAX callbacks */
xmlinit(&ecode, NULL, NULL, NULL, NULL,
        &sax_callback, (void *) &saxctx, NULL, NULL);

/* ----- SAX CALLBACKS ----- */
sword startdocument(void *context)
{
    puts("StartDocument");
    return 0;  /* success */
}

sword enddocument(void *context)
{
    puts("EndDocument");
    return 0;  /* success */
```

```
}

sword startelement(void *context, const oratext *name,
                   const xmlnodes *attrs)
{
    sax_context *saxctx = (sax_context *) context;
    indent(saxctx->depth);
    printf("<%s", name);
    if (attrs)
    {
        for (i = 0; i < numAttributes(attrs); i++)
        {
            attr = getAttributeIndex(attrs, i);
            printf(" %s=\"%s\"", getAttrName(attr), getAttrValue(attr));
        }
    }
    puts(">");
    saxctx->depth++;
    return 0;  /* success */
}

sword endelement(void *context, const oratext *name)
{
    sax_context *saxctx = (sax_context *) context;

    indent(--saxctx->depth);
    printf("</%s>\n", name);
    return 0;  /* success */
}

sword characters(void *context, const oratext *ch, size_t len)
{
    sax_context *saxctx = (sax_context *) context;

    indent(saxctx->depth);
    putchar('"');
    print_string((oratext *) ch, (sword) len);
    puts("\"");
    return 0;  /* success */
}

sword whitespace(void *context, const oratext *ch, size_t len)
{
    sax_context *saxctx = (sax_context *) context;

    indent(saxctx->depth);
    putchar('\'');
```

```
    print_string((oratext *) ch, (sword) len);
    puts("'");
    return 0;   /* success */
}

sword pi(void *context, const oratext *target,
         const oratext *data)
{
    sax_context *saxctx = (sax_context *) context;

    indent(saxctx->depth);
    fputs("PI", stdout);
    if (target)
        printf(" target=\"%s\"", target);
    if (data)
        printf (" data=\"%s\"", data);
    putchar('\n');
    return 0;   /* success */
}

sword notation(void *context, const oratext *name,
               const oratext *publicId,
               const oratext *systemId)
{
    sax_context *saxctx = (sax_context *) context;

    indent(saxctx->depth);
    printf("NOTATION '%s'", name);
    if (publicId)
        printf (" PUB:%s", publicId);
    if (systemId)
        printf(" SYS:%s", systemId);
    putchar('\n');
    return 0;   /* success */
}

sword entity(void *context, const oratext *name,
             const oratext *publidId,
             const oratext *systemId,
             const oratext *notationName)
{
    sax_context *saxctx = (sax_context *) context;

    indent(saxctx->depth);
    printf("ENTITY '%s'", name);
    if (publidId)
```

```
        printf(" PUB:%s", publidId);
    if (systemId)
        printf(" SYS:%s", systemId);
    if (notationName)
        printf(" NAME:%s", notationName);
    putchar('\n');
    return 0;  /* success */
}
```

The following is a sample XML document:

```
<?xml version="1.0"?>
<!DOCTYPE PLAY [
    <!ELEMENT top    (second*)>
    <!ELEMENT second (third*)>
    <!ELEMENT third  (#PCDATA)*>
    <!NOTATION note1 SYSTEM "foo.exe">
    <!NOTATION note2 PUBLIC "bar" "bar.ent">
    <!ENTITY ent SYSTEM "http://www.w3.org/" NDATA n>
]>
<?dummy this is a sample processing instruction?>
<top>
  <second>
    <third>third level</third>
  </second>
</top>
```

and the output from the preceding sample program:

```
StartDocument
NOTATION 'note1' SYS:foo.exe
NOTATION 'note2' PUB:bar SYS:bar.ent
ENTITY 'ent' SYS:http://www.w3.org/ NAME:n
PI target=dummy data=this is a sample processing instruction
<top>
    '\n  '
    <second>
        '\n    '
        <third>
            "third level"
        </third>
        '\n  '
    </second>
    '\n'
</top>
EndDocument
```

XSLT Support

As mentioned previously, XSLT support is integrated into the parser and can be invoked with the *xslprocess* command. An example of such usage is the following:

```
/* Parse the XML document */
if (!(xctx = xmlinit(&ecode, (const oratext *) 0,
                     (void (*)(void *, const oratext *, uword)) 0,
                     (void *) 0, (const xmlsaxcb *) 0, (void *) 0,
                     (const xmlmemcb *) 0, (void *) 0,
                     (const oratext *) 0)))
{
   ...
}

if (ecode = xmlparse(xctx, (oratext *) argv[1], (oratext *) 0,
                 XML_FLAG_VALIDATE | XML_FLAG_DISCARD_WHITESPACE))
{
   ...
}


/* Parse the XSL document */
if (!(xslctx = xmlinit(&ecode, (const oratext *) 0,
                     (void (*)(void *, const oratext *, uword)) 0,
                     (void *) 0, (const xmlsaxcb *) 0, (void *) 0,
                     (const xmlmemcb *) 0, (void *) 0,
                     (const oratext *) 0)))
{
   ...
}

if (ecode = xmlparse(xslctx, (oratext *) argv[2], (oratext *) 0,
                 XML_FLAG_VALIDATE | XML_FLAG_DISCARD_WHITESPACE))
{
   ...
}


/* Initialize the result context */
if (!(resctx = xmlinit(&ecode, (const oratext *) 0,
                   (void (*)(void *, const oratext *, uword)) 0,
                   (void *) 0, (const xmlsaxcb *) 0, (void *) 0,
                   (const xmlmemcb *) 0, (void *) 0,
                   (const oratext *) 0)))
{
   ...
}
```

```
/* XSL processing */
if (ecode = xslprocess(xctx, xslctx, resctx, &result))
{
    ...
}

/* Print the result tree */
printStream(stdout, result, 4, 0);

/* Call the terminate functions */
(void)xmlterm(xctx);
(void)xmlterm(xslctx);
(void)xmlterm(resctx);
```

XML Schema Support

In addition, support for validating XML documents against XML Schemas, in addition to DTDs as in the Java XML Development Kit, has now been implemented. The stand-alone command-line XML Schema processor (named **schema**) is provided in the C distribution in the **bin/** subdirectory. Note that, on Windows NT, the XML shared libraries (DLLs) must be in the same directory as the executable or installed in a location that is in the search path. The XML DLLs are installed by default in the **bin/** directory, so no extra step is necessary when executing **xml** from this directory.

The command-line syntax for use of the stand-alone parser is

schema [*switches*] *document* [*schema*] [*working directory*]

where *document* is the required XML input document, *switches* are optional controls that change the parser's behavior, *schema* the XML Schema, and *working directory* being self-explanatory. If no document is given or if the switches are invalid (or **-h** for Help), a brief usage message is printed:

```
% schema
Usage: schema [flags] <instance> [schema] [working dir]
Where:
     <instance>      is the XML instance document to validate (required)
     [schema]        is the default schema (optional)
     [working dir]   is the working directory for processing (optional)
Flags:
     -O              Always exit with code 0 (success)
     -p              Print instance document to stdout on success
     -v              Show version numbers
```

The XML Schema Processor Library

The XML Schema processor APIs are also provided as a library named **libxsd8.a** (or **libxsd8.dll** on Windows NT), and for Oracle9i, it is named **libxsd9.a** or **libxsd9.dll**. This is the same library used by the stand-alone parser / XSLT processor. The library is intended to run against an Oracle 8.1.6 or later environment.

The library contains APIs for initializing *(schemaInitialize),* loading an XML Schema *(schemaLoad),* validating an XML document against an XML Schema *(schemaValidate),* and terminating the operation *(schemaTerminate).* Typical use would be *xmlinit, xmlparse, schemaInitialize, SchemaValidate,* and *schemaTerminate.* For example:

```
/* Parser */
if (!(ctx = xmlinit(&ecode, (const oratext *) 0,
                    (void (*)(void *, const oratext *, uword)) 0,
                    (void *) 0, (const xmlsaxcb *) 0, (void *) 0,
                    (const xmlmemcb *) 0, (void *) 0,
                    (const oratext *) 0)))
{
    ...
}
if (ecode = xmlparse(ctx, (oratext *) doc, (oratext *) 0,
         XML_FLAG_DISCARD_WHITESPACE))
{
    ...
}
/* Schema */
if (!(scctx = schemaInitialize(ctx, &ecode)))
{
    ...
}

/* Validating XML document against XML Schema */
if (ecode = schemaValidate(scctx, root, (oratext *) schema))
{
    ...
}

schemaTerminate(scctx);
```

The XML Parser, XSLT Processor, XML Schema Processor for C++

The Oracle XML Parser and its integrated XSLT processor and XML Schema Processor for C++ is the C parser and XSLT processor and XML Schema processor underneath, with a wrapper to make it accessible from C++, both coexisting in the same XML library **libxml8.a** (or **libxml9.a** in Oracle9i) and **libxsd8.a** or **libxsd9.a** for the XML Schema Processor. Everything said previously about the C parser and XSLT processor and the XML Schema Processor holds true for the C++ version, except that the C++ wrappers are able to provide the DOM API in an object-oriented manner as was intended, so no renaming of functions is needed. In the C++ DOM, the functions are named and used just as in the DOM specification. See the C++ DOM header **oraxmldom.h** for details on available functions.

The C++ Class Generator

The C++ Class Generator is a tool that generates C++ classes (a source file and header), based on a DTD. The classes are then used in a program to make constructing documents that match the DTD easier.

NOTE
No C class generator exists because C is not an object-oriented language and there is no concept of a class.

The class generator is provided as a stand-alone, command-line executable (**xmlcg**) and a library (**libxmlg8.a** or **libxmlg9.a**). One class is defined in the header file **oraxmlcg.h** named **XMLClassGenerator**. It has one method, **generate**:

```
class XMLClassGenerator
{
    public:
      uword      generate(DocumentType *dtd, char *outdir = (char *) 0);
};
```

To use the method, parse a document and DTD with **xmlparse** or **xmlparsebuf**, and then fetch the DTD with **XMLParser::getDocType** and invoke **generate**. If no output directory (**outdir**) is specified, the generated files will be placed in the current directory. If you want to generate classes based an external DTD and not a complete document, parse the DTD with **xmlparsedtd**, and then proceed as indicated.

One class is generated for each defined element. The class provides methods for constructing element nodes that match the element's definition.

There are two methods of construction: all at once using C++ constructors, or piecemeal using a blank constructor and additional functions. The former creates an element and its children in a single call. The latter creates an empty element. Its children are added one at a time with calls to **addNode** and **addData**.

Providing constructors for every possible combination of children for element definitions that use the * (zero or more) or + (one or more) modifiers is impossible because infinite possible combinations exist. Instead, constructors are only provided that make one of each * or + type. If you need to make an element with a more complicated set of children, start with a blank element and build it up.

For example, given an element with the following definition,

```
<!ELEMENT B (#PCDATA | F)*>
```

the following class will be generated:

```
class B : public Element
{
    public:
        // Constructors
        B(Document *doc);
        B(Document *doc, String data);
        B(Document *doc, F *theF);
        // Assemblers
        void addNode(F *theF);
        // Add data after construction
        void addData(Document *doc, String data);
};
```

Note that all constructors take a **(Document *)** as the first argument because the **Document** class has the methods to build nodes. You can get the **Document** with the **XMLParser::getDocument** method.

The command-line executable is invoked similarly to the parser:

```
xmlcg [switches] document
```

If invalid switches are given (or **-h** for Help) or no document is provided, a usage message is printed:

```
haifa% xmlcg
Error: No document specified
Usage: xmlcg [switches] <document>
    -d <name>        DTD - input is external DTD (must specify name)
    -o <directory>   Output - specify output directory
    -e <encoding>    Encoding - specify input file encoding
    -h               Help - show this usage help
    -v               Version - show Class Generator version#
```

Switches are described in detail in Table 2-8.

Switch	Description
-d *name*	Specifies that the input is an external DTD with the given name, not an XML document.
-o *directory*	Specifies the output directory where generated files are to be placed. If not given, files are put in the current directory.
-e *encoding*	Specifies the default input file encoding. The option works exactly like the -e option to the XML parser; see the previous comments.
-h	Prints the usage help message.
-v	Prints the class generator version then exits.

TABLE 2-8.   *Class Generator Command-line Switches*

CHAPTER
3

Developing for the
Oracle9*i* Database

tarting with Oracle8i, Oracle supports two major programming languages in the database: PL/SQL and Java. Many of Oracle's customers use both PL/SQL and Java to build database applications today. With two languages to program the database, the natural question arises: how do you best use PL/SQL and Java to build XML-enabled applications with Oracle?

As a quick review, PL/SQL provides tremendous capabilities to Oracle database developers, including performance, ease-of-use, seamlessness with SQL, and robustness. Today, PL/SQL is a sophisticated procedural language for developing database applications and is ideally suited for building SQL/data-intensive applications. With Oracle8i, Oracle introduces Java in the database server to provide a robust, scalable platform for this enormously popular general-purpose language. You can use Java to develop multitier, component-oriented applications using Enterprise JavaBeans and *Common Object Request Broker API (CORBA)*, as well as to develop traditional database stored procedures. Oracle8i provides several facilities that simplify how you build XML-enabled applications with PL/SQL and Java, and make it easy to combine applications written in both languages, and Oracle9i extends the flexibility by offering built-in XML SQL and PL/SQL functions, and XML-based messaging capability.

Oracle's complete Java solution offers simplicity, flexibility, and freedom of choice without limiting the power necessary for enterprise applications. Oracle's Java solution combines the best of the traditional world with new Internet standards to produce industrial-strength Java applications.

Oracle provides several components, utilities, and interfaces you can use to take advantage of XML technology in your database applications (see Chapter 2). Which products you use depends on your application requirements, programming preferences, and development and deployment environments. Oracle9i has extended Oracle8i's XML support by including XML SQL and PL/SQL functions, native XML datatype support, and integrated message queuing, along with the native support for Internet Java and XML standards. You can run Oracle XML components and applications built with them inside the database using Oracle JServer—Oracle's built-in Java Virtual Machine. For devices and applications that require a smaller database footprint, you can use Oracle Lite to store and retrieve XML data.

This chapter focuses first on the fundamentals of Oracle JServer architecture and how you can use Oracle's Java XML components within the Oracle JServer. We also discuss various approaches for storing and retrieving XML documents using the XML components, including the new *XMLType* introduced in Oracle9i, along with XPath-based representations to locate data in the database with the new URI support, integration of XML with SQL queries with the new PL/SQL and SQL functions, and usage of the integrated XML message queuing functionality. At the end of this chapter, we discuss how you can use these XML components to develop a simple bookstore Web site.

Oracle9*i*—An XML-Enabled Database

Databases and XML offer complementary functionality for storing data. Whereas databases store data for efficient retrieval, XML offers an easy information exchange that enables interoperability between applications. Oracle8i and Oracle9i, to an even larger extent, enable you to store XML and build XML-enabled applications. Storing XML collections in databases enables you to benefit from database administration tools and procedures, such as backups. You can use them to enforce rules about data and security, and to block operations that compromise data integrity by embedding rules and logic in a database. Also, converting database tables into XML documents enables you to take advantage of XML's features. You can present XML documents as HTML pages with XSLT stylesheets, search them using XML-based query languages, or use them as a data-exchange format.

Oracle's object-relational features enable you to capture the complex structure of XML data. You can operate and manage XML data on a desired level of granularity and lend it readily to efficient construction of dynamic XML documents from the resulting fragments. You can also store XML documents as a single document with its tags in a *XMLType*, in a *Character Large Object (CLOB)*, or as data by distributing it untagged across object-relational tables. Oracle's Internet File System (see Chapter 5) can access XML documents stored in external files or on the Web. You can use Oracle9i's Oracle Text (see Chapter 6) to perform searches on XML documents stored in Oracle. You can index the XML as plain text or as document sections for more precise searches, such as find "Oracle WITHIN title" where "title" is a section of the document or use the new Oracle9i XML datatype *uri-ref* to store and retrieve documents pointed to by the Uniform Resource Indicator (URI). Oracle9i's Oracle Text also provides full-text indexing of documents and the capability to do SQL queries over documents, along with XPATH-like searching. Finally, Oracle9i's Advanced Queuing (AQ) now supports XML-based message queuing in the database, allowing and managing synchronous and asynchronous communications of XML messages defined in the standard internet Data Access Presentation (iDAP) format for both the server and client.

Oracle's JServer and Java XML Components

Oracle offers the industry's broadest and most competitive Java solution—a variety of servers to run Java applications, standard programming interfaces (APIs) to build enterprise applications in Java, and a productive set of tools for deploying Java applications. Oracle offers two Java execution environments—Oracle9i and Oracle internet Application Server. Both servers share a common development model with common APIs, as well as a common deployment and management framework enabling you to build Java applications, which can be easily partitioned across tiers of multitier architecture. Typically, you can deploy data-intensive business logic in the database server and compute intensive logic on the Application Server. In Chapter 4, we discuss developing for the Oracle internet Application Server.

Oracle9i JServer is the industry's most robust enterprise Java server. It has been designed from the ground up as the world's first true enterprise-scale Java programming platform. Oracle9i JServer addresses the technical challenges that have limited Java's widespread adoption for enterprise applications. It provides the fastest, most scalable, reliable, portable, and manageable environment to run Java applications. Oracle's JServer is completely compliant with Java standards supporting the Java Development Kit and passing all the tests required to be certified as "standard Java." Oracle9i is currently shipping with Java support on a large number of operating system and hardware platforms, including Solaris, NT, HP-UX, DEC, AIX, Sequent, and others.

JServer Basics

JServer is tightly integrated with the Oracle database and has a number of components: a byte-code compiler, a garbage collector, an integrated Java class loader, and a Java-through-C compiler, all of which are designed for optimal performance and scalability within the database environment (Figure 3-1). It runs in the same process space and address space as the database kernel itself, sharing a number of the memory heaps for optimal performance. JServer sessions are entirely analogous to traditional Oracle sessions. When you connect to Oracle, you start a database session. The first time during this session that you invoke a Java method, a session-private Java virtual machine is created for the session. A session encompasses the lifetime of all the objects referenced by Java static variables, all the objects referred to by these objects, and so on (their transitive closure). From the point of view of a client/server interaction, each JServer session maintains its own Java state, thereby being perceived as a dedicated JVM. In reality, the Oracle implementation shares almost all the code, infrastructure, and metadata of the active JVM between users.

Unlike conventional JVM, which compiles and loads the Java files, the JServer machine compiles and loads schema objects. The three kinds of Java schema objects, illustrated in Figure 3-2, are

- **Java class schema objects**   Correspond to Java class files
- **Java source schema objects**   Correspond to Java source files
- **Java resource schema objects**   Correspond to Java resource files

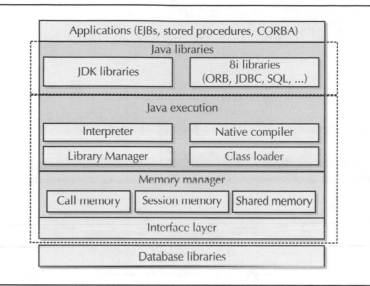

FIGURE 3-1. *The Oracle JServer architecture*

The classes that define a Java application are stored within the Oracle database under a SQL schema of their owner. As these classes/schema objects tend to be long-lived in the database, JServer compiles them into well-optimized native code using *way ahead of time (WAT)* compilation. WAT translates standard Java class binaries generating specialized C programs, which are then compiled (by an embedded, platform-dependent C compiler) to native dynamic libraries. By completely eliminating interpreter overhead and allowing for inlining and object-oriented optimizations, WAT considerably speeds the execution performance of Java applications.

Java XML Components

Oracle provides several components, utilities, and interfaces you can use to take advantage of XML technology in your database applications (see Chapter 2). Among these components are the XML parser, XSL transformation engine, XML class generator, XML Transviewer beans, XSQL Servlet, and XML SQL Utility. The XML parser is a stand-alone XML component that parses an XML document, which can then be processed by an application. The parser supports the *Document Object Model (DOM)* and *Simple API for XML (SAX)* interfaces, and XML namespaces. It can parse XML documents in validating or nonvalidating modes. In nonvalidating modes, the parser verifies that the XML document is well formed. In validating

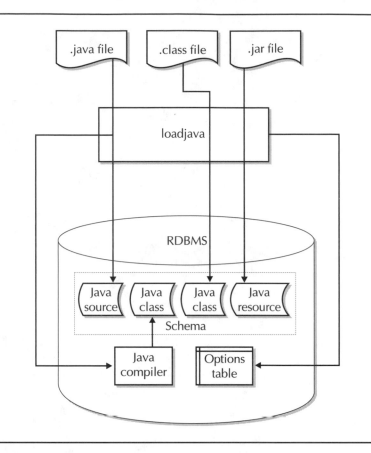

FIGURE 3-2. *Java schema objects*

mode, it also validates the document against the DTD or a XML schema and checks for the validity constraints. The XSL transformation engine is integrated in the XML parser. The transformation engine transforms XML documents using XSL stylesheets. The XML Class Generator creates a set of Java source files from an XML DTD or an XML schema. You can use the generated source files to construct, optionally validate, and print an XML document that is compliant to the input XML DTD or XML schema.

The XSQL Servlet is a tool that processes SQL queries and outputs the result set as XML. This processor is implemented as a Java servlet and takes an XML file containing embedded SQL queries as input. It uses all the previous components to perform its operations, heavily leveraging the XML SQL Utility to return query result sets as XML. The XML Transviewer beans are a set of XML components for Java applications or applets. You can use these beans to parse XML files asynchronously, or to view the XML/XSL files by color-highlighting XML/XSL syntax. You can also apply XSL style sheets to transform an XML document to almost any text-based format, including XML, HTML, and DDL, and view the results of transformations immediately. You can integrate these visual and nonvisual Java components into Oracle JDeveloper to enable developers to create and deploy XML-based database applications quickly.

Java XML components have the flexibility of running as stand-alone Java applications using the JDBC driver to interact with the database or running efficiently inside the Oracle JServer using the finely tuned server-side internal JDBC driver. The stand-alone Java application can reside on the client side or on the Oracle internet Application Server in the middle tier. Normally, in stand-alone Java applications, you use JDBC to establish a connection to the database using the DriverManager class, which manages a set of JDBC drivers. Once the JDBC drivers are loaded, you call the method getConnection, which returns a Connection object representing a database session. All SQL statements are executed within the context of that session. However, the server-side internal JDBC driver runs within a default session and default transaction context. So you are already "connected" to the database, and all your SQL operations are part of the default transaction context. To get a Connection object, in the Java stored procedure, you can use the following statement:

```
Connection c = DriverManager.getConnection("jdbc:default:connection");
```

When developing Java stored procedure applications, be aware that the server-side internal JDBC driver cannot be used to connect to a remote database. You can "connect" only to the server running your Java stored procedure. For server-to-server or client to server connections, use a server side or client side JDBC Thin driver.

As mentioned at the beginning of the chapter, starting with Oracle8i, you can use Java to develop database applications and deploy it in the database as stored procedures. Stored procedures developed in Java run in the same address space as SQL and PL/SQL, so they can seamlessly interoperate with existing PL/SQL applications. Because these Java programs run in the same address space as the database server and can leverage the embedded server-side internal JDBC drivers, they needn't make network round trips to access SQL data and are, therefore, highly optimized to deliver high performance and reduce network traffic. To deploy Java stored programs in the Oracle8i or 9i database, you need to load your Java programs into the database and publish the Java methods to SQL. The database supports a variety of different forms in which you can load a Java program. You can load Java source text, standard Java class files, or Java archives (jar). Java source loaded into the database is automatically compiled by the Java byte-code compiler hosted in the database. You can load Java objects into Oracle in many different ways. First, you should issue a new DDL command of the form "CREATE JAVA ..." from SQL*Plus to load Java source, binaries, or resource files into the database:

```
# Create a directory object on the server's file system
SQL> CREATE DIRECTORY bfile_dir as '/home/user/oracle/xml/parser/v2';
# Then load the Java class using the "CREATE JAVA CLASS ..." statement
SQL> CREATE JAVA CLASS USING BFILE (bfile_dir, 'XMLParser.class');
```

To simplify the loading process, Oracle provides a utility written in Java, called LOADJAVA, that automates the process of loading Java into the database. Because the LOADJAVA utility uses Oracle's JDBC drivers to communicate with the database and load Java into the database, you can load Java program units into the database over the network.

```
loadjava -user scott/tiger@myhost:1521:orcl xmlparserv2.jar
```

Publishing and Calling Java XML Components

Important to note is that the advent of Java stored procedures does not make obsolete stored procedures written in PL/SQL. You can leverage the existing library of PL/SQL stored procedures, while implementing new server-side stored procedures in Java. This approach is enabled because both PL/SQL and Java stored procedures have the same call specification—the latter being published to SQL. At the application level, therefore, it is transparent which technology is employed.

You must publish Java methods in the Oracle data dictionary before calling them from SQL. When you load a Java class into the database, its methods are not published automatically because Oracle does not know which methods are safe entry points for calls from SQL. To publish the methods, you must write call specifications (call specs), which map Java method names, parameter types, and return types to their SQL counterparts. For a given Java method, you declare a function or procedure call spec using the SQL CREATE FUNCTION or CREATE PROCEDURE statement. You publish value-returning Java methods as functions and void Java methods as procedures. Applications call the Java method through its call spec, that is, by referencing the call-spec name. The run-time system looks up the call-spec definition in the Oracle data dictionary, and then executes the corresponding Java method, as illustrated in Figure 3-3.

A call spec and the Java method must reside in the same schema (unless the Java method has a PUBLIC synonym). You can declare a call spec as a

- Stand-alone (top-level) PL/SQL function or procedure
- Packaged PL/SQL function or procedure
- Member method of a SQL object type

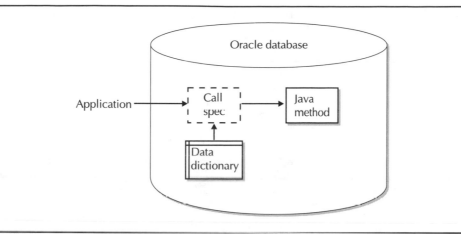

FIGURE 3-3. *Calling a Java method*

A call spec exposes a Java method's top-level entry point to Oracle. Therefore, you can publish only public static methods—with one exception: you can publish instance methods as member methods of SQL object type. The corresponding SQL and Java parameters (and function results) must have compatible datatypes in a call spec. Oracle converts between the SQL types and Java classes automatically.

You can load the following Java source or its class file into the Oracle database and publish its methods as PL/SQL functions. To publish these methods, you can write the following call spec:

```
public class CaseConvert
{
    public static String toUpper(String str)
    {
        return str.toUpperCase();
    }
    public static String toLower(String str)
    {
        return str.toLowerCase();
    }
}

CREATE OR REPLACE FUNCTION toUpper (str VARCHAR2) return VARCHAR2AS LANGUAGE JAVA
NAME 'CaseConvert.toUpper(java.lang.String) returns java.lang.String';

CREATE OR REPLACE FUNCTION toLower (str VARCHAR2) return VARCHAR2AS LANGUAGE JAVA
NAME 'CaseConvert.toLower(java.lang.String) returns java.lang.String';
```

Similarly, you can load the Java XML parser and write the following Java source to parse and validate an XML document stored in a table as a CLOB:

```
public class Validate {
public static String validateCLOB(String xmldoc) {
    SAXParser parser = new SAXParser();
    try {
        .    parser.parse(new StringInputStream(xmldoc));
        return "Valid XML Document";
    } catch (SAXException e) {
        return "Invalid XML Document" + e.getMessage();
    }
}
}

CREATE OR REPLACE FUNCTION validateCLOB (xmldoc CLOB) return VARCHAR2AS LANGUAGE JAVA NAME
'Validate.validateCLOB (oracle.sql.CLOB) returns java.lang.String';
```

Once you publish a Java stored procedure, it looks like a PL/SQL stored procedure. You can invoke it using the SQL name in its call spec from a number of different contexts:

- Inline within any SQL statement:

  ```
  SELECT validateCLOB(XMLDOC) FROM XMLSTORE;
  ```

- From the top level using the CALL form:

  ```
  CALL validateCLOB(:xmldoc) INTO :x;
  ```

- From within a PL/SQL procedure, package, or anonymous blocks using exactly the same syntax used to invoke another PL/SQL procedure:

  ```
  DECLARE
  result  VARCHAR2 [1000];
  xmldoc CLOB;
  BEGIN
  ...
  result := validateCLOB(xmldoc);
  dbms_output.put_line(result);
  ...
  END;
  ```

So far, we have discussed how to develop and deploy Java stored procedures in the Oracle database. With the help of some simple examples, we have demonstrated the steps needed to load, resolve, publish, and invoke Java programs in the database. One of the key applications of Java stored procedures is to use the Oracle database as a repository for XML documents. In the next section, we look at various approaches for mapping database schema to XML documents and vice versa.

Database Schema and XML Documents

XML documents are text that conforms to a hierarchy or tree structure specified by a DTD or XML schema. You can easily store these hierarchical data in an optimal internal form using object-relational tables. All the existing and future internal applications can work with the information in the most efficient way possible. When you retrieve information, for sharing with partners or other applications, you can present the appropriate view of data and document content specific to the task at hand as integrated XML. Oracle8i's and Oracle9i's object views enable you to present data in any number of "logical" combinations, hiding any details of their underlying physical storage. You can effectively transform the structure of one or more underlying tables into a more useful or more appropriate structure for the demands of a specific application. When you link views of information with other views of related information, they quite naturally form "trees" or "graphs" of related data. When you represent database information as XML, the previous related views provide the foundation for many different tree-structured XML documents.

Here, we offer a simple example of mapping a database table to an XML DTD of the following form:

```
<!ELEMENT table (rows)*>
<!ELEMENT rows (column1, column2, ...)>
<!ELEMENT column1 (#PCDATA)>
<!ELEMENT column2 (#PCDATA)>
...
```

However, a database provides even more capability than a DTD for expressing rules. Using DTDs, you cannot define type information other than strings. The database schema defines type information and constraints, such as permissible value ranges. A database schema enables you to define relationships or dependencies. For example, your e-commerce business might receive orders as XML documents. By using a database, you can link customer and order information, and define a rule about not processing orders for closed accounts. In spite of the limitations in DTDs, mapping a database schema to a DTD presents the database as a virtual XML document to the tools that need XML documents as input.

The format for DTDs is an existing worldwide standard and will likely exist and be improved upon for years. However, because of the inherent limitations of DTDs and the increasingly data-oriented role that XML is being asked to assume because of developments in e-business and e-commerce, the W3C standards body is promoting a new standard called XML schema, rather than attempting to push the current DTD standards any further. With the advent of XML schema, you can overcome the limitations of DTDs. XML schemas enable you to specify type information and constraints. Using XML schema, you can map the simple database table into an XML schema of the following form:

```
<schema targetNamespace="someNSURI">
   <element name="table">
     <element name="rows" minOccurs="0" maxOccurs="*">
       <element name="column1">
          <datatype source="string">
             <length  value="1000"/>
          </datatype>
       </element>
       <element name="column2" type="decimal">
         ...
     </element>
   </element>
</schema>
```

To transfer data between an XML document and a database, you must map a document structure to a database schema and vice versa. An XML document structure is associated with a DTD or an XML schema. A DTD is used to describe the elements and attributes. Like DTDs, schemas describe data, but they offer the additional benefit of providing a way to specify the datatype of that data as well, from simple primitive types, such as strings, dates, and integers, to complex structures, such as mailing addresses or points on a graph.

Mapping XML Documents to a Database Schema

When mapping XML documents associated with an XML DTD or a XML schema to a database schema for the purpose of storing XML in Oracle9i, four basic strategies exist:

- Mapping the complete XML document as a single, intact object, such as CLOBs

- Mapping XML elements to object-relational tables and columns in the database schema

- Mapping fragments of XML documents as CLOBs and the rest of it as object-relational tables

- Mapping XML documents to an Oracle *XMLType*

You can choose one of the previous approaches, depending on the structure of the XML document and operations performed by the application. You can also store the XML DTD or schema in the database to validate the XML documents.

XML Documents in CLOBs

Storing an intact XML document in a CLOB or *Binary Large Object (BLOB)* is a good strategy if the XML document contains static content that will only be updated by replacing the entire document. Examples include written text such as articles, advertisements, books, legal, and contracts. Documents of this nature are known as document-centric and are delivered from the database as a whole. Storing this kind of document intact within Oracle9i gives you the advantages of an industry-proven database and its reliability over file system storage. If you choose to store an XML document outside the database, you can still use Oracle9i features to index, query, and efficiently retrieve the document through the use of BFILES, URLs, and text-based indexing.

XML Documents as Object-Relational Data

If the XML document has a well-defined structure and contains data that is updatable or used in other ways, the document is data-centric. Typically, the XML document contains elements or attributes that have complex structures. Examples of this kind of document include sales orders, invoices, and airline flight schedules. Oracle9i, with its object-relational extensions, has the capability to capture the structure of the data in the database using object types, object references, and collections. Two options exist for storing and preserving the structure of the XML data in an object-relational form:

■ Store the attributes of the elements in a relational table and define object views to capture the structure of the XML elements.

■ Store the structured XML elements in an object table.

Once stored in the object-relational form, the data can be easily updated, queried, rearranged, and reformatted as needed using SQL.

The XSQL Servlet or XML SQL Utility then provides the means to store an XML document by mapping it to the underlying object-relational storage and, conversely, provides the capability to retrieve the object-relational data as an XML document. If an XML document is structured, but the structure of the XML document is incompatible with the structure of the underlying database schema, you must transform the data into the correct format before writing it to the database. You can achieve this using XSL stylesheets or other programming approaches; but, depending on your needs, you might want to store the data-centric XML document as an intact single object. Or, you can define object views corresponding to the various XML document structures and define instead-of triggers to perform the appropriate transformation and to update the base data.

XML Documents as Fragment Documents and Object Relational Data

You can use Oracle9i views to view and operate a combination of structured and unstructured XML data as a whole. Views enable you to construct an object on the fly by combining XML data stored in a variety of ways. So, you can store structured data (such as employee data, customer data, and so on) in one location within object-relational tables and store related unstructured data (such as descriptions and comments) within a CLOB. When you need to retrieve the data as a whole, you simply construct the structure from the various pieces of data using type constructors in the view's select statement. The XSQL Servlet then enables retrieving the constructed data from the view as a single XML document.

XML Documents as XMLTypes

Finally, you can store an XML document in an Oracle9i *XMLType,* allowing searches and queries on it using XPATH-like syntax, and its usage in the creation of database table and view columns (since it is actually a hidden CLOB column), and as the parameter and return type of SQL, PL/SQL, and Java functions. For example, the *SYS_XMLGEN* and *SYS_XMLAGG* Oracle SQL functions, which generates an XML document and aggregates a number of XML documents, respectively, can take as a parameter an *XMLType* object and return an *XMLType* object. These functions can be embedded in SQL queries as in a simple *SELECT* statement and return XML:

```
SELECT SYS_XMLGEN(book) FROM bookcatalog WHERE title LIKE '%ELLISON%';
```

and

```
SELECT SYS_XMLAGG(SYS_XMLGEN(book)).getClobVal() book_list FROM
bookcatalog GROUP BY title;
```

where the first would return the XML of a book entry and the second would return a booklist of all the titles of the book entries. Similarly, the new *DBMS_XMLGEN* PL/SQL package, which includes a number of new procedures, converts the result set from SQL queries to an XML stored in an *XMLType,* as in:

```
SELECT SYS_XMLAGG(SYS_XMLGEN(book)).getClobVal() book_list FROM
bookcatalog GROUP BY title
```

resulting in a listing of all the book titles in XML.

Last, table creation using *XMLType* columns and database manipulation language (DML) operations to insert, update, and delete values are allowed with this new datatype, along with datatype member functions such as *existsNode*() and *extract*() that take arguments with XPATH-like syntax to return fragments of XML in the *XMLType,* such as:

```
SELECT book.extract('//title/text()').getStringVal() FROM bookcatalog;
```

and

```
SELECT * FROM bookcatalog where book.existsNode('//book/title') != 0;
```

Mapping a Database Schema to Virtual XML Documents

When mapping a database schema to virtual XML documents, two basic strategies exist:

- Mapping the complete database as a virtual XML document
- Mapping the result set of a query as a virtual XML document

Depending on the application, you may choose one of these approaches. For example, consider an application performing a database copy from a database to another with a different schema. This application can use XSL transformation on the virtual document represented by the first database and insert the result of the transformation into the second database.

Complete Schema

A database consists of a schema associated with each database user. Each schema associated with a user is a collection of schema objects accessible to the user. While mapping a database scheme to a DTD, each user is mapped as a child element of the top-level element identified by the SID of the database instance. An element representing a user schema and its child elements use a unique namespace to avoid conflicts with schema objects defined in other user schema.

The following (simplistic) procedure generates a DTD from a relational schema:

1. For each table, create an element.

2. For each column in a table, create a PCDATA-only child element.

3. For each object or nested table column, create an ELEMENT-content child element with attributes or nested columns as child elements.

For example, the following DTD corresponds to a simple database:

```
<!ELEMENT dbschema (sys, scott, ...)>
<!ATTLIST dbschema
        xmlns CDATA #FIXED "http://www.oracle.com/xml/dbschema"
        sid   CDATA #REQUIRED>
```

```
<!ELEMENT scott (BookList, ...)>
<!ATTLIST scott
        xmlns CDATA #FIXED "http://www.oracle.com/xml/dbschema/scott">
<!ELEMENT BookList (Book)*>
<!ATTLIST Book row_num CDATA #IMPLIED>
<!ELEMENT Book (Title, ISBN, Author, Publisher, (Review)*)>
...
```

Unfortunately, a number of drawbacks exist to mapping a database schema to a DTD. For example, there is no way to predict data types or column lengths definitively from the DTD. The solution to this problem is the use of data types in XML documents using XML schemas. You can also preserve primary key/foreign key constraints in the XML document by using XML schemas.

Query
A result set of a query can be mapped into a virtual XML document, identical to the process of mapping the database to an XML document. The result from the query contains a set of rows, which is mapped to an XML document with the root element ROWSET and each row encapsulated in an element ROW. Each column selected by the query is added as a child of ROW element. You can specify alternative element tags for the ROWSET and ROW element tags. The following example illustrates the mapping of a simple query to an XML document:

```
SQL> select * from scott.BookList;
<!ELEMENT BookList (Book)*>
<!ATTLIST BookList
        xmlns CDATA #FIXED "http://www.oracle.com/xml/dbschema/scott">
<!ELEMENT Book (Title, ISBN, Author, Publisher, (Review)*)>
<!ATTLIST Book row_num CDATA #IMPLIED>
...
```

You can also use a XML schema to specify the XML document structure and data types. The following XML schema corresponds to the previous select query:

```
<schema targetNamespace="someNSURI">
  <type name="Person">
    <datatype name="Lastname" source="string"/>
    <datatype name="Firstname" source='string'/>
  </type>
  ...
  <element name="BookList">
    <element name="rows" minOccurs="0" maxOccurs="*">
      <element name="Title" type="string"/>
      <element name="ISBN" type="ISBN">
      <element name="Author" type="Person">
```

```
     . . .
   </element>
  </element>
</schema>
```

In addition to simple relational queries, you can map nested selects or object navigation queries to an XML document to provide depth in the document. The following example retrieves the **Lastname** attribute from the **Author** object:

```
SQL> select Title, Author.Lastname, ISBN from scott.BookList;
<!ELEMENT BookList (Book)*>
<!ATTLIST BookList
        xmlns CDATA #FIXED "http://www.oracle.com/xml/dbschema/scott">
<!ELEMENT Book (Title, Author_Lastname, ISBN)>
<!ATTLIST Book row_num CDATA #IMPLIED>
. . .
```

The instance of an XML document corresponding to the previous query is:

```
<BookList>
    <Book row_num="1">
        <Title>Introducing XML</Title>
        <Author_Lastname>Smith</Author_Lastname>
        <ISBN>11-0342000123</ISBN>
    </Book>
    <Book row_num="2">
        <Title>XML for web sites</Title>
        <Author_Lastname>Jackson</Author_Lastname>
        <ISBN>15-7812000423</ISBN>
    </Book>
<BookList>
```

Storing and Retrieving XML Data

XML data can be data document-centric or data-centric. Both of these kinds of data documents can originate either in the database or in an XML document. If the data originates from the database, you might want to expose it as XML; and, conversely, If the data originates from an XML document, you might want to store it in a database. An example of the former is the vast amount of legacy data stored in relational databases. An example of the latter is data exposed on the Web as XML that you want to store in your database. Thus, depending on your needs, you may need techniques to transfer data from an XML document to the database, from the database to an XML document, or both. In addition, if applications are to communicate with each other through XML, the built-in support of XML messages in Oracle9*i*'s Advanced Queuing features allows for this.

AQ Support of XML-Based Messages

Oracle9*i*'s AQ features acts as the hub for either native XML or XML defined using iDAP, meaning that such messages can be sent over HTTP or SMTP protocols. In either case, clients such as browsers and servers such as Oracle9*i* can communicate through enqueue, dequeue, publish, and register functionality encapsulated by Oracle-specific tags such as *AQXMLSend, AQXMLReceive, AQXMLPublish, AQXMLRegister, AQXMLReceiveResponse, AQLXMLPublishResponse, AQXMLNotification,* and along with other required elements. For example, a client can construct the following iDAP XML message and send it over HTTP to be processed by Oracle9i:

```
<?xml version="1.0"?>
<Envelope xmlns=http://www.oracle.com/schemas/IDAP/envelope>
    <Body>
        <AQXMLSend xmlns=http://www.oracle.com/schemas/AQ/access>
            <!-- mandatory -->
            <producer_options>
              <!-- mandatory -->
              <destination>BOOKLIST.BOOK_QUEUE</destination>
            </producer_options>
            <!-- mandatory
            <message_set>
              <message>
                <message_number>1</message_number>
                <!-- mandatory -->
                <message_header>
                 <correlation>BOOK</correlation>
                 <sender_id>
                    <agent_name>Juan</agent_name>
                 </sender_id>
                </message_header>
                <message_payload>
                   <Book>
                      <Title>Introducing XML</Title>
                      <Author_Lastname>Smith</Author_Lastname>
                      <ISBN>11-0342000123</ISBN>
                   </Book>
                </message_payload>
              </message>
            </message_set>
        </AQXMLSend>
    </Body>
</Envelope>
```

In this manner, messages can be intelligently managed, so that data about them can be extracted at a later point to help in configuring the architecture and viewing them through SQL.

In the previous section, we discussed various approaches for mapping a database schema to DTD and vice versa. Now, we discuss implementation techniques to accomplish the previous requirement.

Database DOM

Most XML tools work with either the SAX or DOM API. You can get these tools to view a database as an XML document, if there is access to a database using a DOM API. In other words, with a DOM API for databases, you can make the database look like a virtual XML document associated with the DTD derived from the database schema. An element in the DOM model can be loosely interpreted as a single result set (when transferring data from the database to XML) or as a single table or updatable view (when transferring data from XML to the database). You can build a simple DOM tree for a database table by iterating over the rows and columns, and build nodes as you visit them. This procedure can be applied on the complete database or on a result set returned by a query. DOM APIs provide applications random access to the XML documents, and simple implementations can be memory intensive. The memory-efficiency problem can be fixed by using a lazy node construction mechanism (a node in the DOM tree is not built until it is requested).

Although DOM APIs provide a complete navigational access to XML documents, DOM lacks APIs for querying a document. One approach is to use Oracle 9i's Text (see Chapter 6) to perform searches on XML documents stored in the database. In the next section, we discuss a novel approach for querying the database to build dynamic XML pages using SQL queries.

XSQL—XSLT/SQL Server Pages

Many application developers are putting their business data to work over the Web as the Internet drives an explosive demand for flexible information exchange. Developers require standards-based solutions to this problem. SQL, XML, and XSLT are the standards that can get the job done in practice.

SQL is the standard you are already familiar with for accessing appropriate views of business information in your production systems. XML provides an industry-standard, platform-neutral format for representing the results of SQL queries as datagrams for exchange. XSLT defines the industry-standard way to transform XML datagrams into target XML, HTML, or text format as needed.

You can use the XSQL Servlet to build dynamic XML datapages easily from the results of one or more SQL queries. You can then serve the results over the Web as XML datagrams or HTML pages using server-side XSLT transformation. You can also receive XML posted to your Web server and insert it into your database. XSQL Servlet makes use of the Oracle XML parser, the Oracle XSL Transformation Engine, and the Oracle XML SQL Utilities to get the job done.

By combining the power of SQL, XML, and XSLT in the server with the ubiquitously available HTTP protocol for the transport mechanism, you can

- Receive Web-based information requests from any client device on the Web.

- Query an appropriate logical view of business data needed by the request.

- Return the datagrams in XML over the Web to the requester.

- Transform the information flexibly into any XML, HTML, or text format.

Of course, Oracle9i and the Oracle XML Developer's Kit provide all the core technology needed by developers to implement this solution. You can use Oracle XSQL Pages, however, which automate the use of these underlying XML technology components to solve the most common cases without programming.

Oracle XSQL Pages are templates that enable anyone familiar with SQL to declaratively

- Assemble dynamic XML datapages based on one or more parameterized SQL queries.

- Transform the datapages to produce a final result in any desired XML, HTML, or text-based format using an associated XSLT Transformation.

For example, the following URL request serves a list of available flights today for any desired destination city, as shown in Figure 3-4.

http://yourcompany.com/AvailableFlightsToday.xsql?City=SFO

You might write the following XSQL page to retrieve the list from your enterprise database in response to the previous URL request.

```
<?xml version="1.0"?>
<xsql:query connection="demo" xmlns:xsql="urn:oracle-xsql">
    SELECT Carrier, FlightNumber, Origin,
           TO_CHAR(ExpectedTime,'HH:MI') AS Due
      FROM FlightSchedule
     WHERE TRUNC(ArrivalTime) = TRUNC(SYSDATE)
       AND Destination = '{@City}'
  ORDER BY ExpectedTime
</xsql:query>
```

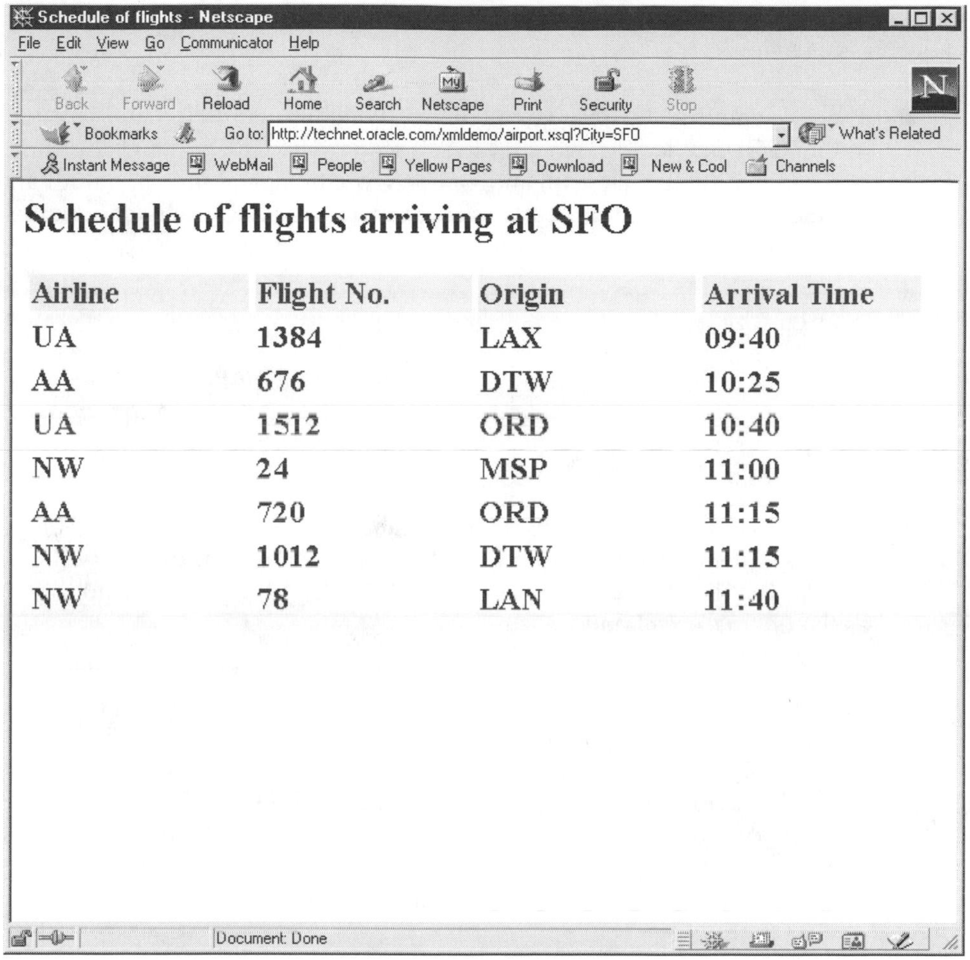
Schedule of flights - Netscape
File Edit View Go Communicator Help
Back Forward Reload Home Search Netscape Print Security Stop
Bookmarks Go to: http://technet.oracle.com/xmldemo/airport.xsql?City=SFO What's Related
Instant Message WebMail People Yellow Pages Download New & Cool Channels
Schedule of flights arriving at SFO
Airline Flight No. Origin Arrival Time
UA 1384 LAX 09:40
AA 676 DTW 10:25
UA 1512 ORD 10:40
NW 24 MSP 11:00
AA 720 ORD 11:15
NW 1012 DTW 11:15
NW 78 LAN 11:40
Document: Done

FIGURE 3-4. *Screenshots of results of airport.xsql*

Architecture of XSQL Pages

The *XSQL Servlet* is a tool that processes SQL queries and outputs the result set as XML. This processor is implemented as a Java servlet and takes an XML file containing embedded SQL queries as input. It uses Oracle's XML Developer's Kit to perform many of its operations.

You can run this servlet in any Web server that supports Java servlets. Figure 3-5 shows how data flows from a client, to the servlet, and back to the client. The sequence of events is as follows:

- The user enters a URL through a browser, which is interpreted and passed to the XSQL Servlet through a Java Web server. The URL contains the name of the target XSQL file (**.xsql**) and, optionally, parameters such as values and an XSL stylesheet name. Or, the user can invoke the XSQL Servlet from the command line, bypassing the browser and Java Web server.

- The servlet passes the XSQL file to the XML parser for Java, which parses the XML and creates an API for accessing the XML contents.

- The page processor component of the servlet uses the API to retrieve the XML parameters and SQL statements (found between the **<xsql:query>** and **</xsql:query>** tags). The page processor also passes any XSL processing statements to the XSLT processor.

- The page processor then constructs a database DOM by sending the SQL queries to the underlying Oracle9i database, which returns the query results. The results are embedded in the XML file in the same location as the original **<xsql:query>** tags.

- If desired, the query results and any other XML data are transformed by the XSLT processor using a specified XSL stylesheet. The data can be transformed HTML or any other format defined by the stylesheet. The XSLT processor can selectively apply different stylesheets based on the type of client that made the original URL request. This HTTP_USER_AGENT information is obtained from the client through an HTTP request.

The XSLT processor passes the completed document back to the client browser for presentation to the user.

Installation of XSQL Servlet

You can install and configure the XSQL Servlet on many different Web servers, such as Oracle9i Lite Portal-to-Go Server, Apache 1.3.9 with JServ 1.0, and Sun JavaServer Web Development Kit (JSWDK) 1.0.1 Web Server.

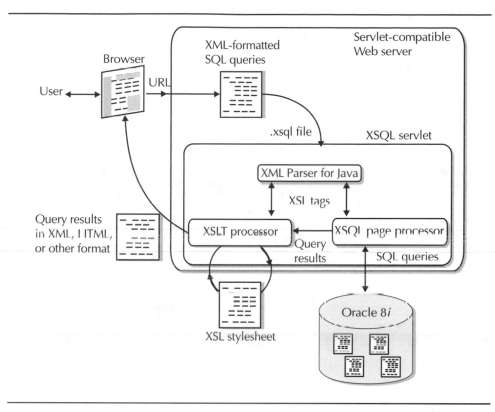

FIGURE 3-5. *Architecture of XSQL pages*

In this section, we briefly describe the installation steps for Apache 1.3.9 Web Server. For detailed instructions for installing XSQL Servlet on many different Web servers, see Chapter 8. The steps for installing the XSQL Servlet are these:

1. Make sure all the JAR files required to run the XSQL Servlet are in CLASSPATH for Apache JServ run-time engine. You should add the following lines to your **jserv.properties** file:

```
# Oracle XSQL Servlet
wrapper.classpath=C:\xsql\lib\oraclexsql.jar
```

```
# Oracle JDBC (8.1.5)
wrapper.classpath=C:\xsql\lib\classes111.zip
# Oracle XML Parser V2 (with XSLT Engine)
wrapper.classpath=C:\xsql\lib\xmlparserv2.jar
# XSQLConfig.xml File location
wrapper.classpath=C:\xsql\lib
```

2. Register the file extension of **.xsql** to map to the Java servlet class named **oracle.xml.xsql.XSQLServlet**. You should add the following lines to your **mod_jserv.conf** configuration file:

```
# Executes a servlet passing filename with proper extension
# property of servlet request.
# Syntax: ApJServAction [extension] [servlet-uri]
# Defaults: NONE
# Notes: This is used for external tools.
#ApJServAction .jsp /servlets/nl.nmg.jsp.JSPServlet
ApJServAction .xsql /servlets/oracle.xml.xsql.XSQLServlet
```

After you register the **.xsql** file extension, restart the Web server and browse an XSQL file to view the XML output or the transformed HTML output.

Dynamic XML Documents from SQL Queries

Oracle XSQL pages are XML datapages with embedded SQL queries to retrieve or insert data. You can build an XSQL page by including an **<xsql:query>** tag in your XML file at the place where you want the SQL to be executed. The **<xsql:query>** element will be replaced by the XML output of your query.

The XSQL Servlet uses a configuration file called **XSQLConfig.xml** to access and authenticate the database connection. A sample configuration file looks as follows:

```
<?xml version="1.0" ?>
<XSQLConfig>
   <connectiondefs dumpallowed="no">
      <connection name="demo">
         <username>scott</username>
         <password>tiger</password>
         <dburl>jdbc:oracle:thin:@localhost:1521:ORCL</dburl>
         <driver>oracle.jdbc.driver.OracleDriver</driver>
      </connection>
   </connectiondefs>
   :
</XSQLConfig>
```

You can define additional connection elements to identify different users or to use different JDBC drivers. The XSQL Servlet expects to find an attribute named "connection" on your XML document's root element whose value must match the name of a connection defined in your configuration file. The simplest use of the **<xsql:query>** tag is

```
<?xml version="1.0"?>
<xsql:query xmlns:xsql="urn:oracle-xsql" connection="demo">
    SELECT 'Hello World' AS "GREETING" FROM DUAL
</xsql:query>
```

The previous XSQL page produces the resulting dynamically created canonical XML document:

```
<?xml version = '1.0'?>
<ROWSET>
    <ROW id="1">
        <GREETING>Hello World</GREETING>
    </ROW>
</ROWSET>
```

You can transform the canonical XML document to a different XML form or to HTML. You can also associate an XSL stylesheet in your XSQL page using a processing instruction:

```
<?xml-stylesheet type="text/html" href="transform.xsl"?>
```

You can use object-relational queries in your XSQL pages. You can also send parameters to these pages using the URL. For example, you can use the object/relational capabilities of Oracle9i to create a user-defined object type called POINT. You can use your new POINT type as the data type of the ORIGIN column in your LOCATION table using the following DDL statements.

```
CREATE TYPE POINT AS OBJECT (X NUMBER, Y NUMBER);

CREATE TABLE LOCATION (
    NAME    VARCHAR2(80),
    ORIGIN POINT
);
```

You can insert a row into this LOCATION table using an INSERT statement with the POINT() constructor:

```
SQL> INSERT INTO LOCATION VALUES ( 'Someplace', POINT(11,17) );
SQL> COMMIT;
```

Then, you can use an XSQL page like the following **point.xsql** to query over the LOCATION table using a parameter *x*-coord.

```
<xsql:query connection="demo" xmlns:xsql="urn:oracle-xsql">
    SELECT name, origin
      FROM location loc
      WHERE loc.origin.x = {@x-coord}
</xsql:query>
```

You can use the following URL to retrieve all locations with *x*-coord value equal to 11.

```
http://yourmachine.com/xsql/demo/point.xsql?x-coord=11
```

```
<ROWSET>
    <ROW num="1">
        <NAME>Someplace</NAME>
        <ORIGIN>
            <X>11</X>
            <Y>17</Y>
        </ORIGIN>
    </ROW>
</ROWSET>
```

This demonstrates how the nested *X* and *Y* attributes in the POINT data type structure of the ORIGIN column appear automatically as nested **<X>** and **<Y>** elements in the XML output.

Support for Conditional SQL Commands in XSQL

Oracle XSQL pages are templates that enable you to assemble dynamic XML datapages based on one or more parameterized SQL queries. The processor then uses XSLT to transform the datapage to produce a final result in any desired XML, HTML, or text-based format.

The following XSQL page shows the use of the *<xsql:ref-cursor-function>* action handler and a parameter value to either retrieve a summary or detailed information on the book list using a stored function with an Oracle Reference Cursor:

```
<?xml version="1.0"?>
```

```
<xsql:ref-cursor-function connection="o817" MyPara="1" xmlns:xsql="urn:oracle-
xsql" xmlns:xsl="http://www.w3.org/1999/XSL/Transform">
```

```
    bookutils.bookdata({@MyPara});
</xsql:ref-cursor-function>
```

The stored function in the Oracle database:

```
create or replace package BookUtils as
type BookCurType is ref cursor;
function BookData(p_Parameter IN NUMBER DEFAULT 1) return BookUtils.BookCurType;
end BookUtils;
/
show errors;
create or replace package body BookUtils as
    function BookData(p_Parameter IN NUMBER) return BookUtils.BookCurType is
        bookcur BookCurType;
    begin
        if p_Parameter=1 then
                open bookcur for select* from scott.booklist;
                else
                open bookcur for select title, author from scott.booklist;
            end if;
        return bookcur;
    end BookData;
end BookUtils;
/
show errors;
```

The Book-Selling Example

In this section, we demonstrate the building of a Web site using XSQL pages, with Oracle9i as the data repository. This section uses the concepts discussed within the chapter to illustrate a "real world" example based on the simple business activity of managing an online book catalog. By following along from design to implementation, you will learn enough to start building XML-enabled Web sites.

Designing the Database Schema

The objective is to develop a simple Web site for managing a book catalog. First, you must identify the data model for storing the catalog in a database. The data model shown in Figure 3-6 illustrates the basic entities—book, authors, reviews—used in this example.

A book has a many-to-many relationship with the author because a book can have many authors (at least one), and each author can have many books. A book also has a one-to-many relationship with reviews. This relationship is optional because a book might not have any reviews. The previous data model can be translated into the following DTD:

```
<!-- DTD for Book Data -->
<!ELEMENT BOOKCATALOG (BOOK)*>
```

```
<!ELEMENT BOOK (TITLE, AUTHOR+, PUBLISHER?, PUBLISHYEAR?, PRICE?,
               REVIEWS*)>
<!ATTLIST BOOK ISBN CDATA #REQUIRED>
<!ATTLIST BOOK BOOKTYPE (Fiction|SciFi|Fantasy) #IMPLIED>
<!ELEMENT TITLE (#PCDATA)>
<!ELEMENT AUTHOR (LASTNAME, FIRSTNAME, EMAIL_ADDRESS)>
<!ELEMENT LASTNAME (#PCDATA)>
<!ELEMENT FIRSTNAME (#PCDATA)>
<!ELEMENT EMAIL_ADDRESS (#PCDATA)>
<!ELEMENT PUBLISHER (#PCDATA)>
<!ELEMENT PUBLISHYEAR (#PCDATA)>
<!ELEMENT PRICE (#PCDATA)>
<!ELEMENT REVIEWS (REVIEWER, RATING, COMMENTS)>
<!ELEMENT REVIEWER (#PCDATA)>
<!ELEMENT RATING (#PCDATA)>
<!ELEMENT COMMENTS (#PCDATA)>
```

The XML document (the book catalog) that is compliant to the previous DTD can be stored in the database in many different ways. The document can be stored as CLOB, and Oracle Text can be used to search and retrieve information from the XML document. The CLOB storage model, or even the *XMLType* that is based on a hidden CLOB, has a limitation. The granularity of updates using a CLOB is the complete document. Another approach to storing the XML document in the database is to map the DTD to a database schema. A simple schema for the previous DTD would contain three entities: a BOOK table, an AUTHOR object, and a REVIEW

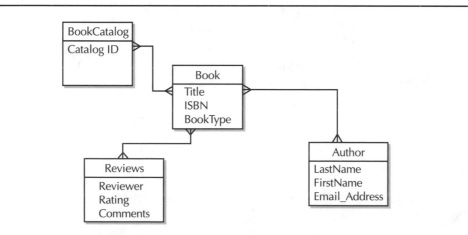

FIGURE 3-6. *Data Model for book catalog*

object. The BOOK table contains the list books and has two nested tables: one for the list of authors and the other for the list of reviews.

After you load the XML document in the database, you need to install the XSQL Servlet and the XDK components on a middle-tier Web server and use JDBC to communicate to the database. Finally, you need to build your Web site using XSQL files to retrieve XML documents and transform them into HTML output.

Designing the Web Site Using XSQL

You can design and build a Web site using JavaScript, Java Server Pages, and dynamic HTML in many different ways. In this section, we present a simple design using only HTML. These steps illustrate the use of XSQL pages to retrieve data from the database. These pages can be used as building blocks in a more advanced Web site design. We present two Web pages from the data in the BOOKCATALOG table:

- A page containing a list of all the books in the catalog

- A page containing a detailed view of a book identified by a ISBN number

Two steps are involved in building a Web page. First, you decide on the data required for the Web page using the XSQL datapage. Then, you decide the HTML formatting using an XSLT transformation. In the case of an advanced Web page design, you could use XSLT to transform the datapage into JavaScript. You can also include the datapage in Java Server Pages and use DOM APIs to retrieve data.

Catalog View

For the catalog view page, you don't need the complete information for each book. You can select only the attributes of the book that you want to present in the catalog view. You can select ISBN number, title, author's last name, publisher, and price using the following XSQL datapage:

```
<?xml version="1.0"?>
<?xml-stylesheet type="text/html" href="catalog.xsl"?>
<xsql:query xmlns:xsql="urn:oracle-xsql"
            connection="demo"
            rowset-element="BOOKCATALOG"
            row-element="BOOK">

    SELECT ISBN, Title, Author.Lastname, Publisher, Price
      FROM scott.BookCatalog

</xsql:query>
```

The previous XSQL page returns a canonical XML document containing the lists of books. The XSQL processor transforms the XML document using the XSLT stylesheet "catalog.xsl" associated in the xml-stylesheet processing instruction.

```xml
<?xml version="1.0"?>
<BOOKCATALOG>
  <BOOK>
    <ISBN>1234-123456-1234</ISBN>
    <TITLE>C Programming Language</TITLE>
    <AUTHOR_LASTNAME>Kernighan</AUTHOR_LASTNAME>
    <PUBLISHER>EEE Editions</PUBLISHER>
    <PRICE>7.99</PRICE>
  </BOOK>
  <BOOK>
    <ISBN>3456-34567890-3456</ISBN>
    <TITLE>C++ Primer</TITLE>
    <AUTHOR_LASTNAME>Lippmann</AUTHOR_LASTNAME>
    <PUBLISHER>McGraw Hill</PUBLISHER>
    <PRICE>4.99</PRICE>
  </BOOK>
  <BOOK>
    <ISBN>2137-598354-65978</ISBN>
    <TITLE>Twelve Red Herrings</TITLE>
    <AUTHOR_LASTNAME>Archer</AUTHOR_LASTNAME>
    <PUBLISHER>Harper Collins</PUBLISHER>
    <PRICE>12.95</PRICE>
  </BOOK>
  <BOOK>
    <ISBN>237864-4787834-3459</ISBN>
    <TITLE>The Eleventh Commandment</TITLE>
    <AUTHOR_LASTNAME>Archer</AUTHOR_LASTNAME>
    <PUBLISHER>Harper Collins</PUBLISHER>
    <PRICE>3.99</PRICE>
  </BOOK>
  <BOOK>
    <ISBN>1230-23498-2349879</ISBN>
    <TITLE>Emperor's New Mind</TITLE>
    <AUTHOR_LASTNAME>Penrose</AUTHOR_LASTNAME>
    <PUBLISHER>Oxford Publishing Company</PUBLISHER>
    <PRICE>15.99</PRICE>
  </BOOK>
</BOOKCATALOG>
```

You can use a simple transformation stylesheet, as the following example shows, to transform the generated XML document into an HTML table. The result of the transformation is shown in Figure 3-7.

```xml
<?xml version="1.0"?>
<xsl:stylesheet version="1.0"
                xmlns:xsl="http://www.w3.org/1999/XSL/Transform">

<xsl:template match="/">
  <HTML>
    <body bgcolor="#FFFFFF" text="#000000">
    <img align="center" src="mylogo.gif" border="0"/>
    <h1 align="center"> Scott's book catalog </h1>
    <xsl:apply-templates/>
    </body>
  </HTML>
</xsl:template>

<xsl:template match="BOOKCATALOG">
  <table align="center" border="10" cellspacing="10" cellpadding="2">
    <th>ISBN</th>
    <th>Title</th>
    <th>Author</th>
    <th>Publisher</th>
    <th>Price</th>
    <xsl:apply-templates select="BOOK"/>
  </table>
</xsl:template>

<xsl:template match="BOOK">
  <tr><xsl:apply-templates/></tr>
</xsl:template>

<xsl:template match="TITLE">
  <td><b><xsl:apply-templates/></b></td>
</xsl:template>

<xsl:template match="AUTHOR_LASTNAME">
  <td><i><xsl:apply-templates/></i></td>
</xsl:template>

<xsl:template match="PUBLISHER">
   <td><xsl:apply-templates/></td>
</xsl:template>

<xsl:template match="ISBN">
   <td><xsl:apply-templates/></td>
</xsl:template>

<xsl:template match="PRICE">
   <td>$<xsl:apply-templates/></td>
</xsl:template>

</xsl:stylesheet>
```

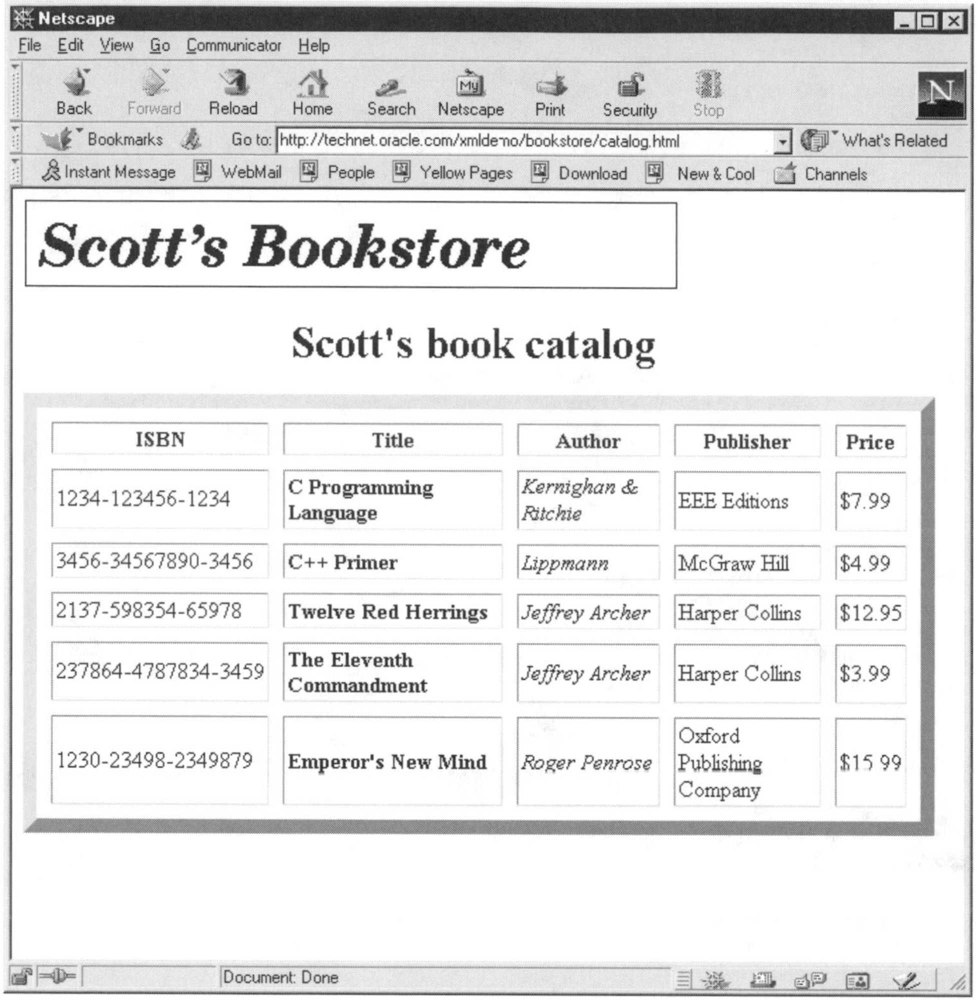

FIGURE 3-7. *Screenshot of book catalog*

Detailed View

You need to retrieve more information to present a detailed view of a book. You can also retrieve all the information and use the XSLT transformation to format the required attributes of the book. The following XSQL datapage retrieves all attributes of the book using a parameter **isbn-no**:

```
<?xml version="1.0"?>
<?xml-stylesheet type="text/html" href="catalog.xsl"?>
<xsql:query xmlns:xsql="urn:oracle-xsql"
            connection="demo"
            rowset-element="BOOKCATALOG"
            row-element="BOOK">

    SELECT *
      FROM scott.BookCatalog
     WHERE ISBN = {@isbn-no}

</xsql:query>
```

The following XML document is retrieved by the XSQL datapage and can be formatted as an HTML page, as shown in Figure 3-8.

```
<?xml version="1.0"?>
<BOOKCATALOG>
  <BOOK>
    <ISBN>2133-23700-5978</ISBN>
    <TITLE>My favorite title</TITLE>
    <AUTHOR>
       <LASTNAME>Smith</LASTNAME>
       <FIRSTNAME>Mark</FIRSTNAME>
       <EMAIL>msmith@mydomain.com</EMAIL>
    </AUTHOR>
    <BOOKTYPE>Fiction</BOOKTYPE>
    <PUBLISHER>Harper Collins</PUBLISHER>
    <PUBLISHYEAR>1982</PUBLISHYEAR>
    <PRICE>12.95</PRICE>
    <REVIEW_LIST>
       <REVIEW>
          <REVIEWER>review@somedomain.com</REVIEWER>
          <RATING>3</RATING>
          <COMMENTS>
             . . .
          </COMMENTS>
       </REVIEW>
       . . .
    <REVIEW_LIST>
  </BOOK>
</BOOKCATALOG>
```

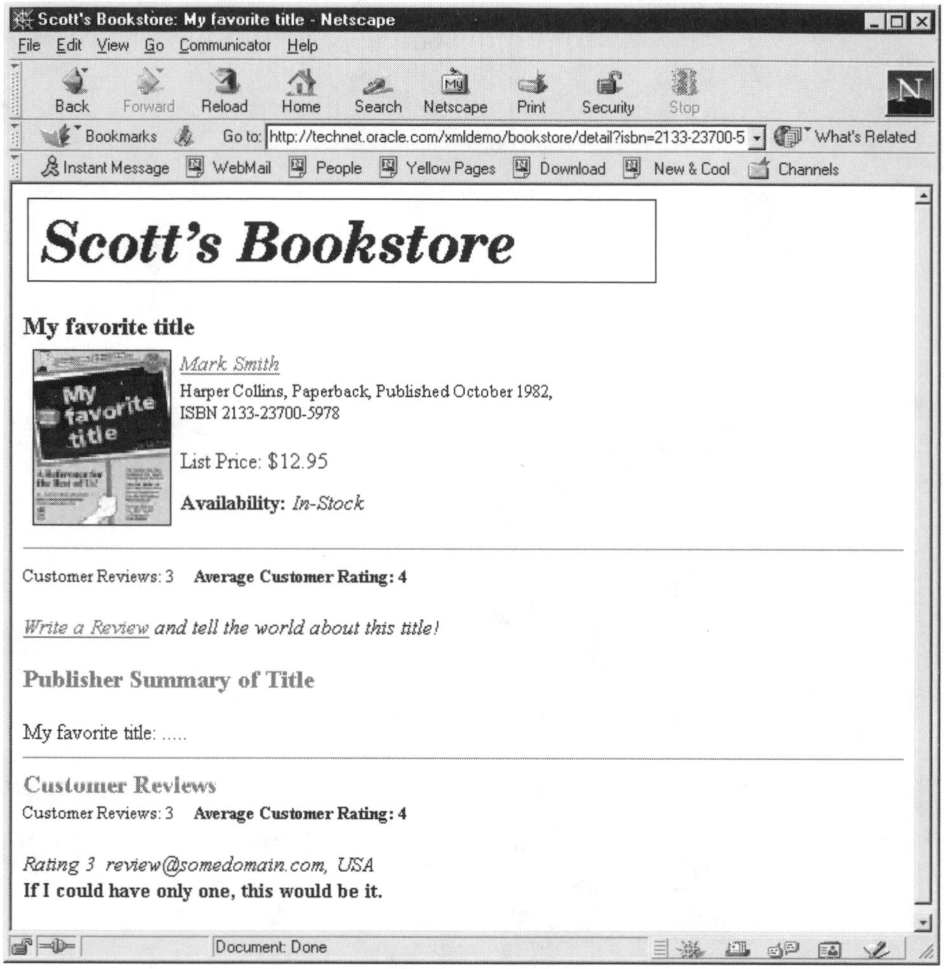

FIGURE 3-8. *Screenshot of details*

CHAPTER
4

Developing for Oracle
Application Servers

he widespread use of Internet technologies has overcome the innate limitations of traditional client/server applications and the corresponding two-tier model. Since the beginning of the Internet, users from IT managers to developers immediately seized on the idea of using a universal Web browser. With a simple mouse click, users could access content such as text, video, graphics, and sound stored in HTML pages. The *Hypertext Transfer Protocol (HTTP)* protocol running over TCP/IP enabled users to access HTML pages stored on any server connected to the *World Wide Web* (the Web). More and more customers started to Web-enable applications that, otherwise, would have never been deployed on the Internet.

The arrival of Java sped up this process. Being inherently platform independent, Java applications could be written once and run anywhere on a machine that had a Java Virtual Machine. Fat clients became obsolete, and client-side Java was used to show the final result of application work. Web browsers could download a Java applet from centrally located servers and run it, allowing new platform-independent applications and data to be distributed to clients on an as-needed basis. In addition, many users found that enterprise applications could be extended to a wider audience of distributed users, as browser-based clients operated over *wide area networks (WANs)* instead of the *local area networks (LANs)* required in traditional two-tier client/server applications.

As previously stated, the two-tier, fat-server model was historically the most common throughout the Web. In this model, almost all the application logic, in addition to HTTP servers with their static HTML pages and *Common Gateway Interface (CGI)* applications, was contained in the server tier. Thin clients as Web browsers formed the client tier. Similarly, client/server database applications were traditionally separated into a relatively thin client tier and a server tier (the database) containing both the application data and the application logic in the form of stored procedures.

While client/server-based Web applications are often suitable for medium-to-large workgroups, they do not scale well. As the number of users and transactions increases into the millions, client/server systems can quickly exceed their performance limits. Another drawback of client/server architectures is their inability to maintain a persistent connection between the client and the database, an especially important consideration for today's Web-based applications. The resulting "stateless" nature of client/server connection requires a client to make a new connection for every transaction, thereby increasing network traffic and decreasing overall performance. Issues related to scalability, maintenance, and connection persistence become a real limitation of client/server architectures, especially for applications distributed across diverse hardware platforms and operating systems.

Recently, a new three-tier model has emerged that isolates much of the application logic in a new flexible middle tier between the client tier (browser) and the server tier (database). More than one middle tier makes the architecture even more object-oriented, which also improves the encapsulation of mission-critical application logic.

The result, known as *n-tier architecture,* allows partitioning of application logic into components that can be easily modified or reused, and deployed across several physical machines on different platforms. Middle-tier servers can also manage connections and make them *state sensitive,* in order that clients and servers can stay connected across multiple transactions, and applications can be distributed across multiple machines and platforms. All this further improves scalability, performance, and overall flexibility.

The use of n-tier architectures is an important first step in the creation of robust enterprise Web applications. To exploit the benefits of n-tier architecture, developers needed an integrated environment for development and deployment of middle-tier components. To meet these requirements, a new product category emerged—the application server. The *application server* is the centerpiece of the middle tier and provides a unified platform for shared enterprise applications. The application server provides vital services, such as security, message brokering, database connectivity, transaction management, and process isolation, while delivering enterprise quality of service.

Oracle Application Server (OAS) and *Oracle9i Application Server (iAS)* integrate all the core services and features required for building, deploying, and managing high-performance, n-tier, transaction-oriented Web applications within an open standards framework. These essential capabilities include:

- HTTP Web Server and support for using other popular Web servers

- Database and legacy access middleware for connection to all major databases

- CORBA ORB support for scalable, cross-platform, distributed-object deployment

- *Transaction Processing (TP) Monitor* capability for load balancing, pooling, and transactions

- Network Services, such as security and directory

- Message-oriented middleware for extensibility that simplifies the enabling of new applications

OAS and iAS offer cross-platform support for network clients, such as HTML and Java, Web servers, and databases, which preserves existing investments in legacy and client/server systems.

This chapter focuses first on the fundamentals of OAS architecture and those of iAS architecture, which is fundamentally different. Then, using a Bookstore application implemented as an OAS servlet, it shows you how to apply XSLT stylesheet transformations to XML documents obtained from a database. The Bookstore application also illustrates the different ways to access the database from OAS. Finally, a section on how to configure the servlet for iAS is included.

Oracle Application Server Architecture

By definition, *Oracle Application Server (OAS)* is a collection of middleware tools and services, and a platform for distributed, server-side applications. OAS implements the middle tier using CORBA, an industry-standard model for distributed object-oriented programming. CORBA specifies the behavior of *Object Request Brokers (ORBs)*. An ORB is responsible for routing requests from clients and other ORBs to CORBA objects. Clients communicate with ORBs using the *Internet Inter-ORB Protocol (IIOP)*, instead of HTTP.

OAS supports access to two types of clients: Web browsers using HTTP for communication and CORBA clients that access JCORBA and EJB applications using IIOP. For CORBA clients, OAS provides a CORBA 2.0–compatible ORB. These clients can be Java applets, cartridges, stand-alone applications, or other JCORBA or EJB objects in the same or different applications.

A group of closely connected OAS machines form a *site*. For each site, a single machine, called the *primary node,* hosts the ORB and *Resource Manager (RM)* proxy and stores configuration data for the entire site. The rest of the site machines are called *remote nodes.*

An OAS contains three major components:

- HTTP listeners
- OAS components
- Application cartridges

HTTP Listeners

A *listener* is an HTTP server that handles requests for static pages and CGI. OAS has its own Oracle Web Listener, but it also supports the following non-Oracle listeners:

- Netscape FastTrack Server
- Netscape Enterprise Server
- Microsoft Internet Information Server (IIS)
- Apache (non-NT)

All requests, other than those for static pages and CGI, are passed to OAS dispatchers for handling. OAS provides listener-specific adapters that enable listeners to work together with dispatchers in a tightly integrated way, thereby optimizing performance.

OAS Components

OAS itself provides a common set of services for applications deployed as cartridges on the server. These services include load balancing; transaction services; error handling; and recovery of failed processes, security, and directory. The OAS dispatchers handle the application requests from HTTP listeners and CORBA/IIOP requests. When a listener receives an HTTP request that does not identify a static HTML page or CGI program, it passes the request to its dispatcher, which assigns a request to a cartridge instance of the appropriate type.

The OAS Dispatcher handles the HTTP requests, managing a pool of cartridge (business components) instances running on one or more nodes. When a request arrives for a particular cartridge, the dispatcher routes the request to one of its cached cartridge instances of the appropriate type. If the dispatcher has no such cartridge instance available, it requests that the OAS create a new cartridge server with an appropriate cartridge instance. The dispatcher then adds this cartridge instance to its cache and assigns the pending request to it. After the request completion, the dispatcher preserves the new cartridge instance, so it is available to handle a new request.

The OAS RM proxy component handles the CORBA/IIOP requests, obtaining JCORBA object references on behalf of external clients. When a client requests an object reference, the RM proxy instantiates, if necessary, the requested object within a JCORBA server and returns the reference to the client. The client then uses the object reference to call methods on the object directly.

One RM proxy per Web site and one dispatcher associated with each listener on each node of a Web site exist.

Application Cartridges

A *cartridge* is Oracle's historical term for a business component. In OAS context, both terms are semantically equivalent, but the term *cartridge* is used to add some Oracle flavor to the described topic. Cartridges are objects managed by and deployed on OAS, sharing libraries that either implement program logic or provide access to program logic stored elsewhere, such as in a database. A *cartridge server* is a process in which one or more cartridge instances run. A *cartridge instance* is a CORBA object running within the cartridge server process that executes cartridge code.

OAS is a platform for a variety of language environments, so most of the cartridges bundled with OAS are targeted for a specific programming language API and library support. OAS 4.0.8 includes the cartridges described in the following sections.

PL/SQL Cartridge

The PL/SQL cartridge runs PL/SQL stored procedures in Oracle databases, using a *Database Access Descriptor (DAD)* to locate the database to which to connect. The cartridge runs files that contain PL/SQL source code, and it loads the contents of the file into the database and executes the code. The PL/SQL cartridge comes with the PL/SQL Web Toolkit, which enables you to get information about the request; to specify values for HTTP headers, such as the content type and cookies; and to generate HTML tags.

JWeb Cartridge

The JWeb cartridge runs Java applications, incorporating a Java Virtual Machine that interprets the bytecodes for the Java application. The JWeb cartridge supports two different methods for database connection and access. The first is the use of Java wrappers of PL/SQL stored procedures and functions. A pl2java tool is used to generate the wrapper Java class, and the stored PL/SQL procedures are called through their wrapped counterpart methods. The second mechanism for database access can be implemented using the *Java Database Connectivity (JDBC)* interface, which enables you to execute SQL statements directly from the application. The JWeb cartridge comes with the JWeb Toolkit, which allows the application to obtain information about the request; to specify values for HTTP headers, such as the content type and cookies; and to generate HTML tags.

JServlet Cartridge

The JServlet cartridge specializes in handling HTTP requests. Different from most other servlet implementations, JServlet shares most JWeb services. One key advantage of OAS JServlet cartridge applications over the single-host servlets is the feature to distribute the same JServlet application automatically across multiple hosts in an OAS site.

C Cartridge

The C cartridge runs C applications, supporting the implementation of callback functions invoked by OAS. The C cartridge comes with the WRB API, which contains functions and data structures that support retrieval of information about the request; specifying values for HTTP headers, such as the content type and cookies; and sending requests to other cartridges.

LiveHTML Cartridge

The LiveHTML cartridge interprets *server-side includes (SSI)* documents. SSI is a standard that enables you to retrieve dynamic data in an otherwise static HTML document. Special tags in LiveHTML documents are used to mark the places where the cartridge substitutes dynamic data. Embedded Perl scripts for generating dynamic data are also allowed.

Perl Cartridge

The Perl cartridge runs Perl scripts. The Perl cartridge also comes with several Perl modules including the DBI/DBD, which enables access to Oracle databases.

Oracle Internet Application Server Architecture

As with OAS, iAS is a collection of services and tools to enable middle-tier deployment of enterprise-level applications. This is where the similarity ends, however, as iAS is a total redesign of many of these services, which can be divided into five sets:

- Communication Services
- Presentation Services
- Business Logic Services
- Data Management Services
- System Services

Figure 4-1 shows a block diagram of the iAS services and their components.

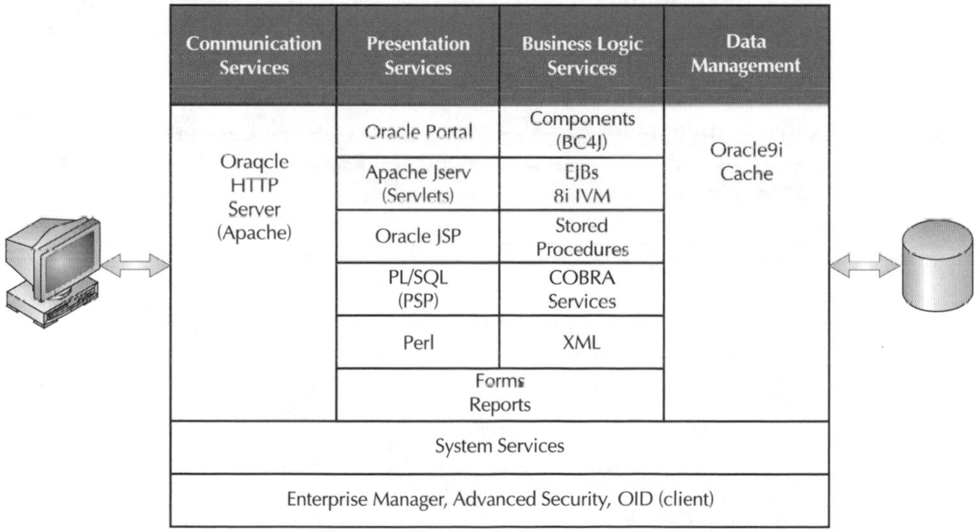

Communication Services	Presentation Services	Business Logic Services	Data Management
Oraqcle HTTP Server (Apache)	Oracle Portal	Components (BC4J)	Oracle9i Cache
	Apache Jserv (Servlets)	EJBs 8i IVM	
	Oracle JSP	Stored Procedures	
	PL/SQL (PSP)	COBRA Services	
	Perl	XML	
	Forms Reports		
System Services			
Enterprise Manager, Advanced Security, OID (client)			

FIGURE 4-1.   *Oracle iAS Services architecture*

iAS Communication Services

The Communication Services handle incoming requests received by the Oracle Internet Application Server. Requests are processed by Oracle HTTP Server or are routed to other services of iAS for processing. These services are made of components that offer support for IIOP, RMI, and Net8. Additionally, Oracle iAS can additionally support mobile and wireless technologies such as the Wireless Access Protocol (WAP).

Oracle HTTP Server

The Oracle HTTP Server is based on the Apache Server. Apache is the industry standard Web listener on the Internet and serves over 60 percent of the world's Internet sites. Therefore, incorporating an Apache-based HTTP server into iAS provides a scalable, available platform that as been thoroughly field tested.

Oracle HTTP Server Modules

Mods are plug-ins to the HTTP Server that extend its functionality either by offering native services (e.g., mod_ssl) or by dispatching requests to external processes (e.g., mod_jserv dispatching to Apache JServ). In addition to the compiled Apache mods provided with Oracle HTTP server, Oracle has enhanced several of the standard mods and has added Oracle-specific mods, which are described in the following sections.

mod_plsql   The mod_plsql module routes HTTP requests for stored procedures to an Oracle8i engine for processing. It executes within the HTTP Server process and is the upgrade to the PL/SQL Cartridge on the Oracle Application Server.

mod_ose   This module routes HTTP requests for Java servlet applications and Java Server Pages (JSPs) configured for the Oracle Servlet Engine (OSE) to an instance running in iAS. Utilizing HTTP tunneling over Net8 as the protocol between the server and servlet engine, mod_ose can leverage Net8's connection manager, load balancing, and firewall support.

mod_ssl   This module provides standard HTTPS that is fully supported by Oracle. It enables secure connections between the HTTP server and a browser client by using an Oracle-provided encryption mechanism over a Secure Sockets Layer (SSL). It may also be used for authentication over the Internet via digital certificates technology.

mod_perl   This module forwards Perl application requests to the Perl interpreter that is embedded in the Oracle HTTP Server. The embedded Perl interpreter saves the overhead from starting an external interpreter process. The code caching feature, in which modules and scripts are loaded and compiled only once, allows the server to run already-loaded and compiled code, therefore incurring less overhead costs in repeated Perl executions. This feature is described in more detail in the "Perl Interpreter" section.

mod_jserv   This module routes all Java servlet and JavaServer Page (JSP) requests to the Apache JServ servlet engine via the Apache JServ protocol (AJP). In the case of JSPs, the OracleJSP run time will manage the execution of the page from within the Apache JServ environment. This process is described in more detail in the "Apache JServ" section.

iAS Presentation Services

The presentation services of Oracle iAS output is a variety of graphical representations, often in the form of HTML. Oracle iAS supports many different ways to generate presentations that can be delivered to the client. These range from low-level programming using Perl scripts and Java servlets to high-level frameworks using Oracle Portal services. The following sections describe the presentation services in Oracle iAS.

Portal Services (Oracle Portal)

Oracle Portal is a tool and corresponding runtime framework for building and managing portals. Portal provides an easy way to let employees or users publish and manage content on the Web. Their portal data can be centrally administered, producing a site-wide consistent look-and-feel, and having internal access to content, transaction, and business intelligence applications. Besides providing this functionality, Oracle Portal also utilizes single sign-on, personalization, and portlet extensibility technologies to provide a simple, integrated view of external content, corporate information, and applications. You can use the Portal Developer's Kit APIs to integrate other applications and syndicated content using Java and XML.

Apache JServ

Apache JServ is a Java servlet engine fully compliant with Sun Microsystems' Java Servlet 2.0 API specification. Like Oracle Portal, Apache JServ is implemented in two central parts. One part is the servlet engine itself, which is composed of 100 percent Java and runs on a version 1.1 or later Java Virtual Machine. The second part is the HTTP server extension, mod_jserv, which runs within the HTTP server process and dispatches HTTP servlet requests over to instances of the servlet engine. This extension communicates with the servlet engine via Apache JServ Protocol (AJP), which runs on top of TCP/IP and enables the servlet engine to run either locally or remotely to the HTTP Server.

OracleJSP

OracleJSP is the interpreter and run-time engine for Java Server Pages (JSPs). JSPs define an easy way to separate presentation and business logic. Knowing no Java but knowing HTML, you can create highly dynamic Web pages. OracleJSP is the JSP container, the program module that translates, executes, and processes JSP pages and delivers requests to them. It runs on Apache JServ or any standard servlet engine that supports version 2.0 or higher of the servlet specification. OracleJSP translates a JSP page into servlet code, which is then compiled and can be invoked in either of two ways: dynamically by the JSP container as a result of a user **.jsp** URL request, or explicitly by the JSP developer. OracleJSP additionally offers exceptional functionality for database applications by extending support to SQLJ, national language support (NLS), and supplementary tag libraries.

PL/SQL Server Pages
PL/SQL server pages are similar to JavaServer Pages, except that they use PL/SQL rather than Java for server-side scripting. Oracle PSP includes the PSP compiler and the PL/SQL Web Toolkit. With PSPs, you can easily author and run database-intensive Web pages as well as integrate existing applications written in PL/SQL.

Perl Interpreter
The Perl run-time environment is embedded in the Oracle HTTP Server process, thus saving the overhead from starting an external interpreter or making IPC calls to execute Perl scripts. When the Oracle HTTP server receives an HTTP request for a Perl script, the request is routed to mod_perl, which in turn routes the request to the Perl interpreter for processing.

iAS Business Logic Services
Oracle iAS provides several ways of developing business logic, utilizing both Java development approaches and high-level model-driven techniques. These approaches include Java technologies such as J2EE, EJB, and Oracle Business Components for Java, as well as rich GUI-oriented approaches such as Oracle Forms and Reports. The following sections describe these major elements that provide business logic services in Oracle Internet Application Server.

The Java engine inside Oracle iAS is the Oracle8i JServer JVM. JServer, originally released as part of the Oracle8i database, addresses the demanding requirements of the server-sde environment.

Oracle Business Components for Java
Oracle Business Components for Java (BC4J) is a 100 percent Java, XML-powered framework that enables productive development, portable deployment, and flexible customization of multitier, database-enabled applications from reusable business components. You can use this framework to design and test business logic in components that automatically integrate with databases. You can reuse this business logic through multiple SQL-based views of data that support different application tasks. Servlets, JavaServer Pages, and thin Java Swing clients can access and update stored data. BC4J is XML-enabled both in the internal structure of its properties files and in its ability to process and work with XML data and documents.

Support for the Java Development Model (J2EE)

Designed as a highly scalable, server-side Java platform, iAS is an enterprise-class 100 percent Java-compatible server environment that supports J2EE (including servlets, JSPs, and Enterprise JavaBeans), CORBA, and database stored procedures. The Oracle9i JServer achieves high scalability through its unique architectural design, which minimizes the burden and complexity of memory management even as the number of concurrent users on the server increases.

Oracle9*i* PL/SQL Engine

The Oracle9i PL/SQL engine is a scalable environment for executing PL/SQL stored procedures, PL/SQL Web applications, and PL/SQL Server Pages (PSPs). The Oracle8i PL/SQL engine runs both on the backend, within the Oracle database process, and on the middle tier, within Oracle iAS. PL/SQL database stored procedures and PSPs can be cached on the middle tier and executed within the Oracle8i PL/SQL engine in Oracle iAS, thus off-loading processing from the backend.

Oracle Forms Services

Oracle Forms Services are included in iAS, providing you the ability to run applications built with Oracle Forms Developer over the Internet or over your corporate intranet. Oracle Forms Services consist of a listener and a run-time engine that runs on iAS in the middle tier. On the client tier, Oracle Forms Services consist of a thin Java-based Forms client applet that provides the user interface for the application. Client and server may communicate through a proprietary protocol directly over sockets (generally appropriate for corporate intranets), or messages may be tunneled over HTTP for use in Internet environments to get through firewalls.

Oracle Reports Services

Oracle Reports is a run-time service to run Oracle Reports applications. Companies need to be able to quickly deploy applications that can dynamically generate data-heavy reports and publish their results in standard Internet formats via the Web. Oracle Reports also provides an option for outputting XML-formatted reports that can then be filtered, transformed, or custom formatted by applying the applicable XSL stylesheets.

Discoverer Viewer

Discoverer Viewer is a run-time environment for running Discoverer workbooks over the Web. It enables users to perform dynamic, ad hoc query and analysis from a standard Web browser. Discoverer heavily leverages XML and XSL to create custom views and formats for its data presentations.

iAS Data Management Services

To reduce the load on the backend database instance, and to avoid network roundtrips for read-only data, Oracle Internet Application Server includes Oracle9i Cache.

Oracle9*i* Cache

Oracle9i Cache is a read-only data and application cache that resides on the middle tier as a component of Oracle Internet Application Server. It improves the performance and scalability of applications that access Oracle databases by caching frequently used data and stored procedures on the middle-tier machine. With Oracle9i Cache, your applications can often process several times as many requests as their original capacity. Processing database queries on the middle tier can reduce the time spent sending and receiving data over the network. This reduces the load on the database server tier, which means that your backend databases can support more users.

A good example of an application that will benefit from Oracle9i Cache is our Bookstore Web site. This Web site keeps a database of all its books, including title, author, reviews, and various other sorts of information. This data is relatively static and may be updated once a day or once a week. The unchanging pages and graphics of the Web site may be served from the file system by the iAS HTTP server on the middle tier. The backend database holds all of the catalog data and thus needs to be queried for every dynamic request. Many requests will be dynamic queries, as users search for books by author, title, subject, or other variables; thus, numerous requests will be made of the database instance. As the user base increases, more and more concurrent requests will be made to the database. In this case, a single database instance will become the bottleneck to scalability if it begins to give slow responses under the heavy load. This bottleneck of a single database may be overcome by offloading query processing to the middle tier, as can be done by caching the catalog data in Oracle9i Cache. All of the catalog queries thus can be serviced locally on the middle tier node, giving better performance by eliminating the network round-trip for each data query. This results in better scalability by offloading work from the database.

iAS System Services

Oracle Internet Application Server includes Oracle Enterprise Manager and Oracle Advanced Security to provide system management and security services. These system services provide a comprehensive management framework for your entire Oracle environment and network security via SSL (Secure Sockets Layer)–based encryption and authentication facilities.

Oracle Enterprise Manager

Oracle Enterprise Manager is the system management tool for centrally managing your Oracle platform. With its graphical console, EM includes Oracle Management

Servers, Oracle Intelligent Agents, common services, and administrative tools. Oracle Enterprise Manager provides a comprehensive systems management platform for managing both Oracle iAS and Oracle8i.

Oracle Advanced Security

Security services for iAS are provided by the Oracle Advanced Security suite. It functions both as network security, protecting enterprise networks and securely extending corporate networks to the Internet, and as the security for directory services to provide enterprise user management and single sign-on.

iAS Client Components

Oracle Database Client Developer's Kit

The Oracle Database Client Developer's Kit contains client libraries for Oracle8i and Java2 Enterprise Edition support (JMS, SQLJ, JDBC, and JNDI). Developers include the libraries in the applications they write. These applications would run on Oracle iAS and access Oracle8i databases.

Oracle XML Developer's Kits

The Oracle XML Developer's Kits discussed in earlier chapters are included as part of iAS. All five XDKs—Java, JavaBeans, C, C++, and PL/SQL—are included to be used for deployment and redistribution of your applications. These components are also used by many of the iAS services both internally and exposing external XML interfaces.

Oracle LDAP Client Toolkit

The Oracle LDAP Client Toolkit is used to develop and monitor LDAP-enabled applications. It supports client calls to directory services that you can use to access your directory data. Applications built with the toolkit can take advantage of the Oracle Internet Directory (OID) and other version 3 LDAP services.

The Bookstore Application as an OAS Servlet

If you want to see the upcoming Bookstore example as an OAS middle-tier application, the following code shows a typical implementation. Bookstore data is stored in an Oracle database. The application logic is implemented as a Java servlet, which resides in OAS and obtains the bookstore data from the database in the form of an XML document. Clients are Web browsers, sending their requests for a specific kind of bookstore data to the OAS servlet and receiving the information in the form of HTML pages. The servlet uses XSLT stylesheets for converting the database XML document into the client HTML page.

The following code illustrates a typical servlet implementation, which in this instance uses XSLT stylesheets to apply to XML documents. A *servlet* is a Java program that receives input from and delivers output to a server. It is invoked from a client browser when a particular servlet's URL is selected. This approach is a common way to install application logic on servers.

```java
import javax.servlet.*;
import javax.servlet.http.*;
import java.io.*;
import java.util.*;
import java.sql.*;
import java.net.*;
import oracle.xml.parser.v2.*;
import org.w3c.dom.*;

public class BookstoreServlet extends HttpServlet
{
    ServletContext context;
    Connection       conn = null;

    public void init (ServletConfig config)  throws ServletException
    {
        super.init(config);

        context = config.getServletContext ();

        // initialize/open database connection
        initDB ();
    }

    public void doGet (HttpServletRequest req, HttpServletResponse res)
            throws ServletException, IOException
    {
        InputStream xmlIn, xslIn;
        String docHTML;

        res.setContentType ("text/html");
        PrintWriter out   = new PrintWriter (res.getOutputStream());

        String xslName    = getXSLName (req);

        // print client HTML header
```

```java
      out.println ("<html>");
      out.println ("<head><title>Booklist</title></head>");
      out.println ("<body>");

      try
      {
         xmlIn  = getXMLfromDB (xmlName);
         xslIn  = getXSL (xslName);
         docHTML = doXSLTransform (xmlIn, xslIn);
      }
      catch (Exception e)
      {
         docHTML = "<H2>Error: " + e.getMessage() + "</H2>";
      }

      out.print (docHTML);
      out.println ("</body></html>");
      out.close();
}

public void destroy () {
   // close DB connection
   closeDB ();
}

String doXSLTransform (InputStream xmlIn, InputStream xslIn)
      throws Exception
{
   DOMParser      parser;
   XMLDocument    xml, out;
   XSLStylesheet xsl;

   try
   {
      parser = new DOMParser();
      parser.setPreserveWhitespace(true);

      // parse input XSL file
      parser.parse (xslIn);
      xsl = new XSLStylesheet (parser.getDocument(), null);

      // parse input XML document
      parser.parse(xmlIn);
      xml = parser.getDocument();

      XSLProcessor  processor = new XSLProcessor();

      // display any warnings that may occur
```

```
        processor.showWarnings (true);
        processor.setErrorStream (System.err);

        // Process XSL
        DocumentFragment result = processor.processXSL (xsl, xml);

        // create an output document to hold the result
        out = new XMLDocument ();

        // create a dummy document element for the output document
        Element root = out.createElement ("root");
        out.appendChild (root);

        // append the transformed tree to the dummy document element

        root.appendChild (result);

        // print the transformed document
        StringWriter  strWriter = new StringWriter ();
        out.print (new PrintWriter (strWriter));
        return strWriter.toString ();
    }
    catch (Exception e)
    {
        return new String ("<H2>Error: " + e.getMessage () + "</H2>");
    }
}

// helper functions
...
}
```

BookstoreServlet Application

The connection to the database is established during the servlet initialization. Two different ways of implementing database access are described later in this chapter. The client requests are received by **doGet()** or **doPut()** servlet methods. These methods are passed two parameters: the client request and the response for it. To begin with, the response type is set:

```
        res.setContentType ("text/html");
```

Thus, the client receives the information in the form of an HTML page. The name of the XSLT stylesheet is obtained from the request. This stylesheet is used to transform the database XML document into a client HTML page. Next, the HTML header is output, and an XML document is obtained from the database. The XSLT stylesheet is read from the servlet storage, and the **doXSLTransform()** method is invoked.

```
PrintWriter out   = new PrintWriter (res.getOutputStream());
...
try
{
    xmlIn  = getXMLfromDB (xmlName);
    xslIn  = getXSL (xslName);
    docHTML = doXSLTransform  (xmlIn, xslIn);
}
catch (Exception e)
{
    docHTML = "<H2>Error: " + e.getMessage() + "</H2>";
}
```

The **XSLTransform()** method instantiates an XSL processor and performs the transformation:

```
XSLProcessor  processor = new XSLProcessor ();
...
DocumentFragment result = processor.processXSL (xsl, xml);
```

In the case of an error, the error message is sent back to the client.

The input XML document could also contain a list of book data as indicated here:

```
...
<booklist>
  <book isbn="1234-123456-1234">
    <title>C Programming Language</title>
    <author>Kernighan and Ritchie</author>
    <publisher>IEEE</publisher>
    <price>7.99</price>
     ...
  </book>
  ...
  <book isbn="1230-23498-2349879">
    <title>Emperor's New Mind</title>
    <author>Roger Penrose</author>
    <publisher>Oxford Publishing Company</publisher>
    <price>15.99</price>
     ...
  </book>
  ...
</booklist>
```

If you apply a client stylesheet to the XML document, an HTML document containing only book titles and prices is generated.

```
...
<xsl:stylesheet version="1.0"
```

```
xmlns:xsl="http://www.w3.org/1999/XSL/Transform" >
 <xsl:output method="xml"/>

 <xsl:template match="/">
     <xsl:apply-templates/>
 </xsl:template>

 <xsl:template match="booklist">
   <BODY BGCOLOR="#CCFFFF">
     <H1 align="center">List of books</H1>
     <table border="0" width="100%" cellspacing="5">
         <tr>
           <td width="83%" bgcolor="FFFF80" align="left">
             <font face="Arial" size="5" color="000080">
               <strong>BOOK</strong>
             </font>
           </td>
           <td width="17%" bgcolor="FFFF80" align="left">
             <font face="Arial" size="5" color="000080">
               <strong>Price</strong>
             </font>
           </td>
         </tr>
         <xsl:apply-templates/>
     </table>
   </BODY>
 </xsl:template>

 <xsl:template match="booklist/book">
     <tr>
       <xsl:apply-templates/>
     </tr>
 </xsl:template>

 <xsl:template match="booklist/book/title">
     <td width="83%" bgcolor="FFFF80" align="left">
       <font face="Arial" size="5" color="000080">
         <strong><xsl:apply-templates/></strong>
       </font>
     </td>
 </xsl:template>

 <xsl:template match="booklist/book/price">
     <td width="17%" bgcolor="FFFF80" align="left">
       <font face="Arial" size="5" color="000080">
           $<xsl:apply-templates/>
       </font>
     </td>
```

```
    </xsl:template>

    <xsl:template match="booklist/book/author">
    </xsl:template>
    <xsl:template match="booklist/book/publisher">
    </xsl:template>

</xsl:stylesheet>
```

Registering the BookstoreServlet Application and Cartridge

The BookstoreServlet application was designed to use the OAS JServlet cartridge because of the advantages offered by this cartridge. No start-up or shutdown of the Java Virtual Machine is required for each request, and the database connections remain open for a session, reducing the overhead of reconnecting to the database with each request. Multiple JServlet cartridges can run on the same virtual machine when they belong to the same application, and instead of creating new instances, free instances of applications are used when available. The JServlet cartridge takes advantage of OAS services, such as load balancing, scalability, monitoring, logging, and session-management capabilities. The JServlet Toolkit is also available to generate HTML and to facilitate database access.

After creating the servlet application, you must register it with the OAS Manager. The OAS Manager connects a JServlet cartridge with the application and provides configuration information, such as a virtual and physical path to the servlet, environment variables, and authentication information. At the end, you must reload the server to activate the servlet registration. The OAS Manager reloads all the Oracle Application Server processes, listeners, and applications.

Invoking the BookstoreServlet Application

The BookstoreServlet can be invoked with the following URL, typed into the client browser:

```
http://<host>:<port>/<servlet_virtual_path>/BookstoreServlet
```

in which a host and port identify a listener that knows about the cartridge. This can be any listener on the application server, except the Node Manager listener. For example, this could be *www listener*, which, by default, resides on port 80.

Another way of invoking the cartridge is from an HTML page, such as this one:

```
...
<HTML>
<HEAD><TITLE>Bookstore </TITLE></HEAD>
```

```
<BODY>
...
  <FORM  METHOD = "GET"
ACTION=HREF="http://jsmith.us.oracle.com:80/oas/jservlets/HelloServlet">
  <A>Run BookstoreServlet</A>
...
```

in which **jsmith.us.oracle.com** is the host, the port number is 80, **/oas/jservlets** is the virtual path, and the servlet input method is **doGet ()**.

The OAS HTTP listener component receives a request for a JServlet cartridge from a client browser. The OAS dispatcher recognizes that the request is for a cartridge and forwards the request to the *OAS Web Request Broker (WRB).* The WRB examines the URL and determines that the request is for a JServlet cartridge because the virtual path (**/oas/jservlets**) is mapped to a JServlet cartridge. The request is passed to the JServlet cartridge. The JServlet cartridge, running in a cartridge server process, receives the request, examines the URL, and finds the name—typically at the end of the URL—of the Java servlet application (class) to invoke. In this example, the name is BookstoreServlet. Next, the JServlet cartridge loads the **BookstoreServlet** class and invokes its entry point method. For servlets, the entry points are the **doGet()** and **doPut()** methods. Finally, the Java servlet application generates a response, including both the HTTP response header and response body, and then returns it through a special output stream (HtmlStream). The JServlet cartridge receives the response and returns it to the WRB. The WRB forwards the response to the client browser that invoked the application.

Database Access

In general, JServlet applications can access databases in two different ways: using JDBC and using the *pl2java* utility.

The first method to access the database is to use the JDBC package or JdbcBeans. JDBC provides a standard interface to access databases from different vendors, allowing you to embed SQL statements as arguments to the access methods. The servlet application directly invokes PL/SQL statements. The following example shows the BookstoreServlet with JDBC database access:

```
...
import java.sql.*;
import oracle.html.*;

public class BookstoreServlet extends HttpServlet
                                 implements SingleThreadModel {
    private Connection conn = null;

    public void init( ServletConfig config ) throws ServletException {
```

```java
   super.init(config);
   ...
   initDB ();
}

initDB ()  {
  try {
     // Load the Oracle JDBC driver
     Class.forName ("oracle.jdbc.driver.OracleDriver");

     String     username = "scott",
                password = "tiger",
                dbURL    = "jdbc:oracle:oci8.@";
     // Connect to the database. To connect to a remote database,
     // insert the connect string after the @ sign in the connection URL.
     conn = DriverManager.getConnection  (dbURL, username, password);
  } catch ( SQLException e ) {
     System.err.println ("Could not establish connection.");
  } catch ( ClassNotFoundException e ) {
     System.err.println ("Could not load database driver.");
  }
}
...

  InputStream getXMLfromDB  ( )  throws Exception
  {
     try {
        // Create a Statement
        Statement stmt = conn.createStatement ();

        // Select the ENAME column from the EMP table
        ResultSet rset = stmt.executeQuery (
                        "select num, xmldoc  from  bookstore");

        // Iterate through the result
        while ( rset.next () )
        {
             buffer.add (rset.getString(2));
        }
     } catch ( SQLException e ) {
        buffer = "A database error occurred";
     }
     return  new StringBufferInputStream  (buffer);
}

void closeDB () {
     try {
        // close the database connection
```

```
      if ( conn != null)
          conn.close();
   } catch (SQLException e) {
        System.err.println ("Error closing database connection.");
   }
 }
  ...
}
```

The second mechanism to access the database is to invoke PL/SQL-stored procedures and functions directly from Java applications running in the context of a JServlet cartridge. The *pl2java* utility is used to generate Java wrapper classes for procedures in a PL/SQL package. For a specified PL/SQL package, *pl2java* generates a single Java wrapper class, which contains a wrapper method for each procedure or function in the package. The signatures of the wrapper methods are the same as the PL/SQL procedures or functions they wrap. This provides a Java class view of PL/SQL packages and allows PL/SQL stored procedures to be called seamlessly.

The following is an invocation of the *pl2java* tool from the command prompt:

```
> pl2java -class bookstore bookstore.sql scott/tiger ...
```

It creates a Java wrapper class named "bookstore" from the PL/SQL package **bookstore.sql**. The user name/password must also be specified. These wrapper classes belong to the **oracle.plsql** package and are derived from the **PValue** base class, which encapsulates the null attribute of PL/SQL values. To pass data between Java and PL/SQL, *pl2java* maps the PL/SQL data types to Java wrapper classes.

The following code shows the BookstoreServlet using a wrapper class for database access.

```
...
import oracle.rdbms.*;

public class BookstoreServlet extends HttpServlet
                        implements SingleThreadModel
{
  private Connection conn = null;

  public void init( ServletConfig config ) throws ServletException
  {
      super.init(config);
      ...
      initDB ();
  }

  initDB () {
    ...
    // Define ORACLE_HOME
```

```
Session.setProperty  ("ORACLE_HOME", System.getProperty("oracleHome"));

    // Create a new database session and logon
    Session session = new Session ();
    session.logon  ("scott", "tiger", "bookstore");
}

public void doPost (...
{
    ...
}

InputStream getXMLfromDB  ()  throws Exception
{
    ...

    // Instantiate Bookstore wrapper class:
    Bookstore  store = new Bookstore  (session);

    // Instantiate a PStringBuffer to get a string from the PL/SQL procedure
    PStringBuffer pBuffer = new PStringBuffer (30);

    // Invoke the PL/SQL procedure
     PBuffer = store.getXML ();

    // Retrieve the return value
    if  (!pBuffer.isNull())
        buffer = pBuffer.intValue();

    return  new StringBufferInputStream  (buffer);
}

    ...
}
```

The database connection is encapsulated by the **Session** class in the **oracle.rdbms** package. The *Session class* provides methods to perform common database tasks: logging on, logging off, commit, rollback, and so forth. Before establishing a connection to an Oracle database, the environment properties have to be defined. Specifically, ORACLE_HOME of the application server is retrieved and assigned as the cartridge's system property "oracleHome" with the **System.getProperty()** method. Next, a Session object is created and logon to the database is executed.

To invoke PL/SQL stored procedures, an object of the wrapper class must be instantiated with a Session object as an argument, binding the wrapper object for the execution of the PL/SQL package in the session. In the case of multiple database sessions, a wrapper class object must be created for each one. PL/SQL procedure parameter values are set by using the wrapper object **setValue()** method. To retrieve the return values, the **getValue()** methods of the wrapper classes are used. For example, the **intValue()** method of the **PInteger** class is used to retrieve an integer value. The corresponding Java object for the PL/SQL table—either an in or an out parameter—is a Java array, along with the elements in the array. This is illustrated by the following fragment of Java code:

```
// Create a PL/SQL table parameter
PStringBuffer pBooks[] = new PStringBuffer[80];
for(int = 0; i < pBooks.length; i++) {
    pBooks[i] = new PStringBuffer (200);
}

// Invoke a PL/SQL procedure
bookstore.get_books (pBooks);
```

All wrapper classes that encapsulate PL/SQL values have a **toString()** method and, therefore, can be concatenated with Java Strings. For example, the previous pBook object can be used directly in a string concatenation:

```
for (int i = 0; i < pBook.length; i++) {
    buffer.add (pBook[i]);
}
```

Using Transaction Service

You can also use the OAS transaction service with the JServlet cartridge. The transaction service works with different database access APIs to coordinate distributed transactions. In this case, the database access APIs are JDBC- and pl2java-generated classes. The transaction service allows you to perform transactions that span requests between resource managers and cartridges. The transaction service is based on *Java Transaction Service (JTS)*.

A typical OAS transaction service scenario starts with a call to **initTS()** to initialize the service. Connection to a resource manager is established using **TransactionService.connectRM()**. Using Session, the transactional DAD is then registered with pl2java classes. In the case of JDBC database access, a DAD name is sent to the wrapper object as a **connectRM()** parameter. The Current object is obtained through **TransactionService.getCurrent()**. The Current object provides the **begin()**, **commit()**, and **rollback()** methods to demarcate transactions. The transaction starts with the **begin()** method. Using **DriverManager.getConnection()**, the database connection is established. Database operations are then performed. Committing or rolling back the transaction is done through either the **commit()** or **rollback()** method. The JServlet is disconnected from the resource manager using the **disconnectRM()** method. At the end, a call to **termTS()** cleans up the service.

Invoking OAS Components

A servlet application running in a JServlet cartridge environment could invoke other applications residing on the same OAS. For example, the Bookstore application could connect to the database through an ECO/Java object. ECO/Java objects are CORBA objects running in OAS processes. Similar to ECO/Java Objects, *Enterprise Java Beans (EJB)* and C++ CORBA applications can be invoked with JServlet applications if they reside on the same OAS.

The Bookstore Application as an iAS Servlet

In iAS, the registering and configuration of servlets is quite different due to the Apache platform for HTTP services. As described previously, iAS includes the JServ servlet engine. The sections that follow describe how to configure Apache and JServ to run the Bookstore demo.

Configuring Apache

Apache comes preset and configured to use the JServ servlet engine. To run the Bookstore application, you should set up the virtual directory. This is done by editing the Apache configuration file named *http.conf* and adding the following line, assuming the application is installed in **C:/Bookstore**:

```
Alias /Bookstore/ "C:/Bookstore/"
```

Configuring JServ

JServ must now be configured to be able to find and run the Bookstore classes. This is done by registering them in the CLASSPATH used by the JServ engine. You edit the JServ configuration file named **jserv.properties**, adding the following entries:

```
wrapper.classpath=C:\Bookstore\lib\xmlparserv2.jar

# Bookstore Servlet wrapper class

wrapper.classpath=C:\Bookstore\lib\Bookstore.class
```

Once Apache is restarted, the application can be accessed via a URL referencing your start page as follows:

```
http://localhost/Bookstore/index.html
```

CHAPTER

5

The Oracle Internet
File System (*i*FS)

he Oracle Internet File System (*i*FS) is a file system and development environment that either runs inside the Oracle8i/9i database or in Oracle9iAS on the middle tier. It provides a means of creating, storing, and managing multiple types of information in a single repository.

To the end user, *i*FS appears as a normal file server, organizing and presenting data as a hierarchy of folders and documents. Its operation is transparent to users; they may never know their documents are stored in a database because *i*FS behaves externally like any typical file, Web, or e-mail server.

Documents within *i*FS are not limited to text. They can be any form of digital data, including spreadsheet and word processor formats, graphics, sound files, presentations, structured formats as in HTML and XML, relational data, and so forth. All types of data and documents can be stored in an *i*FS repository.

The power of *i*FS lies in its consistency: all data can be stored in a single, common repository, which enables enterprise-wide access, as well as simplified content management and administration.

Features

Note that the description of the *i*FS features as well as its functionality and deployment platforms, unless otherwise noted, pertain to the version 1.1.9 that is current at the time of this writing. *i*FS runs inside the Oracle8i/9i Server as a Java application running against the Oracle Enterprise Java Engine, Java virtual machine. It is tightly integrated with other Oracle8i/9i features, such as object types, interMedia Text/Oracle Text, and the Oracle Enterprise Manager administration tool. It also runs in the JVM shipped as part of the Oracle9iAS HTTP server and communicates with the backend database via JDBC. Because it runs within the Oracle8i/9i Server or 9iAS, *i*FS automatically gains the scalability, performance, and security of the server itself. An overview of its architecture and the relationship of each component is shown in Figure 5-1.

Table Storage

Because *i*FS exists within an Oracle8i/9i database or can communicate with one, tables are the fundamental data-storage mechanism. All *i*FS data is stored in tables. This includes the document contents and the metadata about the document. The document content is stored using *Oracle8i/9i's Large Objects (LOBs)* for large unstructured data (text, graphics, video, and so forth), with a capacity of up to 4GB. The *i*FS database schema, part of the *i*FS repository, stores all persistent objects managed by *i*FS as a collection of tables and fields. These are presented as a set of SQL views of the file system, thereby isolating you from dealing directly with the database.

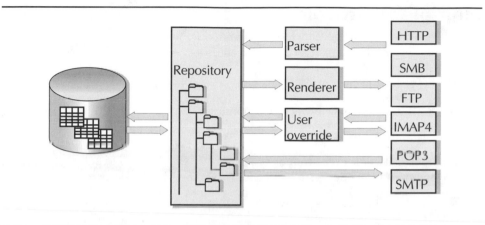

FIGURE 5-1. *An overview of the iFS architecture*

Parsers

When a document is placed into iFS, a parser decomposes ("parses") the document automatically, separating out the content from the metadata and storing the parts in separate columns in a database record. Several built-in parsers (including XML) are provided with iFS, and the user can also create custom parsers.

Renderers

When a stored document needs to be viewed, iFS constructs ("renders") the document from its database storage. *Renderers* are the mechanisms that determine how both parsed and unparsed documents are presented. No matter what the original format of the document when it was entered into iFS, renderers allow that document to be converted to whatever format is best suited to the tool or protocol used to access the document.

Overrides

iFS is implemented as a set of Java classes. To add flexibility, overrides enable you to change or add to the default processing that occurs when a particular method is invoked. By adding custom code to the methods, you can respond to the event that invoked the method and control how the system handles particular content types.

Multiple Protocols

When *i*FS is running inside Oracle8i or on a middle tier, it appears as if it were a normal file system. Contents can be accessed using a variety of protocols:

- HTTP and HTTPS (using any standard Web browser)

- SMB (for access with Microsoft Windows 95, NT, 98, or 2000 clients)

- FTP (File Transfer Protocol)

- SMTP, IMAP4, POP3 (e-mail protocols that enable users to access the files via standard mail clients such as EudoraNetscape Mail, and Microsoft Outlook)

- Custom Protocol Servers written by the user or third parties

Benefits

The internet File System provides a number of advantages over more traditional ways of storing and accessing corporate-wide information:

- **Integrated storage**   Simplifies life for end users, systems administrators, and developers by storing all types of data in a single repository.

- **Familiar interface**   *i*FS presents repository data in the well-known folder/file hierarchy idiom.

- **Universal access**   Data stored in *i*FS can be accessed through any number of protocols, making it available from Web browsers, messaging clients, FTP clients, and so forth.

- **Content management**   *i*FS includes built-in versioning, so all stored documents can have available the multiple versions resulting from document updates. Integrated locking with the familiar check-out/check-in model prevents data from being overwritten.

- **Database functionality**   Because *i*FS is tightly integrated with the Oracle8i/9i database and 9iAS, all database capabilities are automatically available: automatic indexing, fast searching, and context-based searching, plus data backup and restoration.

- **Easy development**   Many desirable features of document-centric applications (security, distributed data storage, search capabilities, and so forth) are built into *i*FS and immediately available with no extra coding needed. With its single data store and single development API, multiple *i*FS-based applications can be quickly developed.

Components

Access to data is provided through multiple protocols, while Java and PL/SQL via Java packages provide the programming APIs for software development.

Administration is through the *Oracle Enterprise Manager (OEM)*, the same tool used to administer the Oracle8i server.

iFS includes the following software components:

- *iFS* server
- *iFS* Java API
- *iFS* Manager for administration (Solaris 2.6 and NT 4.0 platforms)
- *iFS* Web Manager (for browser-based administration on any platform)
- Oracle 8.1.6 or above (required, but not provided with *iFS*)
- Windows client
- Web client

XML

iFS provides built-in support for XML files. An XML parser and renderer are included in *iFS*, and an extensibility mechanism is provided to define new XML-based file types.

When registering a new XML-based file type, a document descriptor is provided that specifies the type's XML structure and how it should be stored in the database. Document descriptors use an XML-based syntax to describe the structure ("schema") of documents of that type. When a document is saved to *iFS*, and it is recognized as one of your defined file types, the document is parsed and the data stored in tables as directed by the descriptor. The same descriptor is then used to render (compose) the XML document on output.

Through the descriptor, you can choose whether an XML document is stored as a series of related database tables and columns, a single text CLOB, or a combination of both. For example, Figure 5-2 shows an insurance claim document that is part structured data (Payee, Data, and so forth) and part structured text markup (DamageReport).

In this example, the structured data would be stored in tables, and the structured text markup as "text blobs."

Once instances of *iFS* file types (including XML-based ones) are stored in the database, you can search their contents using standard SQL queries. These files can be organized, browsed, and versioned using standard tools like Windows Explorer.

```
<?xml version="1.0"?>
    <InsuranceClaim>
      <ClaimID>12345</ClaimID>
      <LossCategory>7</LossCategory>
      <Settlements>
        <Payment>
          <Payee>Borden Real Estate</Payee>
          <Date>12-OCT-1998</Date>
          <Amount>200000</Amount>
          <Approver>JCOX</Approver>
        </Payment>
      </Settlements>
      <DamageReport>
        A massive <Cause>Fire</Cause> ravaged the building and
<Casualties>12</Casualties> people were killed. Early FBI reports
indicate that <Motive>arson</Motive> is suspected.
      </DamageReport>
      :
    </InsuranceClaim>
```

FIGURE 5-2. *XML Insurance Claim document*

Those document parts that are stored as CLOBs in the database can optionally be indexed by the Oracle8i interMedia Text or Oracle9i Text search engine.

interMedia Text/Oracle Text

Oracle8i's *interMedia Text* (formerly *Context*) and the subsequent Oracle9i Text have been improved for enabling developers to pinpoint their searches to a particular section of a document. For XML-based documents, a section is implicitly defined by the XML tags. Because interMedia Text is integrated into the database and the SQL language, you can use SQL to perform queries that involve both the structured data and indexed text.

For example, Figure 5-3 shows a sample query of insurance claim documents (like the previous example shown in Figure 5-2): "How much money has Jim Cox approved to date in settlement payments for arson-related fire claims?"

This demonstrates how, once structured documents such as XML are entered into an Oracle8i/9i database, their contents can be searched and manipulated powerfully using familiar database techniques.

```
SELECT SUM(Amount)
     FROM Claim_Header ch,
          Claim_Settlements cs,
          Claim_Settlement_Payments csp
   WHERE csp.Approver='JCOX'
   AND CONTAINS (DamageReport, 'Arson WITHIN Motive') > 0
   AND CONTAINS (DamageReport, 'Fire WITHIN Cause'  ) > 0
   AND . . . /* Join Clauses */
```

FIGURE 5-3. *Sample query of an insurance claim document*

Document Model

*i*FS is designed around documents—everything in *i*FS is a document.

Documents are composed of structured data elements called *properties,* with an unstructured body. All traditional file systems store additional information about files, such as the filename, modification date, and size. *i*FS extends this model to support content management (versioning and locking), security, and a flexible directory structure.

The body of a document is the content; for example, its text, graphics, audio, or video. The body is itself a property, but different in that it cannot be set through the API, and it is stored as a number of pieces (chunks), rather than as a single unbroken unit.

*i*FS incorporates a number of document types in its implementation:

- Container documents store links to files and implement virtual directories.

- Configuration files are XML documents that store metadata about *i*FS document types.

- Type (**.typ**) documents extend the basic document definition to provide additional properties for custom file formats.

- File Extension (**.fex**) documents define the file extensions that identify document types.

- Parser (**.parse**) and Renderer (**.renderer**) documents identify the Java classes used to store and display data of a particular type.

- *Access Control List (ACL)* documents define read/write privileges for users and groups.

Document Properties

Four basic types of properties are used by *i*FS: versionless, normal, link, and user. Each type is described in its own section.

Versionless Properties

Versionless properties are always the same, regardless of which version of a document is in use. For example, the creation date of a document does not change once the original document is first created. Table 5-1 lists the versionless properties.

Property Name	Data Type	Null Okay?	System?	Description
Creation_ Date	Date	No	Yes	The date the document was created.
Max_ Untagged	Integer	No	No	The number of untagged revisions to retain (this is the purge count).
Project_ID	DocID	Yes	Yes	The documentation identification number of the project to which this file belongs. Files can belong to only one project. If the document is not part of a project, the value is null.
Total_ Revisions	Integer	No	Yes	The total number of revisions of this document to date.
Volume_ID	Integer	No	Yes	The volume identification number for this document.

TABLE 5-1. *Listing of Versionless Properties*

Normal Properties

Normal properties are always the same for a specific version of a document, regardless of how or by whom they are retrieved. They can be changed in subsequent versions, however. Table 5-2 shows the normal properties.

Property Name	Data Type	Null Okay?	System?	Description
Abstract	String(512)	Yes	No	A summary of the document.
ACL	DocID	No	No	The DocID for the Access Control List of this document.
Author	String(60)	Yes	No	The original author (or sender) of the document.
Body_ID	Number(38)	No	Yes	The primary key that identifies this document in the document body table.
Branch_ Tags	Array	Yes	Yes	An array listing all the branches to which this revision is assigned.
Checked_ Out_To	DocID	Yes	Yes	The DocID of the user who has checked out this document.
Content_ Type	String(24)	No	No	The typename of the content type for this document.
Docid	Number(38)	No	No	The unique ID for this document version.

TABLE 5-2.   *Listing of Normal Properties*

Property Name	Data Type	Null Okay?	System?	Description
Generator	String(128)	Yes	No	The name of the application that generated this document body.
ID	Number(38)	No	Yes	The unique ID for this document.
Invalid	Boolean	No	Yes	True if this document is invalid (if there was a parse error or constraint violation).
Is_Current	Boolean	No	Yes	True if this document is the most recent mainline version.
Mime_Type	String(48)	No	No	*MIME (Multipart Internet Mail Extension)* type describing the format of this document.
Mod_Date	Date	No	No	The date on which this document was last modified.
Modified_By	DocID	No	Yes	The DocID of the user who created this version of the document.
Num_Links	Integer	No	Yes	The total number of links to this document.
Owner	DocID	No	Yes	The DocID of the user who owns this document.
Read_Only	Boolean	No	No	True if this document can't be modified.

TABLE 5-2. *Listing of Normal Properties* (continued)

Property Name	Data Type	Null Okay?	System?	Description
Release_ Tags	Array	Yes	Yes	A list of release tags associated with this document version.
Saved_Links	Integer	No	Yes	The number of saved links to this document. A document with saved links cannot be deleted until the saved links are removed.
Size	Integer	No	Yes	The length (in bytes) of the body of this document.
System	Boolean	No	No	True if this document is a file for internal system use.
Title	String(80)	No	No	The title of this document.
Version	String(20)	No	Yes	The system-assigned version identifier for this document.

TABLE 5-2.   *Listing of Normal Properties* (continued)

Link Properties

Link properties are used by container documents and are stored with the container in which a document appears. Table 5-3 lists the link properties.

Property Name	Data Type	Null Okay?	System?	Description
Archive	Boolean	No	No	True if this document version has been archived by a backup facility.

TABLE 5-3.   *Listing of Link Properties*

Property Name	Data Type	Null Okay?	System?	Description
Expires	Date	Yes	No	The date when the link is automatically deleted.
Filename	String(128)	No	No	The filename for this document in the specific container (that is, the link name).
Hidden	Boolean	No	No	True if this document should not normally be displayed in directory listings.
Link_ Serial_ Number	Integer	No	Yes	A serial number assigned to links in the order they are inserted into a container.
Flags	RAW(1)	No	No	Flags used internally by *i*FS.
Saved	Boolean	No	No	True if this link is saved. A document with a saved link cannot be deleted until all saved links are removed.

TABLE 5-3. *Listing of Link Properties* (continued)

User Properties

User properties are stored for each individual user of a document and may be different for each user. For example, the **read** flag is true for users who have read a document, but false for others who have not.

Document Processing

When a document is inserted in *i*FS, it is broken down (parsed) into its component pieces and stored in several database tables.

On insertion, the file extension of the document is compared with currently defined file extensions. If no matching extension is found, a standard parser is used to extract the basic document information from the protocol client (for example, a filename as provided by an FTP program) or through extrapolation (for example, a document's size can be calculated as the document is read in). The document's properties are stored in a generic document table.

If a matching file extension is found, the parser for that type is invoked to extract the additional properties. These custom document properties are then stored in a table for that specific document type.

The entire document, including properties, is loaded into a single column in a table used to store only document bodies. The **BodyID** property in the document type table provides a unique key to the document body record.

When a document is inserted, it can also be indexed for full-text search by the interMedia Text search engine.

The table-based storage of document contents and metadata is designed to be highly efficient to process, but it is vulnerable to user corruption. Users and developers could potentially damage the data structures by directly modifying the table contents, without iFS being aware of it. For this reason, Object Views are provided for each document type. They display a document in a single virtual table ensuring safe data management. Data in iFS should *only* be modified through its standard API or by using Object Views.

Defining Document Types

Type documents (extension **.typ**) are XML files defining the properties that map specific file formats or types to specific database schemas. The definition is used to create the database tables into which the document parts are stored and also to identify the Java classes used to create, manipulate, and store instances of the document type.

A type document serves three functions:

- Defines the type's name

- Identifies the Java classes used to interface an instance of this document type with the iFS repository

- Defines the properties of the document type

Example Type Definition

The following is an example of a simple type definition, first in its entirety, and then with a line-by-line description:

```
<?xml version = "1.0" standalone="yes"?>
<type>
    <title>Simple Type Definition</title>
    <typename>simpletype</typename>
```

```
<dbi_classname>oracle.ifs.demo.simple.SimpleDocumentDBI
</dbi_classname>
<properties>
    <propdef>
        <propname>SimpleProperty</propname>
    </propdef>
</properties>
</type>
```

The meaning of each line is described in Table 5-4.

Standard Type Properties

Type documents are themselves a defined type of *i*FS document, with their own set of unique properties. Generic type information is stored in a table called **content_type**.

Line	Description
<?xml version = "1.0" standalone="yes"?>	Is the standard declaration for XML files
<type>	The root element that starts the type definition
<title>Simple Type Definition</title>	Gives a descriptive name to the type
<typename>simpletype</typename>	Unique name identifier for the type
<dbi_classname>oracle.ifs.demo. simple.SimpleDocumentDBI </dbi_classname>	Names the Java class used to interface the run-time instance of a document of this type with the *i*FS repository
<properties>	Starts the definition of type properties
<propdef>	Begins a property definition
<propname>SimpleProperty </propname>	Defines a property named **SimpleProperty**
</propdef>	Ends the property definition
</properties>	Ends the property definition block
</type>	Ends the type definition

TABLE 5-4. *Type Definition File Description*

Property	Java Type	Database Type	Database Column	Default Value
typename	String	varchar2(64)	typename	No default—a required field
inherits_from	String	varchar2(64)	inherits_from	Document
final_type	Boolean	char(1) [T or F]	final_type	False
tablename	String	varchar2(256)	shd_table	IFS_*typename*
use_existing_table	String	char(1) [T or F]	use_existing_table	False
chunk_size	Integer	integer	chunk_size	*inherits_from*.chunk_size
user_visible	Boolean	char(1) [T or F]	user_visible	True
classname	String	varchar2(1024)	classname	*inherits_from*.classname
dbi_classname	String	varchar2(1024)	dbi_classname	*inherits_from*.dbi_classname

TABLE 5-5. *Listing of all Standard Property Types and Their Default Values*

Table 5-5 lists all standard type document properties and their default values. Only the **typename** property is required. In most cases, the following default values suffice. Detailed descriptions of each property follows:

- **typename** The unique identifier for the document type. This can be up to 64 characters in length, but keeping the length to 15 or fewer characters is best. This type inherits the properties of its parent type (and its parent's parent, and so forth), requiring the typename to be unique within its inheritance path.

- **inherits_from** The name of the type from which the current type is extended. When an existing type is extended, the properties of that type are available to the new type, as well as any additional properties defined.

- **final_type** Types declared as final (T) cannot be extended by other type definitions. The table for a type defined as final has no **derived_rowid** column.

- **tablename** Name of existing table (used in conjunction with the **use_existing_table** property). If **use_existing_table** is true, the **tablename** property must be set to a table already defined in the *i*FS repository.

- **use_existing_table** When set to true, *i*FS does not create a table for this document type. Instead, it is assumed the table has already been defined and is identified by the **tablename** property.

- **chunk_size** The optimal number of bytes to read from or write to the body of this document type. This value should only be explicitly set if the database interface class for this document type (identified by the property **dbi_classname**) overrides the default body-storage mechanism.

- **user_visible** A flag provided to enable developers to hide implementation-specific documents from users at run time. By default, this property is set to true, and documents of the new type are visible to users. Set to false, documents of this type are never seen by users.

- **classname** The Java class that is used to create an in-memory instance of a document of this type at run time. The class for this document must either directly extend the class **oracle.ifs.sdk.Document** or indirectly extend it by extending one of its subclasses.

- **dbi_classname** This property identifies the Java class that is the interface between the database and the in-memory instance of a document of this type. For types that extend from Document, this class must extend **oracle.ifs.sdk.override.DocumentDBI**. For types that extend from Container, the specified class must extend **oracle.ifs.sdk.override.ContainerDBI**.

Custom Type Properties

A type definition can also define new properties aside from the previously listed standard properties. A type definition has a property called *properties,* which is an array of property definition records. Each entry in the array describes one property, with up to a maximum of 1,000 properties able to be described. The values for these attributes are stored in the table **propdef**.

The following is an excerpt from a sample type definition showing an example of a properties declaration, followed by a line-by-line discussion of the declaration in Table 5-6.

```
<properties>
    <propdef>
        <propname> sampleDate </propname>
        <colname> sampleDateColumn </colname>
        <datatype> date </datatype>
    </propdef>
    <propdef>
        <propname> sampleProperty </propname>
    </propdef>
</properties>
```

Code	Description
<properties>	Begins a property definition block
<propdef>	Starts a new property definition
<propname>sampleDate</propname>	Defines a property named sampleDate
<colname>sampleDateColumn</colname>	Creates a new column in the table named sampleDateColumn in the table propdef
<datatype>date</datatype>	Declares the type of data to be stored in the table column
</propdef>	Ends the first property definition
<propdef>	Starts a second property definition
<propname>sampleProperty</propname>	Defines a property named sampleProperty. The column name is the same as the property name by default, and the datatype defaults to String
</propdef>	Ends the second property definition
</properties>	Ends the property declaration block

TABLE 5-6.   *Listing of Properties Declaration and Description of Tags*

Property Attributes

The attributes used to create custom properties are listed in Table 5-7. The only required attribute is **propname**; all others can be derived from their default values. Each attribute is described individually in the following list:

- **propname** The *i*FS name for the property. All references to this property within *i*FS must use this name. This name must be unique within the context of the current properties definition.

- **datatype** Specifies the type of information to be stored in the property. Constants for these values are defined in the class **oracle.ifs.sdk.Type**. Table 5-8 lists the property datatypes defined for *i*FS.

- **max_length** Specifies the maximum length (in characters) of a string property. This property only applies to the datatype "String." When a string property is saved to the database, the length of the string is compared with

Property	Java Type	Database Type	Database Column	Default Value
propname	String	varchar2(40)	Propname	Required; no default
datatype	String	integer	Type	"String"
max_length	Integer	integer	max_length	120
colname	String	varchar2(256)	Colname	propname
user_visible	Boolean	char(1) [T or F]	user_visible	True
tablename	String	varchar2(256)	std_table	propname with an appended sequential integer to make it unique
can_be_null	Boolean	char(1) [T or F]	can_be_null	True
synthetic	Boolean	char(1) [T or F]	Synthetic	False
use_existing_table	Boolean	char(1) [T or F]	use_existing_table	False
properties	Array	integer	Properties	Null
Refers_to	String	varchar2(256)	refers_to	None

TABLE 5-7. *Listing of Property Attributes and Their Default Values*

ifsType Datatype	Column Datatype	Description
ARRAY	Integer	An array of values.
RECORD	Integer	An array of property values.
DOCID	Integer	A unique identifier that can be used instead of a full path to reference an *i*FS document.
BOOLEAN	char(1)	Store in the database as *T* or *F*. Developers can set this to a Boolean or String value, and *i*FS then converts it at run time to the correct value.
BIT	char(1)	0 or 1.
INTEGER	Integer	Whole numbers.
NUMBER	Number	Most flexible numeric type; stores any value.
TIMESTAMP	Date	A date value.
DATE	Date	Same as TIMESTAMP, a date value.
TIME	Date	Same as TIMESTAMP or DATE, a date value.
SHORT	Integer	Same as INTEGER.
LONG	Integer	Same as INTEGER.
DOUBLE	number(38,12)	Double-precision floating-point number.
FLOAT	number(19,6)	Single-precision floating-point number.
VARCHAR	varchar2	A string. Maximum length is determined by the max_length of the property.
STRING	varchar2	Same as VARCHAR.

TABLE 5-0.   *Listing of iFS Property Datatypes*

max_length. If the length of the string is longer than the **max_length** value, it is truncated before being saved to the database.

- **colname**   Specifies the column name for the property. The default is to set the column name to the **<propname>**. If the property is going into a developer-defined table, developers should set this column name to match the column in the table they create.

- **user_visible**   If this attribute is false, the property can only be accessed programmatically and cannot be requested or set by the end user.

- **tablename**   Specifies the table in which to store this property definition.

- **can_be_null**   Specifies whether this property value can be left blank. If true, the database column is constrained to be "not null," and the user must supply a value to create a document of this type.

- **synthetic**   Specifies whether this property is a stored value or a synthetic value. Synthetic properties are calculated at run time by overriding a method in the DBI class for this document type.

- **use_existing_table**   This value determines whether the **TypeDBI** class generates a new table to store the properties of an aggregate property or uses one already created by the developer.

- **properties**   A properties array can contain another properties array. This is used to create another record or array property. The following example demonstrates syntax that creates a standard property for the name of a spouse, followed by a record property used to store the names and ages of children:

```
<properties>
    <propdef>
        <propname> spousename </propname>
    </propdef>
    <propdef>
        <propname> child </propname>
        <datatype> record </datatype>
        <properties>
            <propdef>
                <propname> firstname </propname>
            </propdef>
            <propdef>
                <propname> age </propname>
                <datatype> integer </datatype>
            </propdef>
        </properties>
    </propdef>
</properties>
```

■ **refers_to**   This property is used to reference array or record properties created using the **<declarations>** feature. Declarations have exactly the same attributes as properties, but they are defined separately from the other properties. By declaring arrays separately from the records that use them, the same table can be used to store similar information for more than one property. For example, in an e-mail program, address properties exist for the To, CC, and BCC recipients. The information stored is exactly the same, the only difference being the way it is used at run time. The properties for To, CC, and BCC can be defined to refer to a single array, declared separately. The following XML shows how this is done:

```
<properties>
    <propdef>
        <propname> to </propname>
        <colname> to_addr </colname>
        <datatype> array </datatype>
        <refers_to> addresses </refers_to>
    </propdef>
    <propdef>
        <propname> cc </propname>
        <colname> cc_addr </colname>
        <datatype> array </datatype>
        <refers_to> addresses </refers_to>
    </propdef>
    <propdef>
        <propname> bcc </propname><colname> bcc_addr </colname>
        <datatype> array </datatype>
        <refers_to> addresses </refers_to>
    </propdef>
</properties>
<declarations>
    <propdef>
        <propname> addresses </propname>
        <tablename> addresses </tablename>
        <datatype> record </datatype>
        <use_existing_table> T </use_existing_table>
        <properties>
            <propdef>
                <propname> address </propname>
            </propdef>
        </properties>
    </propdef>
</declarations>
```

File Extensions

All files in *i*FS are processed according to a document type definition. Files are recognized as being a certain type by matching file extensions. A document type definition can be used to process documents with several different extensions. File extensions for a document type are defined in a file extension document (with extension **.fex**). File extension documents are also XML documents.

XML tags used in file extension definitions are described in Table 5-9.

The following is an example of a file extension definition:

```
<?xml version="1.0" standalone="yes"?>
<file_extension>
    <title> Purchase Order Extensions </title>
    <type_of_extension> PurchaseOrder </type_of_extension>
    <mime_type_of_file> text/xml </mime_type_of_file>
    <extensions_list>
        <extension> ipo </extension>
        <extension> opo </extension>
        <extension> purchaseorder </extension>
    </extensions_list>
</file_extension>
```

XML tag	Description
<file_extension>	Outermost tag that encloses the extension definition.
<title>	Descriptive name of the extensions being defined.
<type_of_extension>	A defined content type within *i*FS. This must exactly match a defined typename property in a type file.
<mime_type_of_file>	The MIME type describing the type of information in the document in the standard format *general/specific*. For example, the MIME type of an HTML file is *text/html*.
<extensions_list>	Encloses the individual extension declarations.
<extension>	The file extension being defined. If more than one is wanted, use multiple **<extension>** tags.

TABLE 5-9. *XML File Extension Tags and Descriptions*

Table 5-10 provides a line-by-line description of the preceding tags.

New file extensions are defined by inserting their descriptive **.fex** file anywhere in the *iFS* repository; *iFS* recognizes the **.fex** extension and processes the file, adding the newly defined extensions to the system list. When a file with such a defined extension is then added to the repository, it is processed according to the defined document type.

XML Tag	Description
<?xml version="1.0" standalone="yes"?>	The standard declaration used by all XML files.
<file_extension>	The root element that starts a file extension definition.
<title>Purchase Order Extensions</title>	Sets the descriptive name for the set of file extensions.
<type_of_extension>PurchaseOrder</type_of_extension>	The typename from a type definition file.
<mime_type_of_file>text/xml</mime_type_of_file>	The MIME type of the file (a plain text XML file).
<extensions_list>	Starts the list of extensions.
<extension>ipo</extension>	Defines the extension **.ipo**. *iFS* recognizes any document with this extension as being of type **PurchaseOrder**.
<extension>opo</extension>	Defines a second equivalent extension **.opo**.
extension>purchaseorder</extension>	Defines a third equivalent extension **.purchaseorder**.
</extensions_list>	Ends the list of extensions.
</file_extension>	Ends the file extension declaration and document.

TABLE 5-10. *XML Tags and Descriptions*

Using *i*FS

So far, this chapter has discussed the APIs that *i*FS makes available. These APIs can be used by external Java applications or when *i*FS runs within Oracle8i to provide file services to your application. The following examples illustrate several common file tasks.

Example 1: Creating and Saving Hello World

Creating and saving files in specific directories, such as the current user's home directory, are common tasks applications perform to find configuration or data files. The following code demonstrates the use of *i*FS APIs to create a Java class that will create the file **HelloWorld.txt**; add the content, "Hello World"; and, finally, locate and add it to the current user's home directory.

```
public static void example1()  throws IfsException
{
        LibraryService ifsService = new LibraryService();
        LibrarySession ifsSession;
        ifsSession = ifsService.connect("user","pass","Local");

        DirectoryUser thisUser = ifsSession.getDirectoryUser();
        PrimaryUserProfile userProfile;
        userProfile = ifsSession.getPrimaryUserProfile(thisUser);
        Folder homeFolder = userProfile.getHomeFolder();

        DocumentDefinition newDoc;
        newDoc = new DocumentDefinition(ifsSession);
        newDoc.setName("HelloWorld.txt");
        newDoc.setContent("Hello World");

        Document doc;
        doc = (Document) ifsSession.createPublicObject(newDoc);
        homeFolder.addItem(doc);

        ifsSession.disconnect();
}
```

The current user's home folder is accessed using the **PrimaryUser's Profile.getHomeFolder()** method. To get user objects, the **LibrarySession** class provides the **getPrimaryUserProfile()** method and the **getDirectoryUser()** method. The **getPrimaryUserProfile()** method obtains the **PrimaryUserProfile** object, and the **getDirectoryUser()** method obtains the **DirectoryUser** object used to get the current user's profile. This example also illustrates how to create a new document with

DocumentDefinition() and how to create its name and content with **setName()** and **setContent()**. This document can then be added as an object to the home folder using the **createPublicObject()** and **additem()** methods.

Example 2: Creating a Better Hello World

Moving to a higher-level process, the following example builds upon Example 1 by setting the document's format based upon its extension, creating a single logical unit of work to both create the document and add it to the home folder, and finally incorporating exception handling to report any errors.

```
public static void addToFolder(LibrarySession ifsSession,
                               DocumentDefinition newDoc,
                               Folder homeFolder)
                               throws IfsException
{
    IfsException.setVerboseMessage(true);
    Transaction t = ifsSession.beginTransaction();
    try {
        Collection c = ifsSession.getFormatExtensionCollection();
        Format textFormat = (Format) c.getItems("txt");
        newDoc.setFormat(textFormat);
        Document doc;
        doc = (Document) ifsSession.createPublicObject(newDoc);
        homeFolder.addItem(doc);
        ifsSession.completeTransaction(t);
    }
    catch (IfsException e)
    {
        e.printStackTrace();
        ifsSession.abortTransaction(t);
    }
}
```

Realize that *i*FS needs to know the mime type of a document to index its content correctly. This is specified by passing a Format object that defines the mimeType to the method **DocumentDefinition.setFormat()**. Since *i*FS ships with a collection of the most common predefined Format definitions, you can use the file extension to look up the format with **getFormatExtensionCollection()**.

Transactions are used as a logical body of work. By defining a series of operations to be performed in a single transaction, as is done in this example between the **beginTransaction()** and **completeTransaction()** methods, the entire process can be performed efficiently. Beginning in Oracle9*i*FS 1.2, you can embed custom SQL within the *i*FS file access transaction.

All errors are returned to the **ifsException** class and are handled by the code using the standard **try** and **catch** syntax. In this case, any errors are printed by **printStackTrace()**, and **abortTransaction()** cancels the transaction, rolls back any changes, and frees all memory and resource locks.

Example 3: Working with Files

Folders provide a convenient container for files, and beyond creating and saving, there are a number of operations that applications need to perform. Example 3 illustrates not only how to find a folder given a path but also how to open it and read its contents.

```
public static void readFile(LibrarySession ifsSession,
                        Folder folder,String name)
                        throws IfsException, java.io.IOException

{
    if (folder.checkExistenceOfPublicObjectByPath(name,File.separator))
    {
        PublicObject po;
        po = folder.findPublicObjectByPath(name,File.separator);
        if (po.getClassname().equals(Document.CLASS_NAME)) {
            Document doc = (Document) po;
            BufferedReader r;
            r = new  BufferedReader(doc.getContentReader());
            for (String nextLine = r.readLine();
                nextLine != null;
                nextLine = r.readLine() )
            {
                System.out.println(nextLine);
            }
        }
    }
}
```

To check for a folder's existence prior to trying to access it, the **checkExistanceOfPublicObjectByPath()** method is called and returns true or false. At that point, the **findPublicObjectByPath()** method returns the file object. Finally, you can access and read the file object using the **getContentReader()** method. The example code then prints out the contents.

Example 4: Searching for Files

The final example will illustrate how a simple search on a collection of files returns the paths to the ones matching the search stringcriteria.

```
public static void findMatchingFiles(LibrarySession
                                     ifsSession,String name)
                                     throws IfsException
{
    String search = PublicObject.NAME_ATTRIBUTE+ "= '" + name +"'";
    Selector mySelector = new Selector(ifsSession,Document.CLASS_NAME,search);

    if (mySelector.getItemCount() == 0)
    System.out.println("Search did not find any documents.");
    else {
        for (int i=0;i<mySelector.getItemCount();i++) {
          Document myDoc = (Document)
          mySelector.getItems(i);
          String path = myDoc.getAnyFolderPath();
          System.out.println("Found a Document at: " + path);
          }
        }
    }
}
```

Note that the search string is associated with the **name** attribute declared with the format

NAME ATTRIBUTE + " = " + *filename* + " "

The **Selector** class provides a number of methods for processing the selection, similar to those available for processing a folder list. In this case, **getItems()** and **getItemCount()** are utilized to create the list that is then printed out.

Using *i*FS with XML Files

As previously discussed, the *i*FS repository handles XML files natively. In fact of all the types of files it knows how to process and store, XML files have the greatest flexibility as well as extensibility. This functionality can be broken down into two categories—parsed XML files unparsed XML files. Let's look at these in detail.

Storing Parsed XML Files

The *i*FS repository understands that a file is in XML format principally through its extension being **.xml**. However, new file extensions can be utilized for XML-formatted files as well by defining a subclass of the XML file extension, **.xml**. For example, the purchase order described previously could have the **.po** extension, or a FAQ file may have **.faq**. This works because upon submission of an XML file of, for example, the FAQ type, the *i*FS repository first checks to see if the extension is registered as a subclass of any of its type definitions. In this case, it finds that this file should be in XML format, and if it has a corresponding configuration file, it creates the new objects, such as subclasses, users, or groups that are indicated. Finally if parsing into a table schema is required, the repository invokes the XML parser and checks the document's root element and finds the matching subclass, at which point it creates a new *i*FS object if the document is valid.

The actual parser used can also be defined through the XML Parser Framework. For example, instead of using the SimpleXMLParser that comes with *i*FS, you can register the parser that comes with the XDK for Java with its full W3C Standards support. This registration process is done through the Register option in *i*FS Manager's Object menu, as shown in Figure 5-4.

Besides Oracle parsers and other third-party ones, you can define custom parsers to operate on the XML file in a sequential fashion. First, you need to know that XML files actually have at least two parsers associated with each extension—the *Dispatching Parser* and the *Document Parser*. The Dispatching Parser is used initially to confirm that the file is both well formed and valid against its type definition file. It may also be validated against its DTD. While the well-formed check is turned on by default, DTD validation is not. This is because you may not need to perform this type of validation for many files, especially if applications and not users submit them.

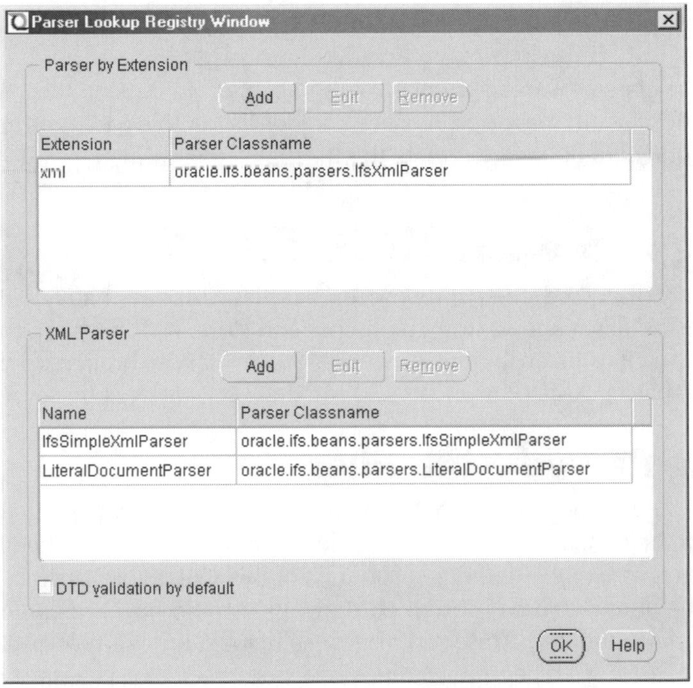

FIGURE 5-4. *Registering an XML parser with iFS Manager*

Validation is turned on from the same Object menu in *i*FS Manager. DTD validation can be expensive; thus, the SAX parser built into the Oracle Parser for Java is an excellent choice for use as the Dispatching Parser. Its event-based operation streams the XML file without the memory cost and start-up delays when using a DOM parser. The validation of the file can be through an embedded DTD or an externally referenced one.

An important point to remember about turning on DTD validation is that no subclass or *i*FS object is created if the submitted XML file is not valid against its DTD. You can, however, trap the exception that is thrown during the validation process to alert the user to fix the error and try to resubmit.

The Document Parser is the one that does the real work creating the defined subclass and its attributes based on the parsed element data. It also stores the document information and its metadata in the appropriate *i*FS repository tables.

Custom parsers can call other parsers to handle specialized or compound XML documents. This gives you fine-grained control over the parsing and subsequent subclass creation process and can extend to creating its DOM to provide full node access. Besides calling other parsers, you can also extend the Document Parser's callback functionality to execute custom Java code. For example, this code can perform other repository operations such as linking the submitted file to others or adding to a summary document.

Storing Unparsed XML Files

There is also the flexibility to store XML files without parsing them and creating *i*FS objects. This is useful if you want to treat the file as only a document and not data—xHTML, JavaDoc, and so forth. The *i*FS repository can be configured in two different ways to accept XML files without parsing them.

If you do not define a subclass associated with the XML file's extension, the file will not be parsed as XML. The repository will still store the file but will store it as a CLOB. This file can still be indexed with *inter*Media Text.

If you do not associate a parser with the XML file's extension, the file will also not be parsed but will be stored as a CLOB. This will occur even if you have associated it with a subclass. Once again, *inter*Media Text can index this file.

Rendering XML Files

As with the parsing framework, *i*FS has an extensible rendering framework that permits reconstructing XML documents. Included in the framework is a basic XML renderer that is used when a user requests an XML document from the repository. When a request is made through, for example, Internet Explorer, *i*FS uses the basic renderer to reconstruct the XML document from its stored subcomponents.

Custom renderers can be registered in a similar manner as custom parsers. This is done through the iFS Manager's Object Registry. In this case, you use the Renderer Registry Lookup Window, as in Figure 5-5.

Name	Operation	Associated ClassObject	Implementation Name
SimpleTextRenderer	RenderAsText		oracle.ifs.server.renderers.SimpleTextRenderer
SimpleXmlRenderer	RenderAsXml		oracle.ifs.server.renderers.SimpleXmlRenderer
FtpXmlRenderer	FtpRenderer	PUBLICOBJECT	oracle.ifs.server.renderers.SimpleXmlRenderer
FtpContentRenderer	FtpRenderer	DOCUMENT	oracle.ifs.server.renderers.ContentRenderer
FtpThrowExceptionRenderer	FtpRenderer	FOLDER	oracle.ifs.server.renderers.ThrowExceptionRenderer
FtpMessageRenderer	FtpRenderer	MESSAGE	oracle.ifs.protocols.email.renderer.RFC822Renderer
CupXmlRenderer	CupRenderer	PUBLICOBJECT	oracle.ifs.server.renderers.SimpleXmlRenderer
CupContentRenderer	CupRenderer	DOCUMENT	oracle.ifs.server.renderers.ContentRenderer
CupThrowExceptionRenderer	CupRenderer		oracle.ifs.server.renderers.ThrowExceptionRenderer
CupMessageRenderer	CupRenderer	MESSAGE	oracle.ifs.protocols.email.renderer.RFC822Renderer
SmbXmlRenderer	SmbRenderer	PUBLICOBJECT	oracle.ifs.server.renderers.SimpleXmlRenderer
SmbContentRenderer	SmbRenderer	DOCUMENT	oracle.ifs.server.renderers.ContentRenderer
SmbMessageRenderer	SmbRenderer	MESSAGE	oracle.ifs.protocols.email.renderer.RFC822Renderer
DavXmlRenderer	DavRenderer	PUBLICOBJECT	oracle.ifs.server.renderers.SimpleXmlRenderer
DavContentRenderer	DavRenderer	DOCUMENT	oracle.ifs.server.renderers.ContentRenderer
DavThrowExceptionRenderer	DavRenderer		oracle.ifs.server.renderers.ThrowExceptionRenderer
DavMessageRenderer	DavRenderer	MESSAGE	oracle.ifs.protocols.email.renderer.RFC822Renderer
EmailXmlRenderer	EmailRenderer	PUBLICOBJECT	oracle.ifs.server.renderers.SimpleXmlRenderer
EmailContentRenderer	EmailRenderer	DOCUMENT	oracle.ifs.protocols.email.renderer.OctetStreamRenderer
EmailThrowExceptionRenderer	EmailRenderer		oracle.ifs.server.renderers.ThrowExceptionRenderer
EmailMessageRenderer	EmailRenderer	MESSAGE	oracle.ifs.protocols.email.renderer.RFC822Renderer

FIGURE 5-5. *Registering a Renderer with iFS Manager*

The renderer's extensibility can be utilized to create custom renderers that apply XSL stylesheets to requested XML documents transforming them into formats compatible with the requesting device. For example, the same XML document can be delivered as HTML, XML, WML, and RTF through applying the appropriate stylesheet. Stylesheets can also be used to filter or add content to the output document.

Custom renderers can also be built to assemble documents from dynamic content such as creating a sales summary report from a table of sales invoices that is materialized in XML and transformed and delivered over HTTP to a requesting browser. The security support in iFS ensures that the requesting user is authorized to view this information.

Additional Important Considerations Regarding XML Files

XML documents can occur in the full range of character encodings. However, it is important to understand that if multiple languages and the character sets are to be supported, judicious selection of the database character set is required. As a rule, UTF8 is recommended if your *i*FS repository needs to support multiple encodings.

Since *i*FS can run either within the database or on the middle tier, it provides a flexible deployment architecture. To scale an *i*FS repository to support many users, you can run as many middle-tier servers as required, all communicating with a single backend database. Further scalability may be attained through the use of the Partitioning option in the Oracle8i Enterprise Edition.

In many cases, you may want to change the behavior of all instances of a set of subclasses. The *i*FS API has a set of classes called Tie classes that reside unexposed at the top of the class hierarchy just below the LibraryObject and can be changed or extended to provide this functionality.

While virtually all *i*FS's configuration and property files are XML based, it is very important that only those permitting direct user modification be edited. The *i*FS Manager is designed to properly manage these files. Additionally, *i*FS supports Access Control Lists (ACLs) to grant or revoke specific file and folder permissions to both users and groups.

CHAPTER
6

Searching XML
Documents with
Oracle Text

atabases are undergoing a revolution. Data in traditional relational databases is rigidly structured, and requests to access that data must always follow the overlaying database schema. These databases are effective for storing structured information, but they are poor at handling and/or searching other data forms. Classical SQL is fine for performing unstructured searches on small column values but is not powerful enough for long text columns. Data searches in an unstructured *Large Data Object (LOB)* have traditionally been inefficient and slow; therefore, the current goal of many database vendors is to provide high-performance accessibility to these complex information types. As these tight restrictions on access to data have been relaxed, databases have also relaxed their rigid restrictions on data structure.

Data stored in today's modern Internet databases take many forms. Video, graphical, and textual information abound, and the size of these types of data is often orders of magnitude greater than structured data. The Internet has introduced the requirement for ad hoc access to data, thereby making XML and HTML documents a common mechanism for Internet text data exchange. Consequently, modern databases backing Web sites must easily handle the searching and retrieval of these documents with scalability and performance.

Oracle Text is a component of Oracle9*i* that allows its users to manage diverse types of data using standard SQL access. Oracle Text, formerly known as interMedia Text or ConText, handles text documents, image, audio, and video as data types; and it enables easy data management, including Internet support for Web authoring tools and Web servers. Specifically, Oracle Text extends the database capabilities to handle textual information, providing seamless search capabilities within a standard SQL query, which is processed entirely within the database kernel and not from an add-on text engine.

This chapter covers the Oracle Text text-indexing architecture with an emphasis on XML-related features, such as XML_SECTION_GROUP; AUTO_SECTION_GROUP; the new PATH_SECTION_GROUP along with the HASPATH() and INPATH() operators introduced in Oracle9*i*; and zone, field, and attribute sections. Variations on the Bookstore application illustrate the practical details of Oracle Text.

Oracle Text as a Next-Generation Text Search Engine

A contemporary relational database system can easily handle all aspects of indexing simple data types, such as integers and small strings. Complex data types, however, such as structured text, spatial, image, video, and audio, require content-based retrieval. They have their own application-specific formats, indexing requirements, and selection predicates. For example, marked-up documents, such as HTML and XML, may require searching by tags or attributes. This raises the need for indexing complex data types and also for specialized indexing techniques.

Oracle's solution for this is to introduce the concept of *indextype*, which, along with an extensible framework, enables defining *indextypes* as required. The *indextype* is analogous to the sorted or bit-mapped index types built into the Oracle Server—with one important difference. *Indextypes* are not built in; the application developer implements them. The framework is based on the idea of cooperative indexing in which interMedia and Oracle9i cooperate to build and maintain indices for data types, such as text, spatial, and *online analytical processing (OLAP)*. interMedia is responsible for defining the index structure, maintaining the index content during load and update operations, and searching the index during query processing. The index structure itself can either be stored in an Oracle database as an *index-organized table (IOT)* or externally as an operating system file. The developer specifies the implementation details for the indextype, whereas the Oracle database kernel implements built-in sorted or bit-mapped indices.

Oracle Text indices may be created on almost any database column. When a document is loaded into one of these columns, the change is automatically detected and it is flagged for indexing. During indexing, which may be performed immediately or on any user-defined schedule, all the words and themes of the document are recorded in the index tables for future retrieval. Text queries are executed against the index and return a hit list of matching documents. Indices are maintained in the database, and all queries are executed within the database using a single API.

The Oracle *Cost Based Optimizer (CBO)* estimates and selects the fastest execution plan, given the run-time properties of the data being queried. The CBO could pipeline rowids satisfying the text predicate, or it could first check if the row with a given rowid satisfies the predicate. The second method uses a special algorithm, introduced in Oracle8i, to access the "inverted" text index for a specified row.

Oracle8i became the first relational database that integrates text querying into the database kernel. This fully integrated system uses the RDBMS kernel to process the entire query, thus earning Oracle Text the title of "Next-Generation Text Search Engine."

Oracle Text Indexing Architecture

The process for handling text with Oracle Text can be viewed as a pipeline to and from various modules, with options available at each stage of the pipeline. The final output of the pipeline is an *inverted index,* which is a list of the words from the document, with each word having a list of documents in which it appears. It is called "inverted" because it is the inverse of the normal way of looking at the text, which is generally represented as a list of documents with each document containing a list of words. Each stage of the indexing pipeline can be customized using the Preference System and/or Section Groups. They are created by using the following special APIs:

```
ctx_ddl.create_preference(...);
ctx_ddl.create_section_group (...);
```

and are plugged into the indexing pipeline using the parameters clause:

```
create index xml_index on Bookstore (xml_text)
            indextype is ctxsys.index
            parameters ('...');
```

The following four sections detail the indexing pipeline stages or modules, the information flow through the pipeline, and the options and commands applicable to each stage. Figure 6-1 gives an overview of the flow of information through the pipeline.

Datastore

The indexing pipeline starts with the *datastore*, which loops over the rows of the table and reads the data out of the column. Rows are not read in any particular order. The text by which Oracle Text indexes can be stored within a database or in file systems and managed by the database. The URL datastore allows a database to manage documents stored remotely on other servers and accessed via HTTP or FTP. This is usually column data, but some datastores use the column data as a pointer to the document data. The URL_DATASTORE, for example, uses the column data as a URL, does a GET, and passes out the returned data. The datastores are created and plugged into the pipeline using the following code snippet:

```
ctx_ddl.create_preference ('xml_urls', 'URL_DATASTORE');
ctx_ddl.set_attribute('xml_urls', 'HTTP_PROXY',
                      'www.proxy.us.oracle.com');
...
create_index xml_index on bookstore (xml_text) ...
   parameters ( 'datastore xml_urls ... ' ) ;
```

Filter

The *filter* takes the document data from the datastore and transforms it into some kind of text representation, such as XML, HTML, or plain text. This is needed when storing binary documents, such as Microsoft Word or Adobe Acrobat files. Oracle Text has filters for more than 100 file formats that can be mixed in a single column. In the following code snippet, the only output of the filters is in HTML format.

In addition, you can plug a custom-built filter or a third-party filter into the pipeline. A *custom-built filter* is simply an executable program or script that takes two arguments, the first being the file containing the formatted input text and the second being the name

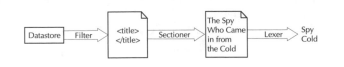

FIGURE 6-1. *Information flow through indexing pipeline*

of the file where the filtered output should be written. Similar to datastores, the filters are created and plugged into the pipeline using the preference system, as shown here:

```
ctx_ddl.create_preference ('xml_filter', 'USER_FILTER');
ctx_ddl.set_attribute ('xml_filter', 'EXECUTABLE', 'xmlfilter.exe');
...
create_index  xml_index  on bookstore (xml_text)
   ...
   parameters ( ''datastore  xml_urls   filter  xml_filter  ... ') ;
```

Sectioner

The *sectioner* takes the output from the filter and converts it to plain text. The conversion process is governed by a section group class type that tells the sectioner how to parse the input. The input from the filter could be analyzed as an XML or HTML document, or as plain text. The section group usually contains one or more sections. By defining a simple mapping, the application developers may give each section a name of their choice. The sectioner recognizes these sections for each text unit and automatically indexes the text as part of them. These sections could be HTML or XML sections or all *<StartTag>* ... *</ EndTag>* sections within an AUTO_SECTION_GROUP. Using the CONTAINS operator, the following statement allows an indexed section search:

```
SELECT pk FROM bookstore
    WHERE  CONTAINS  (xmltext, '(The Spy) WITHIN title') > 0;
```

This query finds the document if it contains XML markup, such as the following:

```
<book>
      <id> 4 </id>
      <author> John LeCarre </author>
      <title> The Spy Who Came in from the Cold </title>
</book>
```

In the case of an empty section group, the sectioner transforms formatted text to plain text, but it doesn't index any section boundaries. The output from the sectioner consists of the section boundaries and the document contents as plain text, which goes to the lexer. Conversion to plain text also includes detecting important section tags, removing "invisible" information, and reformatting the text. The section boundaries then go to the search engine. Section groups are created and plugged using Section Group APIs:

```
ctx_ddl.create_section_group  ('group_name', 'group_type');
...
create index
   ...
   parameters  ('section group  xml_group ...');
```

The sectioner takes the group type into account when it converts the input from the filter into plain output text and when it calculates indices for the section boundaries. As far as XML is concerned, the important section groups are the following:

- **BASIC_SECTION_GROUP**   Only start/end tags are recognized. DOCTYPEs, entities, and tag attributes are not supported. The only processing that occurs is that the markup tags are removed from the output plain text.

- **HTML_SECTION_GROUP**   Obviously, the HTML section group is for HTML. This section group not only supports HTML 4.0 tags, it also handles unknown tags. SCRIPT and STYLE contents and comments are removed; however, contents of the TITLE section are preserved.

- **XML_SECTION_GROUP**   The sectioner parses the input text as an XML document and handles internal entities, internal DOCTYPEs, and tag attributes. The tags are removed, and the internal entities are processed for the output plain text. User-defined sections from the section group are indexed.

- **AUTO_SECTION_GROUP**   Much as with the XML_SECTION_GROUP, the input text is processed as an XML document, but without user-defined sections. Instead, any nonempty tag is automatically indexed as a zone section, with the section name being the same as the tag name.

- **PATH_SECTION_GROUP**   This group is similar to the AUTO_SECTION_ GROUP in respect to tags and attributes within the section. Here, the sectioner also allows the new operators HASPATH() and INPATH() to do XPATH-like searching. In addition, queries within this section are sensitive to the case of the attribute and tag names.

Sections have three important attributes: **tag**, **name**, and **type**. The tag tells the sectioner how to recognize the section. When the sectioner finds a text sequence *<tag>* ... *</tag>*, it automatically indexes it for a search. Tags are unique across the sections of a section group. The section name is referenced in queries. Multiple tags can be mapped to the same name. They are then treated as instances of the same section. As far as XML is concerned, the important section types are the following:

- **ZONE**   Zone sections can repeat, and each instance is treated separately in query semantics. They can enclose other sections—including themselves— and can be enclosed by other sections. In the case of an AUTO_SECTION_ GROUP or PATH_SECTION_GROUP, the sectioner automatically indexes any nonempty tag as a zone section, with the section name being the same as the tag name.

- **FIELD**   The sectioner extracts the contents of this section and indexes them separately. This makes *field* section queries up to three times faster than zone section queries, especially when the section tags occur in every document. This speed comes at the cost of flexibility. Field sections are meant for nonrepeating, nonoverlapping sections. If a field section repeats in the same document, it is treated as a continuation of the section, not a distinct instance. If a field section is overlapped by itself or by another field section, it is implicitly closed at the point where the other section starts. In addition, a maximum of 64 field sections exist in any section group.

■ **ATTRIBUTE**   Attribute sections can be added only to XML_SECTION_ GROUPs. The sectioner indexes the contents of the section attribute and makes them available for querying. In the case of an AUTO_SECTION_GROUP or a PATH_SECTION_GROUP, the sectioner automatically indexes attribute values as attribute sections named *<tag>@<attribute>*.

■ **STOP**   Stop sections can only be used on AUTO_SECTION_GROUPs or PATH_SECTION_GROUPs. The *stop* section indicates that the corresponding *<tag>* should be ignored and not indexed as a section. The number of stop sections per AUTO_SECTION_GROUP or PATH_SECTION_GROUP is unlimited.

Lexer

The *lexer* takes the plain text from the sectioner and splits it into discrete tokens or words. Oracle Text has lexers for white space–delimited languages and specialized lexers for Asian languages, in which segmentation is more complex. The default basic_lexer also includes theme functionality to build unified text/theme indices. Similar to datastores, the lexers are created and plugged into the pipeline using this preference system:

```
ctx_ddl.create_preference     ('my_basic_lexer', 'basic_lexer');
...
create index  xml_index  on  bookstore (xml_text)
   ...
   parameters ('lexer my_basic_lexer  ... ');
```

Finally, Oracle9i takes all the tokens from the lexer and the section offsets from the sectioner and builds an inverted index. An inverted index then stores the tokens and the documents in which these tokens occur.

Working with Oracle Text

The following code shows a typical sequence of SQL statements you might use in Oracle Text to work with structured documents:

```
create table  bookstore (
    pk         NUMBER PRIMARY KEY ,
    xml_text  CLOB
) ;
```

```
insert into bookstore values (111,
  '<Book>
      <Id>4<\Id>
      <Author>John LeCarre</Author>
      <Title>The Night Manager</Title>
  </Book>');
insert into bookstore values (112,
  '<Book>
      <Id>5<\Id>
      <Author>John Grisham</Author>
      <Title>The Client</Title>
  </Book>');

/* ... insert the rest of the  books into the Bookstore */

commit;

begin
   ctx_ddl.create_section_group('xml_sections', 'XML_SECTION_GROUP');
   ctx_ddl.add_zone_section    ('xml_sections', 'titlesec', 'title');
   ctx_ddl.add_zone_section    ('xml_sections', 'authorsec', 'author');
   ctx_ddl.create_preference   ('my_basic_lexer', 'basic_lexer');
   ctx_ddl.set_attribute       ('my_basic_lexer', 'index_text','true');
   ctx_ddl.set_attribute    ('my_basic_lexer', 'index_themes','false');
end;

create index  xml_index  on  bookstore (xml_text)
   indextype is ctxsys.context
   parameters ('lexer my_basic_lexer  SECTION GROUP xml_sections');

select pk  from bookstore
   where contains (xml_text, 'LeCarre WITHIN authorsec') > 0 ;
```

The Bookstore example is a simple Oracle Text SQL example, illustrating the creation and population of a table, a Section Group creation, a textindex creation, and a simple query.

First, a table is created. A primary key is used to identify each document. An XML document is defined as an Oracle *Character Large Object (CLOB)*. Its value is composed of characters belonging to the Oracle9i database character set. The table is populated with book data documents, which could number in the tens of thousands.

Next, an XML_SECTION_GROUP with two zone sections for **<author>** and **<title>** tags is created:

```
ctx_ddl.create_section_group  ('xml_sections', 'XML_SECTION_GROUP');
ctx_ddl.add_zone_section      ('xml_sections', 'titlesec', 'title');
ctx_ddl.add_zone_section      ('xml_sections', 'authorsec', 'author');
```

This section group maps to column xml_text. This tells the Oracle Text engine to assume that the text is a structured XML document. Start tags, end tags, and an internal DTD are recognized as separate elements. Additionally, **<title>** and **<author>** elements are prepared to be indexed for a text search. Next, a text index is built, and a basic_lexer and the section group are plugged in:

```
create_index  xml_index  on bookstore (xml_text)
    indextype is ctxsys.context
    parameters ( 'lexer my_basic_lexer  SECTION GROUP xml_sections');
```

The *indextype* clause instructs Oracle9i to build a text index instead of a regular, B-tree index. Once the index has been created, content-based queries can run against the database of two documents using the contains function:

```
select pk  from bookstore
    where contains  (xml_text,  'LeCarre WITHIN authorsec') > 0 ;
```

This finds all rows in the bookstore table in which the text column has the text **LeCarre** within the element **<author>**. Oracle SQL does not support a *boolean* return (for now), so **> 0** is mandatory. For this example, the result is

```
PK
---------
111
```

The following sections take you through the indexing pipeline using the Bookstore application to illustrate how to apply different Oracle Text techniques.

Datastores

The Oracle Text datastore manages the reading of column data from the database.

The *direct datastore* is the simplest datastore, working with data stored in the indexed column. It doesn't have attributes to customize. The direct datastore is a DEFAULT_DATASTORE, so there is no need to plug it into Oracle Text explicitly; it already exists. The Bookstore example uses direct datastore.

The *file datastore* reads the column data from a file. It opens and reads the file and treats the file contents as an indexed column. The following is the Bookstore example modified to work with file datastore:

```
create table bookstore (
    id          number primary key,
    xml_text  varchar2(2000)
```

```
);
insert into bookstore values    (111, 'book1.xml');
insert into bookstore  values   (112, 'book2.xml');
...
begin
  ctx_ddl.create_preference ('xml_files',  'FILE_DATASTORE');
  ctx_ddl.set_attribute       ('xml_files', 'PATH',  '/xml/files');
  ...
end;
...
create_index  xml_index  on bookstore (xml_text)
   indextype is ctxsys.context
   parameters ('datastore  xml_files lexer my_basic_lexer  SECTION
              GROUP xml_sections');
```

The *URL datastore* reads the column data as a URL. HTTP, FTP, and file protocols are supported. If you want the Bookstore example to work with books stored as URLs, it might look like this:

```
...
begin
   ctx_ddl.create_preference ('xml_urls', 'URL_DATASTORE');
   ctx_ddl.set_attribute ('xml_urls', 'HTTP_PROXY', '<your-proxy-server>');
   ctx_ddl.set_attribute  ('xml_urls', 'Timeout', '300');
   ...
end;
insert into bookstore values (111,  'file://xml/files/book1.xml');
insert into bookstore values (112,  'file://xml/files/book2.xml');
...
create_index  xml_index  on bookstore (xml_text)
   indextype is ctxsys.context
   parameters ( 'datastore  xml_urls  lexer my_basic_lexer  SECTION
              GROUP xml_sections' ) ;
```

The *user datastore* relies on a stored procedure that synthesizes a document. If the books from the Bookstore example are stored as plain text, then a user datastore can be used to convert book data into an XML document. The following code shows the modified Bookstore example using user datastore:

```
create table bookstore (
    pk        number primary key,
    id        integer,
    author    varchar2(80),
    title     varchar2(80),
    xmltext   clob                  /* placeholder for user datastore */
);
insert into bookstore (pk, id, author, title) values (
 111,
 4, 'John LeCarre', 'The Spy Who Came in from the Cold');
```

```
insert into bookstore (pk, id, author, title) values (
 112,
 5, 'John Grisham', 'The Client');
 ...

/* the stored procedure */
create procedure toXML (rid in rowid, tlob in out tlob)
    offset number := 1;
begin
    for book in (select id,author,title,xmltext from bookstore
                 where rowid = rid)
    loop
       synthesize_XML (tlob, book.id, book.author, book.title, offset);
       dbms_lob.append(tlob, book.xmltext);
    end loop;
end toXML;

grant execute on toXML to public;
connect xml/bookstore

begin
  ctx_ddl.create_preference ('xml_proc', 'user_datastore' );
  ctx_ddl.set_attribute      ('xml_proc', 'procedure', 'toXML' );
  ...
end;
...
create_index xml_index on bookstore (xml_text)
   indextype is ctxsys.context
   parameters ('datastore xml_proc lexer my_basic_lexer  SECTION
               GROUP xml_sections') ;
```

The helper procedure synthesize_XML is not shown here. It takes the book data and puts together a temporary XML document *(tlob)*.

```
'<Book><Id>'  ||  book.id  ||  '<\Id><Author>'  ||  book.author  ||
         '</Author><Title>'  ||  book.title  '</Title> </Book>'
```

Next, the tlob is copied into the bookstore xml text. This makes the rest of the SQL almost identical to the previous Bookstore examples. The primary difference is the creation of user datastore, instead of file datastore or URL datastore.

Field and Zone Sections

You can use a slightly modified Bookstore example to illustrate the work with field and zone sections.

NOTE
Only SQL statements related to the current topic are shown.

```
...
insert into bookstore values   (
   111,
   '<Book>
      <Id>4<\Id>
      <Authors>
         <Author1>John Kay</Author1>
         <Author2>Mary Powell</Author2>
      </Authors>
      <Title>Don Juan </Title>
   </Book>'
);
insert into bookstore values   (
   112,
   '<Book>
      <Id>5<\Id>
      <Authors>
         <Author1>Juan Smith</Author1>
      </Authors>
      <Title>One Fine Day </Title>
   </Book>'
);
...
begin
   ...
   ctx_ddl.add_zone_section('xml_sections', 'authors', 'authors');
   ctx_ddl.add_zone_section('xml_sections', 'authorsec', 'author1');
   ctx_ddl.add_zone_section('xml_sections', 'authorsec2', 'author2');
   ...
end;

create_index  xml_index  on bookstore (xml_text)
   indextype is ctxsys.context
   parameters ( 'SECTION GROUP xml_sections  ... ');
```

The query:

```
select pk  from bookstore where
   contains (xml_text, 'Mary within authorsec') > 0;
```

does not find the document. Although Mary is an author, her name does not occur in the '**authorsec**'. Instead of the original setup, if the sections **<author1>** and **<author2>** are mapped to the same section name,

```
begin
   ...
   ctx_ddl.add_zone_section ('xml_sections', 'authorsec', 'author1');
   ctx_ddl.add_zone_section ('xml_sections', 'authorsec', 'author2');
   ...
end;
```

then the query finds the first document because both **<author1>** and **<author2>** are treated as '**authorsec**'.

As was pointed out previously in the chapter, each instance of zone section is treated distinctly. In other words, a query like this:

```
select pk  from bookstore where
    contains  (xml_text, '(Mary and  Powell) within authorsec') > 0;
```

finds the document, but the next query fails:

```
select pk  from bookstore where
    contains  (xml_text, '(Mary and  John) within authorsec') > 0
```

Although the book from the first document has authors with the names Mary and John and they are within '**authorsec**', they are not within the same '**authorsec**'. However, if the outer section **<authors>** was also mapped to the '**authorsec**':

```
ctx_ddl.add_zone_section ('xml_sections', 'authorsec', 'authors');
```

then the last query would succeed because they are both in the outer '**authorsec**'.

If you, as a Bookstore application developer, are interested only in names, and if the section in which they appear is not important for you, then the section setup may look like this:

```
begin
    ...
    ctx_ddl.add_zone_section ('xml_sections', 'authors', 'authors');
    ctx_ddl.add_zone_section ('xml_sections', 'names', 'author1');
    ctx_ddl.add_zone_section ('xml_sections', 'names', 'author2');
    ctx_ddl.add_zone_section ('xml_sections', 'names', 'title');
    ...
end;
```

Now the query:

```
select pk  from bookstore where
            contains  (xml_text, 'Juan within names') > 0
```

finds both documents because Juan is within the first document, **<title>** and within the second document, **<author1>**. Note, this setup can distinguish between names in **<title>** and names in **<author>**. This is achieved by using a nested-within query:

```
select pk  from bookstore where
    contains  (xml_text, '(Juan within names) within authors') > 0;
```

The nested-within query finds the second document because only this document contains Juan within **<authors>**. The nested-within query works only with zone sections. In addition, because of how Oracle Text indexes zone sections, equivalent sections cannot be distinguished. For example, the query

```
select pk  from bookstore where
          contains  (xml_text, '(Juan within authors) within names')
  > 0
```

also succeeds. This happens because the sections bound exactly the same range. The nested-within query does not imply an exact parent-child relationship; the relationship could be a parent-grandchild or great-grandchild. As explained previously in the chapter, each instance of a field section is considered a continuation of the section within a document. If you set up the Bookstore example with field sections:

```
begin
    ...
    ctx_ddl.add_field_section ('xml_sections', 'authors', 'authors');
    ctx_ddl.add_field_section ('xml_sections', 'authorsec', 'author1');
    ctx_ddl.add_field_section ('xml_sections', 'authorsec', 'author2');
    ...
end;
```

then the query:

```
select pk  from bookstore where
          contains  (xml_text, '(Mary and  John) within authorsec') > 0
```

finds the document, although it didn't when '**authorsec**' was a zone section. For each document, the sectioner concatenates the field section instances. The field sections are better with sections such as **<title>**, which do not repeat. They are extracted from the document contents and indexed separately.

This means a non-within query,

```
select pk  from bookstore where
    contains (xml_text, '4') > 0
```

fails to find the document although it contains '**4**'. If it were set up with zone sections, then the query would succeed. This could be changed by making the field section visible. You can do this by setting the optional *boolean* fourth argument **add_field_ section** to TRUE:

```
ctx_ddl.add_field_section  ('xml_section',  'authorsec',  'author1',
                            TRUE);
```

Now, the field section contents are visible to non-within queries. You can accomplish this by double-indexing the word, once as part of the extracted section, and once as part of the document. Of course, this option has its index space cost.

Internal DOCTYPEs are analyzed for XML_SECTION_GROUPs and PATH_SECTION_GROUPs. In this case, you create doctype limited field sections to distinguish between tags from different DOCTYPEs. The tag syntax for this is (<*doctype_name*>) <*tag_name*>:

```
begin
    ctx_ddl.create_section_group('xml_sections', 'XML_SECTION_GROUP');
    ctx_ddl.add_field_section('xml_section'','(Bookstore)authorsec',
                                'author');
    ctx_ddl.add_field_section('xml_section'','(MyBookstore)names',
                                'author');
    ctx_ddl.add_field_section ('xml_section'', 'authorsec',
                                'author');
    ...
end
```

Now, when the sectioner sees an **<author>** tag, it indexes it as the '**authorsec**' section if the DOCTYPE is '**Bookstore**', or as the '**names**' section when the DOCTYPE is '**MyBookstore**'. Both doctype-limited and -unlimited sections can coexist in a section group. The doctype-limited section applies only in its DOCTYPE, but for all other DOCTYPEs, the unlimited section is used. Querying is unaffected by this because the query is done on the section name.

Stop Sections

In the case of AUTO_SECTION_GROUP and PATH_SECTION_GROUP, the sectioner automatically indexes any nonempty tag as a zone section, with the section name the same as the tag name. Some tags may not be important for the application, so indexing them would be a waste of time because they are not useful for searching. For such tags, the AUTO_SECTION_GROUP and PATH_SECTION_GROUP have stop sections, which indicate tags to ignore. For instance, if the Bookstore example is set up with PATH_SECTION_GROUP,

```
begin
    ctx_ddl.create_section_group ('xml_sections', 'PATH_SECTION_GROUP')
    ctx_ddl.add_stop_section ('xml_section', 'Id')
    ...
end
```

then the tag **<Id>** is ignored and is not indexed as a section. The number of stop sections per group is unlimited. Doctype-limiters are also supported. For example,

```
ctx_ddl.add_stop_section('xml_section'', '(MyBookstore)author');
```

ignores the tag **<author>** only inside DOCTYPE '**MyBookstore**'.

Attribute Sections

Attribute sections within XML_SECTION_GROUP and PATH_SECTION_GROUP allow indexing and searching within attribute values. In addition, within a PATH_ SECTION_GROUP, queries take into account case-sensitivity for attribute and tag names. You can modify the Bookstore example to use attribute sections:

```
insert into bookstore values  (
    111,
    '<Book   id     = "4"
             author = "John LeCarre"
             title  =  "The Night Manager" />'
);
insert into bookstore values  (
    112,
    '<Book   id     = "5"
             author = "Juan Smith"
             title  = "The Night Club"/>'
);
 ...
begin
   ctx_ddl.create_section_group('xml_sections', 'XML_SECTION_GROUP');
   ctx_ddl.add_atrr_section('xml_sections', 'authorsec','book@author');
   ctx_ddl.add_atrr_section('xml_sections', 'titlesec', 'book@title');
   ...
end;

create_index  xml index  on bookstore (xml_text)
    indextype is ctxsys.context
    parameters ( 'SECTION GROUP xml_sections  ... ');
```

The attribute name is used in conjunction with the tag name to which it belongs:

<tag_name>@<attribute_name>.

If you run the following sequence of queries against the Bookstore database:

```
select pk  from bookstore where
    contains (xml_text,  'Juan within author') > 0;

select pk  from bookstore where
    contains (xml_text,  '(The Night Manager) within title') > 0;

select pk  from bookstore where
    contains (xml_text,  '(Juan and John) within author') > 0;
```

then the first and second queries find the documents, but the third one fails. It fails because attribute sections within queries can distinguish between occurrences. Note that the first and second queries would fail within a PATH_SECTION_GROUP if the tag names were capitalized:

```
select pk  from bookstore where
     contains  (xml_text,  'Juan within AUTHOR') > 0;

select pk  from bookstore where
     contains  (xml_text,  '(The Night Manager) within TITLE') > 0;
```

Attribute text is considered invisible, so non-within queries, such as the following:

```
select pk  from bookstore where
  contains  (xml_text,  'Juan') > 0;
```

fail to find a document. Attribute section names cannot overlap with zone or field section names. Multiple attribute names mapped to a section name are allowed. Although DTDs are analyzed, the default attribute values specified in them are not supported. In other words, if an actual attribute value is omitted in the document, then the DTD-defined default value is not inserted for indexing.

For AUTO_SECTION_GROUP and PATH_SECTION_GROUP, the sectioner automatically indexes attribute values as attribute sections named *<tag>@<attr>*. For example, the query

```
select pk from bookstore where
     contains(xml_text, '(The Night Manager) within book@title') > 0;
```

searches inside the title attribute value because the title attribute is automatically indexed as an attribute section.

XPATH Searching Within PATH_SECTION_GROUP

Beginning with Oracle9i, two new operators, INPATH() and HASPATH(), were added to allow XPATH-like queries within the PATH_SECTION_GROUP section. For example, instead of the previous example where one is querying against the "title" section, one can issue a query with an XPATH expression to find the expression "Night" within one of the bookstore's "book" child sections, i.e., "title":

```
select pk  from bookstore where
     contains  (xml_text,  'Night within INPATH(//bookstore/book)') > 0;
```

By allowing XPATH expressions to be substituted for section names, the WITHIN operator is thus enhanced for Oracle9i. In addition, tests for attributes are also allowed, so if "Night" appeared in multiple "title" sections but the "title" had "number" attributes to search on, one could retrieve the titles via attribute matching:

```
select pk  from bookstore where
    contains  (xml_text,  'Night within INPATH(//bookstore/book/
title[@number="one"]') > 0;
```

As noted previously, within a PATH_SECTION_GROUP, queries are conscious of case sensitivity of the tag and attribute names.

Finally, similar to how the INPATH() operator can enhance the WITHIN operator, the HASPATH() operator can enhance the CONTAINS operator, allowing searching on XML documents with XPATH expressions. A value of 100 is returned from HASPATH() call if the path exists in the document. For example, the following would return 100 from our bookstore example:

```
select pk from bookstore where
    contains(xml_text, 'HASPATH(bookstore/book/title') > 0;
```

Last, the operator can search XML documents for elements with a certain value, i.e., 'The Night Manager', and return a value of 100 for documents that do have this title value:

```
select pk from bookstore where
    contains(xml_text, 'HASPATH(Book@Title="The Night Manager"])') > 0;
```

Dynamic Add Section

Adding new sections to an existing index without rebuilding the index is useful when documents start coming in with new tags or start getting new **DOCTYPE**s. For example, this is a SQL sequence that adds a new zone section named "names" using the tag **<title>**:

```
alter index xml_index rebuild
parameters  ('add zone section names tag title')
```

and the following is the SQL sequence for adding a new field section named "authors" using the tag **<author>**:

```
alter index xml_index rebuild
   parameters ('add field section authors tag author')
```

The dynamic add section only modifies the index metadata and does not rebuild the index. This means these sections take effect for any document indexed after the operation and do not affect any existing documents. If the index already has documents with these sections, they must be manually marked for reindexing (usually with an update of the indexed column to itself).

NOTE
The current Oracle Text is unable to find and extract fragments of an XML document that satisfy the query conditions. In other words, you must divide large XML documents into meaningful smaller documents before searching. In the future, more intelligent, content-sensitive, fragment-level operations should be able to find and extract meaningful fragments from a single XML document that contains tens of thousands of **<book>** *elements.*

CHAPTER
7

Oracle E-Business
XML Services

he Oracle E-Business Suite of applications offers companies a new
and better way to conduct business. The E-Business Suite combines
Customer Relationship Management (CRM), supply chain management,
and internal operations as a fully integrated solution. The Oracle E-
Business XML Services component, which is part of Oracle CRM and
is available in release 11.5.6 of Oracle Applications, provides a framework and system
infrastructure for deployment, management, and run-time execution of XML Services,
the foundation for developing a new generation of Web-enabled e-business
applications.

XML Services Overview

The XML Services component is new technology that allows CRM developers to
abstract CRM applications functionality as XML services that are accessible by any
authorized source using SOAP-based XML messages. Fundamentally, the applications
have to be designed to take advantage of the XML services as follows:

- Each application creates and publishes a set of XML services. Usually, the
  applications expose their key integration points as XML services.

- Each application creates and publishes a set of events.

- Applications invoke services published by other applications.

- Applications subscribe to all events that the application wants to monitor
  and handle.

- Applications signal the event occurrence to the XML Services component;
  the XML Services component will then invoke all subscribed services to
  handle the event.

The XML Services framework provides a level of abstraction that hides the
details associated with SOAP-based messages and instead lets developers focus
on the development of Java-based services. The framework also takes care of the
authorization model for users to access those services.

XML Services Components

XML Services has five major components.

Administrator Interface

By using the CRM Administrative Console, CRM developers, system integrators, and Oracle Application developers can create, remove, and configure services, invocation points, events, and event subscribers.

SOAP Server

The SOAP Server run-time engine is responsible for executing all XML service requests for services that are deployed in the XML Services repository. The SOAP server engine is implemented as a servlet. This servlet handles all incoming SOAP XML requests. The SOAP servlet translates the incoming SOAP XML requests into Java method invocations. After the requested method is executed, the returned Java object is encoded as a SOAP XML response and sent back to the invoking party.

Client APIs

Application developers use XML Services client APIs to invoke XML services and signal the occurrence of events. The event API is useful to publish event-related information to all subscribers registered for the event. It is also possible to publish the event information to a subset of the subscribers, chosen in terms of the content associated with the event.

Services and Events Repository

XML Services maintains a central repository that holds full information about all registered services, invocation points, events, and event subscribers. It is used by the XML Services run-time engine and is administered using the XML Services administrator interface.

Terminology

The following terms describe important features of the XML Services.

XML Service

An *XML service* is a single logical unit of work that has well-defined inputs and outputs. An XML service can be invoked from any authorized application by sending an XML message as a service request, and receiving an XML message as a response. Each XML service is implemented as a Java method. The XML services are application specific and typically represent well-defined pieces of business logic.

Web Service

Web Service is an XML service that is deployed on the World Wide Web.

Service Group

A *service group* is a group of related XML services. Each service group is implemented as a single Java class. All public methods in this Java class can be services that belong to the service group.

Key Integration Point

A *key integration point* represents an application's functionality that is exposed to the Internet by the means of an XML service. Usually, key integration points implemented as services expose all business functionality that the application wants to expose for use by other related applications. Another way to think of the key integration points is as business APIs that can be used to drive the application functionality programmatically.

Invocation Point

An *invocation point* is a place in the application where the application invokes XML services exposed by another application. The XML Services client API separates the application logic from the service invocation details such as: where is the service deployed, what is the transport protocol used, what are the authentication parameters that are needed to access the service. To invoke a service, the application uses a logical service name that points to the invocation record holding all this information. Therefore, even when the service provider is changed, no changes are needed in the invocation point.

Invocation Record

The *invocation record* holds all the information that is needed to invoke a given service. This includes the URL, where the service is deployed, the service group name, the service name, the user ID, and the password. The invocation record holds detailed information about what parameter types are passed to the service, what type mapping is used for each parameter, and so on. Each invocation record is uniquely identified by its invocation string. This string is also called the logical service name. When the application program uses the XML Services API to invoke a service, the application passes the logical service name for the service that it wants to invoke as the first parameter. This string is used at run time to retrieve the invocation record that fully defines how to invoke the service. Therefore, the invocation record is instrumental in the run-time binding that the XML service client uses when invoking XML services. Through use of run-time binding and a logical service name as a pointer to the invocation record, the application code can be kept unchanged even when important details change, such as who provides the service and what are the access rights.

Event

An *event* is a well-defined Java object that can be produced at some known point in an application when specific circumstances are met. All events are registered in the XML Services events repository. All events are available for event listeners (subscribers) to subscribe to. In XML Services, each event has a unique name. The applications use the XML Services API call to signal to the XML Services component when the event happens. Using the API, the application passes the event name and the event object to the XML Services infrastructure. The XML Services infrastructure will then handle the task of invoking all of the current event subscribers and passing the event object to each subscriber.

Event Subscriber

An *event subscriber* acts as a listener to an event. The event subscribers are implemented as XML services. Each event subscriber service is a normal XML service that takes a single input parameter. This parameter is of the same Java type as the event object type that will be handled. When an event occurs and is signaled by the originating application, all XML services that are event subscribers for that event will be invoked and the event object will be passed as an input parameter. A subscriber XML service is not required to have a return value.

XML Services and SOAP

XML services are SOAP based. Therefore, we must understand SOAP in order to develop, deploy, and use XML services.

What Is SOAP

The Simple Object Access Protocol (SOAP) is a lightweight, XML-based protocol for exchanging information in a decentralized, distributed environment. The SOAP protocol consists of three parts:

- The SOAP Envelope, which defines an overall framework for expressing what is in the message, who should process the message, and whether the processing is optional or mandatory.

- A set of encoding rules for expressing instances of application-defined data types. These rules define a serialization mechanism that converts the application data types to XML and vice versa.

- A SOAP RPC convention for representing remote procedure calls and responses.

The major design goal for SOAP is simplicity and extensibility. SOAP has a looser coupling between the client and the server than some similar distributed computing protocols, such as CORBA/IIOP. All this makes the protocol even more compelling. SOAP is transport protocol independent and can be used with any transport protocol. At the same time, when used with HTTP for remote service invocation over the Internet, SOAP is emerging as a de facto standard for delivering programmatic content over the Web. Currently, the SOAP 1.1 specification is a W3C note. The W3C XML Protocol Working Group has been formed to create a standard that will supersede SOAP.

Since SOAP is XML based, it is platform and operating system independent. It supports communication between a client and a server that use different program languages. SOAP requests are easy to generate, and a client can easily process the responses. By using SOAP, one application can become a programmatic client of another application's services, with the two applications exchanging rich, structured information. SOAP provides a robust programming model that creates the possibility to aggregate powerful, distributed Web services to turn the Internet into an application development platform of the future.

How Does SOAP Work

The SOAP specification describes a standard, XML-based way to encode requests and responses, including:

- Requests to invoke a method as a service, including in parameters

- Responses from a service method, including a return value and out parameters

- Errors from a service

Let's consider the following example: a GetLastTradePrice SOAP request is sent to a StockQuote service. The request takes a string parameter, the company ticker symbol, and returns a float in the SOAP response. The XML document represents the SOAP message. The SOAP Envelope element is the top element of the XML document. XML namespaces are used to disambiguate SOAP identifiers from application-specific identifiers. The example uses the HTTP as the transport protocol. The rules governing XML payload format in SOAP are entirely independent of the fact that the payload is carried in HTTP (because SOAP is transport independent). The SOAP request message embedded in the HTTP request looks like this:

```
POST /StockQuote HTTP/1.1
Host: www.stockquoteserver.com
Content-Type: text/xml; charset="utf-8"
Content-Length: nnnn
SOAPAction: "Some-URI"
```

```
<SOAP-ENV:Envelope  xmlns:SOAP-  ENV="http://schemas.xmlsoap.org/soap/
envelope/"  SOAP-
ENV:encodingStyle="http://schemas.xmlsoap.org/soap/encoding/">
<SOAP-ENV:Body>
<m:GetLastTradePrice xmlns:m="Some-URI">
<symbol>ORCL</symbol>
</m:GetLastTradePrice>
</SOAP-ENV:Body>
</SOAP-ENV:Envelope>
```

What follows is the response HTTP message containing the XML message with the SOAP as the payload:

```
HTTP/1.1 200 OK
Content-Type: text/xml; charset="utf-8"
Content-Length: nnnn

<SOAP-ENV:Envelope xmlns:SOAP-
ENV=http://schemas.xmlsoap.org/soap/envelope/ SOAP-
ENV:encodingStyle="http://schemas.xmlsoap.org/soap/encoding/"/>
<SOAP-ENV:Body>
<m:GetLastTradePriceResponse xmlns:m="Some-URI">
<Price>34.5</Price>
</m:GetLastTradePriceResponse>
</SOAP-ENV:Body>
</SOAP-ENV:Envelope>
```

What Does a SOAP Client Do?

The SOAP client must perform the following steps:

- Gather all parameters that are needed to invoke a service.

- Create a SOAP service request message. This is an XML message that is built according to the SOAP protocol and that contains all of the values of all input parameters encoded in XML. This process is called *serialization of the parameters*.

- Submit the request to a SOAP server using some transport protocol that is supported by the SOAP server.

- Receive a SOAP response message.

- Determine the success or failure of the request by handling the SOAP Fault element.

- Convert the returned parameter from XML to a native data type. This process is called *deserialization.*

- Use the result as needed.

To enable you to avoid dealing with XML and SOAP at a very low level, a number of SOAP clients are available that will do most of this work for you. To facilitate easy application development and to insulate the application developers from all details of using SOAP, XML Services includes a SOAP client API. This API provides an easy way to invoke SOAP services from the XML Services framework. The XML Services SOAP client API supports a synchronous invocation model for requests and responses.

What Does SOAP Server Do?

Any SOAP server follows these general steps while executing a SOAP service request:

- The server receives the service request.

- After parsing the XML request, the server must decide to execute the message or to reject it.

- If the message is to be executed, the server finds out if the service that is requested exists.

- The server converts all input parameters from XML into data types that the service understands.

- The server invokes the service.

- The return parameter is converted to XML and a SOAP response message is generated.

- The response message is sent back to the caller.

XML Services uses the Oracle SOAP implementation that is part of Oracle iAS 1.0.2.2 as its SOAP run-time engine. The Oracle SOAP implementation is based on the Apache SOAP implementation.

Therefore, the XML services are SOAP services and can be invoked by any Apache SOAP–compatible client.

Service Group Guidelines

Be aware of the following rules when combining services into service groups:

- Logically related services that cover specific business areas should be organized into a "service group."

- A service group is deployed under an application.

- From an implementation standpoint, a service group is a Java class and all of its public methods can be exposed as services. Although all public methods of a Java class that implement a service group can be exposed as XML services, the services can be disabled and made inaccessible through the administrative console.

- Since all public methods are candidates for services, the application developer should design the service group classes in such a way that all public methods correspond to legitimate services.

- Although a service group is basically a Java class, keep in mind that the method in this Java class is going to be executed in an RPC model and not all object-oriented concepts will be appropriate. Therefore, the following are *not* allowed:

- Constructor method: The Java class must *not* have a constructor.

- Method overloading: There should be only one method that corresponds to a service.

- Class inheritance: The Java class (service group) should not inherit from other classes except for **java.lang.Object**. Only methods declared in this Java class (not its parent classes) are exposed as services.

- The implementation of the service group (Java class) should also be *thread-safe* and *stateless*.

- The service group registration (or deployment) is done through the E-Business Center.

Service Guidelines

There are a number of issues that the application developer must address before deciding to expose particular application functionalities as services. The following guidelines can direct you:

- The application developer should focus only on the business logic of the service during implementation. The developer will not have to worry about whether the caller is authorized to invoke the service or not. The XML Service framework will perform authentication and authorization checks before the service can be invoked.

- The XML Service infrastructure currently supports synchronous invocation only, and this should be taken into account when creating the service.

- For the parameters and the return value of a service (method), developers are strongly recommended to use the following Java types:

  - **Java primitives**   void, int, long, short, byte, float, double, boolean (note that primitive "char" and primitive objects like java.lang.Integer are not supported)

  - **Java array**   One dimension only

  - **Others**   java.lang.String, java.util.Vector, java.util.Hashtable, and org.w3c.dom.Element

  - **Special types**   Any user-defined Java type whose class is a Java bean that follow these three rules:

- Setter methods for all its fields

- Getter methods for all its fields

- A constructor that does not accept parameters

During execution of a service or invocation of a service, Java types would need to be translated to XML (using SOAP encoding) and vice versa. The XML Services infrastructure supports the translation of Java types in the cases of primitives, arrays, and other types by default, and no additional type translation information is needed. In the case of special types, the XML Services infrastructure provides the option to specify translation information of arbitrary data types by registering Java classes as serializers and deserializers. In the event that your class is Java bean, you can use default values that make use of a class called BeanSerializer, so you as application developer don't have to deal with the complexity of translation between Java types and XML. It is strongly recommended to use the framework's provided default values for data types in the case of special types.

NOTE
For data types nested within a compound data structure such as array, Vector, Hashtable, and Java Bean, the same rules are applied except in the case of org.w3c.dom.Element, which cannot be nested in a compound structure.

In the case that application developers choose to use data types that are not in the preceding list or to specify translation information other than defaults in the case of special types, the following information is required during the registration of the service:

- **Serializer class**   The Java class that implements the translation of the Java data type to SOAP.

- **Deserializer class**   The Java class that implements the translation of SOAP to the Java data type.

- **Encoding Style**   This is a string that is used as a name to identify the set of serializer and deserializer used for a specific data type. When the application developer has more than one set of serializer/deserializer for the same data type, a different encoding style is used to identify the set.

- **Namespace URI**   A string that is used as the XML namespace in the SOAP message. Each data type will be translated into a pair of XML tags in the SOAP message being sent or received, and the namespace URI will be used as the namespace for that pair of XML tags

NOTE
Because of the additional complexity for developers, to use data types that do not belong to the preceding list or to use translation information other than defaults is strongly discouraged.

Security Model

The XML Services infrastructure makes use of the current security model in E-Business Foundation Services.

In other words, username/password-based authentication will be used, and authorization will be based on permissions and roles assigned to the user. For each service, there will be a permission associated with executing the service. The permission will be created automatically when the service group containing the service is deployed into the infrastructure. The name of the permission will be in the format of:

<App short name>_<Service Group Name>_<Service Name>_EXE —all in uppercase

Out of the box, there will be:

- A new user type called "XML_Users." Administrators should create users from this user type for accessing services of the infrastructure.

- Meaningful default roles that group the permissions for executing services.

- For each default role, an enrollment is also created.

At run time, administrators can modify the user type "XML_Users" by adding new roles and enrollments. New users of this user type will get the additional roles and selected enrollments. Typically, these users will be external users (another company) who will come over the Internet.

Service Execution Details

At run time, the following steps are performed to ensure that proper authentication and authorization takes place before a service is executed.

- An authentication check is performed right after a SOAP request arrives. It is based on the username/password in the request.

- A JTF user session is created before executing the service, and the same session will end after the execution of the service.

- An authorization check is performed after creating the user session and before executing the service.

- All the services will be executed synchronously.

- SSL (HTTPS) will be used to secure the transport channel for the response generated by the service.

Invocation Guidelines

The XML Services client API is designed to separate the service invocation from all details that define a particular service. It takes a single Java method call to invoke a service. The following guidelines explain what an application developer must do in application code and what must be done using the XML Services administrative interface.

- The application developer should determine what input parameters to pass to the service to be invoked.

- The application developer should determine what return value the service will return and all the possible errors.

- Invocation name—The application developer must define a logical name for every service invocation. This logical name must be unique across the system to identify this service invocation. The purpose of defining this logical name is to abstract away the service endpoint details from the developer when he or she is writing his code. The details that the logical name abstracts can be configured at the CRM Administrative Console; therefore, the logical name will dynamically bind to these endpoint details at run time. The service endpoint details that will be dynamically bound to the logical name are:

- URL of the target application

- Service group name of the target service

- Service name

- Security credentials required by the target application

- Name, data type, and encoding style for input parameters and return value (names must be unique)

- Type translation information of parameters and return value of the target service

- For invoking a system service, specify the service group name as 'urn:soap-service-manager', the service name as the method name of the system service, e.g., 'get_target_objects', and the Security credentials as NO_AUTHENTICATION (since system services are public services).

- There are two modes of invocation services; the modes are the LOCALHOST mode and the REMOTE mode. If the target URL is specified as 'LOCALHOST', then the LOCALHOST mode will be used; otherwise, the REMOTE mode will be used (even though the network addresses of the client and the server may be the same).

  - **LOCALHOST mode**   If the services are set up in the same instance as where the client is run, the client can be run in the LOCALHOST mode. This mode means that the service request doesn't go through the network but directly translates to a Java API call. No security credential will need to be specified for this mode. No type translation information will need to be entered.

  - **REMOTE mode**   The second way the client can run is in 'remote host' mode. This means that the service request will go through the network to the URL where the XML services are set up. To invoke in this mode, make sure an *authentication profile* has been set up before registering the invocation. Security credentials will need to be created for this mode. Type translation information of parameters will need to be entered, since the request will be translated into XML/SOAP format.

- SSL (HTTPS) will be used to secure the transport channel for the invocation request.

Service Invocation Example

The following lines of code are a stand-alone Java program that calls stock quote service.

```java
import java.util.*;
import oracle.apps.jtf.services.*;                //has to be imported
import oracle.apps.jtf.services.invocation.*;   //has to be imported
import oracle.apps.jtf.base.session.*;

public class ServiceCallExample {
  /**
   * this example program call a service to get Oracle's stock price
   */
  public static void main(String [] args) {
    try {
      //for stand alone program, a stand alone session has to be started
      //before call services.
      //for jsp pages or servlets, startRequest(...) method is used to
      // start session
      ServletSessionManager.startStandAloneSession("JTF", false,
                                    "SYSADMIN","SYSADMIN");
      System.out.println("=================================");
    } catch (Exception e) {
      e.printStackTrace();
    }
    // logical invocation name
    String IN = "oracle.crm.jtf.GET_STOCK_QUOTE";
    //construct all the parameters passed to the service
    Vector params = new Vector();
    try {
      // When using this Param constructor, it is recommended to us
      //"variable.getClass()" instead of "type.class".
      //(in the case of array, java.lang.reflect.Array
      //will not return the correct class of the variable)
      Param parameter = new Param("symbol", symbol.getClass(), "ORCL");
      params.addElement(parameter);
    } catch (ClassNotMatchException e) {
      //This exception is thrown when the parameter type and the value
      //don't match.
      //For example, Param("example", String.class, 3) will cause
      //ClassNotMatchException.
    }
    try{
      //call the service
      ServiceResult result = Client.callService(IN, params);
      if(result==null || result.getFloat()<=0) {//service specificerror
        System.out.println("ORCL is not a valid stock symbol");
      }
```

```
      else { //print out result
          System.out.println("The current stock price of ORCL is"
                    +result.getFloat());
      }
  }
  catch (InvocationException e) {
    //If a service call fails, an InvocationException is thrown. We can
    //tell what happened from the exception's error code,
    //locate the error and then fix it by either
    // changing code or changing the service
    //invocation configuration in the administration.
    int errorCode = e.getErrorCode();
    System.out.println(errorCode);
    System.out.println(e.getMessage());
  }
  try{
    System.out.println("=================================");
    //close the session
    ServletSessionManager.endStandAloneSession();
  }
  catch (Exception e) {
    e.printStackTrace();
  }
  }
}
```

Events Guidelines

Proper use of XML Services events creates applications that expose out-of-the-box application functionality that can be used for integrating or customizing application behavior.

Here are important aspects that you should know about events:

- Event objects are Java objects.

- You must define your event objects to encapsulate all of the data that needs to be passed to the event subscribers when the event takes place.

- The rules for type mapping of data types when defining the event objects are the same as the rules used for service parameters.

- Signaling an event is an asynchronous call, and responses are not expected from subscribers.

- After signaling an event, your application will receive control immediately. The XML Services system will invoke all of the subscribed services in separate threads.

Signal Events Example

The following example illustrates how to use the XML services client API to signal an application event.

```java
import java.util.*;
import oracle.apps.jtf.services.*;              //has to be imported
import oracle.apps.jtf.services.invocation.*;   //has to be imported
import oracle.apps.jtf.base.session.*;

public class EventSignalExample {
  /**
   * This example program signaloracle.crm.oso.NEW_SALES_LEAD_EVENT
   * when a new sales lead comes up.
   * The data type of the event object is LeadInfo which contains
   * information about the new lead like name, address and phone number.
   */
  public static void main(String [] args) {
    try {
      //for stand alone program, a stand alone session has to be
      //started before signal events.
      //for jsp pages or servlets, startRequest(...) method is used to
      //start the session
      ServletSessionManager.startStandAloneSession("JTF", false,
      "SYSADMIN","SYSADMIN");
      System.out.println("==================================");
    } catch (Exception e) {
      e.printStackTrace();
    }
    String eventName = "oracle.crm.oso.NEW_SALES_LEAD_EVENT";
    //construct the event object
    LeadInfo leadInfo = new LeadInfo("John", "500 Oracle parkway",
                                     "650-506-6789");
    Param param = null;
    try {
        //When using this Param constructor, it is recommended to use
        //"variable.getClass()" instead of "type.class".
        //(in the case of array, java.lang.reflect.Array
        //will not return the correct class of the variable)
        param = new Param("lead", leadInfo.getClass(), leadInfo);
    } catch (ClassNotMatchException e) {
        //This exception is thrown when the parameter type and the value
        //don't  match.
        //For example, Param("example", String.class, 3) will cause
        //ClassNotMatchException.
    }
    try {
        //the event is triggered and the event object is sent to all
        //subscribed listeners
```

```
      Client.signalEvent(eventName, param);
   } catch (InvocationException e) {
      //if the event name is not registered, or not configured properly,
      //or the system can not launch threads to call the listeners, an
      //InvocationExcption is thrown.
      //because the invocation of a listener is done asynchronously
      //at a spawned new thread, no InvocationException
      //will be thrown even if errors happen in the invocation.
      int errorCode = e.getErrorCode();
      System.out.println(errcode);
      System.out.println(e.getMessage());
   }
   try{
      System.out.println("===================================");
      //close the session
      ServletSessionManager.endStandAloneSession();
   }
   catch (Exception e) {
      e.printStackTrace();
   }
   }
}
```

Signal Event with Filtered Subscribers Example

The following example shows that the application program can be designed to be aware of the subscribers for a particular event. Based on the details for the event, the application may decide to notify just a subset of listeners. For example, if the application shares sales leads, specific subscribers can be notified, depending on the type of lead.

```
import java.util.*;
import oracle.apps.jtf.services.*; //has to be imported
import oracle.apps.jtf.services.invocation.*; //has to be imported
import oracle.apps.jtf.base.session.*;

public class EventSignalFilterExample {
/**
 * This example program signals an oracle.crm.oso.NEW_SALES_LEAD_EVENT
 *  when a new sales lead comes up.
 * The data type of the event object is LeadInfo which contains
 * information about the new lead like name, address and phone number.
 * This event is associated with a set of listeners which are configured
 * by the admin. In this example, we only want to invoke a subset of the
 * listeners. So we first get all the associated listeners based on the
 * event name, then filter out some listeners based on application-
```

```
* specific logic, then signal the event with the selected list of
* listeners.
*/
 public static void main(String [] args) {
   try {
     //for a stand-alone program, a stand-alone session has to be started
           ServletSessionManager.startStandAloneSession("JTF", false,
                                   "SYSADMIN","SYSADMIN");
     System.out.println("=================================");
   } catch (Exception e) {
     e.printStackTrace();
   }
   String eventName = "oracle.crm.oso.NEW_SALES_LEAD_EVENT";
   //construct the event object
   LeadInfo leadInfo = new LeadInfo("John", "500 Oracle parkway",
                                   "650-506-6789");
   Param param = null;
   try {
     // When using this Param constructor, it is recommended to use
     // "variable.getClass()" instead of "type.class". (in the case of
     // array, java.lang.reflect.Array will not return the correct
     // class of the variable)
     param = new Param("lead", leadInfo.getClass(), leadInfo);
   } catch (ClassNotMatchException e) {
     //This exception is thrown when the parameter type and the value
     //don't match.
     //For example, Param("example", String.class, 3) will cause
     // ClassNotMatchException.
   }

   try {
     //get all the listener logical names of this event
     String [] listeners = Client.getListeners(eventName);
     String [] selectedListeners = new String [5];
     //filter out some listeners based on application-specific logic.
     // putall selected listener logical names in variable
     //"selectedListeners"
     //......
     //the event is triggered and the event object is sent to all
     //selected listeners
     Client.signalEvent(eventName, selectedListeners, param);
   } catch (InvocationException e) {
     //if the event name is not registered, or not configured properly,
     //or the system can not launch threads to call the listeners, an
     //InvocationExcption is thrown. Because the invocation of a
     //listener is done asynchronously at a spawned new thread, no
     //InvocationException will be thrown even if errors happen in the
     //invocation.
     int errorCode = e.getErrorCode();
     System.out.println(errcode);
     System.out.println(e.getMessage());
```

```
    }
    try{
        System.out.println("=================================");
        //close the session
        ServletSessionManager.endStandAloneSession();
    }
    catch (Exception e) {
        e.printStackTrace();
    }
  }
}
```

Services That Are Event Subscribers

Since an event subscriber is a normal XML service and is invoked in the same manner as any other service, all guidelines related to creating a service apply to writing event subscribers.

Deploying a New Service

A number of sample services are included as part of XML Services. We will use the Address Book sample to illustrate all the steps that you must follow in order to deploy and execute a new service.

Here is the Java code for the AddressBook sample:

```
package samples.server.addressbook;
import samples.client.addressbook.*;
import java.util.*;
import java.io.*;
import org.w3c.dom.*;
import org.apache.soap.util.xml.*;
import oracle.soap.util.xml.XmlUtils;
/**
 * See \samples\addressbook\readme for info.
 * Samples assume that variable JTFLogFile is set
 *
 */
public class AddressBook
{
  private static String XML_HOME_VAR = "XML_SERVICE_HOME";
  private static String hashFileName = "hashFile.txt";
  private Hashtable name2AddressTable = new Hashtable();

  private File hashFile = null;

  public AddressBook()
```

```java
{
  // Load Hashtable file
  hashFile = new File(hashFileName);

  addEntry("John B. Good",
          new Address(123, "Main Street", "Anytown", "NY", 12345,
                      new PhoneNumber(123, "456", "7890")));
  addEntry("Bob Q. Public",
          new Address(456, "North Whatever", "Notown", "ME", 12424,
                      new PhoneNumber(987, "444", "5566")));
  try {
      FileInputStream istream = new FileInputStream(hashFile);
      ObjectInputStream p = new ObjectInputStream(istream);
      name2AddressTable = (Hashtable) p.readObject();
      istream.close();
  } catch (EOFException e) {
      name2AddressTable = new Hashtable();
  } catch (Exception e) {
      e.printStackTrace();
  }
}

private void flushHashtable() {
  try {
      FileOutputStream ostream = new FileOutputStream(hashFile);
      ObjectOutputStream p2 = new ObjectOutputStream(ostream);
      p2.writeObject(name2AddressTable);
      p2.flush();
      ostream.close();
    } catch (Exception e) {
      e.printStackTrace();
  }
}

public void addEntry(String name, Address address)
{
  // Put it in hashtable in memory
  name2AddressTable.put(name, address);
  flushHashtable();
}

public Address getAddressFromName(String name)
throws IllegalArgumentException
{
  if (name == null)
  {
    throw new
    IllegalArgumentException("The name argument must not be " +"null.");
  }
  return (Address)name2AddressTable.get(name);
}
```

```java
public Element getAllListings()
{
  Document doc = null;
  try {
    doc = XmlUtils.createDocument();
  } catch (Exception e) {
    e.printStackTrace();
    System.err.println("Error in creating xml document.");
    return null;
  }

  Element bookEl = doc.createElement("AddressBook");
  bookEl.appendChild(doc.createTextNode("\n"));
  for (Enumeration keys = name2AddressTable.keys();
       keys.hasMoreElements();)
  {
    String name = (String)keys.nextElement();
    Address address = (Address)name2AddressTable.get(name);
    Element listingEl = doc.createElement("Listing");
    Element nameEl = doc.createElement("Name");
    nameEl.appendChild(doc.createTextNode(name));
    listingEl.appendChild(doc.createTextNode("\n    "));
    listingEl.appendChild(nameEl);
    listingEl.appendChild(doc.createTextNode("\n    "));
    Element addressEl = doc.createElement("Address");
    Element streetNumEl = doc.createElement("StreetNum");
    streetNumEl.appendChild(
        doc.createTextNode(address.getStreetNum() + ""));
    addressEl.appendChild(doc.createTextNode("\n      "));
    addressEl.appendChild(streetNumEl);
    addressEl.appendChild(doc.createTextNode("\n      "));
    Element streetNameEl = doc.createElement("StreetName");
    streetNameEl.appendChild
               (doc.createTextNode(address.getStreetName()));
    addressEl.appendChild(streetNameEl);
    addressEl.appendChild(doc.createTextNode("\n      "));
    Element cityEl = doc.createElement("City");
    cityEl.appendChild(doc.createTextNode(address.getCity()));
    addressEl.appendChild(cityEl);
    addressEl.appendChild(doc.createTextNode("\n      "));
    Element stateEl = doc.createElement("State");
    stateEl.appendChild(doc.createTextNode(address.getState()));
    addressEl.appendChild(stateEl);
    addressEl.appendChild(doc.createTextNode("\n      "));
    Element zipEl = doc.createElement("Zip");
    zipEl.appendChild(doc.createTextNode(address.getZip() + ""));
    addressEl.appendChild(zipEl);
    addressEl.appendChild(doc.createTextNode("\n      "));
    PhoneNumber phone = address.getPhoneNumber();
    Element phoneEl = doc.createElement("PhoneNumber");
```

```
      phoneEl.appendChild(doc.createTextNode("\n           "));
      Element areaCodeEl = doc.createElement("AreaCode");
      areaCodeEl.appendChild
                      (doc.createTextNode(phone.getAreaCode() + ""));
      phoneEl.appendChild(areaCodeEl);
      phoneEl.appendChild(doc.createTextNode("\n           "));
      Element exchangeEl = doc.createElement("Exchange");
      exchangeEl.appendChild(doc.createTextNode(phone.getExchange()));
      phoneEl.appendChild(exchangeEl);
      phoneEl.appendChild(doc.createTextNode("\n           "));
      Element numberEl = doc.createElement("Number");
      numberEl.appendChild(doc.createTextNode(phone.getNumber()));
      phoneEl.appendChild(numberEl);
      phoneEl.appendChild(doc.createTextNode("\n         "));
      addressEl.appendChild(phoneEl);
      addressEl.appendChild(doc.createTextNode("\n       "));
      listingEl.appendChild(addressEl);
      listingEl.appendChild(doc.createTextNode("\n   "));
      bookEl.appendChild(doc.createTextNode("   "));
      bookEl.appendChild(listingEl);
      bookEl.appendChild(doc.createTextNode("\n"));
    }
    return bookEl;
  }
  public int putListings(Element el)
  {
    Element listingEl = DOMUtils.getFirstChildElement(el);
    int count = 0;

    while (listingEl != null)
    {
      String name = null;
      int    streetNum = 0;
      String streetName = "";
      String city = "";
      String state = "";
      int    zip = 0;
      int    areaCode = 0;
      String exchange = "";
      String number = "";

      Element tempEl = DOMUtils.getFirstChildElement(listingEl);
      while (tempEl != null)
      {
        String tagName = tempEl.getTagName();
        if (tagName.equals("Name"))
        {
          name = DOMUtils.getChildCharacterData(tempEl);
        }
        else if (tagName.equals("Address"))
        {
```

```
Element tempEl2 = DOMUtils.getFirstChildElement(tempEl);
while (tempEl2 != null)
{
  String tagName2 = tempEl2.getTagName();
  String content2 = DOMUtils.getChildCharacterData(tempEl2);
  if (tagName2.equals("StreetNum"))
  {
    streetNum = Integer.parseInt(content2);
  }
  else if (tagName2.equals("StreetName"))
  {
    streetName = content2;
  }
  else if (tagName2.equals("City"))
  {
    city = content2;
  }
  else if (tagName2.equals("State"))
  {
    state = content2;
  }
  else if (tagName2.equals("Zip"))
  {
    zip = Integer.parseInt(content2);
  }
  else if (tagName2.equals("City"))
  {
    city = content2;
  }
  else if (tagName2.equals("PhoneNumber"))
  {
    Element tempEl3 = DOMUtils.getFirstChildElement(tempEl2)
    while (tempEl3 != null)
    {
      String tagName3 = tempEl3.getTagName();
      String content3 =
                   DOMUtils.getChildCharacterData(tempEl3);
      if (tagName3.equals("AreaCode"))
      {
        areaCode = Integer.parseInt(content3);
      }
      else if (tagName3.equals("Exchange"))
      {
        exchange = content3;
      }
      else if (tagName3.equals("Number"))
      {
        number = content3;
      }
      tempEl3 = DOMUtils.getNextSiblingElement(tempEl3);
    }
```

```
        }
          tempEl2 = DOMUtils.getNextSiblingElement(tempEl2);
        }
      }
      tempEl = DOMUtils.getNextSiblingElement(tempEl);
    }
    if (name != null)
    {
      Address address = new Address(streetNum, streetName, city, state,
                                zip, new PhoneNumber(areaCode,
                                                     exchange,
                                                     number));

      addEntry(name, address);
      count++;
    }
    listingEl = DOMUtils.getNextSiblingElement(listingEl);
  }
  return count;
  }
}
```

Here are the Java classes for the **Address** object that is used as a parameter to
AddressBook methods that will be exposed as XML services:

```
public class Address {
    private int        streetNum;
    private String     streetName;
    private String     city;
    private String     state;
    private int        zip;
    private PhoneNumber phoneNumber;
    // constructors and get and set methods not shown
}

public class PhoneNumber {
    private int    areaCode;
    private String exchange;
    private String number;
    // constructors and get and set methods not shown
}
```

To expose the AddressBook methods as XML services, you need to register a
new service group into the XML infrastructure. First, you have to make sure that the
samples directory with the AddressBook source code is in the jserv classpath. After
you compile the AddressBook code, you are ready to deploy the services. We are
assuming that you have the Oracle application instance and XML Services component
already installed and ready to use. To deploy the new services, go to the Oracle E-
Business center, as shown in Figure 7-1, and log in as sysadmin.

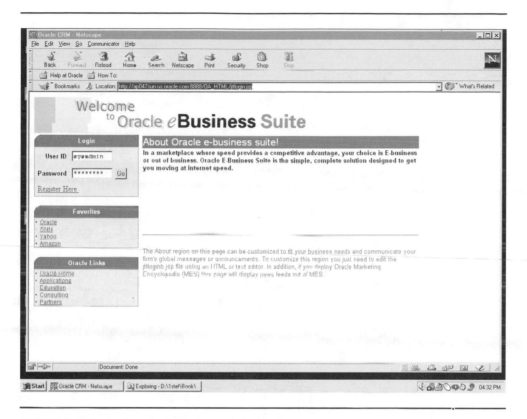

FIGURE 7-1. *Oracle E-Business Suite login page*

After logging in, you will see the page that is shown in Figure 7-2. The XML Services tab will take you to the XML Services administrative pages. As you can see from Figure 7-2, there are four subtabs that you can use to manage services, invocations, events, and authentications.

We are going to register a new service group. To do this, we must select the Services subtab, as shown in Figure 7-2. As you can see from Figure 7-2, the Services page can be used to list, add, and remove service groups. The service groups are listed by application. The service group name is constructed such that there is no name conflict between services belonging to different applications. The full service group name consists of a service group prefix, an application name, and a service group name separated by dots. To deploy a new service group, you must click Create. To remove a service or change the service group prefix, you must click

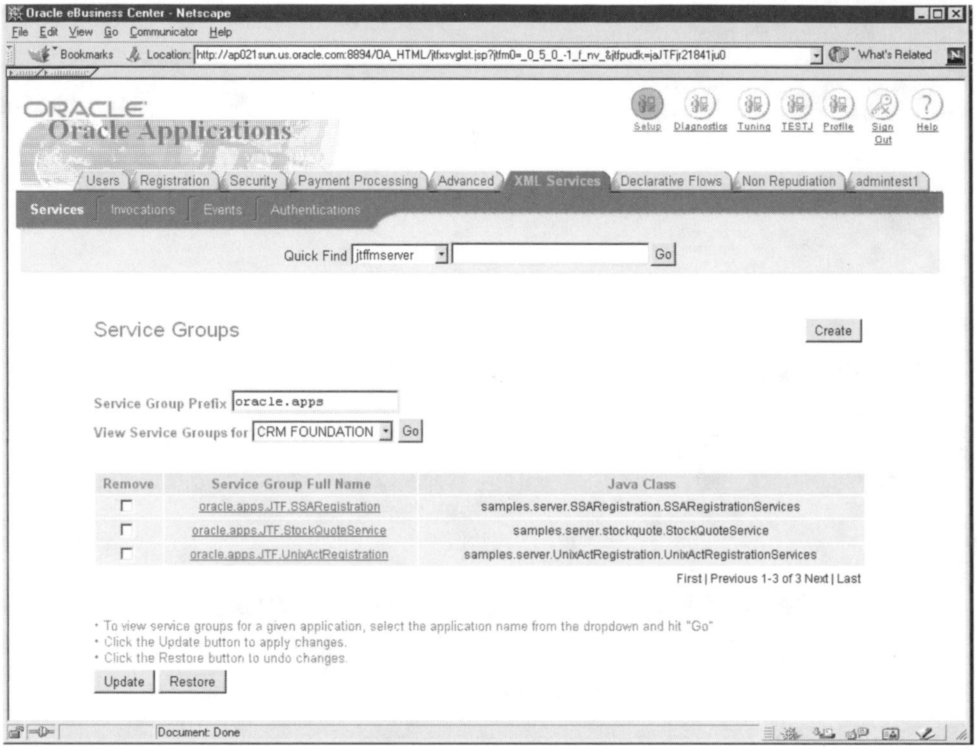

FIGURE 7-2. *XML Services page*

Update. After you choose to create a service group, you will be taken to a page that is used to deploy a Java class as new service group. This page is shown on Figure 7-3.

As shown in Figure 7-3, you can enter AddressBook as name for the service group. Taking into account the service group prefix, the fully qualified name for the service group will be oracle.apps.JTF.AddressBook (JTF is the three-letter abbreviated name for the CRM Foundation). You must use that same group name later when creating invocation records for services from this group. The Java class that implements this service group is **samples.server.addressbook.AddressBook**, and you must enter this name in Java Class entry field. You can also enter a short description about the newly defined service group. Now you are ready to move to the next step in deploying this service group by clicking Scan Class. This will lead you to the page. The Create Service Group page will gather all the information from you that is needed to fully describe the new service group. The screen on Figure 7-4 shows the first half of this page.

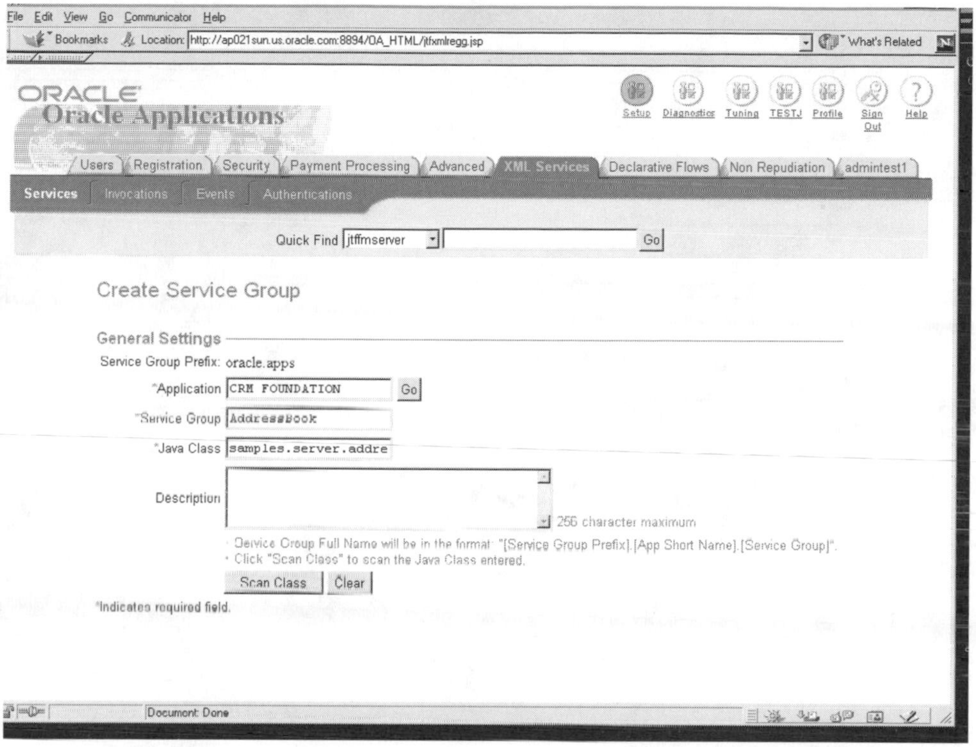

FIGURE 7-3. *Create a new service group*

As you can see, the four public methods from **AddressBook.java** are shown as possible candidates for services in this service group. You can enable these services by clicking the Enable check box. The methods that are not enabled as services will not be available and can't be executed as services. At any time, you can use the page from Figure 7-2 to list all service groups per CRM application. By clicking the service group name, you will be taken to the Service Update page, which is very similar to the one shown in Figure 7-4. There you can disable the services that are not needed in this particular installation. After you've selected the methods that will become services, the next step is to register the type mappings for all of the parameters that the newly added services will use. The **addEntry** method uses the **Address** class as input parameter. The **Address** class uses the **PhoneNumber** class. You must define type mappings for all nonprimitive Java classes exchanged as parameters. Therefore, you must define type mappings for these two classes. There are two other parameters: **String** is the input parameter for **getAddressFromName**, and **org.w3c.doc.Element** is

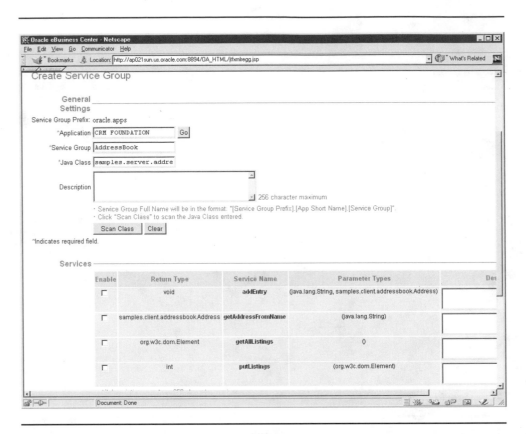

FIGURE 7-4. *Selecting services as part of a service group*

the input parameter for **putListing** and the return parameter for **getAllListings**. XML services use the default SOAP encoding for all primitive Java types, and you do not need to define encoding for it. **org.w3c.doc.Element** is a special case when used as a parameter to XML services. To allow XML services to get access to arbitrary XML data, which must be handled without any change by your service (Java method), there is a special encoding type, named XML Encoding. By using XML Encoding for parameters that are XML elements in the body of the SOAP request, you assure that these parameters are passed as org.w3c.dom.Element object to your Java methods. For example, the method **putListing** takes **org.w3c.dom.Element** as its single parameter. See the iSOAP example that is included in this chapter for putListing service as a good illustration of how to pass custom XML data to a service. You can go back to the source code for **AddressBook.java** and look at the **putListing** method to see how **putListing** handles the address list to retrieve the address information.

```
POST /soap/servlet/soaprouter HTTP/1.0
Host: 130.35.57.119
content-type: text/xml
user-agent: Oracle-Soap-Client/1.0 HTTP/1.0
soapaction: ""
Content-Length: 1362


<SOAP-ENV:Envelope xmlns:xsi="http://www.w3.org/1999/XMLSchema-instance"
xmlns:xsd="http://www.w3.org/1999/XMLSchema" xmlns:SOAP-
ENV="http://schemas.xmlsoap.org/soap/envelope/">

<SOAP-ENV:Header>
<AuthenticationType="1">
        <UserName>sysadmin</UserName><PassWD>sysadmin</PassWD>
</Authentication>
</SOAP-ENV:Header>
<SOAP-ENV:Body>
<ns1:putListings xmlns:ns1="oracle.apps.JTF.AddressBook" SOAP-
ENV:encodingStyle="http://schemas.xmlsoap.org/soap/encoding/">
<XMLDoc
        SOAP-ENV:encodingStyle="http://xml.apache.org/xml-soap/literalxml">
<AddressBook>
  <Listing>
    <Name>Mary Smith</Name>
    <Address>
      <StreetNum>888</StreetNum>
      <StreetName>Broadway</StreetName>
      <City>Somewhere</City>
      <State>FL</State>
      <Zip>07654</Zip>
      <PhoneNumber>
        <AreaCode>222</AreaCode>
        <Exchange>333</Exchange>
        <Number>4444</Number>
      </PhoneNumber>
    </Address>
  </Listing>
  <Listing>
    <Name>Dave Davis</Name>
    <Address>
      <StreetNum>919</StreetNum>
      <StreetName>Baker Lane</StreetName>
      <City>Sunnytown</City>
      <State>UT</State>
      <Zip>43434</Zip>
      <PhoneNumber>
        <AreaCode>789</AreaCode>
        <Exchange>654</Exchange>
        <Number>3210</Number>
```

```
      </PhoneNumber>
    </Address>
  </Listing>
</AddressBook>
</XMLDoc>
</ns1:putListings>
</SOAP-ENV:Body>
</SOAP-ENV:Envelope>


HTTP/1.1 200 OK
Date: Thu, 24 May 2001 21:43:18 GMT
Server: Apache/1.3.9 (Unix) ApacheJServ/1.1
Set-Cookie: JServSessionIdsoap=t53nsgi63c.j1; path=/
Set-Cookie: crmdev07_etftech=E6E42E5131C13A1F; domain=.oracle.com; path=/
Set-Cookie: crmdev07_etftech=-1; domain=.oracle.com; path=/
Set-Cookie:
ses=202EDDEEC14477F632A4148902C07038EC21642401E2F42E194B705147F0CFA286639FFD
3C5DF18E06C88901701CF2F55CC755C73CCEB85F68E8950CBF3B;
expires=Mon, 23-Jul-2001 21:43:19 GMT; domain=.oracle.com; path=/
Content-Length: 429
Connection: close
Content-Type: text/xml; charset=UTF-8


<SOAP-ENV:Envelope xmlns:SOAP-
ENV="http://schemas.xmlsoap.org/soap/envelope/"
xmlns:xsi="http://www.w3.org/1999/XMLSchema-instance"
xmlns:xsd="http://www.w3.org/1999/XMLSchema">
<SOAP-ENV:Body>
<ns1:putListingsResponse xmlns:ns1="oracle.apps.JTF.AddressBook" SOAP-
ENV:encodingStyle="http://schemas.xmlsoap.org/soap/encoding/">
<return xsi:type="xsd:int">2</return>
</ns1:putListingsResponse>
</SOAP-ENV:Body>
</SOAP-ENV:Envelope>
```

XML Services uses XML encoding as the default encoding for **org.w3c.doc.Element**
Java types, so you don't need to specify encoding for the **org.w3c.doc.Element**
parameter. Figure 7-5 shows the encoding selection of the Add New Service page
for parameters used in the AddressBook service group.

After you enter the type mappings (or select the defaults, as in this example),
click Create to deploy the newly created service group into the XML Services
repository. The services that you just registered can be used in two modes: local
mode and remote mode. To perform local service invocations, you must create an
invocation record and select "localhost" as the authentication profile. If you want to
perform remote service invocation that is SOAP based and uses XML messaging for
service invocation, you must create an authentication profile and an invocation
record. The local mode can be selected when the Java client runs on the same

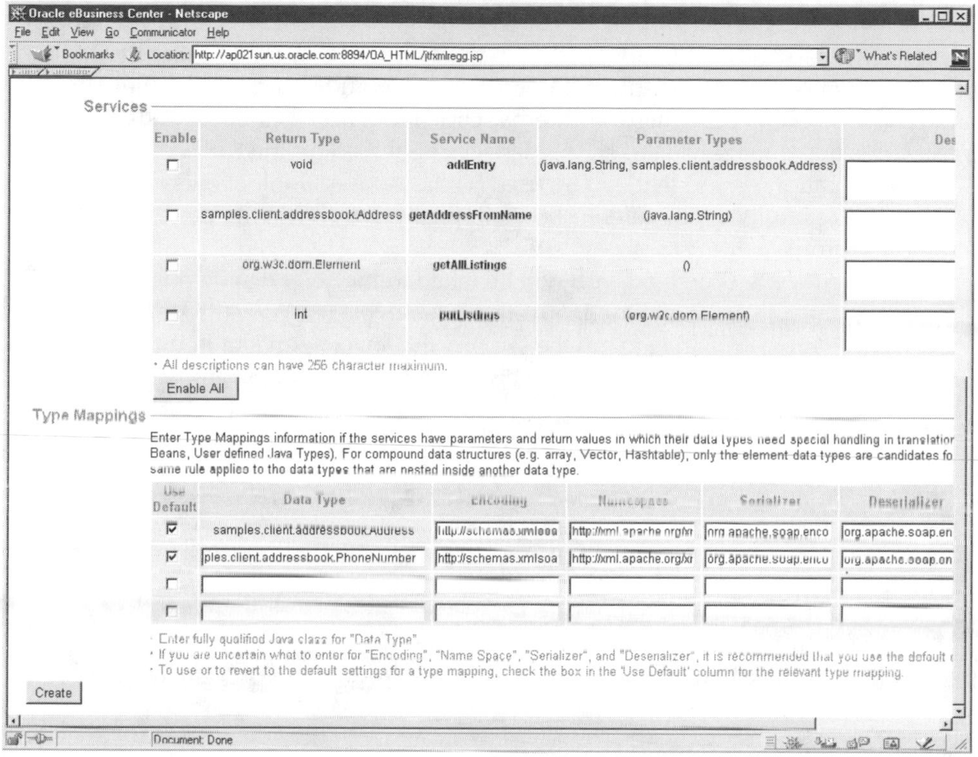

FIGURE 7-5. *Selecting type mapping for parameters*

instance of the E-Business Suite. In this case, the service call does not use SOAP and the service invocation is performed as a local Java call. This results in very efficient service invocation. The local mode is an important feature of the XML Services framework. The framework can be used to deploy interface services. In this way, all applications are built independently and interact with other applications by using interface services (or key integration points) exposed by the applications. When the applications run on the same local instance, the performance will be very good, since every service call is equal to a Java method call. At the same time, since interapplication dependencies are in the form of service invocations and services, any application can be replaced with a third-party application by just reimplementing the services that the old application exposes to others for use. Furthermore, the new application can be deployed over the Internet on a different URL; this will just require rewiring the service invocation records to point to the new URL, where the replacement services are deployed.

Creating an Authentication Profile

No external services can be invoked from the E-Business instance using the XML Services client APIs without using a reference to the authentication profile. The authentication profile defines the external URL and a list of valid user IDs and passwords that can be used to access services deployed on this URL. Let's create an authentication profile that can be used by the AddressBook clients to access AddressBook services. The screen shown in Figure 7-6 shows the page used to create the profile.

After the profile is created, you will be taken to the screen shown in Figure 7-7. This screen lists all available authentication profiles.

The last step in preparing to run the samples that invoke services in the AddressBook service group is to create invocations for each of the services in the group.

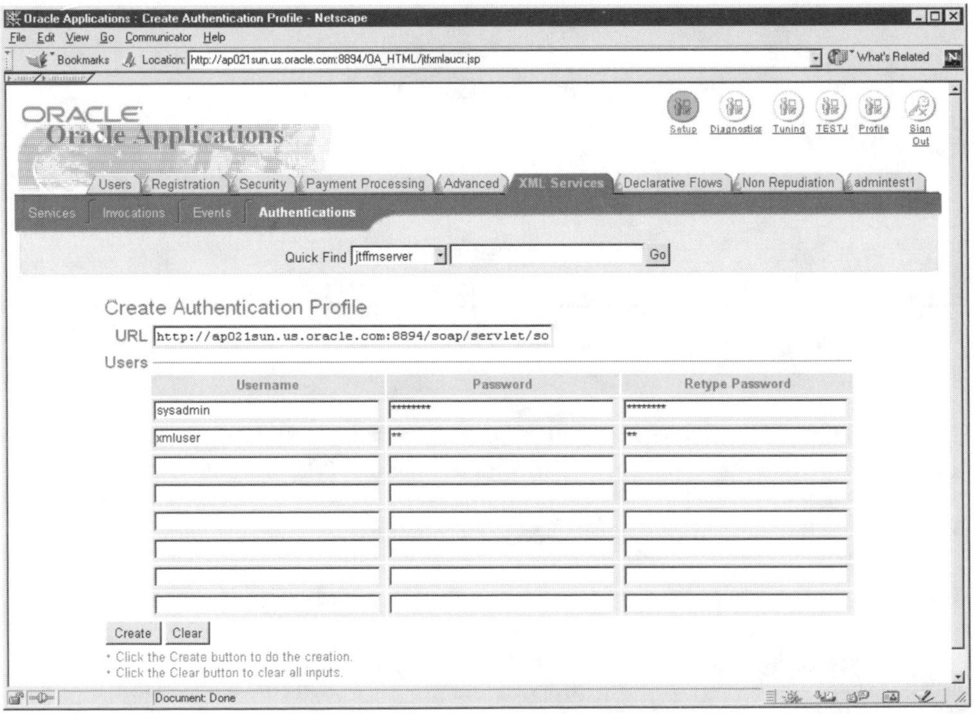

FIGURE 7-6. *Creating an authentication profile*

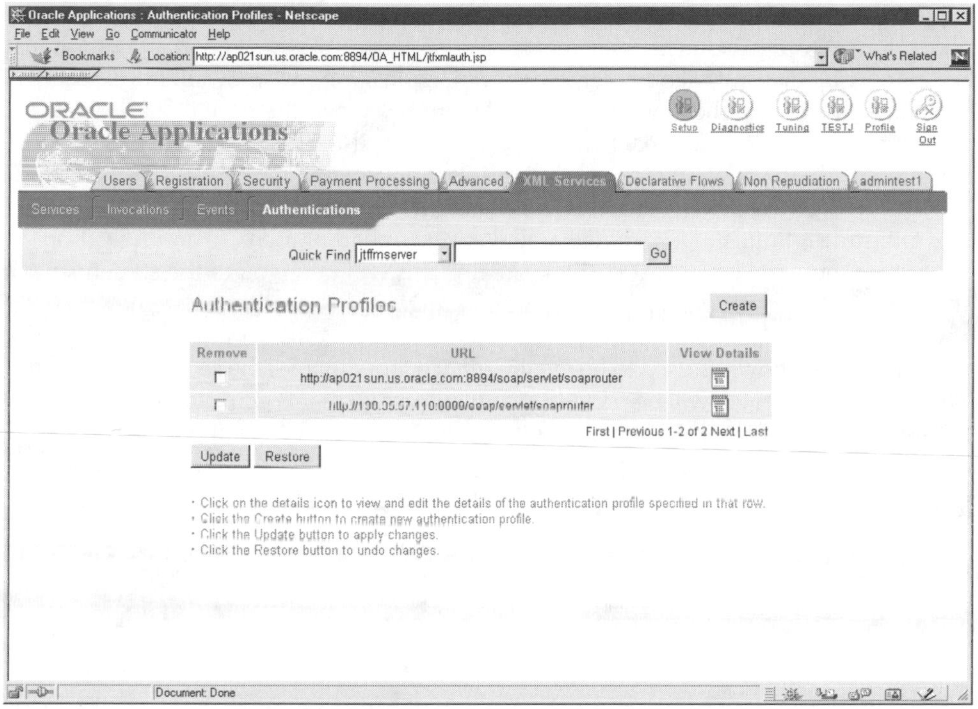

FIGURE 7-7. *Authentication profiles*

Creating an Invocation Record

As we mentioned before, when your application invokes a service using the XML
Services client API, you must specify two parameters: a logical service name string and
a Vector that contains Params objects for each of the parameters you are passing to the
service. (A Param object holds Java objects together with the Java object type and name
and is used as a parameter wrapper.) You don't specify any information about where the
service is, what the service name is, or what authentication information is needed to
invoke the service. All this information is stored in the service invocation record. The
logical service name string is simply the key to the service invocation record. This
record contains all of the information that the XML Services infrastructure needs at run
time to invoke the service. The run-time binding is very useful. The application code
does not specify service endpoint details but deals with logical aspects of service

invocation only. What is more important, the services can be easily replaced with equivalent services (services with the same calling signature) by just changing the invocation record to point to a different service provider. Another important point is that if we know all the invocation points for a given application, we know all the external interfaces that this application depends on. Figure 7-8 shows the page that is used to manage service invocation records. This page shows a list of all invocation records in the system. The invocation records are listed per application.

The AddressBook service group exposes four services: GetAddressFromName, GetAllListings, PutListing, and getName. Let's go ahead and create an invocation record for the getName service. Click Create. This will take you to the screen shown in Figure 7-9. This screen is the first part of a page that is used to create new invocation records.

The screen shown is used to define the service group name, the service name, the URL where the service will be provided, and the user ID that is going to be used when accessing the service. The password for this user ID is kept in the authentication profile.

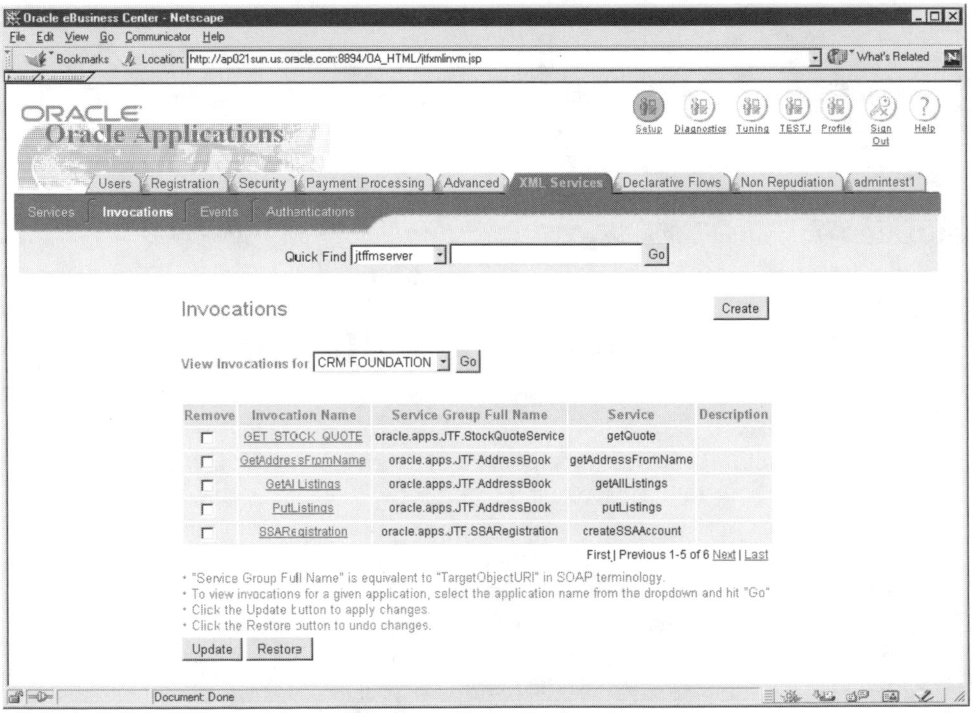

FIGURE 7-8. *List of all invocations for CRM Foundation*

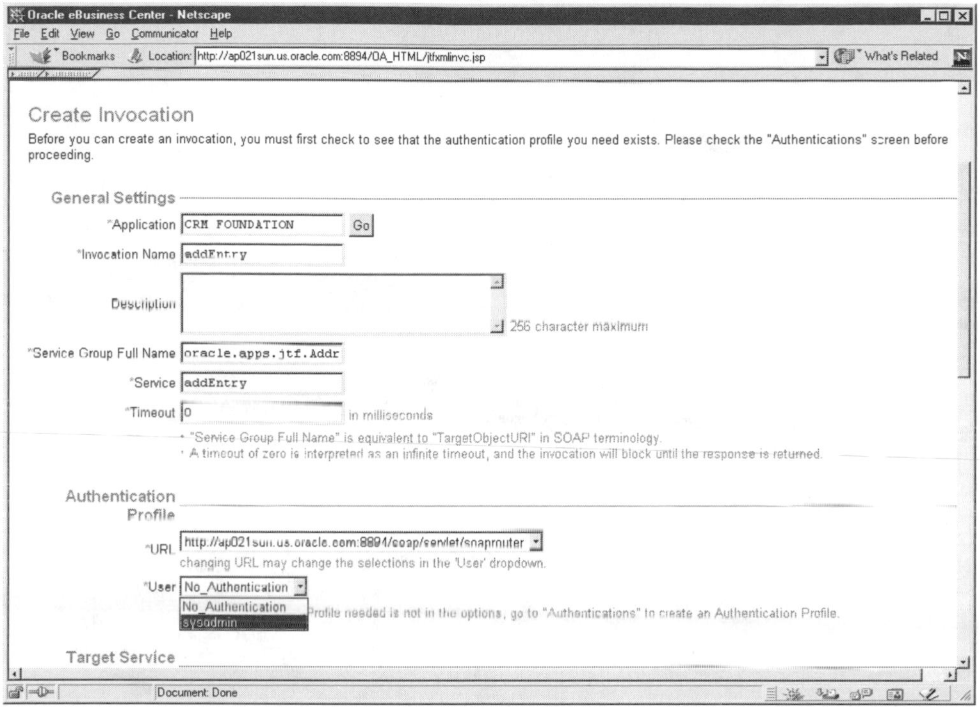

FIGURE 7-9.   *Create Invocation—Part 1*

The screen shown in Figure 7-10 shows the second part of the invocation page. You must enter all parameter names and Java types that are going to be passed to the addEntry service in the Target Service Signature table. In addition, the return data type and the encoding of the return object must also be specified. The Type Mapping table tells the CRM SOAP client how to convert the Java types that are passed as parameters to XML. The default type mapping that you select uses SOAP encoding and the standard SOAP serializer and deserializer class called BeanSerializer. This class will be used to convert your parameters from Java to XML and from XML to Java.

Running a Sample Service

We just deployed the AddressBook service group. There are four services in this group. We also created an invocation record for one of the services. You must

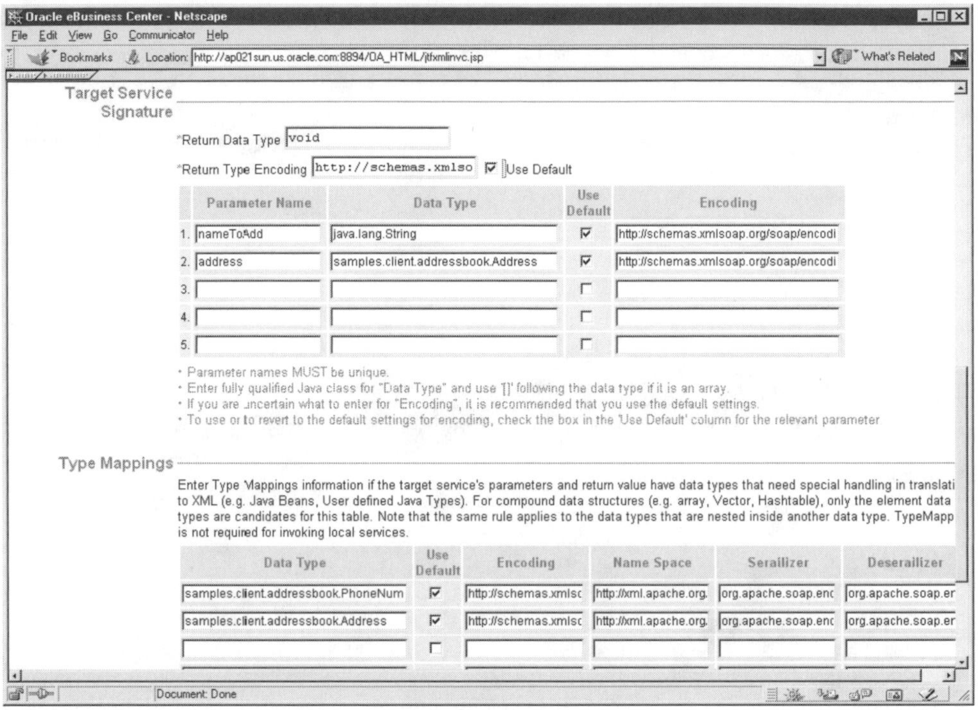

FIGURE 7-10. *Create Invocation—Part 2*

create invocation records for all of the samples before running the samples. There is a readme file for each sample that tells you exactly what parameters you must use when creating the invocation records. Finally, we are now ready to invoke the addEntry service. Here is the Java sample that invokes the addEntry service:

```
package samples.client.addressbook;
// Include the XML Service Infrastructure client API
import oracle.apps.jtf.services.invocation.*;
import oracle.apps.jtf.base.session.*;
import java.io.*;
import java.util.*;
import java.net.*;
import org.w3c.dom.*;
import org.apache.soap.util.xml.*;
import org.apache.soap.*;
import org.apache.soap.encoding.*;
import org.apache.soap.encoding.soapenc.*;
```

```java
import org.apache.soap.rpc.*;

/**
 * Put a new address into the address book.
 *
 */


public class PutAddress
{
  public static void main(String[] args) throws Exception
  {
    if (args.length != 9)
    {
      System.err.println("Usage:");
      System.err.println("  java " + PutAddress.class.getName() +
                         " name streetNumber " +
                         "streetName city state zip areaCode " +
                         "exchange number");
      System.exit (1);
    }
    // Start JTF session to access registered invocation
    ServletSessionManager.startStandAloneSession("JTF", false, "SYSADMIN"
                                                 "SYSADMIN");


    // process the arguments
    String nameToRegister = args[0];
    PhoneNumber phoneNumber = new PhoneNumber(
    Integer.parseInt(args[6]), args[7], args[8]);
    Address address = new Address(Integer.parseInt(args[1]),
                                  args[2],
                                  args[3],
                                  args[4],
                                  Integer.parseInt(args[5]),
                                  phoneNumber);

    // Build argument vector
    Vector params = new Vector();
    params.addElement(new Param("nameToRegister", String.class,
                                nameToRegister));
    params.addElement(new Param("address", Address.class,
                                address));

    ServiceResult result = null;
    try {
      // Execute the call
      result = Client.callService("AddEntry", params);
    }
    catch (Exception e) {
        System.out.println("Error occur in invocation AddEntry");
```

```
        e.printStackTrace();
        return;
    }

  System.out.println("Entry is added successfully");

   // End JTF session
   ServletSessionManager.endStandAloneSession();
  }
}
```

Figure 7-11 shows the command that we used to run the sample.

Tunnel is a sample port tracing application that comes with Oracle SOAP. We used a slightly modified version of this application to monitor and capture the data exchanged between the SOAP client and the SOAP server. You can see the Tunnel source if you download the SOAP source code from http://xml.apache.org. Figure 7-12 shows the request message that our PutAddress sample sent to the XML Services SOAP server. Figure 7-13 shows the response message.

Following the addEntry sample, here are the steps that take place:

1. The application invokes the service using the XML Services API in Java. The application supplies the invocation name along with the list of parameters to invoke the service.

2. XML Services looks up invocation metadata and calls the SOAP server API with the endpoint information and the parameter list supplied by the application. Besides endpoint information (URL, service group name [class], service name [method]), the metadata also includes authentication information (username/password). This information is also part of the SOAP message.

3. The SOAP server marshals the Java parameters data into a SOAP request message.

```
(skiritzo) addressbook- java ${JAXP} ${JTFDBCFILE} ${FWLogFile} ${JTFLogFile} s
amples.client.addressbook.PutAddress "John Doe" 123 "Main Street" AnyTown SS 12
345 800 555 1212
Entry is added successfully
(skiritzo) addressbook- █
```

FIGURE 7-11. *Running the PutAddress sample*

4. The SOAP server sends the SOAP message through the transport adapter.

5. The SOAP server at the receiver gets the SOAP message from the transport protocol.

6. This SOAP server unmarshals the message and calls the XML Services service provider, supplying the authentication information, the service group name (class), the service name (method), and the list of parameters to it.

FIGURE 7-12.   *The addEntry SOAP service request message*

7. The XML Services service provider looks up the services metadata (including the invoker credential) and invokes the service if the invoker is authorized to do so.

8. Reply process flow follows the same steps.

Invocation and Event APIs

This section contains the Java APIs that application developers use to invoke XML services and signal events using the XML Services framework.

Class oracle.apps.jtf.services.invocation.Client

```
public class Client extends Object
```

This class contains the APIs for the application developers to call a service or signal an event.

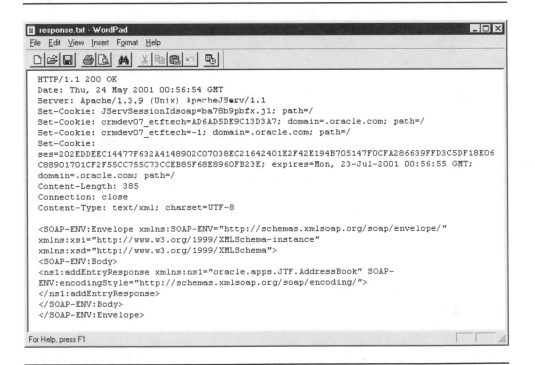

FIGURE 7-13. *The addEntry SOAP service response message*

Constructors

Client

Public Client()

Methods

callService

public static ServiceResult callService(String SLN, Vector params) throws InvocationException

Call a service using the service logical name.

Parameters: String SLN: service logical name. This logical name is dynamically bound at run time to the metadata (server URL, service group ID, service ID, user ID, password, etc.) needed for a service invocation. All this metadata is stored as an invocation record. The service logical name is used to retrieve the invocation record that holds all information needed to invoke the service.
     Vector params: a Vector of Param objects. Each one contains the name, data type, and value of one of the parameters passed to the service.
Returns:
     ServiceResult: the return object of the service execution

Throws: InvocationException

signalEvent

public static void signalEvent(String eventName, Param eventObj) throws InvocationException

Signal an event using the event name. All associated event listeners (services) are invoked asynchronously.

Parameters: String eventName: event name. From this name, all its associated listeners are dynamically located.
     Param eventObject: the parameter to be passed to the event listeners
Returns:
     void

Throws: InvocationException when the event name is not registered or XML Services infrastructure is failing to spawn threads for the listener invocation

getListeners

```
public static String[] getListeners(String eventName)
```

Get the list of listeners' logical names associated with a given event name.

Parameters: String eventName: name of the event
Returns:
     String []: listeners' logical names. If the event name is not registered, return null. If no listener is registered with the event name, return an empty array.

signalEvent

```
public static void signalEvent(String eventName, String
selectedListeners[], Param eventObj) throws InvocationException
```

Signal an event using the event name. An associated event listener (service) is invoked asynchronously if it is also in the list of listeners passed in.

Parameters: String eventName: event name. From this name, all its associated listeners are dynamically located.
     String [] listeners: a list of listener logical names
     Param eventObject: the parameter to be passed to the event listeners
Returns:
     void

Throws: InvocationException when the event name is not registered or the call fails to spawn threads for the listener invocation

Class oracle.apps.jtf.services.invocation.Param

```
public class Param extends Object
```

To call a service or signal an event, a Param object has to be constructed for every parameter to pass. The parameter name, the data type and the value of the parameter are stored in the Param class.

Constructors

Param

```
public Param(String name, Class type, Object value) throws
ClassNotMatchException
```

Parameters: String name: parameter name
Class type: data type
Object value: value of the parameter

Throws: ClassNotMatchException if the parameter value object is not
assignment-compatible with the parameter type
See the XML Services Java documentation for more constructors for the
Param object.

Methods

getName

```
public String getName()
```

Get the parameter name.
Returns:
String: parameter name

setName

```
public void setName(String name)
```

Set the parameter name.

Parameters: String name: parameter name

getType

```
public Class getType()
```

Get the data type.
Returns:
Class: data type

getObject

```
public Object getObject()
```

Get the parameter value.
Returns:
getBoolean

`public boolean getBoolean()`

> Get the parameter value.
> Returns:
>   boolean: parameter value

getInt

 `public int getInt()`

> Get the parameter value.
> Returns:
>   int: parameter value

getByte

 `public byte getByte()`

> Get the parameter value.
> Returns:
>   byte: parameter value

getChar

 `public char getChar()`

> Get the parameter value.
> Returns:
>   char: parameter value

getDouble

 `public double getDouble()`

> Get the parameter value.
> Returns:
>   double: parameter value

getFloat

 `public float getFloat()`

> Get the parameter value.

Returns:
    float: parameter value

getLong

```
public long getLong()
```

Get the parameter value.
Returns:
    long: parameter value

getShort

```
public short getShort()
```

Get the parameter value.
Returns:
    short: parameter value

setObject

```
public void setObject(Object value) throws ClassNotMatchException
```

Set the parameter value.

Parameters: Object value: parameter value

Throws: ClassNotMatchException if the parameter value object is not assignment-compatible with the parameter type

setBoolean

```
public void setBoolean(boolean value) throws ClassNotMatchException
```

Set the parameter value.

Parameters: boolean value: parameter value

Throws: ClassNotMatchException if the parameter type is not boolean

setInt

```
public void setInt(int value) throws ClassNotMatchException
```

Set the parameter value.

Parameters: int value: parameter value

Throws: ClassNotMatchException if the parameter type is not int

setByte

```
public void setByte(byte value) throws ClassNotMatchException
```

Set the parameter value.

Parameters: byte value: parameter value

Throws: ClassNotMatchException if the parameter type is not byte

setChar

```
public void setChar(char value) throws ClassNotMatchException
```

Set the parameter value.

Parameters: char value: parameter value

Throws: ClassNotMatchException if the parameter type is not char

setDouble

```
public void setDouble(double value) throws ClassNotMatchException
```

Set the parameter value.

Parameters: double value: parameter value

Throws: ClassNotMatchException if the parameter type is not double

setFloat

```
public void setFloat(float value) throws ClassNotMatchException
```

Set the parameter value.

Parameters: float value: parameter value

Throws: ClassNotMatchException if the parameter type is not float

setLong

```
public void setLong(long value) throws ClassNotMatchException
```

Set the parameter value.

Parameters: long value: parameter value

Throws: ClassNotMatchException if the parameter type is not long

setShort

```
public void setShort(short value) throws ClassNotMatchException
```

Set the parameter value.

Parameters: short value: parameter value

Throws: ClassNotMatchException if the parameter type is not short

Class oracle.apps.jtf.services. invocation.ServiceResult;

Constructors

ServiceResult

```
public ServiceResult(Class type, Object returnValue)
```

Methods

getBoolean

```
public boolean getBoolean()
```

Get the return value.
Returns:
boolean: return value

getByte

```
public byte getByte()
```

> Get the return value.
> Returns:
> byte: return value

getChar

```
public char getChar()
```

> Get the return value.
> Returns:
> char: return value

getDouble

```
public double getDouble()
```

> Get the return value.
> Returns:
> double: return value

getFloat

```
public float getFloat()
```

> Get the return value.
> Returns:
> float: return value

getInt

```
public int getInt()
```

> Get the return value.
> Returns:
> int: return value

getLong

```
public long getLong()
```

Get the return value.
Returns:
  long: return value

getObject

```
public Object getObject()
```

Get the return value.
Returns:
  Object: return value

getShort

```
public short getShort()
```

Get the return value.
Returns:
  short: return value

getType

```
public Class getType()
```

Get the data type of the return value.
Returns:
  Class: data type

CHAPTER
8

Oracle and XML
in Action

hile XML provides an enabling framework for a wide array of applications, it is only an enabling technology—it is not an application in itself. Until there is an agreed-upon schema or DTD, applications cannot use XML to reliably exchange or render data. In this chapter, we will examine two application areas in which these agreements do exist and discuss the specific implementations.

XML has been tightly linked to the Internet for a number of significant reasons. Because the content of an XML document is simply text, exchanging documents is easy over existing Internet protocols, across operating systems, and through firewalls. This capability gives rise to two major application areas—delivering content to a wide range of Internet-enabled devices and interchanging e-business data.

Before looking at these application areas in detail, we need to examine two Oracle Java components, which were introduced in Chapter 3, that make use of the XML infrastructure components: the Oracle XML SQL Utility and the Oracle XSQL Servlet.

Oracle XML SQL Utility

Many applications benefit from having their data reside in databases and querying these databases when data is required. An XML-enabled database benefits from being able to have these queries return data already marked up in XML in accordance with the database schema. The XML SQL Utility is a set of Java classes that accept these application queries, passing them through JDBC to the database and returning the resulting data in an XML format corresponding to the database schema of the query. As a complementary process, the XML SQL Utility can also accept an XML document conformant to the database schema and save the data untagged in the database across this schema.

In addition to reading and writing XML data into JDBC-enabled databases, the XML SQL Utility can create the DTD that represents the queried database schema. This DTD can then be used in application development with Oracle's Class Generators, as demonstrated in Chapter 2. Also, because the XML SQL Utility requires JDBC to connect to the database, there are separate versions for JDBC 1.1 and 1.2.

Retrieving XML-Formatted Data

Because there are similar hierarchical data relationships between them, a relational database schema can be modeled in XML. Let's assume we have a database of book listings in which a **BookList** table is set up with the following columns: BookID, Title, Author, Publisher, Year, ISBN, and Description. The following is a typical query that an application would make to the database:

```
SELECT Title, Author, Publisher, Year, ISBN FROM BookList WHERE BookID
= 1234;
```

If this query is submitted through the XML SQL Utility, the database returns the following result:

```
<?xml version="1.0"?>
<ROWSET>
  <ROW id="1">
    <TITLE>The Difference Between God and Larry Ellison: Inside Oracle
          Corporation</TITLE>
    <AUTHOR>Mike Wilson</AUTHOR>
    <PUBLISHER>William Morrow and Co.</PUBLISHER>
    <YEAR>1997</YEAR>
    <ISBN>0688149251</ISBN>
  </ROW>
</ROWSET>
```

This output can be in the form of a string if the application simply wants to write it to a file or in the form of a DOM object, which can be directly passed to the Oracle XML parser for transformation by its XSLT processor. Providing a DOM output eliminates a parsing operation that would otherwise need to be done before applying any XSL transformations.

As shown in the following code segment, queries can be submitted by passing them to the **oracle.xml.sql.query.OracleXMLQuery** class:

```
/** Simple example of using Oracle XMLSQL API; this class queries the
 database with "select * from Booklist" in scott/tiger schema;
 then from the results of query it generates an XML document */

import java.sql.*;
import java.math.*;
import oracle.xml.sql.query.*;
import oracle.jdbc.*;
import oracle.jdbc.driver.*;

public class read_sample
{
//========================================
// main() - public static void
public static void main(String args[]) throws SQLException
{
  String tabName = "Booklist";
  String user = "scott/tiger";
  DriverManager.registerDriver(new oracle.jdbc.driver.OracleDriver());
```

```
//init a JDBC connection by passing in the user
  Connection conn =
    DriverManager.getConnection("jdbc:oracle:oci8:"+user+"@");

// init the OracleXMLQuery by using the initialized JDBC connection
// and passing in "Booklist" as tabName
  OracleXMLQuery qry =  new OracleXMLQuery(conn,"select * from "
    +tabName );

// get the XML document in the string format which allows us
// to print it
  String xmlString = qry.getXMLString();

// print out the result to the screen
  System.out.println(" OUTPUT IS:\n"+xmlString);

// Close the JDBC connection
    conn.close();
  }
}
```

An alternative command-line interface is also provided in the XML SQL Utility, which is useful in generating the DTD associated with a particular database schema. Assuming everything has been properly installed, the complete listing of command-line options is available by simply executing the following command:

```
java oraclexml
```

The following command line illustrates how to create the DTD associated with a particular schema being queried:

```
java oraclexml getxml -user "scott/tiger" -withDTD "SELECT *
    FROM BookList"
```

For the Booklist table shown previously, the XML SQL Utility would output the following DTD embedded in the XML document produced from the query:

```
<!ELEMENT BOOKLIST (BookID, Title, Author, Publisher, Year, ISBN,
    Description)>
<!ELEMENT BookID (#PCDATA)>
<!ELEMENT Author (#PCDATA)>
<!ELEMENT Publisher (#PCDATA)>
<!ELEMENT Year (#PCDATA)>
<!ELEMENT ISBN (#PCDATA)>
<!ELEMENT Description (#PCDATA)>
```

Saving XML-Formatted Data

Once a schema is created in the database, the XML SQL Utility can begin saving data to it as long as the XML-formatted data conforms to the DTD generated from the schema. The XML SQL Utility provides the ability to map the XML documents to table rows. The storage uses a simple mapping to map the element tag names to columns with XML strings converted to the appropriate data types through default mappings. In a case in which the XML element has child elements, it is mapped to a SQL object type.

To save the XML-formatted data, the XML SQL Utility initiates an insert statement binding all the values of the elements in the VALUES clause of the insert statement. The contents of each row element are mapped to a separate set of values.

Returning to the BookList example earlier in the chapter, the generated SQL statement to store an entry formatted in XML would be the following:

```
INSERT INTO BOOKLIST (BookID, TITLE, AUTHOR, PUBLISHER, YEAR, ISBN,
     DESCRIPTION) VALUES (?,?,?,?,?,?,?) and BIND the values,
BOOKID -> 1234
TITLE -> The Difference Between God and Larry Ellison: Inside Oracle
          Corporation
AUTHOR -> Mike Wilson
PUBLISHER -> William Morrow & Co.
YEAR -> 1997
ISBN -> 0688149251
Description -> Account of Larry Ellison;
```

The following sample code shows how this can be done from a Java program:

```
/** Simple example of using Oracle XMLSQL API; this class inserts the
 data from an XML document into the database*/

import oracle.xml.sql.dml.*;
import java.sql.*;
import oracle.jdbc.driver.*;
import oracle.jdbc.*;
import java.net.*;

public class save_sample
{
  //=======================================
  //  main() - public static void
  public static void main(String args[]) throws SQLException
  {
    String tabName = "BOOKLIST";       // table into which to insert
    String fileName = "sampdoc.xml";  // file containing the xml doc
    DriverManager.registerDriver(new oracle.jdbc.driver.OracleDriver());
```

```
    // init a JDBC connection by passing in the user and password
    Connection conn =
      DriverManager.getConnection("jdbc:oracle:oci8:scott/tiger@");

    // Init the OracleXMLSave class by passing in the JDBC connection
    // and the "BOOKLIST" table name.
    OracleXMLSave sav = new OracleXMLSave(conn, tabName);

    // Point to the XML file, sampledoc.xml, to save using a URL
    URL url = sav.createURL(fileName);

    // Save the data populating rows in the BOOKLIST table and
    // return the number of rows written
    int rowCount = sav.insertXML(url);

    //Print out the confirmation of the successful insertion
    System.out.println(" successfully inserted "+rowCount+
            " rows into "+ tabName);

    // Close the JDBC connection
    conn.close();
  }
}
```

As with **getXML**, there is also a command-line version for the save function called **putXML**. This is useful for bulk-loading XML data. The following command line will load an XML document containing book listings conformant to our example DTD:

```
java oraclexml putXML -user "scott/tiger" sampdoc.xml BookList
```

Performing Updates with the XML SQL Utility

Updates differ from inserts in that they may apply to more than one row in the table. The XML element to be updated might match more than one row if the matching columns are not key columns in the table. Therefore, updates require a list of key columns that the utility uses to identify the row to update. This is illustrated in the following example of a book listing update:

```
<ROWSET>
  <ROW num="1">
    <BOOKID>1234</BOOKID>
    <TITLE> The Difference Between God and Larry Ellison: Inside Oracle
            Corporation </TITLE>
    <AUTHOR>Mike Wilson</AUTHOR>
    <PUBLISHER>William Morrow and Co.</PUBLISHER>
    <YEAR>1997</YEAR>
    <ISBN>0688149251</ISBN>
```

```
    </ROW>
</ROWSET>
```

This XML update results in the following SQL statement passing in the BookID and the key columns:

```
UPDATE BOOKLIST SET TITLE = ?, AUTHOR = ? WHERE BOOKID = ?
      and bind the values,
      BOOKID -> 1234
      TITLE -> The Difference Between God and Larry Ellison: Inside
                Oracle Corporation
      AUTHOR -> Mike Wilson;
```

Note that we need not update all of the columns in the original XML document. The following sample code shows how this can be done from a Java program:

```java
/** Simple example of using Oracle XMLSQL API; this class updates the
 database data from an XML document submitted into the database*/

import oracle.xml.sql.dml.*;
import java.sql.*;
import oracle.jdbc.driver.*;
import oracle.jdbc.*;

public class ListUpdate
{
  //========================================
  //  main() - public static void
  public static void main(String argv[]) throws SQLException
  {
    String tabName = "BOOKLIST";        // table into which to insert
    DriverManager.registerDriver(new oracle.jdbc.driver.OracleDriver());

    // init a JDBC connection by passing in the user and password
    Connection conn =
      DriverManager.getConnection("jdbc:oracle:oci8:scott/tiger@");

    // Init the OracleXMLSave by class passing in the JDBC connection
    // and the "BOOKLIST" table name.
    OracleXMLSave sav = new OracleXMLSave(conn, tabName);

    // init the key column used for the update
    String [] keyColNames = new String[1];
    keyColNames[0] = "BOOKID";
    sav.setKeyColumnNames(keyColNames);

    // Assume that the user passes in this document as the first argument!
    sav.updateXML(argv[0]);
    sav.close();
  }
}
```

Performing Deletes with the XML SQL Utility

The XML SQL Utility also supports deletes of XML documents. It identifies the rows to be deleted by using the key columns in the same way it does for updates. If one or more key columns are not given, it will still try to match the columns in the document. The following is the XML document and the corresponding equivalent delete SQL statement generated:

```
<ROWSET>
  <ROW num="1">
    <BOOKID>1234</BOOKID>
    <TITLE> The Difference Between God and Larry Ellison: Inside Oracle
           Corporation </TITLE>
    <AUTHOR>Mike Wilson</AUTHOR>
    <PUBLISHER>William Morrow and Co.</PUBLISHER>
    <YEAR>1997</YEAR>
    <ISBN>0688149251</ISBN>
  </ROW>
</ROWSET>


DELETE FROM BOOKLIST WHERE TITLE = ? AND AUTHOR = ? AND PUBLISHER = ? AND YEAR = ?
AND ISBN = ? AND BOOKID = ?
      binding,
      BOOKID <- 1234
      TITLE <- The Difference Between God and Larrry Ellison: Inside
               Oracle Corporation
      AUTHOR <- Mike Wilson
      PUBLISHER <- William Morrow & Co.
      YEAR <- 1997
      ISBN <- 0688149251;
```

The following example shows how this delete can be done from Java, using the BookID as a key column:

```
/** Simple example of using Oracle XMLSQL API; this class deletes the
 database data from an XML document submitted into the database */

import oracle.xml.sql.dml.*;
import java.sql.*;
import oracle.jdbc.driver.*;
import oracle.jdbc.*;

public class ListDelete
{
  //========================================
  // main() - public static void
  public static void main(String argv[]) throws SQLException
  {
    String tabName = "BOOKLIST";      // table into which to delete data
```

```
   DriverManager.registerDriver(new oracle.jdbc.driver.OracleDriver());

 // init a JDBC connection by passing in the user and password
   Connection conn =
     DriverManager.getConnection("jdbc:oracle:oci8:scott/tiger@");

 // Init the OracleXMLSave class by passing in the JDBC connection
 // and the "BOOKLIST" table name.
   OracleXMLSave sav = new OracleXMLSave(conn, tabName);

 // init the key column used for the update
   String [] keyColNames = new String[1];
   keyColNames[0] = "BookID";
   sav.setKeyColumnNames(keyColNames);

 // Assume that the user passes in this document as the first argument!
   sav.deleteXML(argv[0]);
   sav.close();
 }
}
```

Installing the XML SQL Utility

Installing the XML SQL Utility on a client or server is no different than installing any
other Java library. Because it is packaged in a **.jar** archive, when using **xsu111.jar** or
xsu12.jar, you must explicitly declare its filename and path in the CLASSPATH for
your session. The XML SQL Utility depends upon the Oracle XML parser for Java v2,
and its jar is included in the archive and must likewise be declared in the CLASSPATH.
An **env.bat** file for Windows and an **env.csh** file for Unix are provided to help set up
the session environment. Finally, the proper set of JDBC classes, 1.1 or 1.2, must be
available to connect to the database.

In applications in which the XML SQL Utility will be communicating with an
Oracle 8i database, an additional installation option is available. Due to the inclusion
of the JServer Java Virtual Machine within 8i, you can load the XML SQL Utility jar
into the database, where it can be called by internal or external procedures. Since
8.1.6 shipped with a Java 1.1–compliant JServer, you would load the **xsu111.jar**; for
8.1.7, which was Java 1.2 compliant, you would use the **xsu12.jar**. In this configuration,
the utility benefits from an in-memory JDBC connection that dramatically reduces
the retrieval times for large XML documents.

To assist in the installation with 8i, an **oraclexmlsqlload.bat** file for Windows
and an **oraclexmlsqlload.csh** file for Unix are provided. When run, these scripts
load all of the classes from the **oraclexmlsql.jar** except for the OracleXML
command-line class. They will also load the XML parser for Java v2 and execute
the **xmlgensql.sql** script that creates the **xmlgen** PL/SQL package and runs the test
script, **oraclexmltest.sql**. This package allows the XML SQL Utility to be used
from SQL or from within a PL/SQL procedure.

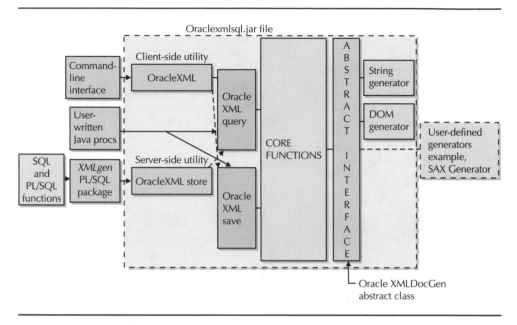

Oraclexmlsql.jar file

FIGURE 8-1. *XML SQL Utility architecture*

Extending the XML SQL Utility

While the XML SQL Utility currently supports both DOM and String outputs, it can be extended to support other forms, including SAX. Figure 8-1 shows its architecture from a function block point of view.

The core functions are wrapped with an abstract layer, **OracleXMLDocGen**, to generate the XML document. In the current implementation, this abstract class is extended by **OracleXMLDocGenDOM** to generate a DOM output, and by **OracleXMLDocGenString** to generate a String output of the XML document. Additional classes can extend the OracleXMLDocGen class to support other representations.

Oracle XSQL Servlet

Building upon the functionality of the XML SQL Utility and the XML parser is the XSQL Servlet introduced in Chapter 3. Written in Java, this servlet provides a high-level declarative interface to developers and Webmasters to render data across the Internet dynamically and in custom formats. Able to run with the servlet engines of most Web servers, the XSQL Servlet delivers the capability to transform a single data source automatically in terms of the client browser and the format best suited to its capabilities and those of the platform.

The XSQL Pages

The heart of the XSQL Servlet is the XSQL page. This page is simply an XML file that contains specific elements to direct the action of the servlet. The following **booklist.xsql** file is a simple XSQL page:

```
<?xml version="1.0"?>
<?xml-stylesheet type="text/xsl" href="booklist.xsl"?>
<xsql:query connection="demo" xmlns:xsql="urn:oracle-xsql">
  select * from Booklist
</xsql:query>
```

Figure 8-2 shows the process flow when an Internet browser requests this page and the Web server hands over the request to the XSQL Servlet after it registers the **xsql** extension with the server. The servlet then hands the page to the XML parser to retrieve its instructions. In this case, it is asked to open a JDBC connection with the alias of **demo** and submit the query "Select * from Booklist." It does this by passing this data to the XML SQL Utility, which performs the query as described previously and returns the result as an XML DOM object. Finally, the servlet passes the stylesheet reference along with the DOM object to the XML parser's XSLT processor to apply the transformation to HTML for display in the client's browser.

The essential elements of the file are the **<xsql:query>** element, which includes the database connection information within its **connection** attribute and the SQL query within its body. The connection value is an alias contained within the **<connectiondefs>** section of the **XMLConfig.xml** file:

```
<connectiondefs>
    <connection name="demo">
       <username>scott</username>
       <password>tiger</password>
       <dburl>jdbc:oracle:thin:@localhost:1521:ORCL</dburl>
       <driver>oracle.jdbc.driver.OracleDriver</driver>
    </connection>

    <connection name="xmlbook">
       <username>xmlbook</username>
       <password>xmlbook</password>
       <dburl>jdbc:oracle:thin:@localhost:1521:ORCL</dburl>
       <driver>oracle.jdbc.driver.OracleDriver</driver>
    </connection>

    <connection name="lite">
```

```
      <username>system</username>
      <password>manager</password>
      <dburl>jdbc:Polite:POlite</dburl>
      <driver>oracle.lite.poljdbc.POLJDBCDriver</driver>
   </connection>
</connectiondefs>
```

This section from the default **XMLConfig.xml** file shows the declaration of the database connection string and the JDBC driver that will be used by the XML SQL Utility. As this file resides on the server in a directory not accessible to the client, this information remains secure.

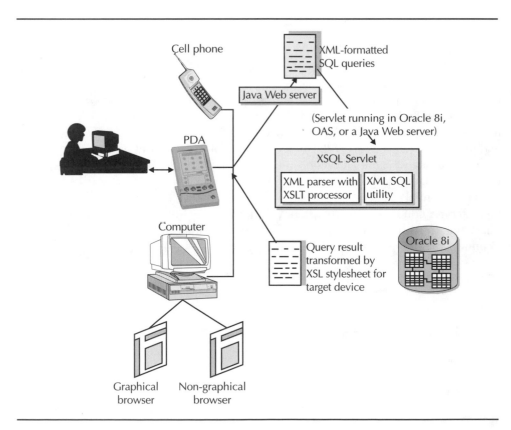

FIGURE 8-2. *XSQL page process*

Installing the XSQL Servlet

The XSQL Servlet is available from the OTN at **technet.oracle.com/tech/xml** and is designed to be quite flexible in its installation and setup. It may be used in any 1.1 or greater JVM and with any JDBC-enabled database. Specific testing has been done with JDK 1.1.8 and 1.2.2 on Windows and several Unix platforms, including Solaris, Linux, and HP-UX. The following is the list of supported and tested servlet engines:

- Allaire JRun 2.3.3

- Apache 1.3.9 with JServ 1.0 and 1.1

- Apache 1.3.9 with Tomcat 3.1 Beta1 Servlet Engine

- Apache Tomcat 3.1 Beta1 Web Server + Servlet Engine

- Caucho Resin 1.1

- NewAtlanta ServletExec 2.2 for IIS/PWS 4.0

- Oracle8i Lite Web-to-Go Server

- Oracle Application Server 4.0.8.1 (with "JSP Patch")

- Oracle8i 8.1.7 Beta "Aurora" Servlet Engine

- Sun JavaServer Web Development Kit (JSWDK) 1.0.1 Web Server

See Chapter 9 for full instructions on installing the XSQL Servlet and the included demos.

Submitting Queries to the XSQL Servlet

The XSQL Servlet is designed to create dynamic Web pages from database queries. The XSQL pages can be linked to any Web site and can contain one or more queries whose results will replace the respective **<xsql:query>** section in the page. These results can be further customized through the use of attributes within the **<xsql:query>** tag. Table 8-1 shows the various options available.

Parameters can also be passed into the query from the HTTP request line. By prefixing an @ to the parameter name, the XSQL Servlet will search the HTTP request parameters and then the **<xsql:query>** attributes to find a match. Once a match is found, a straight lexical substitution is performed. The following is an

Attribute Name	Default	Description
rowset-element	<ROWSET>	Element name for the query results. Set equal to the empty string to suppress printing a document element.
row-element	<ROW>	Element name for each row in the query results. Set equal to the empty string to suppress printing a row element.
max-rows	Fetch all rows.	Maximum number of rows to fetch from the query. Useful for fetching the top-N rows or, in combination with skip-rows, the next-N rows from a query result.
skip-rows	Skip no rows.	Number of rows to skip over before returning the query results.
id-attribute	id	Attribute name for the id attribute for each row in the query result.
id-attribute-column	Row count value	Column name to supply the value of the id attribute for each row in the query result.
null-indicator	Omit elements with a NULL value.	If set to y or yes, causes a null-indicator attribute to be used on the element for any column whose value is NULL.
tag-case	Use the case of the column name or alias from the query.	If set to upper, UPPERCASEs the element names for columns in the query result. If set to lower, lowercases the element names for columns in the query result.

TABLE 8-1. *Attribute Options for the <xsl:query> Element*

example of an XSQL page using this function when the HTTP request line is **http://localhost/xsql/demo/booksearch.xsql?year=2001**:

```
<?xml version="1.0"?>
<xsql:query xmlns:xsql="urn:oracle-xsql" connection="demo"
    SELECT TITLE, AUTHOR, DESCRIPTION FROM BOOKLIST
      WHERE YEAR = {@year}
</xsql:query>
```

Queries that return no rows can also be handled by adding an optional **<xsql:no-rows-query>** element within the **<xsql:query>** tags. This allows the user to see a formatted page instead of the raw error. The following is an example that initially tries to retrieve the listings corresponding to the author's name; failing that, it attempts to do a fuzzy match on the submitted name:

```
<?xml version="1.0"?>
<xsql:query xmlns:xsql="urn:oracle-xsql" connection="demo"
    SELECT TITLE, AUTHOR, DESCRIPTION FROM BOOKLIST
      WHERE AUTHOR = UPPER ('{@author}')

  <xsql:no-rows-query>
    SELECT TITLE, AUTHOR, DESCRIPTION FROM BOOKLIST
      WHERE AUTHOR LIKE UPPER ('%{@author}%')
      ORDER BY AUTHOR
  </xsql:no-rows-query>

</xsql:query>
```

Transforming the XSQL
Output with Stylesheets

The real power of the XSQL Servlet lies in its capability to dynamically transform query results by applying XSL stylesheets. The stylesheet declaration is included in the XSQL file and is applied once the XML output from the query is received. It most commonly transforms query results into HTML, as can be seen in the following example; however, the stylesheet can perform any text-based transformation. The following XSQL page and its associated stylesheet will return the results to the requesting browser as an HTML table:

Searchauthor.xsql
```
<?xml version="1.0"?>
<xsql-stylesheet type="text/xsl" href="totable.xsl"?>
<xsql:query xmlns:xsql="urn:oracle-xsql" connection="demo"
    SELECT Title, Author, Description FROM Booklist
      WHERE Author = UPPER ('{@author}')

  <xsql:no-rows-query>
    SELECT Title, Author, Description FROM Booklist
      WHERE Author LIKE UPPER ('%{@author}%')
      ORDER BY Author
  </xsql:no-rows-query>
```

```
</xsql:query>
```

Totable.xsl
```
<html xmlns:xsl="http://www.w3.org/1999/XSL/Transform">
  <head>
    <title>Book Listing</title>
  </head>
  <body>
    <table border="1" cellspacing="0">
        <tr>
         <th><b>Author</b></th>
         <th><b>Title</b></th>
         <th><b>Description</b></th>
        </tr>
      <xsl:for-each select="ROWSET/ROW">
        <tr>
         <td><xsl:value-of select="TITLE"/></td>
         <td><xsl:value-of select="AUTHOR"/></td>
         <td><xsl:value-of select="DESCRIPTION"/></td>
        </tr>
      </xsl:for-each>
    </table>
  </body>
</html>
```

Figure 8-3 shows the query result and subsequent transformation.

Multiple stylesheet declarations are also supported. In such instances, the XSQL Servlet chooses the transformation method by matching the **user-agent** string in the HTTP header to an optional **media** attribute in the **<xml-stylesheet>** element. The match is case insensitive, and the first match in file order is the one applied. The following example shows how multiple browsers are supported.

```
<?xml version="1.0"?>
<?xml-stylesheet type="text/xsl" media="lynx" href="booklist-lynx.xsl" ?>
<?xml-stylesheet type="text/xsl" media="msie" href="booklist-ie.xsl" ?>
<?xml-stylesheet type="text/xsl" href="booklist.xsl"?>

<xsql:query connection="demo" xmlns:xsql="urn:oracle-xsql">
  select * from BOOKLIST
</xsql:query>
```

Note that the last stylesheet declaration has no **media** attribute. It will be applied to any HTTP requests that do not match the others and thus acts as the default

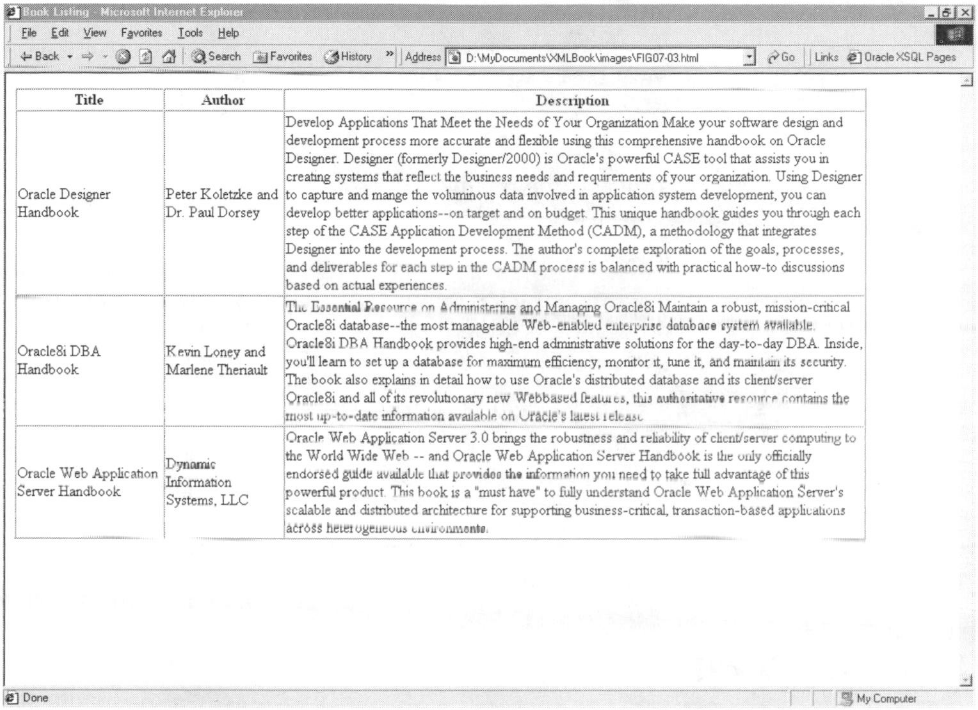

Title	Author	Description
Oracle Designer Handbook	Peter Koletzke and Dr. Paul Dorsey	Develop Applications That Meet the Needs of Your Organization Make your software design and development process more accurate and flexible using this comprehensive handbook on Oracle Designer. Designer (formerly Designer/2000) is Oracle's powerful CASE tool that assists you in creating systems that reflect the business needs and requirements of your organization. Using Designer to capture and mange the voluminous data involved in application system development, you can develop better applications--on target and on budget. This unique handbook guides you through each step of the CASE Application Development Method (CADM), a methodology that integrates Designer into the development process. The author's complete exploration of the goals, processes, and deliverables for each step in the CADM process is balanced with practical how-to discussions based on actual experiences.
Oracle8i DBA Handbook	Kevin Loney and Marlene Theriault	The Essential Resource on Administering and Managing Oracle8i Maintain a robust, mission-critical Oracle8i database--the most manageable Web-enabled enterprise database system available. Oracle8i DBA Handbook provides high-end administrative solutions for the day-to-day DBA. Inside, you'll learn to set up a database for maximum efficiency, monitor it, tune it, and maintain its security. The book also explains in detail how to use Oracle's distributed database and its client/server Oracle8i and all of its revolutionary new Webbased features, this authoritative resource contains the most up-to-date information available on Oracle's latest release
Oracle Web Application Server Handbook	Dynamic Information Systems, LLC	Oracle Web Application Server 3.0 brings the robustness and reliability of client/server computing to the World Wide Web -- and Oracle Web Application Server Handbook is the only officially endorsed guide available that provides the information you need to take full advantage of this powerful product. This book is a "must have" to fully understand Oracle Web Application Server's scalable and distributed architecture for supporting business-critical, transaction-based applications across heterogeneous environments.

FIGURE 8-3. *Formatted output from the SearchAuthor.xsql page*

stylesheet. Table 8-2 shows the allowable attributes that can be added to the **<xml-stylesheet>** element and their functions.

The final way to apply a stylesheet is to pass its URL as an HTTP parameter as follows:

```
http://localhost/yourdatapage.xsql?param1=value&xml-stylesheet=yourstyle.xsl
```

This technique is especially useful for prototyping and development. By replacing the stylesheet URL with **none**, you ensure that the raw XML document is sent without any stylesheet processing.

Attribute	Required	Description
type	Yes	Must be set to the value **text/xsl**; otherwise, the **<?xml-stylesheet?>** instruction is ignored by the XSQL Page Processor.
href	Yes	Indicates the relative or absolute URL of the stylesheet to be used.
media	No	If set, this attribute's value is used to perform a case-insensitive match on the **User-Agent** string of the requesting browser, so the appropriate stylesheet is used, depending on the requesting software/device.
client	No	If set to **yes**, will download the raw XML to the client and include the **<?xml-stylesheet?>** processing instruction for processing in the browser. If not specified, the default is to perform the transform in the server.

TABLE 8-2. *Attribute Options for the <xml:stylesheet> Element*

Inserting XML Documents with the XSQL Servlet

Leveraging the full capability of the XML SQL Utility, an XSQL page can also be set up to insert XML documents into a database. An XML document can be submitted to the **OracleXMLSave** class of the XML SQL Utility by employing the Action Element, **<xsql:insert-request>**. As discussed previously, the schema must already exist in the database to save a document. While at first this may be considered a limitation, the XSQL Servlet's capability to apply a stylesheet to the XML document on submission provides the necessary functionality to filter or transform documents as needed.

Returning to the book listing example presented earlier in the chapter, an XSQL page can be set up to accept book listings not only in the prescribed format of the database but also from virtually any text-based format. For example, consider the case in which a local bookseller would like to list his books on the pages, but his book listings use a different set of tags from the database schema. By creating an XSL stylesheet and applying it on receipt of his listings, his selections could be accommodated. The following XSQL page could accept the book feed from "Joe's Books" via HTTP and transform it into the Booklist database schema by applying the **joesbooks.xsl** stylesheet and then submitting the resulting XML to the **OracleXMLSave** class for insertion:

```
<?xml version="1.0">
<xsql:insert-request xmlns:xsql="urn:oracle-xsql"
            connection = "demo"
            table = "BOOKLIST"
            transform = "joesbooks.xsl"/>
```

However, one more item must be set up to allow this example to function properly. The database generates the BookID column; therefore, this column's entry must be created for each new insertion. This can be done by setting up a trigger on the Booklist table that generates this ID whenever an insertion is made. The following SQL script will create a new BookID when each new listing is added, assuming you have already created a sequence named **bookid_seq**:

```
CREATE TRIGGER booklist_autoid
BEFORE INSERT ON BOOKLIST FOR EACH ROW
BEGIN
    SELECT bookid_seq.nextval
    INTO :new.BookID
    FROM dual,
END;
```

Other Action Elements that are supported by the XSQL Servlet and their functions are listed in Table 8-3.

Action Element	Description
<xsql:query>	Execute an arbitrary SQL statement and include its result set in canonical XML format.
<xsql:dml>	Execute a SQL DML statement or PL/SQL anonymous block.
<xsql:set-stylesheet-param>	Set the value of a top-level XSLT stylesheet parameter. The parameter's value can be set by supplying the optional **value** attribute or by including a SQL statement as the element content.
<xsql:insert-request>	Insert the (optionally transformed) XML document that has been posted in the request into a database table or view. If HTML form has been posted, then the posted XML document is materialized from HTTP request parameters, cookies, and session variables.

TABLE 8-3.   *Action Elements and Their Functions for XSQL Pages*

Action Element	Description
<xsql:include-xml>	Include arbitrary XML resources at any point in your page by relative or absolute URL.
<xsql:include-request-params>	Include key information such as HTTP parameters, session variable values, and cookies in your XSQL page for addressing them in your stylesheet.
<xsql:include-xsql>	Include the results of one XSQL page at any point inside another.
<xsql:include-owa>	Include the results of executing a stored procedure that makes use of the *Oracle Web Agent (OWA)* packages inside the database to generate XML.
<xsql:action>	Invoke a user-defined action handler, which is implemented in Java, for executing custom logic and including custom XML information into your XSQL page.
<xsql:ref-cursor-function>	Include the canonical XML representation of the result set of a cursor returned by a PL/SQL stored function.
<xsql:set-page-param>	Set a page-level (local) parameter that can be referred to in subsequent SQL statements in the page. The value can be set using a static value, the value of another parameter, or the results of a SQL statement.
<xsql:include-param>	Include a parameter and its value as an element in your XSQL page.
<xsql:set-session-param>	Set an HTTP session-level parameter. The value can be set using a static value, the value of another parameter, or the results of a SQL statement.
<xsql:set-cookie>	Set an HTTP cookie. The value can be set using a static value, the value of another parameter, or the results of a SQL statement.
<xsql:insert-param>	Insert the value of a single parameter containing XML. Can optionally supply a transform to get it in canonical format.

TABLE 8-3. *Action Elements and Their Functions for XSQL Pages* (continued)

Updating Data with the XSQL Servlet

Many applications require that data or documents be updated instead of wholly replaced. In a similar manner to the way the BookID was automatically generated, you can use a form of trigger to provide this functionality.

Oracle 8i makes available an INSTEAD OF trigger, which allows a stored procedure in PL/SQL or Java to be called whenever an INSERT of any kind is attempted. These triggers utilize Oracle 8i's Object Views to be associated with the INSERT.

For example, if you wanted to have the Booklist table be updatable, you could initially search for the unique combination of title and author and, if one is found, perform an UPDATE instead of doing an INSERT. To set this up, you must create an Object View corresponding to the Booklist table. This can be done using the following SQL:

```
CREATE VIEW Booklistview AS
SELECT * FROM Booklist;
```

Next, the trigger needs to be created and associated with this view. In this example, PL/SQL is being used, but the job could also be done with a Java stored procedure.

```
CREATE OR REPLACE TRIGGER insteadOfIns_booklistview
INSTEAD OF INSERT ON booklistview FOR EACH ROW
DECLARE
  notThere BOOLEAN := TRUE;
  tmp      VARCHAR2(1);
  CURSOR chk IS SELECT 'x'
                FROM BOOKLIST
                WHERE TITLE = :new.title
                AND AUTHOR  = :new.author;
BEGIN
  OPEN chk;
  FETCH chk INTO tmp;
  notThere := chk%NOTFOUND;
  CLOSE chk;

  IF notThere THEN
    UPDATE INTO Booklist(TITLE,
                         AUTHOR,
                         PUBLISHER,
                         YEAR,
                         ISBN,
                         DESCRIPTION)
```

```
        VALUES (:new.title,
               :new.author,
               :new.Publisher,
               :new.Year,
               :new.ISBN,
               :new.Description);
   END IF;
END;
```

Finally, the XSQL file needs to be changed as follows to update the Booklistview instead of the Booklist table.

```
<?xml version="1.0">
<xsql:insert-request xmlns:xsql="urn:oracle-xsql"
            connection = "demo"
            table = "Booklistview"
            transform = "joesbooks.xsl"/>
```

As a final note, since the uniqueness is being checked in terms of the combination of the title and author, a unique index can be created to speed up the check and improve performance. The following SQL statement will create the index:

```
CREATE UNIQUE INDEX booklist_index ON booklist(Title, Author);
```

While the previous example explained how to perform an update using the trigger functionality of an object view, you can also use the XML SQL Utility update capability from the XSQL Servlet using the following very simple **.xsql** file:

```
<?xml version="1.0"?>
<xsql:dml connection="demo" xmlns:xsql="urn:oracle-xsql">
  update Booklist set status='S' where BookID = '1';
</xsql:dml>
```

This example illustrates the simplicity and power of the XSQL's XML-based interface.

An XML-Powered Web Site

Traditional Web sites have had to have their content preformatted for an anticipated screen size with little in the way of automatic client detection and customization possible. Most sites that try to accommodate different browsers are limited to a user selecting between "frames" and "non-frames" or "text" and "text+images" versions. These pages are typically stored statically and must be updated manually, introducing the possibility of errors or missing data. Any changes in formatting has to be replicated across every page.

The introduction of cascading stylesheets improved this situation by off-loading much of the HTML formatting to a separate file. While this support removes much of the formatting from the source HTML file, it still depends upon a static source file with HTML formatting. To deliver true data sources, rendered dynamically through stylesheets to browsers, has been the goal of many e-commerce companies hoping to speed the delivery of their current data. Pursuit of this strategy has resulted in enterprise-level databases such as Oracle being added to Web site backends.

The XML-Enabled Solution

In Chapter 3, we introduced the use of XML's capability to describe data in a structured way coupled with XSL's capability to perform virtually any text-based transformation on that data, delivering the solution of a true, single, unified data repository. This data repository can serve as a backend for a presentation system, be it a browser, PDA, cell phone, or pager. Embedded links, instead of calling static Web pages, can generate database queries returning up-to-the-minute content.

On the backend, databases can accept a variety of data feeds, including those formatted in XML, and store the data for immediate use. Content repositories can also be created containing reusable document fragments or modules that can be assembled by XSL stylesheets on demand to vastly simplify online document publishing. This content and presentation separation also simplifies the production process, as presentation designers can work on the stylesheets without the risk of introducing content errors.

A real-world example of such a Web site is a real-estate aggregation site where listings from a variety of *multiple listing services (MLSs)* can be assembled in one place. The scenario is that you have a Web site that accepts these MLS listings from a variety of sources, each with its own XML format. An XSL stylesheet unique to the source is applied to the XML feed, which is then transformed to a normalized format for insertion into a database. A summary of this data is presented to requesting browsers that can then search for or expand a particular listing.

The Design Requirements

To properly design this Web site, two general design requirements must be met: The database must have the capability to accept XML and do the appropriate XSL transformation for the source. It also must be able to dynamically render the listings in a variety of ways in a scalable manner with high performance.

The system must also be able to handle a variety of image formats and be able to select the appropriate type for display on the requester's system or display no images at all in the case of a cell phone or pager. The system would ideally not only respond to direct requests but also generate messages in response to receiving listings that met preset criteria. This can be especially useful to real-estate agents searching for new listings to present to clients.

The Architecture

This system is ideally suited to be designed with a database as its repository. In this case, you can use Oracle 8i to store both the data and the images, if required. Object views are set up to link the data with the images to present a complete listing to Internet browsers after XSL transformation with the appropriate stylesheet.

Figure 8-4 shows a diagram of the overall architecture of the real-estate site. XML data feeds are accepted by the XSQL Servlet, transformed into a normalized format, and saved to the database.

Clients using a browser can search the listings or display available listings in accordance with several preset criteria. The format is automatically keyed to the requesting browser's capabilities. Additionally, notifications can be sent out in the event of a change in the status of or an update to a listing.

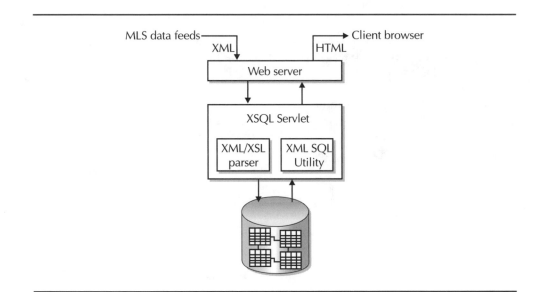

FIGURE 8-4. *Function diagram of the Real Estate site*

An Example Implementation

To implement this system, you must first design a normalized MLS schema. For the purpose of this example, the following DTD will represent the data model:

```
<!ELEMENT LISTING (ListingID, MLS_Number, Address, Area, City, State,
                   Zipcode, Description, AskPrice, Agent, ImageURI,
                   Category, Status)>
<!ELEMENT ListingID (#PCDATA)>
<!ELEMENT MLS_Number (#PCDATA)>
<!ELEMENT Address (#PCDATA)>
<!ELEMENT Area (#PCDATA)>
<!ELEMENT City (#PCDATA)>
<!ELEMENT State (#PCDATA)>
<!ELEMENT Zipcode (#PCDATA)>
<!ELEMENT Description (#PCDATA)>
<!ELEMENT AskPrice (#PCDATA)>
<!ELEMENT Agent (#PCDATA)>
<!ELEMENT ImageURI (#PCDATA)>
<!ELEMENT Category (SFH | CONDO | APTBLDG | DUP | THM | COM | LOT)>
<!ELEMENT Status (A | P | S | C)>
```

This DTD can serve as the template to create the stylesheets that are keyed to the specific MLS services. For example, if the NorCal service used **Neighborhood** instead of **Area**, and **Zip** instead of **Zipcode**, the following stylesheet could perform the transformation:

```
<?xml version="1.0"?>
<ROWSET xmlns:xsl=http://www.w3.org/1999/XSL/Transform
        xsl:version="1.0">
  <xsl:for-each select="Norcal/LISTING">
  <ROW>
  ...
  <Area><xsl:value-of select="Neighborhood"/></Area>
  ...
  <Zipcode><<xsl:value-of select="Zip"/></Zipcode>
  ...
  </ROW>
 </xsl:for-each>
</ROWSET>
```

Once all of the stylesheets have been created, an XSQL page can be set up to accept each service and apply the appropriate transformation, as shown in the following XSQL page, which uses the **<xsql:insert-request>** Action Element described in the earlier section "Inserting XML Documents with the XSQL Servlet."

```
<?xml version="1.0"?>
<xsql:insert-request xmlns:xsql="urn:oracle-xsql"
            connection = "demo"
            listingview = "LISTING"
            transform = "norcal.xsl"/>
```

XSQL pages can also be used on the client side to query the listings and produce various pages, such as a summary page based on **Area** or **Zipcode**, as well as refining the searches with price ranges or property type, as shown in Figure 8-5.

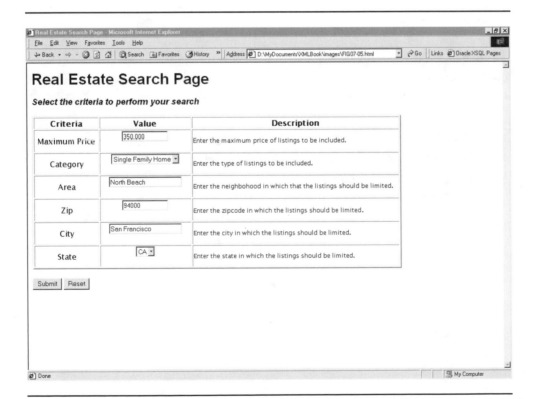

FIGURE 8-5. *Sample MLS listing search page*

You can perform these searches by creating links to XSQL pages that perform the specific queries or by using the **@parameter** technique to pass the criteria to a generic XSQL page.

With the proliferation of Web-enabled cell phones, PDAs, and pagers, this site can also meet their unique and limited display requirements by utilizing the **user-agent** string in the HTTP header and the **media** attribute in the stylesheet declaration. The following XSQL example supports the Palm Pilot, the Unwired Planet cell phone, and standard browsers:

```
<?xml version="1.0"?>
<?xml-stylesheet type="text/xsl" media="Palm" href="ListingPP.xsl"?>
<?xml-stylesheet type="text/xsl" media="Mozilla" href="ListingMZ.xsl"?>
<?xml-stylesheet type="text/xsl" media="UP" href="ListingWML.xsl"?>
<?xml-stylesheet type="text/xsl" href="Listing.xsl"?>

<xsql:query connection="demo" xmlns:xsql="urn:oracle-xsql">
  select * from Listingview WHERE
          Zipcode=94065
</xsql:query>
```

Extending the Example

Using the INSTEAD OF INSERT trigger described in the earlier section "Updating Data with the XSQL Servlet," you can make this Web site proactive by having it notify registered users of new listings, pending sales, and closings as they are inserted or updated. The stored procedure called by the trigger could query an interest registration table of e-mail addresses and send a broadcast e-mail to those registered for a particular listing, area, zip code, and so on.

A full-service site could link in financial information to alert clients or agents to loan approvals, title clearances, and other notifications during the real-estate transaction. Finally, with the upsurge in home auctions, this site could be extended to support hosting an auction service, accepting bids and notifying bidders across a wide array of communication devices.

Oracle Portal-to-Go

A product that already implements much of the functionality described in this example is Oracle's Portal-to-Go. Primarily designed for wired and wireless service providers, Portal-to-Go permits a single content repository to serve a wide array of devices, utilizing gateways to provide the custom formatting specific to the requesting device.

Figure 8-6 displays the architecture of Portal-to-Go. XML-formatted information feeds are connected to an Oracle 8i database, storing content in a normalized manner. Oracle9i Dynamic Services, which crawls Web sites, and returning data in XML, can deliver additional feeds.

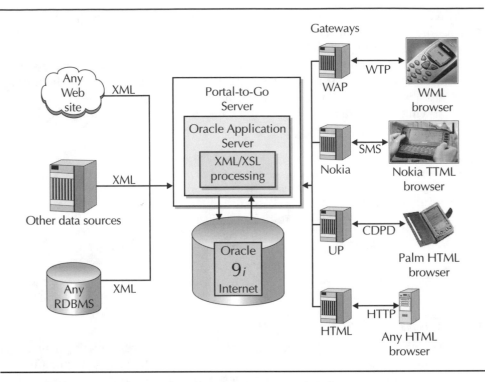

FIGURE 8-6. *Oracle Portal-to-Go architecture*

On the output side, device-specific gateways are set up to allow intelligent interaction with a variety of two-way wired and wireless devices. Users can customize their own views and content selections. Through the use of portlets, that are well defined areas of HTML/XML in a web page providing basic access to an information resource, users can even operate in disconnected mode, which is ideal for many wireless users.

XML-Powered Messaging for E-Business

The requirement to exchange data between applications and enterprises is growing daily. Historically, this data exchange required a high level of technological agreement about data types, structures, transport protocols, and so forth. Services such as CORBA delivered this capability but were limited in their capability to use the Internet, pass through firewalls, and set up ad hoc sessions. What was needed was a method for applications to send and receive data in text form across a variety of transports and protocols and in a self-describing manner. Given this, applications would not need rigorous adherence to a technology stack to communicate. This would then allow companies to integrate applications across the Internet, meeting the demands of industry-consolidation trends and opening a whole new service area for application hosting.

The XML-Enabled Solution

The rise of XML and its related technologies of XSL, XML Schema, XML Query, and XPath make the possibility of true application integration across enterprises a reality. Whether by purchase order or update message, applications need to exchange structured data. XML-formatted data eliminates the need for metadata and its structure to be inferred through hard-coded application logic. XML Schema definitions or DTDs can be included to validate the messages. XSL stylesheets can transform these messages into specific application-compliant formats. Finally, all of this processing can be done by generic components built to the open standards. These standards give the companies that use them to develop products the confidence that they will be widely supported and used.

Because this is such a widespread application area, let's return to the Booklist example and create an online bookstore that utilizes these various XML technologies. The scenario is that we have an online used bookstore for which we would like to both receive listings of books for sale and permit clients to purchase books over the Internet. We would also like to aggregate the book listings from other used bookstores to promote to a national clientele.

The Design Requirements

To properly design this Web site and application, we need to design data models for the different objects that will be utilized. Because the database is going to serve as primary storage and is the most constrained component when it comes to modeling, we should design the database schema first. From there, the XML SQL Utility is used to generate the DTDs that map properly. Then the Class Generator converts these DTDs to the DOM classes that are used in the application front end to create the XML documents that will be inserted by the XML SQL Utility into the database.

The system must be able to accept book listings from individual sellers as well as bulk listings from other booksellers. It also needs to present book listings to prospective buyers, process sales transactions, and notify sellers. Finally, it must handle payments from buyers and to sellers.

Consideration must be given to the overall performance in the design requirements. While the retrieval of the data in XML format scales well, complex transformations and the requirement of one thread per stylesheet instance can produce a significant bottleneck under heavy loads. Minimizing the stylesheet processing and employing middle-tier caches, such as Oracle's iCache, can mitigate much of this bottleneck.

The Architecture

This system can be implemented using Oracle 8i as the data repository and Oracle Application Server as both the Web server and the middle tier. Clients can interact with the site using standard browsers. Booksellers will be able to submit XML-formatted listings and receive sales notifications. Figure 8-7 shows a functional diagram of the system.

To insert a book listing into the store, a seller enters data into a *Java Server Page (JSP)* that calls the DOM classes to generate the XML document to be inserted. This document is then parsed and its data inserted into the Booklist schema. Additionally, the seller's account information is inserted into an Account schema. Clients are presented with the book listings by category or as the result of searches by interacting with HTML pages generated from the XSQL Servlet. Book purchases capture and store the transaction in the database and notify the seller via e-mail.

While this is by no means a complete application and architecture, the discussion and example implementation of its various parts serve as a good representation of the use of XML and as a foundation for many similar applications.

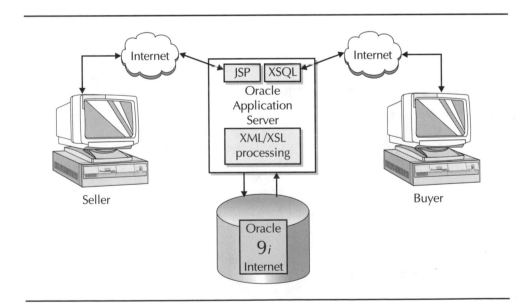

FIGURE 8-7. *Functional diagram of online bookstore*

An Example Implementation

By extending the Booklist schema introduced earlier in the chapter and adding a
Client schema, we can discuss the specifics of the implementation. The following
is the XML DTD that represents the extended book listing:

```
<!ELEMENT BOOKLIST (BookID, Title, Author, Publisher, Year, ISBN,
                    Description, Category, Cost, Status)>
<!ELEMENT BookID (#PCDATA)>
<!ELEMENT Title (#PCDATA)>
<!ELEMENT Author (#PCDATA)>
<!ELEMENT Publisher (#PCDATA)>
<!ELEMENT Year (#PCDATA)>
<!ELEMENT ISBN (#PCDATA)>
<!ELEMENT Description (#PCDATA)>
<!ELEMENT Category (FICTION | NONFICTION | REFERENCE | TECHNICAL)>
<!ELEMENT Cost (#PCDATA)>
<!ELEMENT Status (A | S)>
```

This DTD can then serve as input to the Class Generator to create the set of
DOM classes that can create conformant XML documents. The following is an
example command line:

```
Java samplemain booklist.dtd
```

It will create Java source files for all of the elements, which can then be compiled
into Java classes using the Javac compiler. Next, a JSP is created using these classes,
as illustrated in the following listing:

```
<HTML>
  <HEAD>
    <TITLE>Book Submission</TITLE>
  </HEAD>
<BODY bgcolor = "#ffffff">
<%@ page import="java.io.*" %>
<%
String Title = request.getParameter("TITLE");
String Author = request.getParameter("AUTHOR");
String Publisher = request.getParameter("PUBLISHER");
String Year = request.getParameter("YEAR");
String ISBN = request.getParameter("ISBN");
String Description = request.getParameter("DESCRIPTION");
String Category = request.getParameter("CATEGORY");
String Cost = request.getParameter("COST");
String status = new String("A");  // A for available
```

```
try {
    out.println(author + " " + TITLE + " " + CATEGORY + " " + ISBN
                + " " + PUBLISHER + " " + YEAR + " " + DESCRIPTION
                + " " + COST +" "+ STATUS);

    Booklist entry = new Booklist();
    oracle.xml.parser.v2.DTD dtd = entry.getDTDNode();
    TITLE t = new TITLE(TITLE);
    AUTHOR a = new AUTHOR(AUTHOR);
    PUBLISHER p = new PUBLISHER(PUBLISHER);
    YEAR y = new YEAR(YEAR);
    ISBN i = new ISBN(isbn);
    CATEGORY c = new CATEGORY(CATEGORY);
    COST ct = new COST(COST);
    STATUS st = new STATUS(STATUS);

    entry.addNode(t);
    entry.addNode(a);
    entry.addNode(p);
    entry.addNode(y);
    entry.addNode(i);
    entry.addNode(c);
    entry.addNode(ct);
    entry.addNode(st);
    entry.print(new FileOutputStream("result.xml"));
    }
catch (Exception e) {
    out.println("...." + e + "..e.");
    e.printStackTrace(new PrintWriter(out));
}
%>
</BODY>
</HTML>
```

Using JavaScript and providing a fill-in form interface, this JSP can be called from an HTML page. The following HTML page is an example of this; it produces the book submission form shown in Figure 8-8.

```
<html>
<head>
  <title>Book Submission Form</title>
</head>
<body bgcolor="#ffffff">
<script language="JavaScript">
  function checkRequiredFields() {
    var frmR = window.document.frmReport;
    if (frmR.title.value == "") {
```

```
        alert("Please enter a value for the title");
        return false;
      }
      if (frmR.author.value  == "") {
        alert("Please enter the author");
        return false;
      }
      if (frmR.publisher.value  == "") {
        alert("Please enter the publisher");
        return false;
      }
      if (frmR.year.value  == "") {
        alert("Please enter the Year");
        return false;
      }
      if (frmR.isbn.value  == "") {
        alert("Please enter the ISBN number");
        return false;
      }
      if (frmR.description.value  == "") {
        alert("Please enter the description");
        return false;
      }
      if (frmR.category.value  == "") {
        alert("Please enter the category - Fiction, Nonfiction,
              Reference, or   Technical");
        return false;
      }
      if (frmR.isbn.cost  == "") {
        alert("Please enter the cost");
        return false;
      }
   frmR.action = "procSell.jsp";
   frmR.submit();
   return true;
}
/script>
</p>
<h3><img src="openbook.gif"> Oracle Used Books Store  
<a href=""><font size="-1"><i>Main</i></font></a></h3>
<br>
<br>
<br>
<h4>Seller Form</h4>
<form name="frmReport">
  <table width="90%" align="center">
    <tr>
      <td><div align="left"><p><font color="red">*</font>Title</td>
```

```
      <td><input type="text" name="TITLE" value size="60"></td>
    </tr>
    <tr>
      <td><div align="left"><p><font color="red">*</font>Author</td>
      <td><input type="text" name="AUTHOR" value size="60"></td>
    </tr>
    <tr>
      <td><div align="left"><p><font color="red">*</font>Publisher</td>
      <td><input type="text" name="PUBLISHER" value size="60"></td>
    </tr>
    <tr>
      <td><div align="left"><p><font color="red">*</font>Year</td>
      <td><input type="text" name="YEAR" value size="4"></td>
    </tr>
    <tr>
      <td><div align="left"><p><font color="red">*</font>ISBN</td>
      <td><input type="text" name="ISBN" value size="20"></td>
    </tr>
    <tr>
      <td<div align="left"><p><font color="red">*</font>
          Description</td>
      <td><input type="text" name="DESCRIPTION" value size="200"></td>
    </tr>
    <tr>
      <td><div align="left"><p><font color="red">*</font>Category</td>
      <td><input type="text" name="CATEGORY" value size="12"></td>
    </tr>
    <tr>
      <td><div align="left"><p><font color="red">*</font>Cost $</td>
      <td><input type="text" name="COST" value size="6"></td>
    </tr>
  </table>
  <p><br>
    <input type="button" value="Submit" onClick=
        "checkRequiredFields();">
    <input type="reset" value="Reset">
  </p>
 </form>
</body>
</html>
```

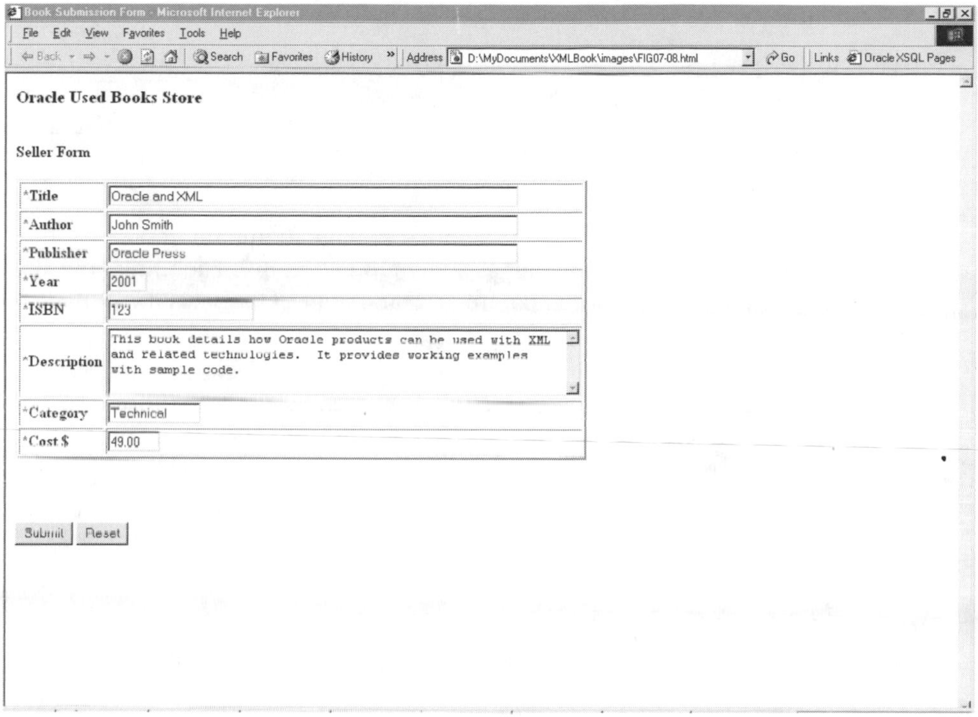

FIGURE 8-8. *Example book submission form*

The following is an example of the XML document produced by the JSP and passed to the XML SQL Utility for insertion:

```
<?xml version="1.0"?>
<Booklist>
  <BookID>001234</BookID>
  <Title>The Difference Between God and Larry Ellison: Inside Oracle
      Corporation</Title>
  <Author>Mike Wilson</Author>
```

```
<Publisher>William Morrow & Co.</Publisher>
<Year>1997</Year>
<ISBN>0688144251</ISBN>
<Description>Account of Larry Ellison</Description>
<Category>Computer</Category>
<Cost>30.00</Cost>
<Status>A</Status>
</Booklist>
```

To design the buyer Web page, we use an XSQL page to initially represent a query based on the categories available, as shown in Figure 8-9. Each link could call a specific page as follows, or the parameter capability of the servlet can pass the category to a generic page.

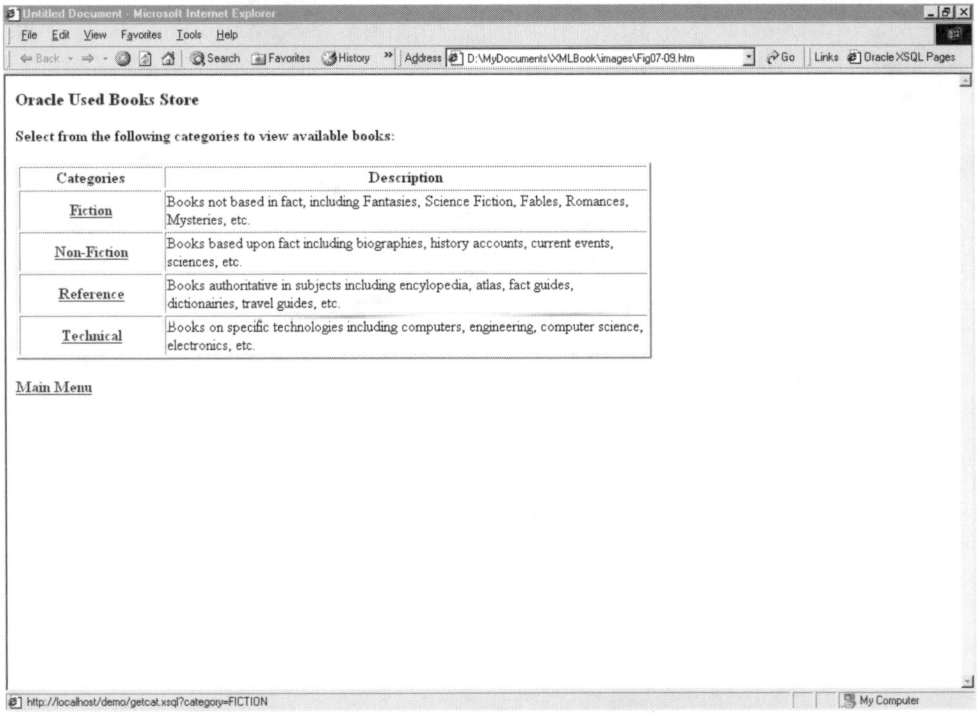

FIGURE 8-9. *Bookstore category submission page*

```
<?xml version="1.0"?>
<xsql-stylesheet type="text/xsl" href="categorydetail.xsl"?>
<xsql:query xmlns:xsql="urn:oracle-xsql" connection="demo"
    SELECT Title, Author, Description, Cost FROM Booklist
      WHERE Category = FICTION
</xsql:query>
```

The **categorydetail.xsl** stylesheet can then format the display of listings and add the form action to allow for the purchase. By utilizing the update capability detailed previously, the Status column can be changed from A, available, to S, sold, and the trigger procedure could be extended to send an e-mail notification of the sale by using the **utl_smtp** package.

The remaining task is to set up a form to create accounts on the system and keep track of submissions and sales. You can do this using the XML SQL Utility, Class Generator, and JSP architecture of the book submission. The implementation is left to the reader, but the following example XML file is provided to get started:

```
<Client>
    <ClientID>123456</ClientID>
    <Name>Mike Wilson</Name>
    <Address>123 Main St.</Address>
    <City>San Francisco</City>
    <State>CA</State>
    <Country>USA</Country>
    <Zipcode>94000</Zipcode>
    <Email>mwilson@anyhere.com</Email>
    <Date>03-MAY-2002</Date>
    <Time>22:00</Time>
    <Status>A</Status>
    <Account>
      <Buy>
          <BookID>103454</BookID>
          <Date>04-JUN-2003</Date>
          <Time>11:05</Time>
      </Buy>
      <Sell>
          <BookID>001234</BookID>
          <Date>03-MAY-2002</Date>
          <Time>22:00</Time>
      </Sell>
    </Account>
</Client>
```

Extending the Example

The bookstore example, while simple, can be easily extended in a number of areas. On the client side, you could add a search function that uses the "fuzzy match" capability described previously. Java or PL/SQL stored procedures could call into an authorization service to verify credit information and return a card approval number. By accepting XML book listings from other vendors, the site could act simply as an aggregator, leaving it up to the sellers to actually process the shipment.

While this example showed a consumer-to-business relationship, the same technology and architecture could be used for a business-to-business site. Wholesalers and manufacturers could present their inventories for businesses to bid, or conversely, businesses could post a purchase order that would trigger messages to be sent to vendors to bid on fulfillment.

In the case of application-to-application messaging, the XML SQL Utility's classes can be called directly to read and write data. Taking advantage of Oracle 8*i*'s *Advanced Queuing (AQ)* and Oracle Workflow, routing logic can be applied to prioritize and send the messages in the proper order. See the following section on the Oracle Integration Server for more details.

Oracle Integration Server

The *Oracle Integration Server (OIS)* is a suite of products designed to provide the generic XML-based messaging infrastructure that allows easy implementation of application integration across intranets or the Internet. Figure 8-10 shows the architecture of OIS. Note that this is based on a hub-and-spoke architecture that simplifies administration and management by reducing the routing. Adapters are built or provided to generate the XML message payload that is accepted by *Oracle Message Broker (OMB)*. OMB then packages the message in a Java Messaging Service envelope and routes it to the hub. This type of transport has the advantage of being transparent to firewalls, as well as providing control over service quality and resource usage.

Once the message arrives at the hub, as shown in Figure 8-11, it is queued and submitted to the rules engine within Oracle Workflow for proper routing. XSL stylesheets are utilized to transform the message into the destination's desired format, and it is requeued and sent via OMB to one or more receiving applications.

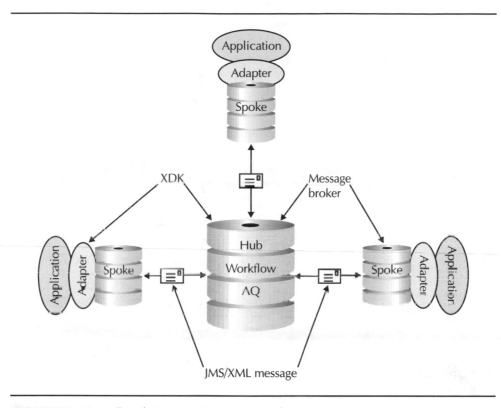

FIGURE 8-10. *Oracle Integration Server architecture*

This type of messaging, enabled by the XML open standards, permits applications to be loosely coupled and to communicate asynchronously, placing the integration logic in the hub instead of hard-coded into the applications.

As can be seen from the examples, XML and databases are closely linked at many levels of application integration. The missing piece that allows this to occur seamlessly is the XML schema standard. Already, vendor-neutral groups, such as XML.org and the Open Applications Group, have begun to create repositories

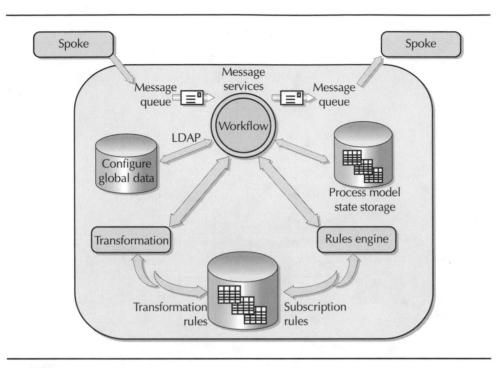

FIGURE 8-11. *Oracle Integration Server Hub architecture*

of specific industry DTDs and schemas to permit businesses in the same market segment to exchange data easily. The addition of simple and complex data types to the XML technology stack will permit precise data mappings in an open standard. This will only speed the adoption of XML as the data interchange format.

CHAPTER
9

A Case Study Using Oracle's XML-Enabled Technology Stack

hroughout this book, we have presented the wide range of Oracle's products that have become XML-enabled, and we have introduced many of the XML standards. In this chapter, we will explore the development and deployment of a real-world application that utilizes these standards with the Oracle XDKs and the new XML features of Oracle9i. In this application, we explore the important capabilities of XSLT, the XML Class Generator, the XSQL Servlet, the XML SQL Utility, Oracle Text, and new XML datatypes and operators introduced in Oracle9i.

An XML-Enabled FAQ Web Site

A frequent requirement for companies that maintain a Web presence is to have a support area for their products. This area may range from simple electronic versions of their owner's manuals to a moderated discussion forum. A popular support area feature is to have a FAQ (frequently asked questions) section for each product. This is the application that is the subject of this case study; it is illustrated in Figure 9-1.

Visitors to the site will be able to see all the FAQ subject areas on the home page and can also search and select from the most frequently viewed FAQs. Whenever the list of FAQs appears, users can see the answers as well as find related FAQs by following the presented links. Inside each FAQ answer are links to an online glossary for technical or special terms. This functionality will be described in detail later in the chapter. Web site administrators are able to load the new FAQs into the database and get statistical data for each FAQ such as the hit count and the last update time.

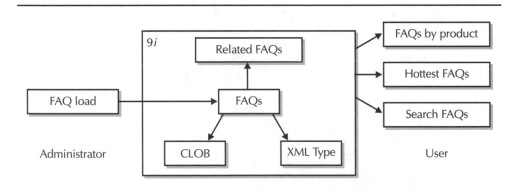

FIGURE 9-1. *Application function diagram*

The Application Requirements

As you have no doubt realized by now, the Oracle XML-enabled products and components are quite extensive and include software development kits in the disparate programming languages of C, C++, PL/SQL, and Java. However, underneath they all provide XML functionality that is programming- language agnostic. This gives rise to an awkward model for providing technical support because many questions that are XML-based can be equally applicable across all of the XDKs, yet there are many language-specific questions that only make sense in one. Therefore, providing an Oracle9i XML FAQ site that can store all questions within a database and designing the schema in a way that FAQs can be tagged as relevant for one or more of the XDKs as well as the XML-enabled database features is a basic requirement for this site.

Besides simply displaying a listing of FAQs per XDK and feature, users would expect a search facility. Since we plan to store the FAQs in Oracle9i, we can take advantage of the Oracle Text (formerly interMedia Text) search engine with its XML support. We will also need a mechanism for submitting FAQs, which can be provided by a Web form.

In most cases, the content for Web sites is delivered from HTML pages stored in file systems on servers. For this application, we will deliver as much of the content as possible from the database. This will give us maximum manageability of the content while at the same time demonstrating most of the Oracle9i XML functionality.

The Application Design

Since this case study describes an application that is designed to be part of a larger Web site, we will focus only on the Web pages that will be part of the FAQ section. Figure 9-2 shows a diagram of the section and the application development and runtime architecture.

Note that the figure shows two types of processing from the database—development and runtime. The application development process flows from the database schema through the XML SQL Utility to create the XML Schema, which is then processed by the class generator to create the application classes. These classes will be then used to build the application based upon the XSQL Servlet. At runtime the application will accept text input in the form of questions and answers and create an XML document that will flow through the Web server to XSU and be deposited into the database. In these next sections, we will walk through the design of this application from start to finish using most of the features of the Oracle9i database and XDK.

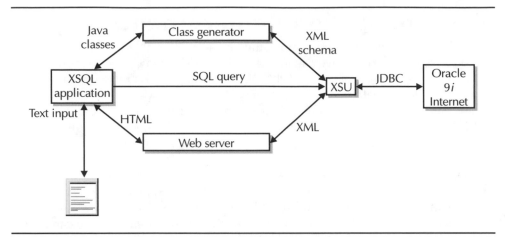

FIGURE 9-2. *Diagram of FAQ application development and runtime*

The Database Schema Design

For this application, we will leverage the database as much as possible. This will require creating a schema to store not only the question and its associated answer but also metadata that will permit associating the FAQ with XML components and features as well as tracking the submissions and selections. We will also store keywords and their definitions to create a glossary of technical terms. Finally, we will support linking to related FAQs and provide performance enhancements utilizing CLOBs in cache tables.

The database schema will be a simple one and will consist of an **xmlfaq_ xmltype** table with category, question, questionde (detailed question), answer, language, sendby, and createtime columns. The answer and questionde columns will be created as an XMLType to permit storing and indexing the answers as XML documents. The following script will create this schema:

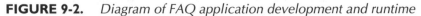

```
Rem Script to create XML Faq Schema
CREATE TABLE xdkfaq_xmltype(
    question     VARCHAR2(4000) NOT NULL,
    questionde   sys.xmltype NOT NULL,
    answer       sys.xmltype NOT NULL,
    category     VARCHAR2(30),
    language     VARCHAR2(4000),
    id  NUMBER,
    createtime   VARCHAR2(30),
```

```
   CONSTRAINT  xdkfaq_xmltype_pk PRIMARY KEY (id)
);
create sequence xdkfaqid_seq start with 1;
```

The next table in the schema, which will be very similar, will be used for ease of displaying the questions and answers in a browser. To store FAQs, the following **xdkfaq** table is created:

```
CREATE TABLE xdkfaq(
    question      VARCHAR2(4000) NOT NULL,
    questionde    VARCHAR2(4000) NOT NULL,
    answer        VARCHAR2(4000) NOT NULL,
    category      VARCHAR2(32) NOT NULL,
    language      VARCHAR2(10) NOT NULL,
    createtime    VARCHAR2(20) NOT NULL,
    diff          NUMBER,
    id            NUMBER NOT NULL,
    hits          NUMBER,
    sendby        VARCHAR2(10),
    CONSTRAINT xdkfaq_pk  PRIMARY KEY (id)
);
create sequence xdkfaqgl_seq start with 1;
```

The question, questionde, and answer columns are used to store FAQs. The category, language, createtime, hits, and sendby columns will be used by the administrator to manage the FAQs that will also be used for searching.

In this table, we also have an ID column that will be the unique ID of each FAQ. Creating the sequence xdkfaqid_seq with the SQL statement in the last line generates the ID. Then for each FAQ's input, the ID will be generated by using this sequence in the trigger, such as:

```
   select xdkfaqid_seq.nextval
   into :new.ID
   from dual;
```

To create the glossary, we need to create a table that can be linked to specific rows using the DBURIType. The link column will be the DBUri-ref link pointing to the content of the glossary item. The following script will create this table:

```
CREATE TABLE xdkfaq_glossary(
    id       NUMBER NOT NULL,
    name     VARCHAR2(30),
    link     VARCHAR2(100),
    content  VARCHAR2(4000),
    CONSTRAINT xdkfaq_gloss  PRIMARY KEY (id)
);
```

Finally, we want this Web site to perform. To ensure this, we can create a cache that can be used when displaying a fixed set such as the top 20 FAQs. The following script creates two tables to implement the cache:

```
CREATE TABLE xdkfaq_ccache(
   category   VARCHAR2(32) NOT NULL,
   content    CLOB NOT NULL,
   CONSTRAINT xdkfaqccache_pk PRIMARY KEY (category)
);
```

Note that we start with the database schema design and then create the necessary XML schema from the database schema. This is dictated because the database will likely be the more constrained of the two, and in most cases where the XML is stored as data, stripped of its tags, there will be alternative SQL accesses/updates to this data that the design will need to take into account.

Generating the XML Schema

Once we have the database schema designed and created, we can use the XML SQL Utility to generate the associated XML Schema. To do this, we can simply issue the following query via XSU:

```
select category, question, answer, language, sendby, createtime from xdkfaq
```

The following is the listing of the XML schema generated from the preceding query:

```
<xsd:schema xmlns:xsd="http://www.w3.org/2000/10/XMLSchema">
  <xsd:element name="ROWSET">
   <xsd:complexType>
    <xsd:sequence>
     <xsd:element name="ROW" minOccurs="0" maxOccurs="unbounded">
      <xsd:complexType>
       <xsd:sequence>
        <xsd:element name="CATEGORY" type="xsd:string" minOccurs="0"/>
        <xsd:element name="QUESTION" type="xsd:string" minOccurs="0"/>
        <xsd:element name="ANSWER" type="xsd:string" minOccurs="0"/>
        <xsd:element name="LANGUAGE" type="xsd:string" minOccurs="0"/>
        <xsd:element name="SENDBY" type="xsd:string" nullable="true"
         minOccurs="0"/>
        <xsd:element name="CREATETIME" type="xsd:string" minOccurs="0"/>
       </xsd:sequence>
       <xsd:attribute name="num" type="xsd:integer"/>
      </xsd:complexType>
     </xsd:element>
```

```
     </xsd:sequence>
    </xsd:complexType>
   </xsd:element>
  </xsd:schema>
```

Note that the mapping from the database to the XML Schema creates elements from the table columns instead of attributes. Since XML Schemas can only type attributes as XML simple types, this mapping to elements provides a much richer data typing capability, which is essential once we start developing more sophisticated schemas specifying nested tables, ranges, and so on.

Generating the Java Classes

Now that we have the XML Schema corresponding to the database schema, we can use the Java Class Generator to generate the classes that we can then use in Java applications, applets, or Java Server Pages (JSP) to insert XML data back into the database. This can be done quite easily by using **oracg.bat** from the command line. The following is the command line for **xmlfaq.xsd** file:

```
java oracg -c -s xmlfaq.xsd -p rowset
```

This command will produce the **rowset.java** class source code file. Though the listing is too long to reproduce here, the following is a fragment to show the type of classes generated:

```
/**
 * Adds the local element
 * @param QUESTION the element node
 * @exception  InvalidContentException if the element is not valid.
 */
public void addQUESTION(ROWSET.ROWSET_Type.ROW.ROW_Type.QUESTION theQUESTION)
         throws InvalidContentException
             {
                 super.addElement(theQUESTION);
             }
/**
 * Adds the local element
 * @param ANSWER the element node
 * @exception  InvalidContentException if the element is not valid.
 */
public void addANSWER(ROWSET.ROWSET_Type.ROW.ROW_Type.ANSWER theANSWER)
         throws InvalidContentException
             {
                 super.addElement(theANSWER);
             }.
```

You should note that the code is commented to make it easier to use and extend.

Storing XML Documents as XMLType

Before creating the application itself, we need to introduce the Oracle9i XMLType. In Oracle9i, a new system-defined datatype called XMLType is provided for handling XML documents. XMLType can be used *inside the server* in PL/SQL and SQL. In this application, we will use this new datatype to:

- Store XML documents as XMLTypes

- Generate XMLType data using SYS_XMLGEN and SYS_XMLAGG

- Extract data using **Extract()** and **ExistsNode()** from XMLType

- Perform searches with XML documents stored as XMLType by creating functional indexes

To store an XML document as an XMLType, we can simply define a column of XMLType as we did previously. We can then use the XMLType constructor to create an XMLType instance before inserting the document into the column by using SYS_XMLGEN or SYS_XMLAGG.

Generating XML Using SYS_XMLGEN and SYS_XMLAGG

The SYS_XMLGEN and SYS_XMLAGG functions are native SQL functions that can be used not only to instantiate an XMLType, but also to generate or aggregate XML documents from within SQL queries. The following query uses SYS_XMLGEN to extract all keywords and return them in a set of XML documents where each corresponds to one answer with ROW as the root:

```
select sys_xmlgen(f.answer.extract('//keywords')).getStringVal()
  from xdkfaq_xmltype f;
```

The next query uses SYS_XMLGEN to extract the same keywords but returns them all aggregated into a single XML document with ROWSET as the root containing all of the ROWs.

```
select sys_xmlagg( sys_xmlgen(f.answer.extract('//keywords'))).getStringVal()
  from xdkfaq_xmltype f;
```

Extracting Data by Using Extract() and ExistsNode() from XMLType

The preceding queries use the **Extract()** function from XMLType. This function can be used to retrieve portions of an XML document stored as an XML type. It will return nodes of the XML document, as the following query and its result show:

```
select extract(e.answer,'keywords').getStringVal()
    from xdkfaq_xmltype e
    where existsNode(e.answer,'code')>0;
```

This is a fraction of the result:

```
<keywords>importNode</keywords>
<keywords>adoptNode</keywords>
<keywords>document fragment</keywords>
<keywords>owner document</keywords>
```

Using XMLType for Related FAQs

For the FAQs Web site we can take advantage of the XMLType to build the related FAQs' functionality. These FAQs are based on the "keywords" element within the answer. There are two ways to implement this. In the first way, we will build a table to store the relations between FAQs, as in the following listing:

```
CREATE TABLE xdkfaq_urimanage(
    keyword  VARCHAR2(300) NOT NULL,
    faqid    NUMBER NOT NULL,
    CONSTRAINT faquri_pk PRIMARY KEY (keyword,faqid)
);
```

The data is input via the trigger in the INSERT SQL statement within the following code fragment:

```
key_typea  sys.xmlType;
….
key_typea := sys.xmltype.createxml(:new.answer);
  if key_typea.existsNode('//keywords') =1 THEN
    LOOP
      v_temp:= key_typea.extract('//keywords['||i||']/text()');
      EXIT WHEN v_temp IS NULL;

      key := v_temp.getStringVal();
      i := i+1;
```

```
      -- Insert new content to xdkfaq_query
      INSERT INTO xdkfaq_urimanage(keyword,faqid) VALUES(key,:new.id);
    END LOOP;
  END IF;
```

Thus the XSQL page will be as follows:

```
<?xml version="1.0"?>
<?xml-stylesheet type="text/xsl" media="mozilla" href="xsl/faqrelative.xsl"?>
<page  connection="xdkdemo" xmlns:xsql="urn:oracle-xsql">
<xsql:set-page-param  name="SIG" value="{@sig}" />
<xsql:query>
    <![CDATA[
     select faq.id,
            faq.question,
        cursor(select question, id,
            sys_dburigen(faq1.ID,faq1.answer).getUrl() as quri,
            sys_dburigen(faq1.ID,faq1.answer).getUrl() as auri
            from xdkfaq faq1
            where faq1.id in (select distinct(uri.faqid)
                from xdkfaq_urimanage uri
            where uri.keyword in ( select keyword
                        from xdkfaq_urimanage
                        where faqid = {@id})
            and uri.faqid != {@id}))
      as relatives
     from xdkfaq faq
     where faq.id = {@id}
     ORDER BY question
    ]]>
</xsql:query>
<xsql:include-param name="SIG" />
</page>
```

The other approach takes advantage of the performance improvement from
using functional indexes on XMLType and retrieves the related FAQs with the
following XSQL page:

```
<?xml version="1.0"?>
<?xml-stylesheet type="text/xsl"  href="xdkfaqrelative.xsl"?
<page connection="xdkdemo" xmlns:xsql="urn:oracle-xsql">
<xsql:dml>
 alter session set query_rewrite_enabled=true
</xsql:dml>
<xsql:dml>
 alter session set query_rewrite_integrity=trusted
</xsql:dml>
<xsql:include-owa>
    show_related({@id});
</xsql:include-owa>
</page>
```

The PL/SQL procedure **show_related** is as follows:

```
CREATE OR REPLACE PROCEDURE show_related (p_id in NUMBER) IS
    I    NUMBER :=1;    -- relative FAQ variables
    key_typea        sys.xmlType;
    key    VARCHAR2(300);
    v_temp      sys.xmltype;
    v_temp1     sys.xmltype;
    v_result   VARCHAR2(4000);
    v_question VARCHAR2(4000);
BEGIN
    htp.p('<ROWSET>');
    htp.p('<ROW>');
    htp.p('<ID>');
    htp.print(p_id);
    htp.p('</ID>');
    htp.p('<QUESTION>');
    select f.questionde.extract('/question/text()').getClobVal()
      into v_question from xdkfaq_xmltype f where id = p_id;
    htp.print(v_question);
    htp.p('</QUESTION>');
    htp.p('<RELATIVES>');
    ----------------------------------------------------------
    -- Get relative faq for each keyword
    ----          ---------------------------------------------
    select answer into key_typea from xdkfaq_xmltype  where id = p_id;
    if key_typea.existsNode('//keywords') =1 THEN
    LOOP
        v_temp:= key_typea.extract('//keywords['||i||']/text()');
        EXIT WHEN v_temp IS NULL;

        key := v_temp.getStringVal();
        i := i+1;
        select sys_xmlagg(sys_xmlgen(relative_type(e.question,
          e.id),sys.xmlgenformattype.createformat('RELATIVES_ROW'))
            ).extract('/ROWSET//RELATIVES_ROW').getClobVal() into v_result
        from xdkfaq_xmltype e
        where e.id != p_id and e.id in (
        select f.id from xdkfaq_xmltype f
        where f.answer.extract('/answer//keywords/text()').getClobVal() like '%'||key||'%');
        htp.print(v_result);
      END LOOP;
    END IF;
    htp.p('</RELATIVES>');
    htp.p('</ROW>');
    htp.p('</ROWSET>');
EXCEPTION
    when others then
    BEGIN
        htp.p('</RELATIVES>');
        htp.p('<error>exception</error>');
        htp.p('</ROW>');
        htp.p('</ROWSET>');
    END;
END show_related;
```

Creating the Web Application

This FAQ Web application will be developed using the XSQL Servlet as its underlying engine. This servlet, introduced in Oracle8i and refined in Oracle9i, is a robust and flexible platform for this type of application. We will use it in the following ways:

- To generate the static content from pages stored in the database

- To accept FAQs for inclusion in the database

- To provide a keyword search interface

- To display the results from the various queries in the browser

- To manage the database connections

We have already covered the XSQL Servlet's capability to display static content. Figure 9-3 shows the entry page of our application where the actual content, in xHTML, and its stylesheet are retrieved from the database cache table by passing the page name to the XSQL Servlet.

Submitting FAQs

To be able to submit FAQs, we will use the classes we generated with the Class Generator in an XSQL action handler. Before we can do this, we must first create a form for the user to enter the FAQ data. Figure 9-4 shows the form created by retrieving **submit.xml** from the database and transforming it with **submit.xsl**.

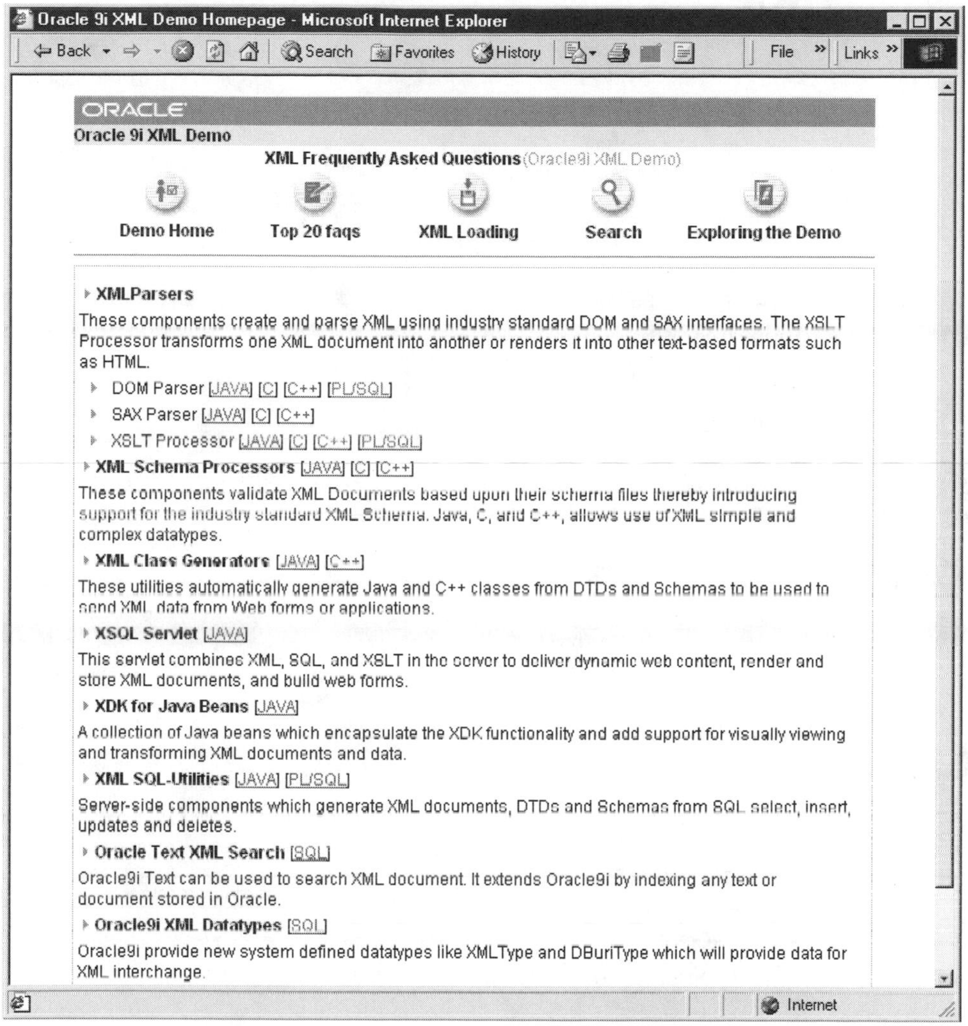

FIGURE 9-3. *The FAQ entry page*

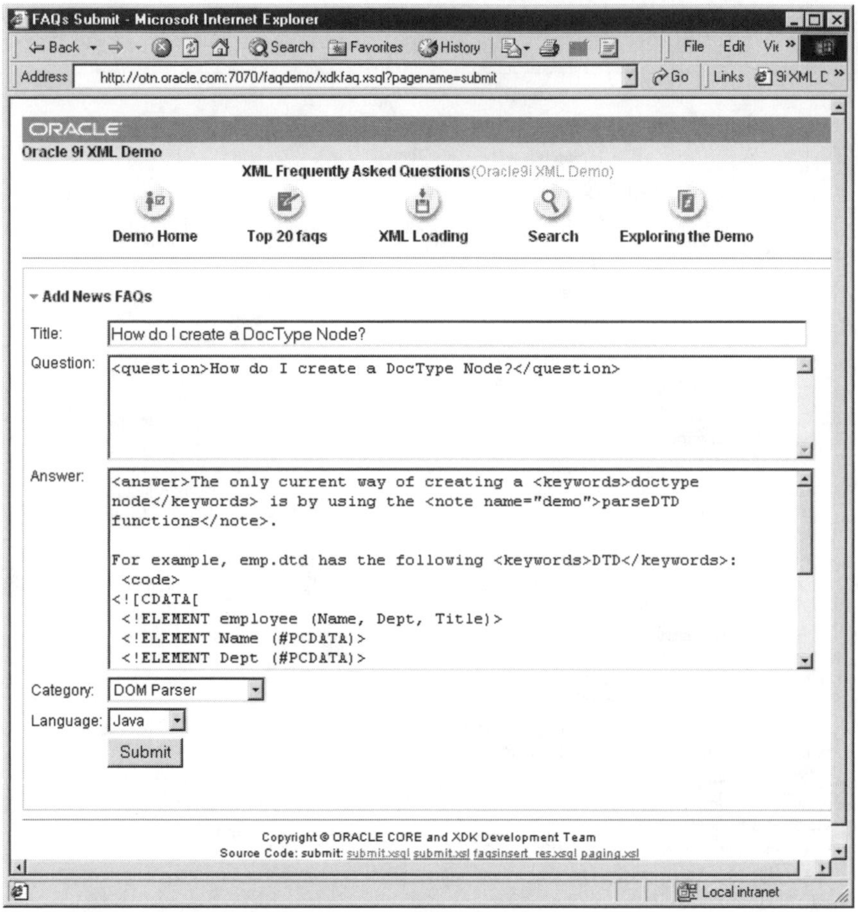

FIGURE 9-4. *FAQ Submission Form*

The following fragment is the active part of this page; it shows how data is passed to a second XSQL page, **faqsinsert_res**, that calls the action handler.

```
<tr>
  <td colspan="2" height="366">
    <form method="post" action="xdkfaq.xsql?pagename=faqsinsert_res"
     name="addfaqs">
      <table width="60%" border="0">
        <tr>
          <td width="5%">Title:</td>
          <td width="95%">
            <input type="text" name="title" size="80"
```

```
              value="How do I create a DocType Node?">
      </td>
    </tr>
    <tr>
      <td width="5%" valign="top">Question:</td>
      <td width="95%">
        <textarea name="question" cols="70"
         rows="5">&lt;question&gt;&lt;/question&gt;</textarea>
      </td>
    </tr>
    <tr>
      <td width="5%" valign="top">Answer:</td>
      <td width="95%">
        <textarea name="answer" cols="70" rows="10">
        &lt;
        answer&gt;
        The only current way of creating a &lt;keywords&gt;
        doctype node&lt;/keywords&gt;
        is by using the &lt;note name="demo"&gt;
        parseDTD functions&lt;/note&gt;.
        For example, emp.dtd has the following
        &lt;keywords&gt;DTD&lt;/keywords&gt;:&lt;code&gt;&lt;
        ![CDATA[
          &lt;!ELEMENT employee (Name, Dept, Title)&gt;
          &lt;!ELEMENT Name (#PCDATA)&gt;
          &lt;!ELEMENT Dept (#PCDATA)&gt;
          &lt;!ELEMENT Title (#PCDATA)&gt;
        ]]&gt;
        &lt;/code&gt;
        You can use the following code to create a doctype node:
        &lt;code&gt;
        parser.parseDTD(new FileInputStream(emp.dtd), "employee");
        doc = parser.getDocument();
        /* doc has the dtd as its child or dtd = parser.getDoctype();*/
        &lt;/code&gt;&lt;/answer&gt;</textarea>
      </td>
    </tr>
    <tr>
      <td width="5%">Category:</td>
      <td width="95%">
        <select name="comp">
          <option value="domparser">DOM Parser</option>
          <option value="saxparser">SAX Parser</option>
          <option value="xslt">XSL Processor</option>
          <option value="schema">Schema Processor</option>
          <option value="xsu">XML SQL Utility</option>
          <option value="xsql">XSQL Servlet</option>
          <option value="soap">SOAP</option>
          <option value="jbeans">Java Beans</option>
        </select>
      </td>
```

```
      </tr>
      <tr>
        <td width="5%">Language:</td>
        <td width="95%">
          <select name="lang">
            <option value="java">Java</option>
            <option value="c">C</option>
            <option value="cpp">C++</option>
            <option value="plsql">PL/SQL</option>
            <option value="xml">XML</option>
          </select>
        </td>
      </tr>
      <tr>
        <td width="5%" valign="top" height="8"> </td>
        <td width="95%" height="8">
          <input type="submit" name="Submit" value="Submit">
        </td>
      </tr>
    </table>
  </form>
```

The following source for **faqsinsert_res.xsql** is quite simple and to the point:

```
<?xml version="1.0" ?>
<!-- <?xml-stylesheet type="text/xsl" href="xsl/faqsinsert_res.xsl"?>
-->
<page connection="xdkdemo" xmlns:xsql="urn:oracle-xsql">
<webpage title="Insert FAQs Items">
  <xsql:action handler="FAQsInsertDemo" />
  </webpage>
  </page>
```

The **FAQsInsertDemo** action handler is a Java class utilizing our generated classes and a JDBC connection to insert the FAQ into the database. The following is the source for that class:

```
import java.sql.*;
import java.net.*;
import oracle.xml.xsql.*;
import oracle.xml.sql.dml.OracleXMLSave;
import javax.servlet.http.*;
import oracle.xml.parser.v2.*;
import org.w3c.dom.*;
import java.io.*;
import org.xml.sax.SAXParseException;
import java.io.StringReader;
import oracle.xml.parser.v2.XMLOutputStream;
import oracle.xml.classgen.CGXSDElement;
```

```java
import oracle.xml.classgen.SchemaClassGenerator;
import oracle.xml.classgen.InvalidContentException;
import ROWSET;
public class FAQsInsertDemo extends XSQLActionHandlerImpl
{
  ByteArrayInputStream bInput= null;
  String m_title=null;
  String m_question=null;
  String m_answer=null;
  String m_status=null;
  String m_comp=null;
  String m_lang=null;
  public void handleAction(Node root) throws SQLException
  {
    if(getPageRequest().getRequestType().equals("Servlet"))
    {
      /*
      ** get request parameters
      */
      XSQLServletPageRequest xspr =
(XSQLServletPageRequest)getPageRequest();
      HttpServletRequest req = xspr.getHttpServletRequest();
      m_title = req.getParameter("title");
      m_question = req.getParameter("question");
      m_answer = req.getParameter("answer");
      m_status = req.getParameter("status");
      m_comp = req.getParameter("comp");
      m_lang = req.getParameter("lang");
      /*
      ** XML well-formedness check and validation of question and answer
      */
      DOMParser dp = new DOMParser();
      try {
        dp.parse(new StringReader(m_question));
      }
      catch (SAXParseException spe){
        this.reportError(root,"Please check the question"+
                    " Input, it needs to be well-formed.\n Error:"
                    +spe.getMessage());
        return;
      }
      catch(Exception e){}
      try {
        dp.parse(new StringReader(m_answer));
      }
      catch (SAXParseException spe){
        this.reportError(root,"Please check the answer"+
                    " Input, it needs to be well-formed.\n
                    Error:"+spe.getMessage());
        return;
      }
```

```
catch(Exception e){}
/*
** User Generated Classes to build XML document
*/
ByteArrayOutputStream baos = new ByteArrayOutputStream();
DataOutputStream output = new DataOutputStream(baos);
XMLOutputStream  out = new XMLOutputStream(output);
try {
   ROWSET.ROWSET_Type rstype = new ROWSET.ROWSET_Type();
   ROWSET.ROWSET_Type.ROW.ROW_Type rtype =
   new ROWSET.ROWSET_Type.ROW.ROW_Type();
   Integer num_in = new Integer(1);
   rtype.setNum(num_in);
   /*
   * Set data for the ROW
   */
   ROWSET.ROWSET_Type.ROW.ROW_Type.CATEGORY category =
       new ROWSET.ROWSET_Type.ROW.ROW_Type.CATEGORY();
   category.setType(m_comp);
   rtype.addCATEGORY(category);

   ROWSET.ROWSET_Type.ROW.ROW_Type.QUESTION question =
       new ROWSET.ROWSET_Type.ROW.ROW_Type.QUESTION();
   question.setType(m_title);
   rtype.addQUESTION(question);
   ROWSET.ROWSET_Type.ROW.ROW_Type.QUESTIONDE questionde =
       new ROWSET.ROWSET_Type.ROW.ROW_Type.QUESTIONDE();
   questionde.setType(filter(m_question));
   rtype.addQUESTIONDE(questionde);
   ROWSET.ROWSET_Type.ROW.ROW_Type.ANSWER answer =
       new ROWSET.ROWSET_Type.ROW.ROW_Type.ANSWER();
   answer.setType(filter(m_answer));
   rtype.addANSWER(answer);
   ROWSET.ROWSET_Type.ROW.ROW_Type.LANGUAGE language =
       new ROWSET.ROWSET_Type.ROW.ROW_Type.LANGUAGE();
   language.setType(m_lang);
   rtype.addLANGUAGE(language);

   ROWSET.ROWSET_Type.ROW.ROW_Type.DIFF diff =
       new ROWSET.ROWSET_Type.ROW.ROW_Type.DIFF();
   diff.setType(new Integer(1));
   rtype.addDIFF(diff);
   ROWSET.ROWSET_Type.ROW row = new ROWSET.ROWSET_Type.ROW();
   row.setType(rtype);
   rstype.addROW(row);
   ROWSET rowset = new ROWSET();
   rowset.setType(rstype);

   rowset.print(out);
   out.flush();
```

```
      /*
      ** Print out to ByteArrayInputStream
      */
      byte[] data = baos.toByteArray();
      out.close();
      bInput = new ByteArrayInputStream(data);
      }catch(InvalidContentException ex)
      {
        this.reportError(root,ex.getMessage());
        //e.printStackTrace();
        return;
      }
      catch(IOException e)
      {
       this.reportError(root,e.getMessage());
       //e.printStackTrace();
       return;
      }
      /*
      ** Connect to Database and send the data
      */
      try {
        Connection conn = xspr.getJDBCConnection();
        OracleXMLSave sav = new OracleXMLSave(conn,"xdkdemo.xdkfaq");
        sav.insertXML(bInput);
        sav.close();
        /*
        ** Output generated xml file to the screen
        */
        String outtemp=baos.toString();

        Element e =
           getActionElement().getOwnerDocument().createElement("InputDoc");
        addResultElement(e,"CONTENT",outtemp);
        root.appendChild(e);
        bInput.close();
        conn.close();
      }
      catch(Exception e){
       this.reportError(root,"Exception caught "+e.getMessage());
       return;
      }
    }
}
public static String filter(String input)
{
    if (input == null) return "";
    StringBuffer filtered = new StringBuffer(input.length());
    char c;
    for( int i=0; i<input.length(); i++)
```

```
        {
        c = input.charAt(i);
        if(c == '<')
        {
                filtered.append("&lt;");
        }
        else if(c == '>')
        {
                filtered.append("&gt;");
        }
        else if(c == '"')
        {
                filtered.append("&quot;");
        }
        else if(c == '&')
        {
                filtered.append("&amp;");
        }
        else
        {
                filtered.append(c);
        }
        }
        return (filtered.toString());
    }
}
```

Searching for FAQs

Now that we have a mechanism for inserting FAQs, we need a way to retrieve them.
This can be done once again with an XSQL page using the capabilities of Oracle Text
in conjunction with XMLType. Figure 9-5 shows the search form that we will use. You
should note that we will be searching by both category and keyword, where the category
is supplied by a drop-down box of the various XML components and the keyword(s)
is free text.

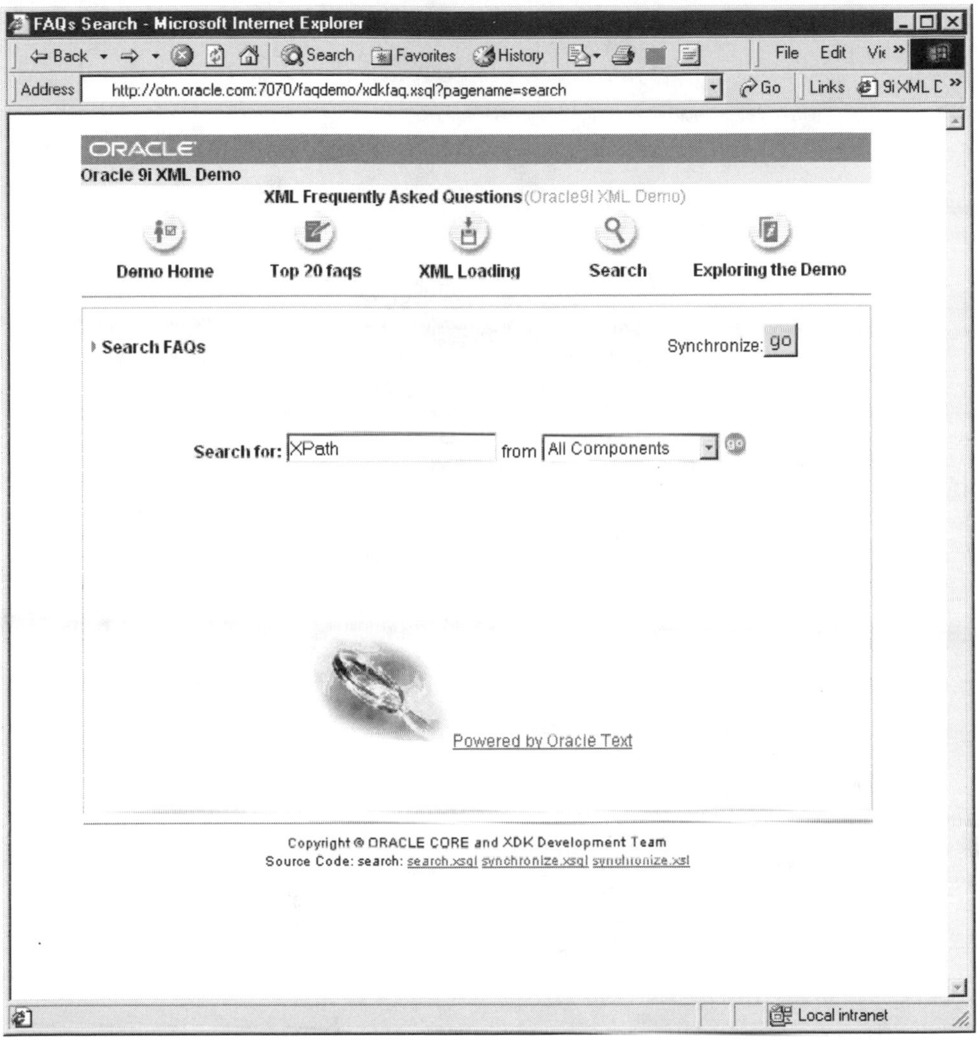

FIGURE 9-5. *The FAQ search form*

The following listing is the active part of the page; it uses the Form method to pass the parameters of the search into an XSQL page that does the actual querying of the database.

```
<form method="post" name="find">
  <b>Search for:</b>
  <input type="text" name="search"> from
  <SELECT name="category" size="1">
          <OPTION value="all" selected>All Components</OPTION>
          <OPTION value="domparser">DOM Parser</OPTION>
          <OPTION value="saxparser">SAX Parser</OPTION>
          <OPTION value="xslt">XSLT Processor</OPTION>
          <OPTION value="schema">Schema Processor</OPTION>
          <OPTION value="classgen">Class Generator</OPTION>
          <OPTION value="xsql">XSQL Servlet</OPTION>
          <OPTION value="jbeans">Java Beans</OPTION>
          <OPTION value="xsu">XML SQL Utility</OPTION>
          <OPTION value="xmltype">XMLType</OPTION>
          <OPTION value="dburi">DBUri</OPTION>
          <OPTION value="oracletext">Oracle Text</OPTION>
  </SELECT>
  <A href="xdkfaq.xsql?pagename=faqsearch"
   onClick="if(document.find.category.value=='all')
   search_loc = 'xdkfaq.xsql?pagename=faqsearch&amp;search='
   + document.find.search.value;
   else search_loc =
   'xdkfaq.xsql?pagename=faqsearch_cat&amp;search='
   +document.find.search.value+'&amp;cat=
   '+document.find.category.value;
   document.location.href = search_loc;
   return false;"
   onMouseOver="self.status='xdkfaq.xsql?pagename=faqsearch';
   return true;"
   onMouseOut="self.status=''; return true;">
   <img src="images/go.gif" width="16" height="17" border="0"
    alt="Click to search.">
  </A>
</form>
```

The **faqsearch.xsql** shown on the following listing passes two queries to the database through the XSU and the JDBC driver:

```
<?xml version="1.0" ?>
<page id="1" connection="xdkdemo" xmlns:xsql="urn:oracle-xsql">
  <xsql:set-page-param name="query" value="{@search}" />
<xsql:action handler="Paging" rows-per-page="10"
```

```
   url-params="xdkfaq.xsql?pagename=xdkfaqsearch&">
<![CDATA[
       SELECT count(question) FROM xdkfaq
       WHERE contains(answer,'{@search}')>0
  ]]>
  </xsql:action>
<xsql:query skip-rows="{@paging-skip}" max-rows="{@paging-max}">
<![CDATA[
       SELECT * FROM xdkfaq WHERE contains(answer,'{@search}')>0
       ORDER BY hits DESC
  ]]>
  </xsql:query>
  <xsql:include-param name="query" />
  </page>
```

The first query retrieves the number of FAQs satisfying the search in order that a large number can be paged. The second query actually retrieves the FAQs.

Using HASPATH and INPATH for XMLType Searches

Notice also that we used the CONTAINS operator in the preceding query. If we want to do a specialized search on a specific branch of the answer stored as an XMLType, we can use the new HASPATH and INPATH operators to facilitate finding and retrieving only hits from that branch.

Suppose, for example, we put this in one of the FAQ answers:

```
<answer>
The parser validates a document against its <keywords>DTD</keywords>.
</answer>
```

Then you can use following SQL query to search only answers where "DTD" is a keyword:

```
select * from xdkfaq where contains(answer,'DTD inpath(/answer/keywords')>0;
```

The HASPATH operator functions in a similar fashion to the **ExistsNode()** operator in XMLType and can be used to limit a search, as the following query illustrates:

```
select * from xdkfaq
       where contains(answer,'haspath(/answer/keywords)')>0;
```

Using Functional Indexes to Improve Search Performance

When the parameters of a search are known, we can significantly improve its performance by using a *functional index* to precalculate the results. In our case, we have answers in XML that can contain keywords marked up as <keyword>term </keyword>. The XMLType functions, such as **ExistsNode()**, **isFragment()**, and **getNumberVal()**, can all benefit from the use of functional indexes. The following script illustrates how a functional index is created:

```
create index quef_idx on xdkfaq_xmltype
      (substr(sys.xmltype.getStringVal(
       sys.xmltype.extract(answer,'/answer/keywords/text()')),1,255));
       select sys_xmlagg(
       sys_xmlgen(relative_type(e.question.getStringVal(),e.id),
       sys.xmlgenformattype.createformat('RELATIVES_ROW'))
       ).extract('/ROWSET//RELATIVES_ROW').getStringVal()
    into v_result
    from xdkfaq_xmltype e
    where e.id in
       (select f.id
        from xdkfaq_xmltype f
        where f.answer.extract('/answer//keywords/text()').getStringVal()
                like '%'||key||'%');
```

This functional index allows us to search for relative FAQs while the main search was taking place. Without it, the queries would take minutes instead of achieving the subsecond performance we get by using the functional index.

Linking Directly to Database Content with URI-Refs

Prior to Oracle9i, content could be navigated within an Oracle database only via SQL. New in Oracle9i is the capability to navigate and retrieve data with URI references. The DBUri-Ref is a local ref (URL) within the database. After providing the DBUri, you can retrieve the referenced content by using SQL Query. You can also generate a DBUri-Ref from SQL Query in order to build links to content stored in the database. The following SQL query uses the new **sys_dburigen** function to create links to FAQs whose id = 5:

```
select sys_xmlagg(
      sys_xmlgen(sys_dburigen(id,answer))).extract('//URL/text()').getStringVal()
      from xdkfaq where id = 5;
```

For our FAQ application, we use DBUri-Refs to build up the glossary indexes for the FAQs.

Building the Glossary

Earlier in the chapter, you saw the script that built the table **xdkfaq_glossary** for the keywords we want to have linked to online definitions. Next we need to generate the XML files with glossary name and DBUri links. We do this by creating a trigger on the FAQ table that adds a link to all of the <keywords/> elements within the Glossary file. This is done with the following XSL stylesheet and SQL script:

```
<?xml version="1.0" ?>
<xsl:stylesheet xmlns:xsl="http://www.w3.org/1999/XSL/Transform" version="1.0">
<xsl:output method="xml" indent="yes" />
<xsl:template match="node()|@*">
  <!
   Copy the current node
  -->
<xsl:copy>
 - <!--
   Including any attributes it has and any child nodes
  -->
<xsl:apply-templates select="@*|node()" />
</xsl:copy>
</xsl:template>
<xsl:template match="keywords">
<keywords>
<xsl:if test="document('glos.xml')/glossarys/link[@name=current()/text()]">
<xsl:attribute name="link">
<xsl:value-of select="document('glos.xml')/glossarys/link[@name=current()/text()]" />
</xsl:attribute>
</xsl:if>
<xsl:apply-templates />
</keywords>
</xsl:template>
</xsl:stylesheet>


------------------------------------------------------------------------
FAQDBGlossary.sql
 Create Glossary for the input XML document
 grant javauserpriv to xdkdemo
 grant javasyspriv to xdkdemo
 modify the uri:/private/tomcat/webapps/xdkdemo/source/faq/sql
------------------------------------------------------------------------
```

```
CREATE OR REPLACE PROCEDURE MakeGlossary(xmlbuf IN VARCHAR2,resbuf IN OUT NOCOPY VARCHAR2) AS

  p xmlparser.Parser;
  dir varchar2(100) :='/private/public_html/xdk/source/sql/faq/glossary';

  xmldoc xmldom.DOMDocument;

  proc xslprocessor.Processor;
  ss xslprocessor.Stylesheet;
  xsldoc xmldom.DOMDocument;
Begin
 new parser
   p := xmlparser.newParser;
   xmlparser.setBaseDir(p,dir);

 -- parse xml buffer
    xmlparser.parseBuffer(p, xmlbuf);

-- get document
    xmldoc := xmlparser.getDocument(p);

 -- parse xsl buffer
    xmlparser.parse(p, dir ||'/'||'glos.xsl');

 -- get document
    xsldoc := xmlparser.getDocument(p);

 -- make stylesheet
    ss := xslprocessor.newStylesheet(xsldoc,dir);

 -- process xsl from doc
    proc := xslprocessor.newProcessor;

    xslprocessor.processXSL(proc,ss,xmldoc,resbuf);

    xmldom.freeDocument(xmldoc);
    xmldom.freeDocument(xsldoc);
    xslprocessor.freeStylesheet(ss);
    xslprocessor.freeProcessor(proc);

    xmlparser.freeParser(p);
end;
/
show errors;
```

Figure 9-6 shows a FAQ answer with "XPath" displayed as a link to a glossary definition. Clicking the word will pass it as a parameter into another XSQL page, **faqdburi_show.xsql**, appended to the DBURI_Ref, **/PUBLIC/ XDKFAQ_GLOSSARY/ROW**.

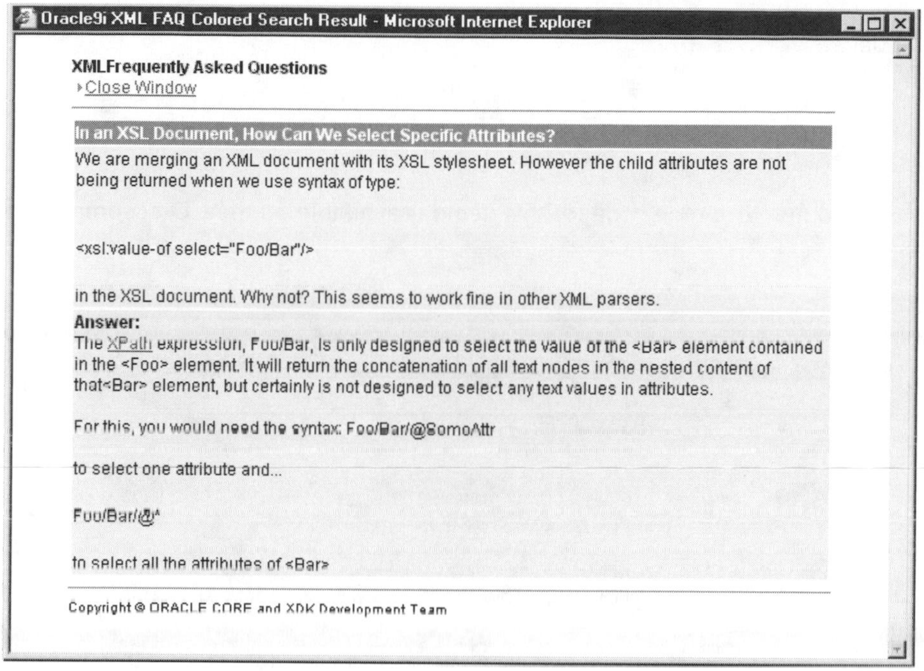

FIGURE 9-6.   *FAQ answer showing DBURI link*

Extending the Application

In the previous section, the groundwork was laid to create a real-world XML-enabled application using the Oracle9i XML functionality and components in the XDK. This case study can be easily extended or modified. One such extension that I will discuss in this last section is to provide a "Top 20" list of FAQs based upon the number of hits. This is a very commonly requested Web application. Figure 9-7 shows the completed page that is actually generated from a CLOB updated hourly based upon the number of hits each question receives.

This page also supplies the relative FAQs associated with each question from their own CLOB cache, as was previously shown. The following code listing shows the XSQL page that generates Figure 9-7:

```
<?xml version="1.0" ?>
<page connection="xdkdemo" xmlns:xsql="urn:oracle-xsql">
<webpage title="Top 20 Frequently Asked Question">
<xsql:query max-rows="20">
<![CDATA[
```

```
SELECT *
  FROM XDKFAQ
ORDER BY hits DESC
]]>
</xsql:query>
</webpage>
</page>
```

The complete source code for this demo is available on the CD accompanying this book.

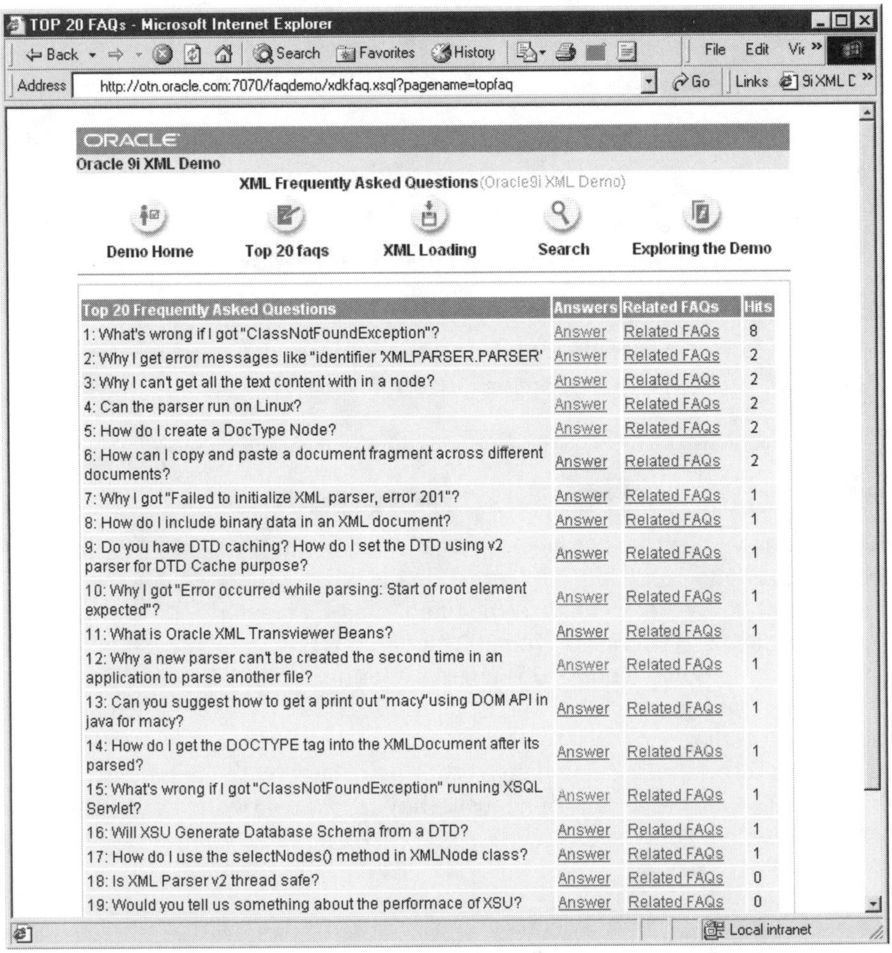

FIGURE 9-7. *Top 20 FAQ Page*

CHAPTER
10

XML-Based Applications Offered on OTN

number of XML-based applications are hosted on the *Oracle Technology Network (OTN)* site. This is a good place for you to test-drive Oracle XML technology and to review the latest XML examples to solve real-life problems. The OTN URL is **http://otn.us.oracle.com**. You can use the vertical navigation bar on the left for getting around OTN. From OTN, you need to find the link to the XML home page, but the XML home page is not directly accessible from the OTN main page. You can get to the XML home page either by clicking the Technologies link on the navigation bar or by directly entering the URL, **http://otn.oracle.com/tech/xml/xdkhome.html**.

The XML home page hosts all the currently available Oracle XML products, packaged as the Oracle XML Developer's Kits. There are currently five XDKs available based upon different languages. There are XDKs for Java, JavaBeans, C, C++, and PL/SQL. To help you understand how to use each of the products in the Oracle XML Developer's Kit, demo sample applications, which were developed by Steve Muench, are included to help ensure that the respective products are installed and function properly.

In addition to these demo samples, a number of sample applications are hosted directly on the XML home page, providing a live interactive XML demonstration running directly over the Web. These sample applications are designed to illustrate how Oracle XML technology can be used for solving real-life problems. In this chapter, we review these OTN applications, explaining what they do and how they work. At the end of this chapter, you'll learn how to install and run these applications on your own computer.

Accessing the XML Applications

To get to the XML applications posted on OTN, click the Live XML Demo link, as shown in Figure 10-1.

This loads the page shown in Figure 10-2, which lists a number of demo applications using XML and Oracle9*i*.

Let's look more closely at the page shown in Figure 10-2. The page is built using two frames: The top frame holds the title, Oracle XSQL Servlet Demos, and links to the OTN and the XML demo home pages. This frame stays always on top and can be used as a navigation bar to get back to this page or to get to OTN at any time when running the demos. The bottom frame holds a four-column table that lists the available applications. The first column contains the name for the application and serves as a link to launch it.

The second column contains an icon that shows either **ie5** or **any**. This icon indicates which browser the application requires to be run and viewed properly. Therefore, not all the applications can run in any browser. Some of the applications are specifically designed to show how Internet Explorer 5 (IE5) and its built-in XML support can be used to work together with Oracle's server-side XML technology.

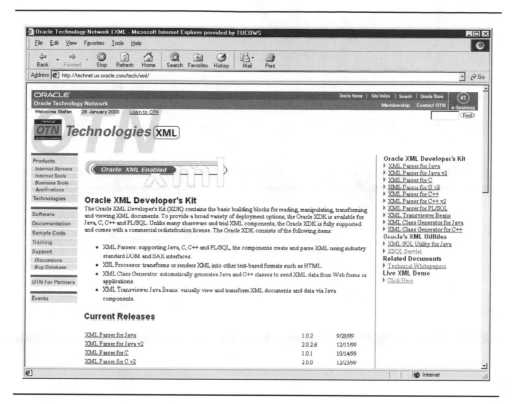

FIGURE 10-1.   *XML Home and Live XML Demo link*

The third column displays an icon that links to a page displaying the relevant source code for the corresponding application when available. By examining this code, you can find the particular query used and the format of the application's XSQL page to show you interactively all the relevant information about the source code used by the application. Finally, the fourth column gives you a short explanation about what the application does and highlights special aspects of the application.

Clicking any application link in the first column launches the application page in the bottom frame of the screen. If you would like to see the applications in a new browser window without frames, you can launch the applications by right-clicking with your mouse. On browsers that support this function, a list of options will appear. Selecting the Open in New Window option will open a new window for the application without using frames. Using this method, you can run more than one application simultaneously. Also, the address field of the new browser window will show the URL that invokes the selected application. This can be useful if you wish to experiment with adding or changing the URL parameters that launch the applications.

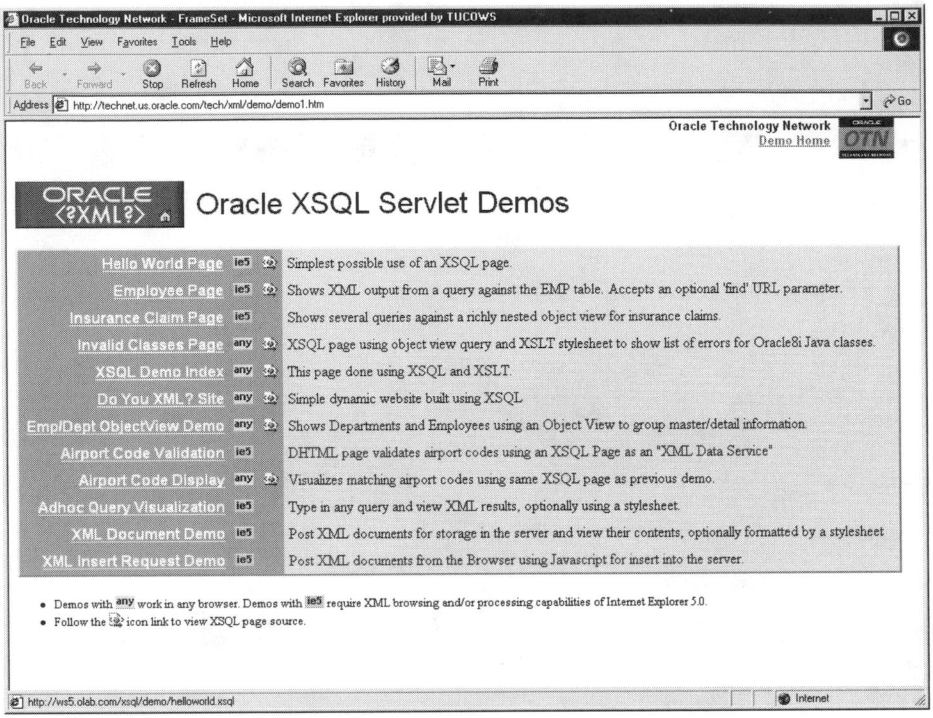

FIGURE 10-2. *Oracle XML Servlet Demos*

What the XML Applications Demonstrate

Oracle8i/9i and the Oracle XML Developer's Kits support all of the core technologies needed to use the power of combining SQL, XML, and XSL on the server. The components of each XML Developer's Kit provide great flexibility and power, enabling you to easily develop Java, C, C++, or PL/SQL applications using these core technologies.

Many typical classes of applications exist, which you can build without using any programming at all. You can do this by using a simple, yet powerful, template-based scripting language that can deliver most of the functionality for a fraction of the time and the cost associated with developing custom software modules. The XML applications on the XML home page illustrate this alternative approach, which does not require programming or at least eliminates a great part of it.

The XML applications previewed here are built on standard templates called *Oracle XSQL pages.* The XSQL Servlet supports these XSQL pages. This XSQL Servlet can be installed on any Web server that supports servlets and used with any JDBC-enabled database. Working with Oracle 8i or 9i databases, you can tap into the full power of the Oracle XSQL pages and create powerful, yet reasonably simple, applications.

If you are familiar with SQL, you can use the XSQL pages together with associated XSL transformation files to produce HTML, XML, or virtually any text file, as a result of one or more database queries. To create the XSQL pages and the associated XSL transformation files, which are, in fact, XML documents, all you need is a text editor. An XSQL page is simply a well-formed XML document with the extension **.xsql**. The XSQL page contains a query and an optional reference to one or more XSL stylesheets that are applied to the XML data retrieved from the database.

Once you have built an XSQL page and loaded it on your Web server, it can be requested by a browser with a URL of the form:

```
http://yourserver.com/EmpXSQLPage.xsql?dept=30
```

On the server, the XSQL Servlet handles the request, which generally includes the following steps:

1. Parsing the XSQL page and retrieving all relevant information regarding this request

2. Establishing a connection to an Oracle8i/9i database using an alias

3. Submitting the query(s) specified in the XSQL page to the XML SQL Utility (XSU)

4. XSU formatting the query result data into an XML document, which is passed back to the servlet

5. Applying the XSL transformation to the XML document if an XSL stylesheet is specified

6. Returning the resulting document to the browser

If the applied stylesheet transforms the XML data from the database request into HTML format, it can be shown directly in any browser. Figure 10-3 shows how the XSQL pages are processed on the server.

You can download the XSQL Servlet and the XML SQL Utility as part of the XDK for Java. Complete instructions for installing the XSQL Servlet appear at the end of this chapter, in the section "Installing and Running the XML Applications."

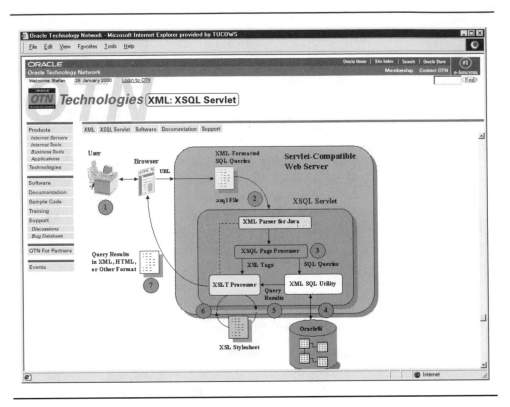

FIGURE 10-3. *XSQL pages processing diagram*

The XML Applications

In this section of the chapter, we will examine each of the applications offered on the OTN site in greater detail.

Hello World Application

The Hello World application is the simplest example of using an Oracle XSQL page on your Web site. Upon running the Hello Word application, you get a screen, as shown in Figure 10-4.

IE5 has a feature called Direct Browsing, which allows IE5 to display XML files automatically, in the same way it does HTML or GIF files. Because XML files do not have predefined presentations, IE5 uses a built-in XSL stylesheet to convert to an HTML display. When the XML file does not refer to a specific XSL stylesheet that IE5 can use for the visual representation, a default and hidden stylesheet is used to provide

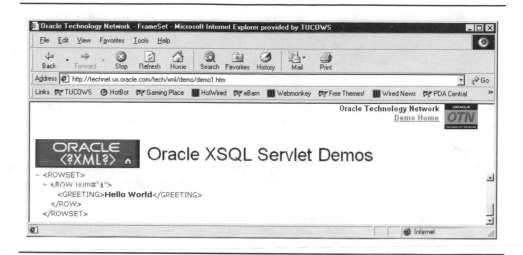

FIGURE 10-4. *Hello World output screen*

a tree-based view of the XML content. This is exactly what you can see in Figure 10-4. The output of our application is an XML document, which IE5 displays as a tree view.

Let's analyze how the Hello World application actually works. When you select the Hello World link, the browser requests the URL **http://ws5.olab.com/xsql/ demo/helloworld.xsql**. This file is shown in Figure 10-5. You can display the file source code by selecting the Source icon (represented by the image of a camera).

The file shown in Figure 10-5 is an XSQL page. The **.xsql** extension indicates to the Web server to use the XSQL Servlet to handle this request. Let's return to the Hello World output screen. To see the actual data that comes back to the browser as a result of running the Hello World application, right-click the lower portion of the screen, where the XML document is shown, and then select View Source. The page source is displayed in a Notepad window, as shown in Figure 10-6.

Referring again to Figure 10-5, note that this page actually has only one element.

```
<xsql:query connection="demo" xmlns:xsql="urn:oracle-xsql">
 SELECT 'Hello World' AS greeting FROM DUAL
</xsql:query>
```

After parsing this XSQL page, the XSQL Servlet looks to find elements with an **<xsql:query>** tag. The XSQL Servlet then treats the text in the **<xslq:query>** tag as a SQL statement and submits it to the database for execution, using the information contained in the **connection** attribute to log on. In this case, the result of the query is automatically formatted as an XML file and sent back to the browser.

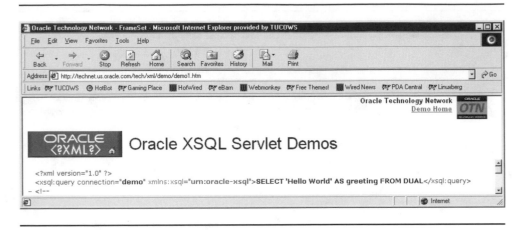

FIGURE 10-5. *Hello World XSQL page source*

The structure of this output XML document is based on the internal structure of the database schema that returned the query results. Columns are mapped to top-level elements. Scalar values are mapped to elements with text-only content, object types are mapped to elements with attributes appearing as subelements, and collections are mapped to lists of elements. Finally, object references and referential constraints are mapped to XML IDREFs.

For the Hello World application, the resulting data set contains a single column—greeting—and one row with one element—Hello World. The XSQL Servlet formats this data set to the XML file, as shown in Figure 10-6.

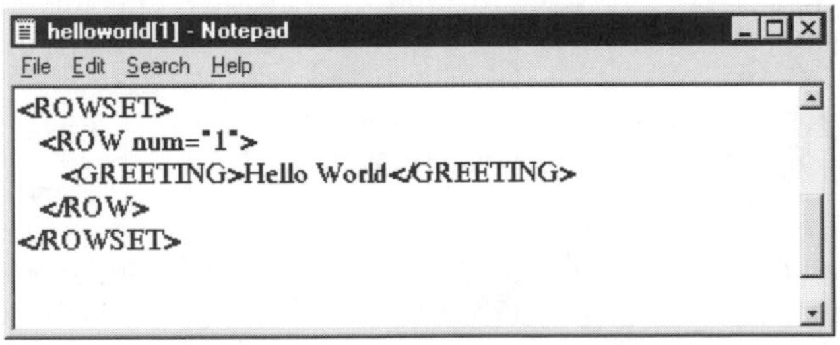

FIGURE 10-6. *Hello World—the data returned from the server*

Here is another simple example of creating an XML document from a query, submitted to the XSQL Servlet:

```
<xsql:query connection="demo" xmlns:xsql="urn:oracle-xsql">
SELECT DEPTNO, ENAME FROM EMP WHERE DEPTNO = 7654;
</xsql:query>
```

It generates the following XML document:

```
<?xml version="1.0"?>
<ROWSET>
  <ROW id="1">
    <DEPTNO>7654</DEPTNO>
    <ENAME>STEVE</ENAME>
  </ROW>
  <ROW id="2">
    <DEPTNO>7654</DEPTNO>
    <ENAME>JOHN</ENAME>
  </ROW>
  <ROW id="3">
    <DEPTNO>7654</DEPTNO>
    <ENAME>MARRY</ENAME>
  </ROW>
</ROWSET>
```

Now look at the format of the output XML document. By default, ROWSET is the element name of the XML document element. ROW is the element name for each row in the query result. Data, such as contained in EMPNO and ENAME, is also represented as elements nested within the ROW node.

In general, data is represented as elements, and attributes are used to constrain the data where needed. If an application requires a different set of tags or formatting, an XSL stylesheet can perform the transformation dynamically, as you'll see in the next section.

Now look again at the **<query>** tag in file **helloworld.xsql**:

```
<xsql:query connection="demo" xmlns:xsql="urn:oracle-xsql">
```

The attribute **connection="demo"** defines where to find the information needed to connect to the database. The XSQL Servlet uses the configuration file, **XSQLConfig.xml**. This file can have multiple entries where each one represents a separate database connection. Each database connection entry contains all the necessary information needed to connect and log in to the desired database. The **XSQLConfig.xml** file is an XML file with the following special format:

```
<?xml version-"1.0" ?>
<connectiondefs dumpallowed="no">
```

```
<connection name="demo">
  <username>scott</username>
  <password>tiger</password>
  <dburl>jdbc:oracle:thin:@localhost:1521:ORCL</dburl>
  <driver>oracle.jdbc.driver.OracleDriver</driver>
</connection>
<connection name="lite">
  <username>system</username>
  <password>manager</password>
  <dburl>jdbc:Polite:POlite</dburl>
  <driver>oracle.lite.poljdbc.POLJDBCDriver</driver>
</connection>
</connectiondefs>
```

When installing the XSQL Servlet, you can edit this file to create new entries for your specific database connections. Each connection entry contains elements for the user name, password, database URL, and the JDBC driver to be used for servicing this connection.

As you can see, the Hello World application is simple—a single XML document with a **.xsql** extension that contains a database query. Once this XSQL page is requested by the browser, the XSQL Servlet produces the result as an XML file. The XSQL Connection Pool handles the task of establishing a connection to the database. The Servlet submits the query through the XML SQL Utility that returns the results in XML. Because the Hello World XSQL page did not refer to a stylesheet to be used for XSL transformation of the output XML file, the browser receives the response to the requested XSQL page in XML format.

Employee Page Application

The Employee Page application demonstrates how you can do a database query and let the server side format the query results in HTML. This allows any browser to display the result in your desired customized format. Figure 10-7 shows the result screen after running the Employee Page application.

This application uses one important feature of the Oracle XSQL pages: the capability to request the transformation of the resulting XML into HTML. This formatting occurs on the server by the XSQL Servlet, as opposed to the formatting IE5 does when it renders XML on the client. In both cases, the formatting is achieved by applying an XSL stylesheet to an XML file. When you select the Employee Page link on the screen shown earlier in

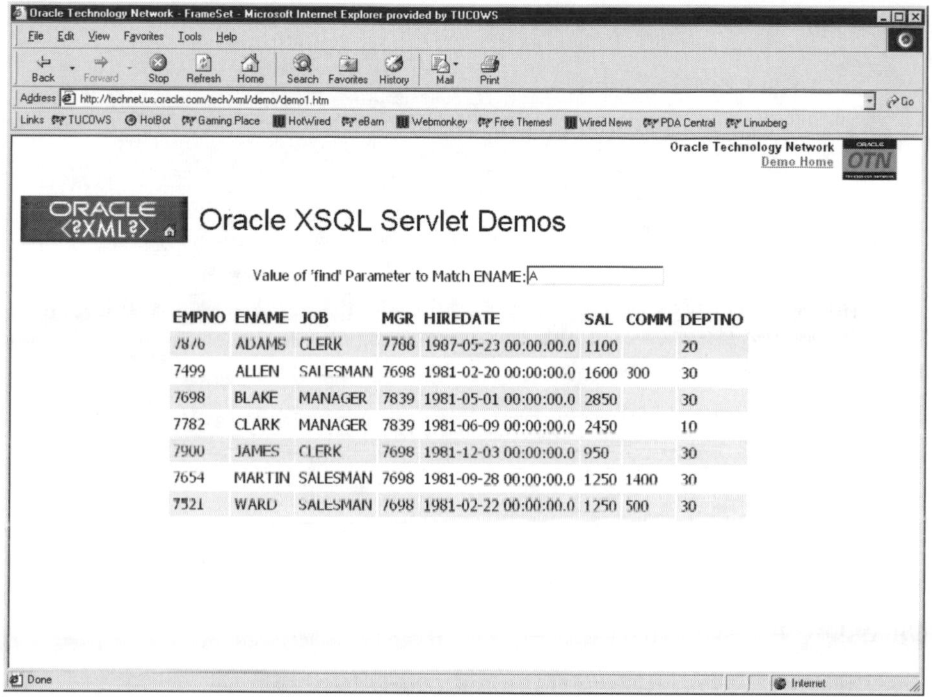

FIGURE 10-7. *Employee Page application results*

Figure 10-4, the browser requests an XSQL page file, **emp.xsql**, which contains the following XML elements:

```
<?xml-stylesheet type="text/xsl" href="emp.xsl"?>
<xsql:query connection="demo" xmlns:xsql="urn:oracle-xsql"
            find="%"
            sort="ENAME"
   null-indicator="yes" >
      SELECT * FROM EMP
      WHERE ENAME LIKE '%{@find}%'
      ORDER BY {@sort}
</xsql:query>
```

If the line declaring the stylesheet were not included, the XSQL Page processor would return the following XML document:

```
<?xml version="1.0"?>
<ROWSET>
    <ROW num="1">
        <EMPNO>7876</EMPNO>
        <ENAME>ADAMS</ENAME>
        <JOB>CLERK</JOB>
        <MGR>7788</MGR>
        <HIREDATE>1987-05-23 00:00:00.0</HIREDATE>
        <SAL>1100</SAL>
        <COMM NULL="YES"></COMM>
        <DEPTNO>20</DEPTNO>
    </ROW>
    <ROW num="2">
        . . . the data for the second row of the result . . .
    </ROW>
    . . . additional rows may follow . . .
</ROWSET>
```

Now look at what happens when this stylesheet declaration is included in the **emp.xsql** XSQL page:

```
<?xml-stylesheet type="text/xsl" href="emp.xsl"?>
```

This is a processing instruction, which tells the XSQL Servlet to apply an XSL transformation as dictated by **emp.xsl** before sending the result page back. The processing instruction defines the name of the XSL stylesheet to be used by the Oracle XSQL Servlet for transforming the resulting XML document into HTML (or any text-based) document. Therefore, when we request an XSQL page with this processing instruction included, the browser received back an HTML document that showed the desired data as a table.

To summarize, the Employee Page application consists of two text files:

- **emp.xsql** This is an XML file containing the SQL request and a reference to **emp.xsl**, as well as a reference to an alias that provides the connection information for the desired database.

- **emp.xsl** This file is an XSL stylesheet that defines an XSL transformation to be used by the XSL Processor.

The XSQL Servlet creates the final output by passing the result XML file and the declared XSL file that the XSL Processor included in the Oracle XML Parser. The XSQL Servlet receives the result data in XML by passing the SQL query to the Oracle XML SQL Utility. It is important to know in detail how the resulting data should be formatted into an XML file to create a meaningful XSL stylesheet that transforms the intermediate XML format into the final format wanted by the client.

Insurance Claim Application

The Insurance Claim application demonstrates multiple ways in which the XSQL pages can be used in a real-world scenario in the insurance industry. These examples output data in XML that results from queries against tables containing user-defined types. The *Unified Modeling Language (UML)* model of an insurance claim is shown in Figure 10-8.

You can run five different examples based on the page shown in Figure 10-8. The lower right-hand part of the screen consists of two frames: the upper frame shows the source XSQL page when you click the Source link for each example; the lower frame shows the resulting XML document returned to the browser after running the corresponding XSQL page. Figure 10-9 shows the source XSQL page and the result received for Example One.

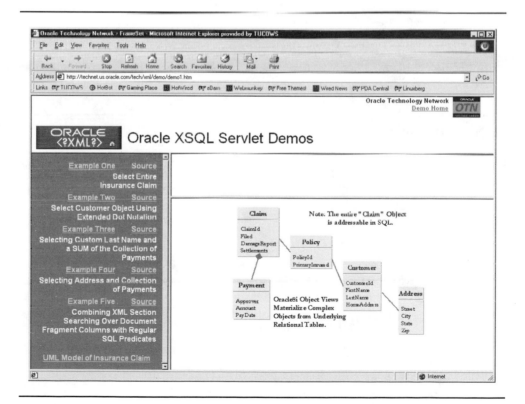

FIGURE 10-8. *UML Model of an Insurance Claim*

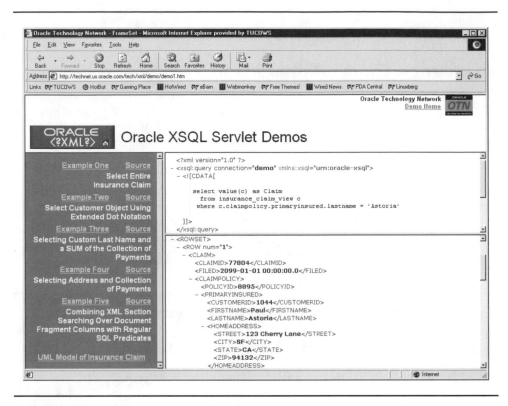

FIGURE 10-9. *Running Example One*

NOTE
Note the use of the CDATA section to hold the query. The CDATA section must be used when the query contains text or characters that could otherwise be recognized as a markup.

The following listing is the SQL used to create the tables, views, and user-defined types used by all examples in the Insurance Claim application. For each example, we can use this DDL together with the query in the example's XSQL page to understand how the XSQL Servlet generates XML from data sets containing user-defined types.

```
create type address_t as object( Street varchar2(80),
        City Varchar2(80), State VARCHAR2(80), Zip NUMBER )/
```

```
create type policyholder_t as object( CustomerId number, FirstName
        varchar2(80), LastName varchar2(80), HomeAddress address_t)/
create type policy_t as object( policyID number, primaryinsured
        policyholder_t)/
create type payment as object( PayDate DATE, Amount NUMBER,
        Approver VARCHAR2(8))/
create type settlements_t as table of payment/
create type insurance_claim_t as object ( claimid number, filed date,
        claimpolicy policy_t, settlements settlements_t,
        damageReport varchar2(4000) /* XML */)/
create table policyholder( CustomerId number, FirstName varchar2(80),
        LastName varchar2(80), HomeAddress address_t,
        constraint policyholder_pk primary key (customerid))/
create or replace force view policyholder_view of policyholder_t
        with object OID (customerid)
        as select customerid, firstname, lastname, homeaddress
        from policyholder/
create table policy( policyid number, primarycustomerid number,
        constraint policy_pk primary key (policyid),
        constraint customer_fk foreign key (primarycustomerid)
        references policyholder)/
create or replace force view policy_view of policy_t
        with object OID (policyid)
        as select p.policyid, (SELECT value(phv) from policyholder_view phv
        WHERE phv.customerid = p.primarycustomerid) as primaryinsured
        from policy p/
create table insurance_claim( claimid number, filed date,
        claimpolicy number, damageReport varchar2(4000) /* XML */,
        constraint insurance_claim_pk primary key (claimid),
        constraint policy_fk foreign key (claimpolicy) references policy)/
create table settlement_payments( claimid number, PayDate DATE,
        Amount NUMBER, Approver VARCHAR2(8),
        constraint claim_fk foreign key (claimid) references
        insurance_claim)/
create or replace force view insurance_claim_view of insurance_claim_t
        with object OID (claimid) as select c.claimid,c.filed,
        (SELECT value(pv) from policy_view pv
        WHERE pv.policyid = c.claimpolicy),
        CAST(MULTISET(SELECT PAYMENT(sp.paydate,sp.amount,sp.approver)
        as Payment from settlement_payments sp
        WHERE sp.claimid = c.claimid) AS settlements_t), c.damagereport
        from insurance_claim c/
create index ctx_xml_i on insurance_claim(damagereport)
        indextype is ctxsys.context
        parameters('LEXER Demo SECTION GROUP demo_xml')/
```

Example One uses the following SQL in its XSQL page:

```
select value(c) as Claim
        from insurance_claim_view c
        where c.claimpolicy.primaryinsured.lastname = 'Astoria'
```

The XSQL Servlet generates this XML file in response:

```
<?xml version="1.0"?>
<ROWSET>
<ROW num="1">
  <CLAIM>
    <CLAIMID>77804</CLAIMID>
    <FILED>1999-01-01 00:00:00.0</FILED>
    <CLAIMPOLICY>
      <POLICYID>8895</POLICYID>
        <PRIMARYINSURED>
          <CUSTOMERID>1044</CUSTOMERID>
          <FIRSTNAME>Paul</FIRSTNAME>
          <LASTNAME>Astoria</LASTNAME>
          <HOMEADDRESS>
            <STREET>123 Cherry Lane</STREET>
            <CITY>SF</CITY>
            <STATE>CA</STATE>
            <ZIP>94132</ZIP>
          </HOMEADDRESS>
        </PRIMARYINSURED>
    </CLAIMPOLICY>
    <SETTLEMENTS>
      <SETTLEMENTS_ITEM>
        <PAYDATE>1999-01-05 00:00:00.0</PAYDATE>
        <AMOUNT>7600</AMOUNT>
        <APPROVER>JCOX</APPROVER>
      </SETTLEMENTS_ITEM>
    </SETTLEMENTS>
    <DAMAGEREPORT>The insured's <;VEHICLE>car<;/VEHICLE>broke
through the guard rail and plummeted into a ravine. The cause
was determined to be <;CAUSE>faulty brakes<;/CAUSE> Amazingly
there were no casualties. </DAMAGEREPORT>
  </CLAIM>
  </ROW>
  <ROW num="2">
    . . . the data for row number 2 follows . . .
  </ROW>
</ROWSET>
```

The rest of the examples use different queries but are built using the same technique. Of particular note is Example Five because it combines a number of database capabilities. Let's take a look at the query.

```
select sum(n.amount) as TotalApprovedAmount
  from insurance_claim_view v, TABLE(v.settlements) n
 where n.approver = 'JCOX'
   and contains(damageReport,'Brakes within Cause') > 0
```

This query has a where clause that is looking for claims that have specific XML markup in their damageReport. We can run this query by utilizing the support for XML within Intermedia Text. Further operations are then done on the claims that satisfy this clause along with having JCOX as the approver.

Invalid Classes Application

The XSQL page for the Invalid Classes application uses an object view query and a XSL stylesheet to show a list of errors for Oracle9i Java classes. The output screen for this application is shown in Figure 10-10.

Here is the SQL that creates the user types and the view used in the application:

```
create type "XSQLJavaClassError" as object ( "Message" varchar2(4000) );
create type "XSQLJavaClassErrors" as table of "XSQLJavaClassError";
create view "XSQLJavaClassErrorView" as
        select replace(dbms_java.longname(uo.object_name),'/','.')
        "ClassName",
        CAST(MULTISET(SELECT "XSQLJavaClassError"(ue.text)
        FROM user_errors ue WHERE name = uo.object_name
        ORDER BY ue."SEQUENCE") AS "XSQLJavaClassErrors") AS "Errors"
        from user_objects uo where object_type = 'JAVA CLASS'
        and status = 'INVALID'
        order by replace(dbms_java.longname(object_name),'/','.');
```

To understand the CREATE VIEW statement, you need to have some information about the package **DBMS_JAVA** that comes with Oracle8i and 9i. When initializing JServer, that is the Java Virtual Machine that runs within the Oracle server, the **initjvm.sql** script creates the PL/SQL package **DBMS_JAVA**. Some of the APIs within **DBMS_JAVA** are for your use, while others are currently for internal use only. Of the many included, we discuss only the one used in the previous SQL:

```
FUNCTION longname (shortname VARCHAR2) RETURN VARCHAR2
```

The **longname** function returns the longname from a Java schema object. Because Java classes and methods can have names exceeding the maximum SQL

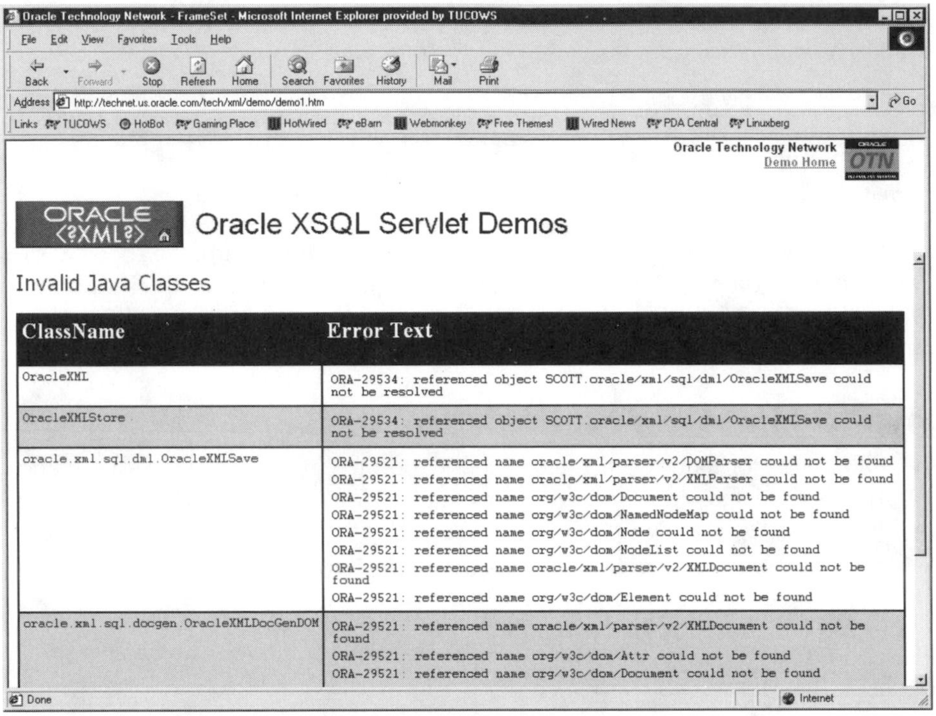

FIGURE 10-10. *Invalid Classes application*

identifier length, JServer uses abbreviated names internally for SQL access. This function simply returns the original Java name for any (potentially) truncated name. An example of this function is to print the fully qualified names of classes that are invalid for some reason.

```
select dbms_java.longname (object_name) from user_objects
        where object_type = 'JAVA CLASS' and status = 'INVALID';
```

NOTE
Refer to the Oracle8i or 9i Java Stored Procedures Developer's Guide for a detailed example of the use of this function and ways to determine which Java schema objects are present on the server.

The XSQL page that does the database query has the following two elements:

```
<?xml-stylesheet type="text/xsl" href="invalidclasses.xsl"?>
<xsql:query connection="demo" tag-case="lower" xmlns:xsql="urn:oracle-xsql">
          select * from "XSQLJavaClassErrorView"
</xsql:query>
```

The declared XSL stylesheet, **invalidclasses.xsl**, is applied by the XSQL Servlet to the XML document representing the query data set. The resulting HTML document is sent back to the browser. This application is similar to the Employee Page application, but uses a view created from the tables USER_ERROR and USER_ OBJECT. This application shows how easy creating reports for a particular user schema and publishing them on the Web is in a custom format.

XSQL Demo Index

The applications reviewed so far have shown how flexible and easy using this template-based approach is for Web publishing. This should come as no surprise: the Demo Index Page shown earlier in Figure 10-2 and used to navigate the demo applications, is also built using this simple XSQL pages technology. Figure 10-11 shows the XSQL page used, as well as the corresponding XSL stylesheet that actually builds the HTML for the page in Figure 10-2.

Here is the SQL used to create and load the tables used by this page:

```
create table xsqldemolist(title varchar2(200), description varchar2(4000),
          url varchar2(200), sourceurl varchar2(200), ie5only varchar2(1) );
insert into xsqldemolist values ('Hello World Page',
          'Simplest possible use of an XSQL page.', 'helloworld.xsql',
          'helloworld-xsql.xml', 'Y');
insert into xsqldemolist values ('Employee Page',
          'Shows XML output from a query against the EMP table. Accepts an
          optional'
          || '''find'' URL parameter.', 'emp.xsql?find=A',
          'empsource.html', 'Y');

insert into xsqldemolist values ('Insurance Claim Page',
          'Shows several queries against a richly nested object view for insurance
          claims.',
          'xsqlov.htm', 'None',  'Y');
insert into xsqldemolist values ('Invalid Classes Page',
          'XSQL page using object view query and XSLT stylesheet  to show list of'
          || 'errors for Oracle9i Java classes.', 'invalidclasses.xsql',
          'invalidclassessource.html', 'N');
insert into xsqldemolist values ('XSQL Demo Index',
          'This page done using XSQL and XSLT.', 'index.xsql',
          'indexsource.html', 'N');
insert into xsqldemolist values ('Do You XML? Site',
```

```
          'Simple dynamic website built using XSQL', 'doyouxml.xsql',
          'doyouxmlsource.html', 'N');
insert into xsqldemolist values ('Emp/Dept ObjectView Demo',
          'Shows Departments and Employees using an Object View to
          group master/detail information.',
          'empdept.xsql', 'empdeptsource.html', 'N');
insert into xsqldemolist values ('Airport Code Validation',
          'DHTML page validates airport codes using an XSQL Page as an "XML Data
           Service"',
          'airport.htm', 'None', 'Y');
insert into xsqldemolist values ('Airport Code Display',
          'Visualizes matching airport codes using same XSQL page as previous
          demo.',
          'airport.xsql?xml-stylesheet=airport.xsl',
          'airportsource.html', 'N');
insert into xsqldemolist values ('Adhoc Query Visualization',
          'Type in any query and view XML results, optionally using a
          stylesheet.',
          'sqltoxml.html', 'None', 'Y');
insert into xsqldemolist values ('XML Document Demo',
          'Post XML documents for storage in the server and view their contents,'
          ||'optionally formatted by a stylesheet',
          'docdemo.html', 'None', 'Y');
insert into xsqldemolist values ('XML Insert Request Demo',
          'Post XML documents from the Browser using JavaScript '||
          'for insert into the server.', 'newsstorydemo.html', 'None', 'Y');
```

As you can see from this example, Oracle9i is the natural place to keep all your Web site's data and pages. The next application demonstrates this specific capability.

Do You XML? Site

The Do You XML? Web site, which is an internal Web site at Oracle, demonstrates how a database of stored data can serve as a repository for a Web site driven by the XSQL Servlet and XML to HTML stylesheets. Figure 10-12 shows the Do You XML? site.

This site illustrates several functions of the XSQL Servlet that are well suited to delivering dynamic Web content on a device-specific basis. The following is the **doyouxml.xsql** that powers the site:

```
<?xml version="1.0"?>
<?xml-stylesheet type="text/xsl" media="mozilla" href="doyouxml.xsl" ?>
<?xml-stylesheet type="text/xsl" media="MSIE 5" href="doyouxml.xsl" ?>
<?xml-stylesheet type="text/xsl" href="doyouxml.xsl" ?>
```

Note the three stylesheet declarations. Using the **media** tag in the HTTP header from the requesting browser, the XSQL Servlet can apply the appropriate stylesheet, assuring that the user, whether using a full browser or a WAP phone, will see a

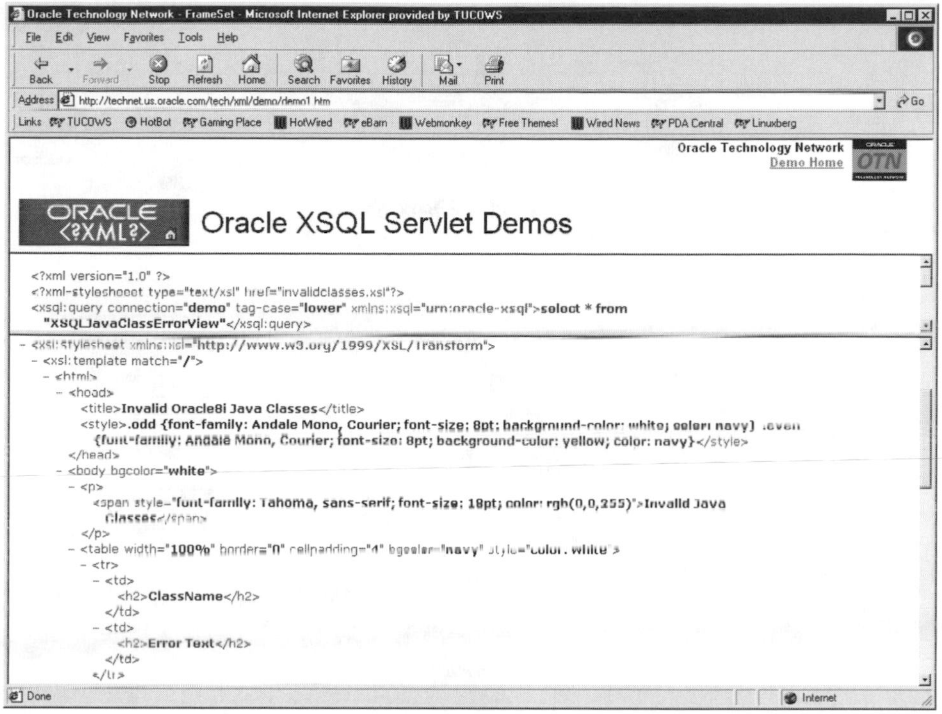

FIGURE 10-11. *The XSQL page and XSL transformation used by XSQL Demo Index*

device-appropriate page without the need to store multiple static versions that are difficult to keep in sync and updated.

```
<datapage connection="demo" xmlns:xsql="urn:oracle-xsql">
```

As previously mentioned, the datapage element specifies an alias to the actual database connection located in the **XSQLConfig.xml** file, which should be kept in a secure location accessible by only the server. It also defines the "xsql" namespace, which will prevent name collisions within an XSQL file, since all of the keywords are thus prefixed, as in the following "xsql:query" element:

```
<xsql:query rowset-element="" row-element="INFO"><![CDATA[
   select count(*) as "TOTAL", '{@cat}' as cat from site_entry
   where categories like '%'||UPPER('{@cat}')||'%' and permanent is null
]]>
</xsql:query>
```

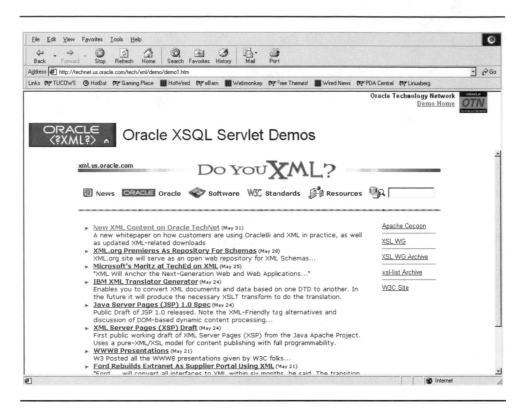

FIGURE 10-12. *Do You XML?*

This first query counts the total number of entries in the listing and will be used to retrieve each group of six entries.

```
<xsql:query rowset-element="SiteStructure" row-element="Category" ><![CDATA[
    SELECT name "Name", icon "Icon" FROM site_category ORDER BY id
]]>
</xsql:query>
```

This second query creates the top navigation bar including both the text and the icons from the database. Should the Web page be requested by a device with limited or no graphics capabilities, the applied stylesheet could simply ignore the icon graphics in its template that builds the navigation bar.

```
<xsql:query
    category="NEWS"  rowset-element="MAINITEMS"
    row-element="ITEM" max-rows="6" skip="0"
```

```
    skip-rows="{@skip}" >
<![CDATA[
    select title,id,description,url,to_char(timestamp,'Mon DD') timestamp
    from site_entry where categories like '%'||UPPER('{@cat}')||'%'
    and permanent is null order by id desc
]]>
</xsql:query>
```

This third query is a bit more complex, as it sets up variables that will later be incremented to retrieve the subsequent sets of entries. Note that it is retrieving entries by categories that match those in the navigation bar and displaying their respective timestamp.

```
<xsql:query
    rowset-element="SIDEBARITEMS" row-element="ITEM"
    max-rows="5" category="NEWS">
<![CDATA[
    select title,id,description,url,to_char(timestamp,'DD-MON-YYYY') timestamp
    from site_entry where categories like '%'||UPPER('{@cat}')||'%'
    and permanent > 0 order by id desc
]]>
</xsql:query>
</datapage>
```

This fourth and final query creates the "quick navigation" sidebar items by passing in preset variables to the query to retrieve the first five news items.

Employee/Department Object View Application

This application combines elements from the Insurance Claims application, in which the result data sets containing user types were converted to XML, with the Employee Page application, in which the results were formatted using XSL stylesheets. The output screen from this application is shown in Figure 10-13.

You can select the source link icon for this application and examine the three source files used to build it. The first frame, as shown in Figure 10-14, shows the XSQL page used by this application. The second frame in the same figure shows the XSL stylesheet used to apply the transformation on the output XML file. This transformation formats the query result data set into data cells of a table in the HTML page. The third frame enables you to examine the SQL and the data used to create the database tables that drive this application.

Airport Code Validation Application

The Airport Code Display application lets you find your destination city by entering a three-letter airport code or lets you find the airport code by entering the city name. The application uses a single form field for text input.

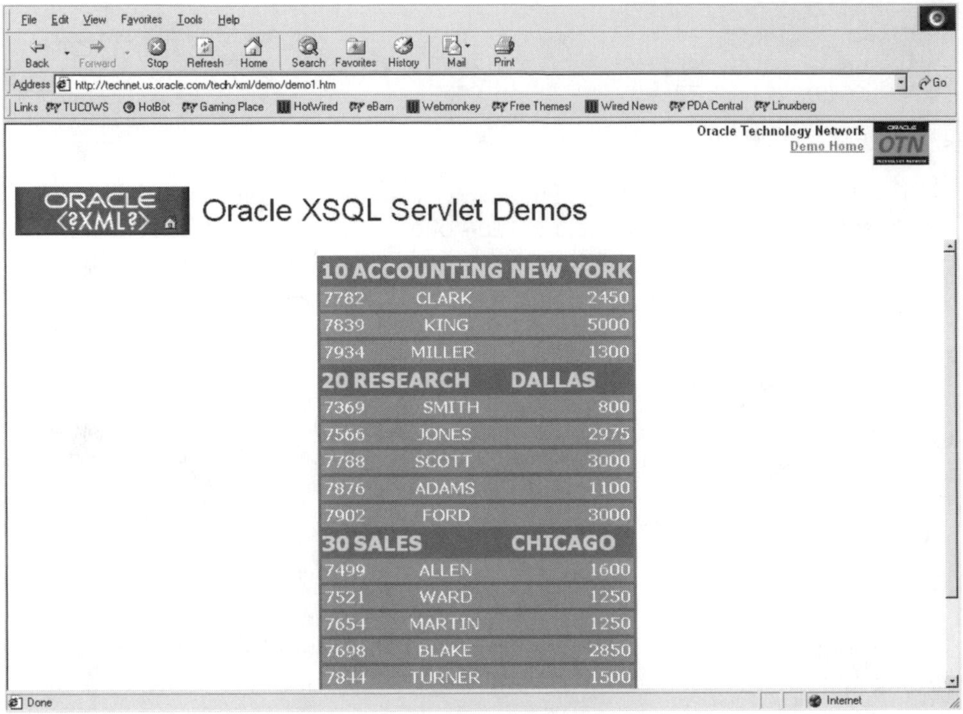

FIGURE 10-13. *Employee/Department Object View*

Here is how this application works. When you type a string in the input field and press TAB, the application searches the AIRPORT table for the three-letter airport code matching your input. If an airport with the same code is found, the application shows the airport code and its closest city name. If not, the application assumes the string you entered is a city name and searches the AIRPORT table for all records containing this string in the city name. Then, the first ten records are shown in a drop-down box, enabling you to select the city with an airport code for which you are searching. Figure 10-15 shows the output screen when the airport code entered is **SFO**.

This application uses JavaScript on the client, along with data islands to interact with the server. The application uses XML as datagrams to get a response when an airport code is entered. If the search for the code is successful, an OK datagram is returned. The XML for an OK datagram is shown on the screen in Figure 10-15. When the search for the airport code fails, an XML datagram with an Error indication is returned. This Error datagram contains ten matches that are the result output of a

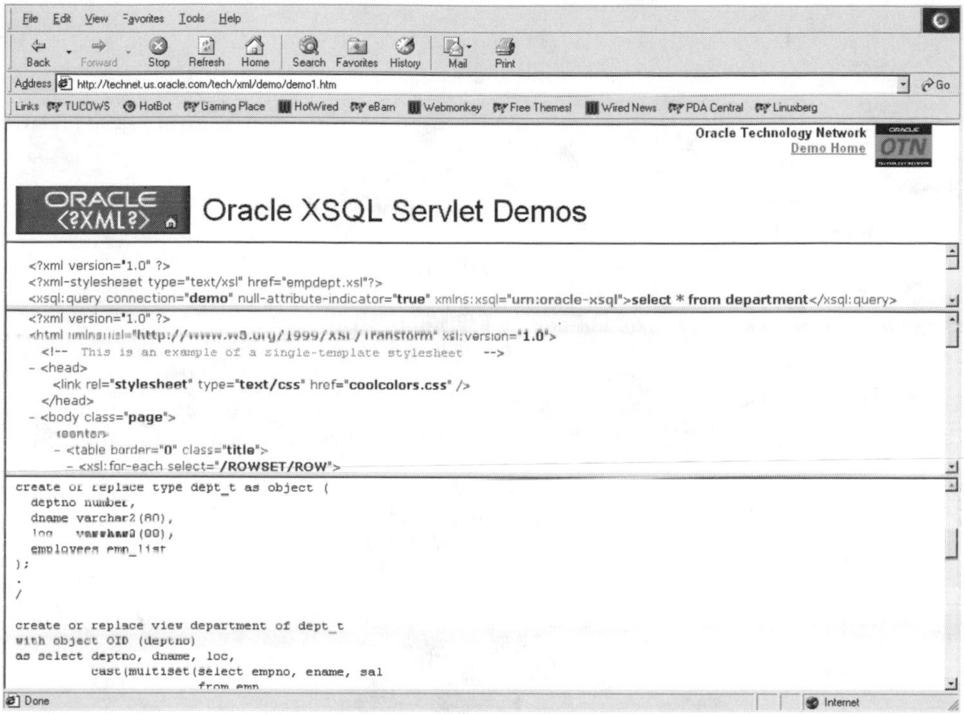

FIGURE 10-14. *Source files for Employee/Department Object View*

second query, which is executed only when the first query returns a null data set. This second query tries to find records in which the city name may contain the string entered. The two queries defined in the XSQL page for this application are as follows:

```
<?xml version="1.0"?>
<xsql:query xmlns:xsql="urn:oracle-xsql" connection="demo" airport-"SFO"
        rowset-element="Ok" max-rows="1" row-element="Airport" >
        SELECT tla "Code", description "Description" FROM AIRPORT
        WHERE tla = UPPER('{@airport}')
<xsql:no-rows-query
        max-rows="10" rowset-element="Error" row-element="Airport" >
        SELECT tla "Code", description "Description" FROM AIRPORT
        WHERE UPPER(description) LIKE UPPER('%{@airport}%') ORDER BY tla
</xsql:no-rows-query>
</xsql:query>
```

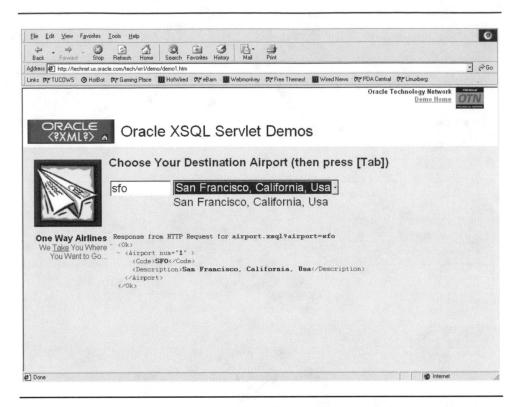

FIGURE 10-15. *Find the city with the airport code SFO in the Airport Demo application*

Figure 10-16 shows what would happen if we were looking for the airport code for Paris and actually entered the string **PARI**. What we see is the Error datagram returned in XML format. This XML data contains the first ten records returned by the second query defined in the element with the tag **<xsql:no-rows-query>**.

If you look at Figure 10-17, you can see that the data from the Error datagram was loaded into the drop-down box shown on the page. This box can then be used to narrow your selection. How does all this happen? The answer lies in the JavaScript used to collect this information from the incoming XML.

Let's examine some portions of the HTML and the JavaScript code from the Airport demo page to see how all this works. The following HTML creates a form named **airport** with these XML elements: the input text entry field named **code** (identified in the JavaScript as **airport.code**), a selection element named **lookup** (identified as **airport.lookup**), and a description element that is loaded to show the airport

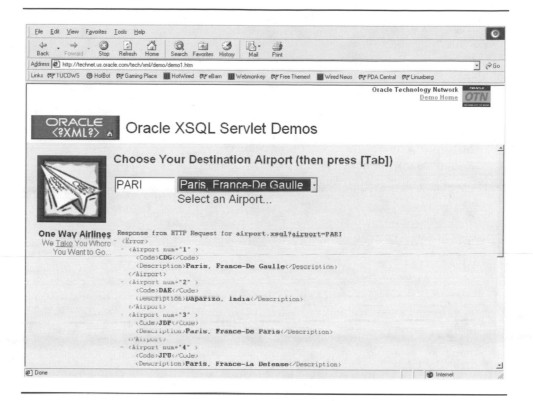

FIGURE 10-16.   *The requested string matches more than one city*

description. The name for this element is **description**, and the element is referred from JavaScript as **airport.description**.

```
<form  id="airport" method="GET" action="">
<div align="left">
<table border="0" height="89">
<tr>
  <td valign="top">
  <input style="font-family:Arial; font-size: 18pt" id="code" name="code"
         type="text" size="8" onchange="validateAirport()"><br>
</td>
<td valign="top">
  <select style="font-family:Arial; font-size: 18pt"
    onchange="setAirportCode(this)" name="lookup" size="1">
  </select><br>
```

```
<div class="st" style="font-family:Arial; font-size:18pt" id="description">
</div>
</td>
</tr>
</table>
</div>
</form>
```

NOTE
*The **airport.code** element sets the **onchange** attribute as **onchange="validateAirport()"**. This executes the function **validateAirport()** any time a new entry is made in the airport code field.*

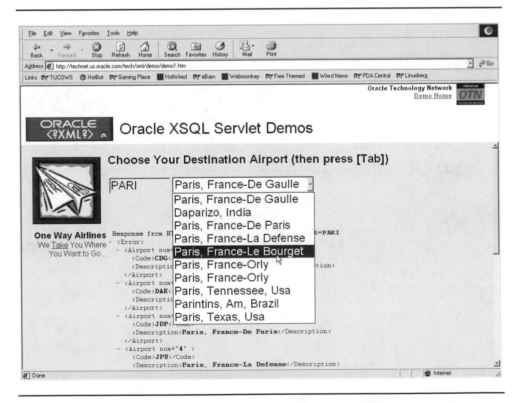

FIGURE 10-17. *Using JavaScript on the client to fill in the drop-down box with suggestions for possible selection in the Airport demo*

The following HTML creates an XML fragment or data island, which can be used as a template to load and contain the XML result received from the server:

```
<xml id="airportCodes">
</xml>
```

This empty XML fragment is only a placeholder for now. The important thing to remember is this XML data can be referred to by the name **airportCodes** in the JavaScript embedded in the page.

Now look at the way the **validateAirport()** function works. As previously discussed, this function is run by IE5 any time you enter an airport code and press the TAB key. Here is the code for the function:

```
<script>
function validateAirport() {
  event.returnValue = true;
  removelistoptions();
  if ( airport.code.value != "" ) {
    airportCodes.async = false;
    url = "airport.xsql?airport=" + airport.code.value;
    airportCodes.load( url );
    var DE = airportCodes.documentElement;
    result.innerHTML = DE.transformNode(ie5default.documentElement);
    urlexample.innerHTML = " Response from HTTP Request for <b
    style='color:blue'><pre>"+url+"</pre></b>";
    if ( DE.nodeName == "Ok" ) {
      description.innerText = DE.selectSingleNode("//Description").text;
      var newOption = new Option;
      newOption.text  = DE.selectSingleNode("//Description").text;
      newOption.value = DE.selectSingleNode("//Code").text;
      airport.lookup.options.add( newOption, 0 );
      airport.lookup.options[0].selected = true;
    } else {
      var matches = DE.selectNodes("Airport");
      if (matches.length == 0) {
        description.innerText = "Invalid Code, No Suggestions...";
      } else {
        if (matches.length == 1) {
          airport.code.value =
          matches.item(0).selectSingleNode("Code");
          description.innerText =
          matches.item(0).selectSingleNode("Description");
          var newOption = new Option;
          newOption.text  =
          matches.item(0).selectSingleNode("Description").text;
          newOption.value =
          matches.item(0).selectSingleNode("Code").text;
          airport.lookup.options.add( newOption,0 );
```

```
                airport.lookup.options[0].selected = true;
                setAirportCode(airport.lookup.options);
          } else {
             for ( ctr = 0; ctr < matches.length ; ctr++ ) {
                 var newOption = new Option;
                 newOption.text  =
                 matches.item(ctr).selectSingleNode("Description").text;
                 newOption.value=
                 matches.item(ctr).selectSingleNode("Code").text;
                 airport.lookup.options.add( newOption,ctr );
                 airport.lookup.options[0].selected = true;
                 description.innerText = "Select an Airport...";
             }
          }
        }
      }
    }
  }
}
function setAirportCode(s) {
  airport.code.value = s.options[s.selectedIndex].value;
  description.innerText = s.options[s.selectedIndex].text;
}
</script>
```

Let's focus on these two lines of code:

```
url = "airport.xsql?airport=" + airport.code.value;
airportCodes.load( url );
```

The first line of code generates the URL for the XSQL page used by the application. The second line of code does all the magic, which includes:

■ Requesting the server side to execute the XSQL page defined by the URL

■ Handling the XSQL page by the XSQL Servlet and returning a datagram XML file

■ Assigning this XML data to the XML object named **airportCodes** (remember the previous island definition?)

The JavaScript code after **airportCodes.load(url)** can now access the returned datagram.

Here is the way the application interprets what happened with the request:

```
var DE = airportCodes.documentElement;
...some code skipped...
        if ( DE.nodeName == "Ok" ) {
```

```
...now we know that OK datagram arrived
        } else {
...now we know that Error datagram arrived, let's get the airport data...
        var matches = DE.selectNodes("Airport");
...much more code skipped...
    }
```

The following lines make it clear how the lookup drop-down box is filled with the data from the XML elements of the received datagram:

```
newOption.text  = matches.item(ctr).selectSingleNode("Description").text;
newOption.value = matches.item(ctr).selectSingleNode("Code").text;
        airport.lookup.options.add( newOption,ctr );
```

Airport Code Display Application

This application uses the same XSQL page as the Airport Code Validation application. Figure 10-18 shows the resulting page when **LAX** was entered.

Figure 10-19 shows the resulting page when **PARI** was entered.

Figure 10-20 shows the screen with the source code for the XSQL page and for the XSL stylesheet. In contrast to the previous application, this one does not depend on the built-in XML support in IE5 and, thus, can work with any browser.

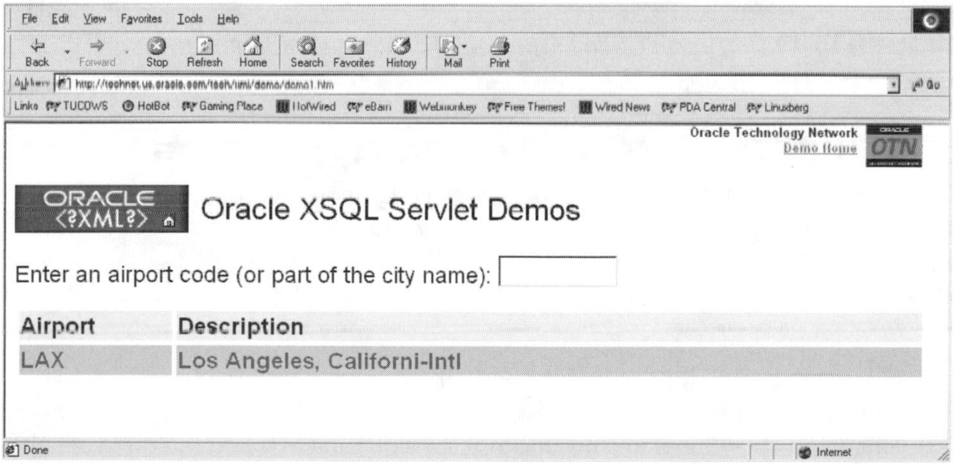

FIGURE 10-18. *Airport Code Display application—LAX entered*

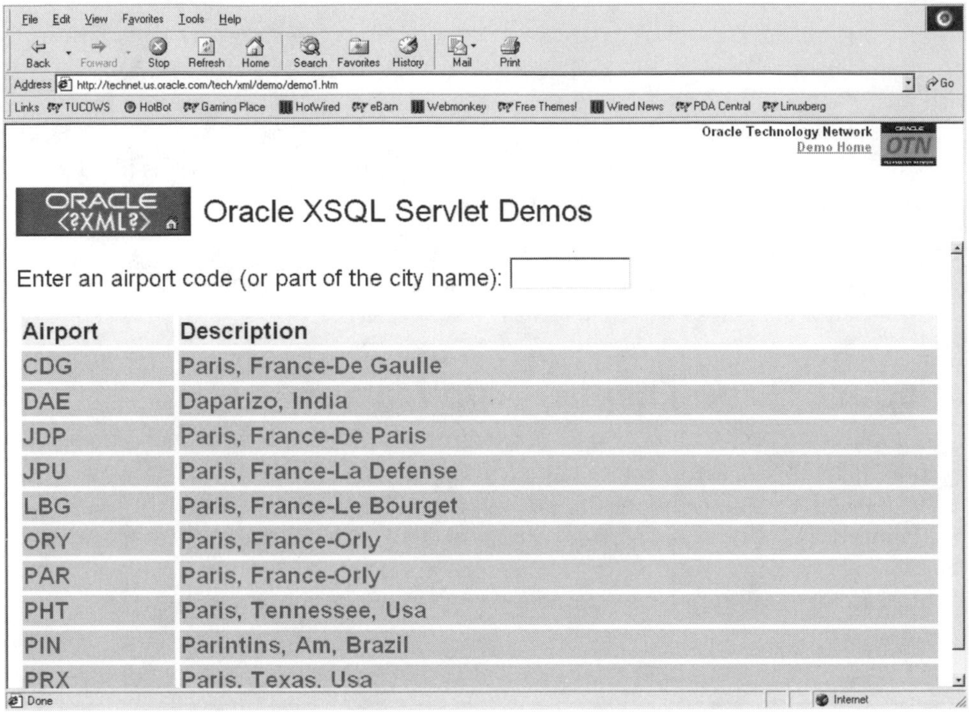

FIGURE 10-19. *Airport Code Display application—PARI entered*

Ad Hoc Query Visualization Application

This application puts most of the topics covered by the previous applications all together on a single screen. Figure 10-21 shows how this visual application enables the user to perform the following:

■ Enter a query.

■ Select a stylesheet to be applied to the resulting XML data.

When you click Show Results, the SQL runs on Oracle9i and the query result is shown in a frame in the left-hand corner of the screen. If you are interested in the schema used by this application, refer to the SQL listing for the Insurance Claim application discussed previously in the section "Insurance Claim Application."

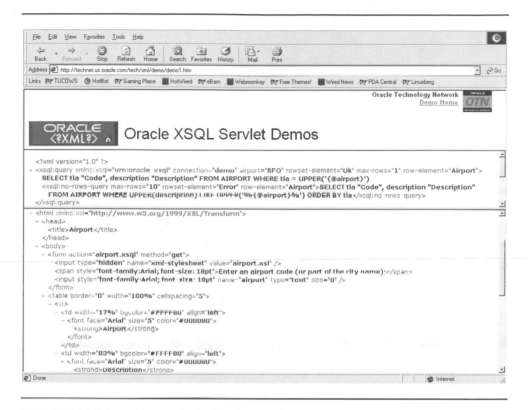

FIGURE 10-20. *Airport Code Display application—source pages*

XML Document Demo

This is a complex example that saves XML documents to the server. It shows a list of all the previously saved documents. If you select a document, the application displays it using the optionally supplied stylesheet to transform the result. The application screen is shown in Figure 10-22.

The list of saved documents is shown in the lower left-hand side, while the frame to the right shows the selected document. Selecting the stylesheet links listed in the FORMATTED column results in the document being shown in the HTML resulting from the selected XSL stylesheet. If you select the DOCID link, the XML document is shown without server transformation.

The screen shown in Figure 10-23 shows how a new document is added.

This application uses the built-in XML support in IE5. It also uses embedded JavaScript for light-weight client-side processing and user-input handling. This

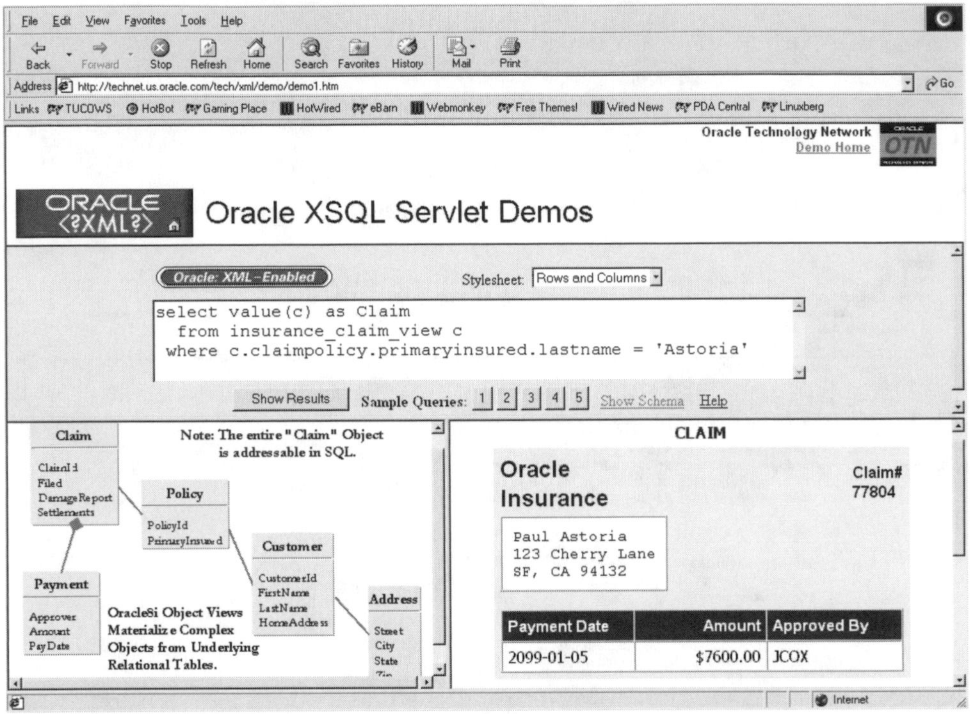

FIGURE 10-21. *Ad hoc Query Visualization application*

application is similar to, but more complex than, the Airport Code Validation application covered previously. Look at the JavaScript for the page to find the differences:

```
var test = new ActiveXObject("Microsoft.XMLDOM");
test.async = false;
test.loadXML(val);
```

Here, an ActiveX object is used to load the XML and do the parsing instead of using XML data islands, as was done in the Airport Code Validation application. The

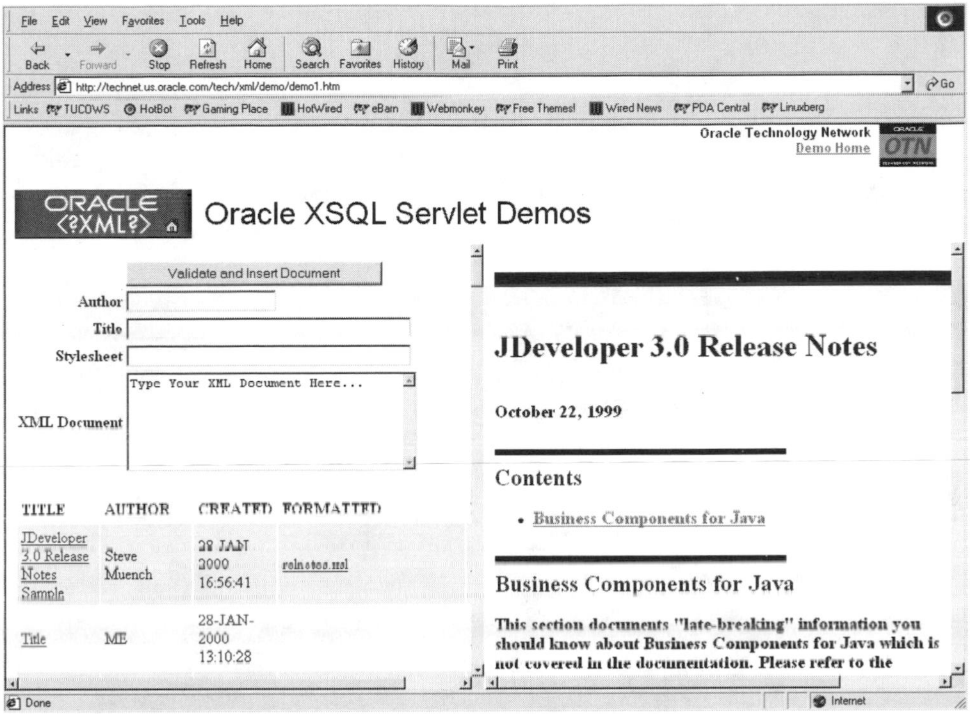

FIGURE 10-22. *XML Document Demo application*

application shows how JavaScript, the XMLDOM ActiveX object, and HTML forms are merged together with XML, SQL, Oracle XSQL pages, and Oracle8i/9i.

XML Insert Request Demo

The XML Insert Request application enables you to post a news story consisting of an XML file with a headline and a URL of the page with the news as elements. Figure 10-24 shows this application.

This application demonstrates how you can send XML from the browser for storage on the server. This involves using one important feature of the XSQL Servlet

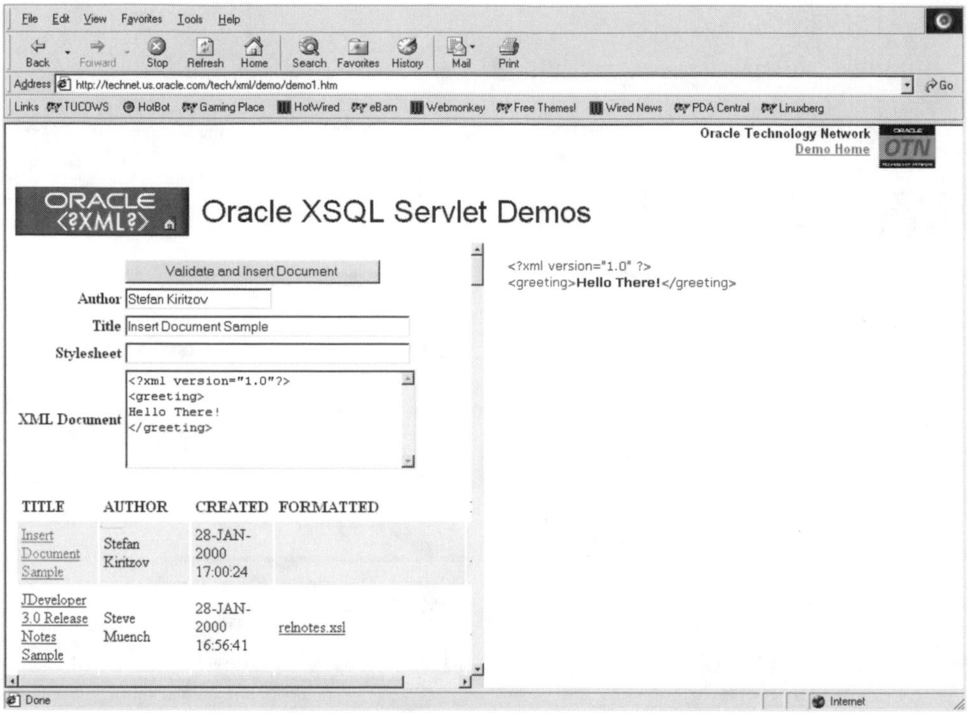

FIGURE 10-23. *Adding a new document to the XML Document Demo application*

that enables you to use XML to update database tables. Here is the application's HTML page, which includes the JavaScript that does the work:

```
<HTML>
<BODY>
<SCRIPT>
  function PostOrder (xmldoc)
  {
    var xmlhttp = new ActiveXObject ("Microsoft.XMLHTTP");
    xmlhttp.open("POST", "insertnewsstory.xsql",false);
    xmlhttp.send(xmldoc);
    return xmlhttp.responseXML;
  }
function submitInfo(){
 var xmldoc  = new ActiveXObject ("Microsoft.XMLDOM");
 xmldoc.async = false;
 xmldoc.loadXML(xmldocText.value);
```

```
 var response = PostOrder(xmldoc);
 alert(response.documentElement.xml);
 parent.bottom.location = "newsstorylist.xsql";
}
</SCRIPT>
<b>Type in an XML Document to Post:<b><br>
<TEXTAREA rows="12" style="width:100%" cols="70" NAME="xmldocText"
><moreovernews>
 <article>
  <url> http://otn.oracle.com/tech/xml </url>
  <headline_text> Oracle Releases XML Parser </headline_text>
  <source> Oracle </source>
 </article>
</moreovernews></TEXTAREA>
<P><INPUT TYPE=button Value="Post XML Document"
    onclick="submitInfo()">
</BODY>
</HTML>
```

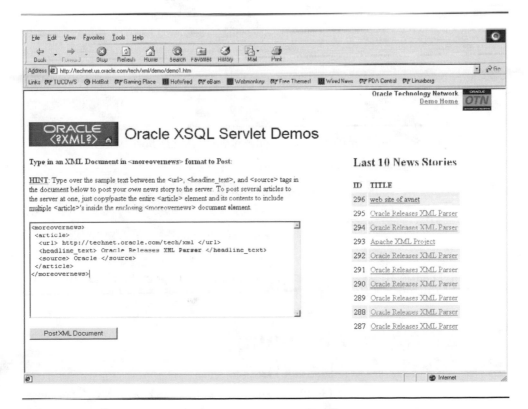

FIGURE 10-24. *XML Insert Request Demo application*

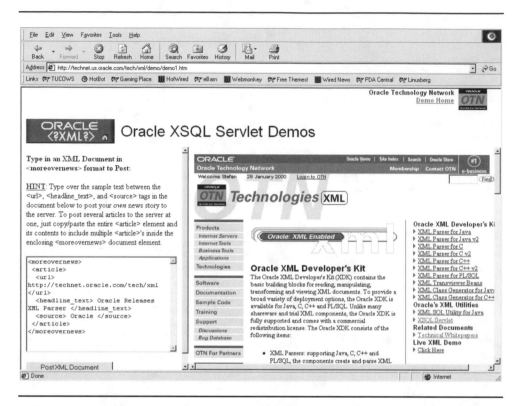

FIGURE 10-25. *XML Insert Request Application—Oracle does XML!*

Here is the XSQL page that requests the insert operation:

```
<?xml version = '1.0'?>
<xsql:insert-request connection="demo" xmlns:xsql="urn:oracle-xsql"
  table="newsstory" transform="moover-to-newsstory.xsl"/>
```

Finally, Figure 10-25 shows what happens when you select the first news story from the list on the left from Figure 10-24.

Installing and Running the XML Applications

The XML applications covered in this chapter are part of the Oracle XSQL Servlet, which is part of the XDK for Java. Download the XDK from the Oracle Technology

Network XML home page by clicking the link named XDK for Java on the screen shown earlier in this chapter in Figure 10-1, and follow the instructions detailed in this section. Figure 10-26 shows the XDK for Java home page.

Download either xdk_java_x_x_x_x_x.zip for Windows or xdk_java_x_x_x_x_x.tar.gz for UNIX, and follow these steps:

NOTE
The content of the files is the same.

1. Choose a directory to extract the downloaded file to.

   ■ If you are using Windows, you might select C:\, in which case you would change the directory to **C:**, and then extract the downloaded archive file using WinZip.

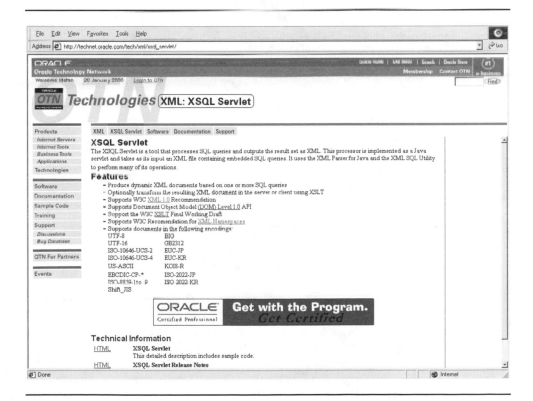

FIGURE 10-26. *XSQL Servlet home page*

■ If you're using UNIX, you would use the following command:

```
tar xvfz xdk_java_9_0_1_0_0.tar.gz
```

2. The files will expand under the subdirectories **/bin**, **/lib**, **/xdk**.

3. All JAR and ZIP files needed to run the XSQL Servlet are in the lib subdirectory. Make sure those files are in the CLASSPATH for your Web server's Java Servlet run-time engine. For example, if you are using Apache JServ, add the following lines to your **C:\Apache\Jserv\conf\jserv.properties** file:

```
# Oracle XSQL Servlet
wrapper.classpath=C:\xdk\lib\oraclexsql.jar
# Oracle JDBC (8.1.5)
wrapper.classpath=C:\xdk\lib\classes12.zip
# Oracle XML Parser V2 (with XSLT Engine)
wrapper.classpath=C:\xdk\lib\xmlparserv2.jar
# Oracle XML SQL Components for Java
wrapper.classpath=C:\xdk\lib\xsu12.jar
# XSQLConfig.xml File location
wrapper.classpath=C:\xdk\lib
```

4. The next step is to register the file extension of **.xsql** to map to the Java Servlet class named **oracle.xml.xsql.XSQLServlet**. To do this in Apache, add the following lines to your **C:\Apache\Jserv\conf\mod_jserv.conf** configuration file:

```
# Executes a servlet passing filename with proper extension
# in PATH_TRANSLATED property of servlet request.
# Syntax: ApJServAction [extension] [servlet-uri]
ApJServAction .xsql /servlets/oracle.xml.xsql.XSQLServlet
```

5. Copy the files in the demo subdirectory to a convenient directory under your Web server's virtual root. For example, if you are using Apache on Windows, use the following command:

```
xcopy /s c:\xdk\xdk\demo\java\xsql\demo C:\Apache\htdocs\xsql\
demo
```

6. The demos are set up to use the SCOTT schema on a database on your local machine (in other words, the machine where the Web server is running). If you are running a local database and have a SCOTT account with a password of TIGER, then you are all set. Otherwise, you need to edit the **.\xdk\lib\XSQLConfig.xml** file to correspond to your values for username, password, dburl, and driver values for the connection named "demo", as shown here:

```
<?xml version="1.0" ?>
<XSQLConfig>
      :
  <connectiondefs dumpallowed="no">
    <connection name="demo">
      <username>scott</username>
      <password>tiger</password>
      <dburl>jdbc:oracle:thin:@localhost:1521:ORCL</dburl>
      <driver>oracle.jdbc.driver.OracleDriver</driver>
    </connection>
    <connection name="lite">
      <username>system</username>
      <password>manager</password>
      <dburl>jdbc:Polite:POlite</dburl>
      <driver>oracle.lite.poljdbc.POLJDBCDriver</driver>
    </connection>
  </connectiondefs>
      :
</XSQLConfig>
```

7. To set up the database tables used in the examples discussed in this chapter, run all of the SQL scripts in the demo subdirectory. SQL scripts have an extension of **.sql**. For example, to set up the data tables used by the Airport Demo application, use this command:

```
sqlplus scott/tiger @airport.sql
```

8. Restart your Web server. After that, you can launch Internet Explorer 5 and navigate to **http://yourserver/xsql/demo/helloworld.xsql**. If everything was installed successfully, you will see the application screen shown previously in Figure 10-2. Now the applications will run on your machine.

Another easy way to run the applications is to use the *Oracle Web-to-Go Web server*. Oracle's Web-to-Go is a single-user Web server targeting mobile applications. Because it supports Servlets fully, you can run the XSQL Servlet with this Web server. If you are using JDeveloper 3.x, then you already have Web-to-Go on your system. Assuming that your JDeveloper 3.x home directory is **d:\jdev**, the script listed next will start the Web-to-Go Web server using the configuration settings specified in the **d:\jdev\lib\webtogo.ora** file. If this is not true on your machine, you will need to change the scripts accordingly.

```
@@echo off
setlocal
set JDEV_HOME=d:\jdev3
set PATH=%JDEV_HOME%\bin;%PATH%
```

```
set CP=%JDEV_HOME%\java\lib\classes12.zip
set CP=%CP%;%JDEV_HOME%\lib\webtogo.jar
set CP=%CP%;%JDEV_HOME%\lib\xmlparserv2.jar
set CP=%CP%;%JDEV_HOME%\lib\classgen.jar
set CP=%CP%;%JDEV_HOME%\lib\ojsp.jar
set CP=%CP%;%JDEV_HOME%\jswdk-1.0\lib\servlet.jar
set CP=%CP%;C:\xsql\lib
set CP=%CP%;C:\xsql\lib\classes111.zip
set CP=%CP%;C:\xsql\lib\oraclexsql.jar
set CP=%CP%;C:\xsql\lib\oraclexmlsql.jar
set CP=%CP%;C:\xsql\lib\xmlparserv2.jar
jre -classpath %CP% oracle.lite.web.JupServer
endlocal
```

Save this script as a file named **wtg.bat**, and use the **wtg** command to start the Web-to-Go server. But before starting Web-to-Go, you must edit the file **d:\jdev3\ lib\webtogo.ora**.

In the [FILESYSTEM] section, add this line:

```
ROOT_DIR=C:\
```

This line sets the physical directory to act as the Web server's virtual document root.

In the [MIMES] section, add this line:

```
xsql=text/html;handler=oracle.xml.xsql.XSQLServlet
```

This line registers the XSQL Servlet's class file as the handler for files with an ***.xsql** extension.

In the [MIMES] section, add these lines as well:

```
xml=text/xml
xsl=text/xml
```

These lines set the default MIME type for XML and XSL files.

The entire source of the *modified* **webtogo.ora** file follows:

```
[WEBTOGO]
PORT = 7070
USE_SYSTEM_CLASSPATH=YES
DEBUG=YES
[FILESYSTEM]
ROOT_DIR=C:\
TYPE=OS
[MIMES]
html=text/html
xml=text/xml
xsl=text/xml
```

```
jsp=text/html;handler=oracle.jsp.JspServlet
xsql=text/html;handler=oracle.xml.xsql.XSQLServlet

[APPLICATIONS]
xmlfile=.\wtgapp.xml

[SERVLET_PARAMETERS]
```

After modifying the **webtogo.ora** file, you can launch the Web-to-Go Web server by running the **wtg.bat** file. Then start Internet Explorer 5 and navigate to **http://yourserver/xsql/demo/helloworld.xsql**. If Web-to-Go is installed successfully, you will see the application screen shown earlier in Figure 10-2. Now the applications will run on your computer using Web-to-Go and your Oracle8i or 9i database.

CHAPTER
11

Future Trends

ccording to Forrester Research, business-to-business e-commerce in the U.S. alone is estimated to exceed $1 trillion in 2003, an amount ten times larger than business-to-consumer e-commerce. How is that possible? Suppose businesses and entire industries shift their buying and selling to electronic exchanges on the Internet, so that parts made by suppliers could always be made available and sold competitively over the Web via an industry-specific eBay type of forum. Rather than purchasers having no knowledge of what a broad range of suppliers may be offering and when they may be offering certain components, such information would always be available online. Does this give the demand side an advantage? Not really, since suppliers' excess inventory could be sold, components could be made to order, and suppliers could realize potential sales by joining such an exchange. The automotive industry already has had players such as Ford Motor Company, GM, and Daimler-Chrysler team up on such exchanges.

Who else would benefit from such large electronic exchanges over the Internet besides the supply/demand businesses involved? Obviously, database companies, because large amounts of data and huge numbers of transactions need to be handled over the Internet, and such software is needed by all players involved in the exchange. Larry Ellison's mantra of "The Internet Changes Everything" is obviously true for Oracle. Software application companies who come up with standardized applications for specific industries would benefit, as well as consulting companies geared toward helping set up such electronic exchanges. On the hardware side, companies who make large data-storage devices would obviously benefit, along with PC and networking companies. Finally, companies involved with XML would benefit, because these exchanges would most likely standardize on a data exchange format, i.e., XML, that could be sent and retrieved from databases; these XML companies would facilitate the integration of such technology by offering services, tools, or products to the businesses involved in these exchanges.

While all of the these objectives may seem coldly commercial, the technology needed to make such things happen probably came from a spark of creativity, the feeling of pure fun at having created something. Indeed, applications for such technology need not happen only in the business arena; for example, exchanges could be built for trading information between conservationists concerned with endangered species or between children in classrooms.

For the most part, the fundamental concepts of XML are fairly straightforward, the applications of the ideas are incredible, and the implications of further development simply breathtaking. For those immersed in this area, the possibilities are endless and the future of the industry extremely bright. Whether or not XML turns out to be another SGML is another question, but as long as innovation in applications and open standards continues, and breakdowns in the XML industry and technology do not occur at a rapid clip, this will be a fertile area for many years down the road.

This chapter will focus on these standards bodies and the XML-related work they are doing. We will then look at industry-wide schemas and XML's influence on the Internet.

The Role of Standards Bodies

Open software standards. Three simple words that convey meaning far beyond what's stated. For example, in an ideal situation, with open software standards, software developers could write programs with components from different vendors and not fear interoperability problems. The problem of being locked to a particular vendor would go away. The role of the World Web Consortium, OASIS, and other standards bodies is to then come up with enough quality functionality to satisfy a majority of the software development community. And because requirements change at different times for different parts of the community, these standards bodies must be constantly attuned to the needs of its users and respond with additional functionality specifications or risk the possibility of becoming obsolete. These software standards are especially important when certain industries need to standardize on new technologies such as XML. Not having such standards or having deficient standards would make it very difficult for businesses to interoperate on the Internet. The standards produced by the W3C and OASIS are the key to pointing the way toward future work and applications.

The Role of the W3C

Currently, the most important standards body for the XML industry is the W3C. According to their Web site:

> The World Wide Web Consortium was created in October 1994 to lead the World Wide Web to its full potential by developing common protocols that promote its evolution and ensure its interoperability . . . . By promoting interoperability and encouraging an open forum for discussion, W3C commits to leading the technical evolution of the Web.

Basically, the W3C is a consortium composed of W3C employees and companies, such as Oracle, IBM, Microsoft, and Sun Microsystems, that pay membership dues to place their representatives on a number of committees that produce open software standards specifications according to developers in the industries code. In short, it is a very powerful consortium.

While it is true that some member companies do not wait for the committees to formalize such specifications and develop company-proprietary APIs, and that some APIs—such as the SAX APIs developed by Dave Megginson—don't fall under the auspices of the W3C, developers know that open standards are the way to go.

Once the W3C comes out with API specifications, developers will flock to it unless those specifications are horribly flawed. And once the industry developers flock to it, company-proprietary APIs often fall by the wayside. The implications are that many companies can then participate in an industry mechanism, such as an electronic exchange, rather than one company dictating what others should do.

The W3C's home page, located at **http://www.w3.org**, is shown in Figure 11-1.

As you can see, the left-hand side of the page has links to a number of W3C committees and technologies. The right-hand side contains links to the mission statement, how to get involved, W3C member area, W3C team, past news and a search engine of the W3C site and public mailing list archives. The top and bottom have links to Activities, Technical Reports, Site Index, About W3C, and Contact. Finally, the middle of the page lists current news and specification releases. We will highlight some of these links to explore the impact of W3C's contributions to the future of XML.

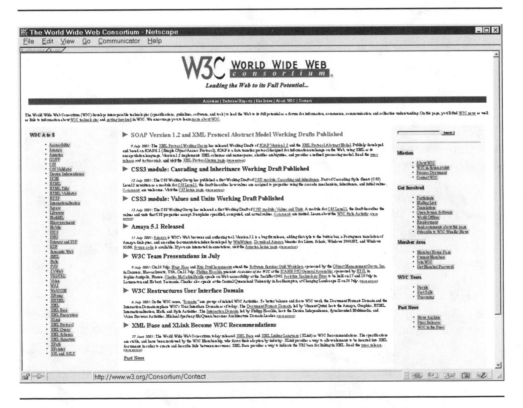

FIGURE 11-1. *World Wide Web Consortium Web site (Copyright 1994–2001, W3C [MIT, INRIA, KEIO]. All rights reserved.)*

Documents Formats Domain

Formerly part of the User Interface Domain, the Documents Formats Domain has some of the previous domain's goals to "improve all user/computer communications on the Web" and to work on "formats and languages that will present information to users with more accuracy and a higher level of control," namely that of "improving the technology that allows Web users to effectively perceive and express information." Currently, this Web page lists the following domain activities:

Amaya   This is a W3C-developed Web client that is both a browser and an authoring tool. Its purpose is to act as a test instrument and demonstration of some of the new specs and Web formats and protocols.

Graphics   In October 1996, the W3C published Portable Network Graphics (PNG), a format for bitmapped images, and they are now developing Scalable Vector Graphics (SVG), an open vector graphics format written in XML. With the Internet depending more and more on graphics rather than text, we can expect the W3C to come out with additional recommendations and specifications in this area in the years to come.

Hypertext Markup Language (HTML)   Hypertext Markup Language—known as HTML—is the current standard for Web pages; however, the W3C is now designing XHTML, the next generation of HTML to take advantage of XML applications. In addition, a subgroup working on XForms, a mechanism to transform data as XML and reducing the need for scripting, has also been spun off.

Internationalization   To handle multibyte character-set languages, such as Chinese and Japanese, the W3C has also turned its attention toward Unicode as the language of XML, thus being able to handle languages throughout the world without having to sacrifice interoperability. To satisfy the needs of the international community, work on providing internationalization features will continue.

Math   Created by the W3C in 1998, Mathematical Markup Language (MathML) was a recommendation to allow mathematical expressions in HTML and XML documents. Following that up was MathML 2.0, the latest recommendation for this language.

Style Sheets   The W3C continues to enhance the *Cascading Style Sheets (CSS)* language to provide more control over the presentation of Web pages. With the publication of the Extensible Stylesheet Language (XSL) specification, presentation of XML documents will also be steered into directions that go far beyond presentation, allowing enhanced functionality for the transformation of XML documents.

Interaction Domain

Formerly part of the User Interface Domain, the Interaction Domain is the other group spun off from the previous domain, with its goal of "exploring new ways to access Web information." Currently, this Web page lists the following domain activities.

Device Independence   Given the popularity of personal computers, cell phones, Palm devices, GPSs, and other future hand-held devices, all to interoperate seamlessly across the Web, the W3C has targeted this as another promising area in the future.

Synchronized Multimedia   This area of the W3C focuses on the *Synchronized Multimedia Integration Language (SMIL)* as a mechanism for integrating audio, video, text, and graphics. The SMIL specification is currently a recommendation.

Voice Browser   Given the popularity of MP3 and such sites as the Napster, it is no wonder the W3C is devoting resources to how audio will affect the Internet. From call centers to music to voice mail on the Web, this will be another fruitful area of investigation for the W3C.

Some of the additional activities underway include "voice" XML and digitizing and tagging speech appropriately while offering APIs to navigate the data. Indeed, the XML applications for mobile technology and television (imagine tagged television content!) are mind-boggling.

The Technology and Society Domain

The mission of the Technology and Society Domain is to understand "society's ethical and legal issues from a new international perspective in light of new technology—partly by changing the technology, and partly by educating users about the technology's benefits, costs, and limits." Currently, the Web page lists the following domain activities.

Metadata   Formed in 1997, this group's activity is key to the W3C's work on how to protect intellectual property on the Internet using encryption and digital signatures on the *Resource Description Framework (RDF)*. As content and e-commerce proliferate on the Web, the question of how to protect such intellectual property is an important one, and the W3C is fully involved.

XML Signature (xmldsig)   XML Signature is one of the areas the W3C launched to protect and identify the IP of XML documents. Areas that the W3C is investigating are

- XML signature requirements
- XML signature core syntax and processing

Platform for Privacy Preferences (P3P)   The P3P initiative is about providing consumer protection on the Internet to guard against the invasion of privacy of Internet users, while making sure the Internet is still attractive for e-commerce. To this end, the W3C group thinks up mechanisms such as privacy policy notices that can be posted on Web sites to alert consumers. As highlighted by issues concerning consumer privacy on the Internet, the W3C can make a significant contribution in this area.

Public Policy Role   The W3C also has a group working on initiatives to inform the public and government policymakers about the Internet's capabilities to address international restrictions.

Electronic Commerce   E-commerce—capitalism on the Internet—is an entire paradigm shift concerning the selling and purchasing of goods and services over the Web. The W3C has a group that considers the problems and priorities for e-commerce and possible solutions. Obvious issues are bandwidth and consumer protection; this particular W3C group monitors this facet of the evolving medium.

Security   Security goes hand in hand with e-commerce and is an issue that faces the Internet as a whole. If users do not trust that the information being transmitted on the Internet is secure, they will be reluctant to use such a medium, thus affecting the growth of the Internet.

Obviously, e-commerce has played a major role in highlighting the importance of security on the Web. As more and more thinking goes into how far the Web can become commercialized and move away from being a pure information medium, XML signatures to tag content and prevent intellectual property piracy will become more of a looming concern, particularly with content such as movies and songs being delivered over the Internet.

Architecture Domain

The mission of the Architecture Domain is to "exploit the power of computing in our everyday lives" as part of the evolution of the Web. Currently, the Web page lists the following domain activities.

Document Object Model (DOM)   The Document Object Model is a standardized API that allows access to the traversal, retrieval, and updating of XML documents. As time goes on, more and more database applications will appear, as DTDs morph into XML schemas and XML schemas map to database schemas.

Jigsaw   Another testing mechanism for the W3C, Jigsaw is a W3C-developed, Java-based, object-oriented Web server.

XML: Structured Document Interchange   Extensible Markup Language (XML) is a meta-markup language based on SGML. More powerful than HTML, XML is playing an increasingly important role in e-commerce, as its structured data can be manipulated, stored, retrieved from database-backed Web sites, and then transmitted to other Web sites.

XML Protocol   This group is developing technologies to allow communication via XML in a distributed environment. Thus, architectures along with a XML messaging format would be investigated, such as the Simple Object Access Protocol (SOAP).

Hypertext Transfer Protocol (HTTP)   The W3C has been a leader in promoting the Hypertext Transfer Protocol (HTTP), which enables cross-platform, cross-enterprise, multimedia-information exchange over the Internet. Since 1990, the W3C has done its best to improve HTTP in terms of additional functionality and better performance, and it will continue to do so to help accommodate the increasing traffic on the Internet.

URI (Uniform Resource Identifiers)   The role of this group is to "monitor, provide guidance, and review" other organizations' documents concerning global identifier mechanisms for the Web. Thus, investigations into persistent URIs, Metadata, new URI schemes, and internationalized identifiers will be investigated.

Seminal work occurs in the Architecture domain, as evidenced by the creation of XML itself, so expect other crucial work to also come from this area in the future. For example, W3C conferences (**http://www.www10.org**), such as the conference detailed in Figure 11-2, can be expected to turn up additional areas of research.

At this conference, you can discover where some of the future trends may lie, with papers on Web performance, security for XML documents, richer queries for XML, document-publishing formats, Web searching with PDAs, storage of Web pages in databases, Web profiling, XML usage scenarios, hyperlink analysis, more efficient searching mechanisms, better tools to create and search Web sites, voice and video formats and portals on the Web, next-generation Web architectures, Web caching of multimedia data, Web data mining, advertising on the Web, and Web page user analysis.

Thus, the fruits of "enhancing the infrastructure of the Web and increasing its automation" is a dynamic and fluid development driven by forces both internal and external to the W3C. The hope is that this work becomes part of the open standards as espoused by the W3C.

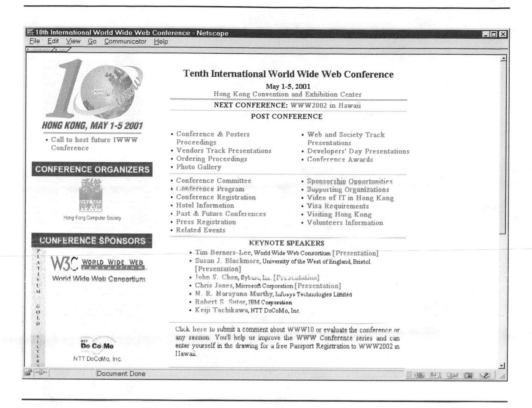

FIGURE 11-2. *World Wide Web Consortium w9 Web site (Copyright 1994–2001, W3C [MIT, INRIA, KEIO]. All rights reserved.)*

Web Accessibility Initiative (WAI)

The mission of the Web Accessibility Initiative is to pursue "accessibility of the Web through five primary areas of work: technology, guidelines, tools, education and outreach, and research and development" for people with disabilities. Currently, the Web page lists activities concerning each of these five areas. As Tim Berners-Lee, the W3C director and inventor of the World Wide Web, puts it, "The power of the Web is in its universality. Access by everyone regardless of disability is an essential aspect."

W3C Open Source Software

Open source code is available for download from the W3C site. Obviously, we wish more of the specifications had code available, but sites such as the Apache

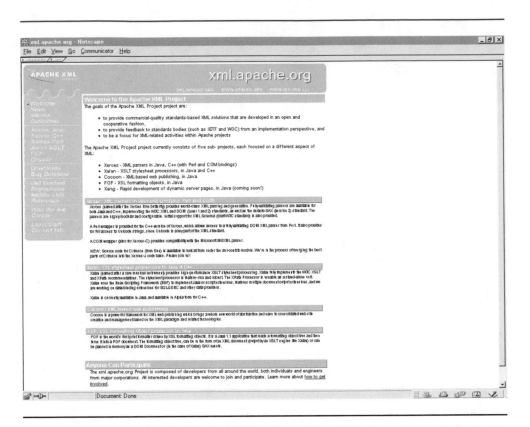

FIGURE 11-3. *Apache's XML Web site (Copyright 2001, The Apache Software Foundation. All rights reserved.)*

Software Foundation (**http://xml.apache.org**) are alternatives. Apache's XML Web site, shown in Figure 11-3, lists open source, downloadable Java/C++ XML/XSLT processors, Java XML-based Web publishing (Cocoon), Java XSL formatting objects (FOP), and rapid development of dynamic Java server pages (Xang).

Indeed, this even applies to industry-specific DTDs or XML schemas that are stored and standardized by consortiums such as RosettaNet, shown in Figure 11-4, at **http://www.rosettanet.org**.

In addition, many W3C member companies also offer free downloadable software from company Web sites, such as Oracle's **http://technet.oracle.com/tech/xml** Web site.

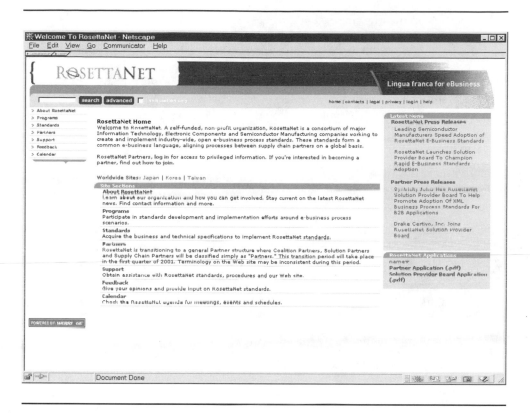

FIGURE 11-4. *RosettaNet's Web site (Copyright 2001, RosettaNet. All rights reserved.)*

The Role of OASIS

The other organization that will most influence the XML industry in the future is the Organization for the Advancement of Structured Information Standards (OASIS). According to their Web site:

> OASIS . . . is a nonprofit, International consortium dedicated to accelerating the adoption of product-independent formats based on public standards, which include SGML, XML, HTML and CGM . . . .

It focuses on making these standards easy to adopt, recommending specific application strategies. Finally, it provides a forum for members to "create, receive, coordinate, and disseminate information describing methodologies, technologies and implementations of the standards." Depending on which recommendations and strategies are adopted by OASIS, companies in the industry would likely incorporate them into the product creation processes.

The OASIS home page, which is shown in Figure 11-5, is located at **http://www.oasis-open.org**.

The OASIS Web site contains links to information about its organization, library, calendar, site map, members, and news. Similar to the W3C, OASIS is a consortium that is composed of sponsoring companies, such as Oracle, IBM, Microsoft, and Sun

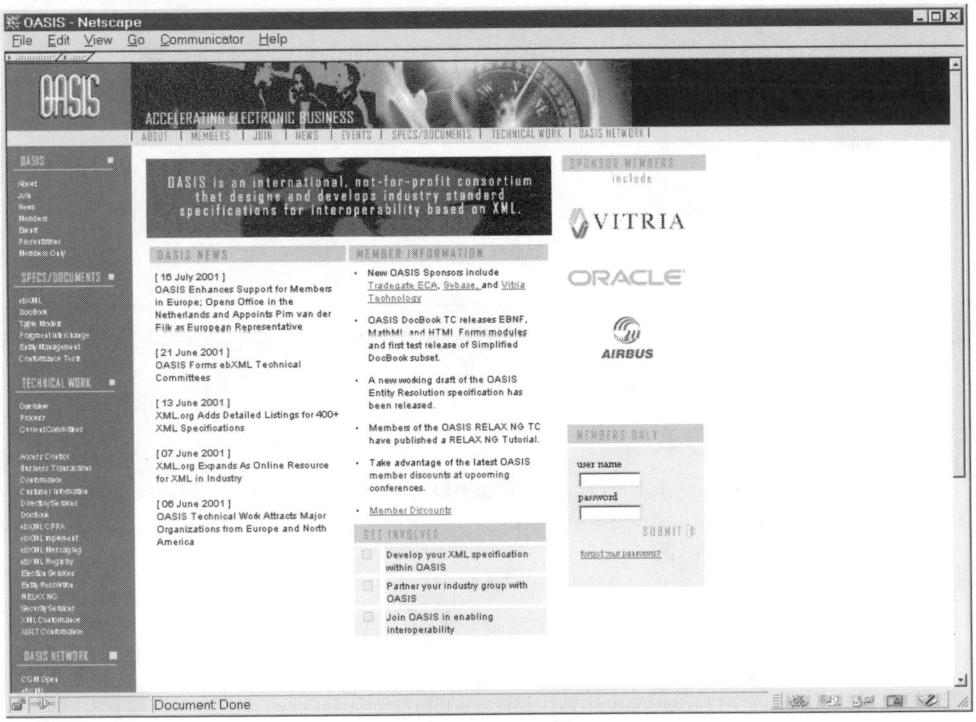

FIGURE 11-5. *OASIS Web site (Copyright 2001, OASIS. All rights reserved.)*

Microsystems, that pay dues. While many software developers in the XML industry may identify OASIS with the OASIS/NIST (National Institute of Standards and Technology) XML conformance test suite, OASIS also operates an XML Web portal for the industry, XML.ORG, in which up-to-date news about XML applications in industrial and commercial settings is broadcast, along with reference repositories for XML specifications such as schemas.

XML.ORG's home page, shown in Figure 11-6, is located at **http://www.xml.org**.

OASIS and its XML portal, XML.ORG, complement and work in conjunction with standards bodies, such as the W3C, that produce specifications, so that more and more reference material—for example, test suites and XML schemas—may be available in a common location for the XML industry in the future. Whether or not

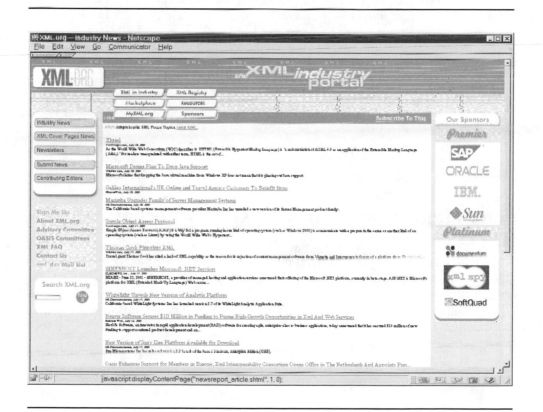

FIGURE 11-6. *XML.ORG Web site, the top of the page (Copyright 2001, xml.org. All rights reserved.)*

these reference materials evolve into more reference source code implementations is a different issue, but the continuing addition of functionality specifications and repositories will hopefully fulfill the needs of the XML industry and propel the industry to its expected heights.

Industry-Wide Schemas for XML

As briefly mentioned in the introduction to the chapter, certain industries will create and have created electronic exchanges on the Internet to buy and sell goods, in essence creating massive electronic trading communities. To facilitate this, the backbone of the data being stored, retrieved, and sent across the wire will be in XML. While certain industries will standardize on DTDs and XML schemas to govern the XML data format—e.g., a DTD or XML schema to describe brake parts for suppliers—such a mechanism is not an absolute requirement given the power of XSL to transform XML documents. Having different XML data formats in a particular industry will give rise to performance issues and custom converters, however.

Granted, the difficulty in getting different suppliers of brake parts to standardize on data formats will be problematic; but if such a standardization does happen and this data standardization based on industry-specific DTDs or XML schemas spreads across wholly different industries, the creation of these exchanges will grow very, very quickly. To this end, different companies, organizations, industries, and the U.S. government have attempted to create repositories of DTDs or XML schemas for specific industries. These will be discussed in the following section.

The Major Players in the XML Schema/ DTD Arena

OASIS and RosettaNet come to mind immediately. Both have mechanisms set up on their Web sites to allow submission of DTDs and XML schemas. For RosettaNet, the classifications must follow categories defined by the North American Industry Classification System (NAICS), a comprehensive list for different business sectors, as shown in Figure 11-7.

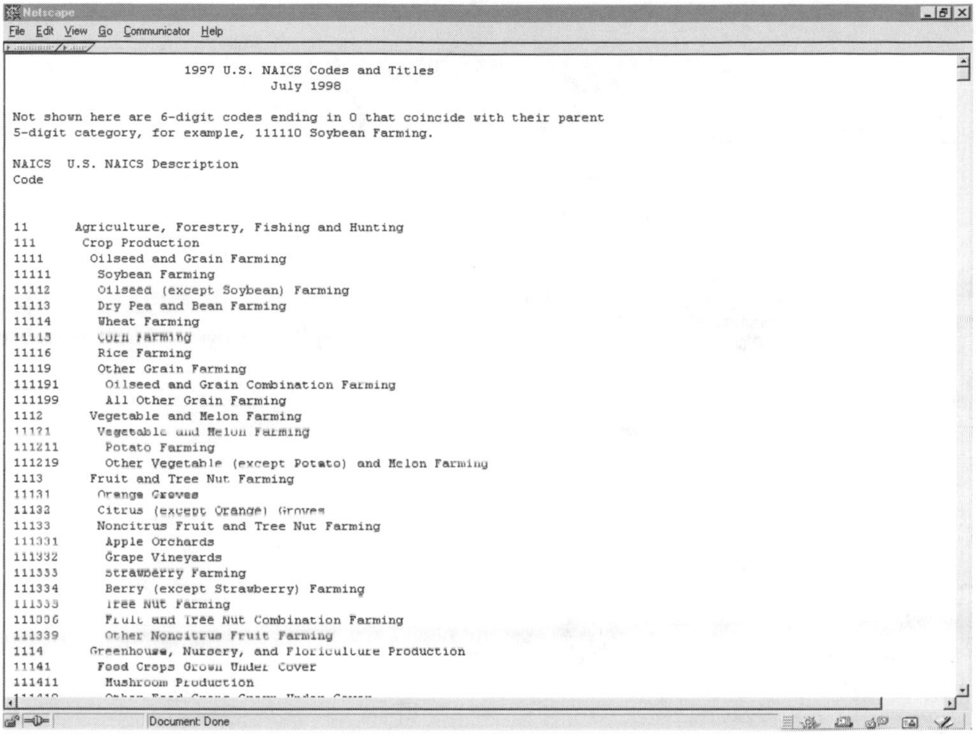


```
                    1997 U.S. NAICS Codes and Titles
                                July 1998

Not shown here are 6-digit codes ending in 0 that coincide with their parent
5-digit category, for example, 111110 Soybean Farming.

NAICS  U.S. NAICS Description
Code


11      Agriculture, Forestry, Fishing and Hunting
111      Crop Production
1111      Oilseed and Grain Farming
11111      Soybean Farming
11112      Oilseed (except Soybean) Farming
11113      Dry Pea and Bean Farming
11114      Wheat Farming
11115      Corn Farming
11116      Rice Farming
11119      Other Grain Farming
111191      Oilseed and Grain Combination Farming
111199      All Other Grain Farming
1112      Vegetable and Melon Farming
11121      Vegetable and Melon Farming
111211      Potato Farming
111219      Other Vegetable (except Potato) and Melon Farming
1113      Fruit and Tree Nut Farming
11131      Orange Groves
11132      Citrus (except Orange) Groves
11133      Noncitrus Fruit and Tree Nut Farming
111331      Apple Orchards
111332      Grape Vineyards
111333      Strawberry Farming
111334      Berry (except Strawberry) Farming
111335      Tree Nut Farming
111336      Fruit and Tree Nut Combination Farming
111339      Other Noncitrus Fruit Farming
1114      Greenhouse, Nursery, and Floriculture Production
11141      Food Crops Grown Under Cover
111411      Mushroom Production
```

FIGURE 11-7. *NAICS Web site, http://www.census.gov/epcd/naics/naicscod.txt (Copyright 2001, U.S. Census Bureau. All rights reserved.)*

In addition, two industry organizations also come to mind: Microsoft's BizTalk and DTD.com. Microsoft's BizTalk is a Microsoft-led effort to come up with and disseminate the BizTalk version of business-oriented XML schemas. The BizTalk Web site is shown in Figure 11-8.

Similarly, DTD.com also has DTD and XML schema repositories for developers to share, along with tools to create, edit, and validate these content models. Their Web site is shown in Figure 11-9.

FIGURE 11-8. *BizTalk Web site, http://www.biztalk.org (Copyright 2001, BizTalk. All rights reserved.)*

An Example of an Industry-Specific DTD/XML Schema Effort

FinXML is an organization created to capture the DTD/XML schemas for financial services companies. As stated on their Web site:

> FinXML™ is an XML based framework developed to support a single universal standard for data interchange within the Capital Markets, allowing a financial institution to communicate the details of highly structured financial transactions in electronic form within its own organizations as well as to others on the Internet.

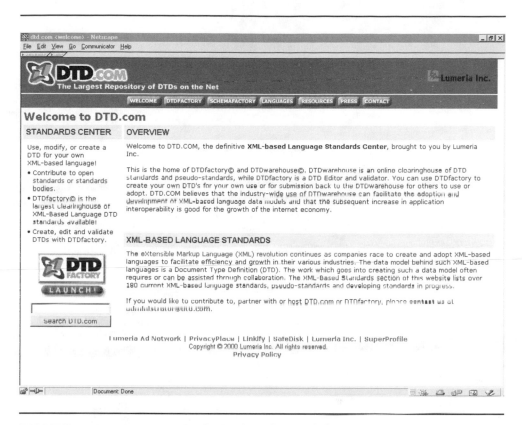

FIGURE 11-9. *DTD.com Web site, http://www.dtd.com (Copyright 2001, Lumeria. All rights reserved.)*

The consortium backing FinXML is composed of parties involved in the Capital Markets, with a keen interest in standardizing the "vocabulary" that describes financial transactions and other aspects associated with them. For those member institutions that are part of the consortium, the FinXML Web site is a valued resource for current news, specifications, and implementations. And since FinXML is based on standards put forth by the International Swaps and Derivatives Association, Inc. (ISDA), BizTalk, and cXML, consortium members have the ability to "interoperate" with each other, rather than coming up with their own proprietary "vocabularies." Thus, those in the consortium are extremely interested in propagating FinXML throughout the Capital Markets industry.

The FinXML Web site is shown in Figure 11-10.

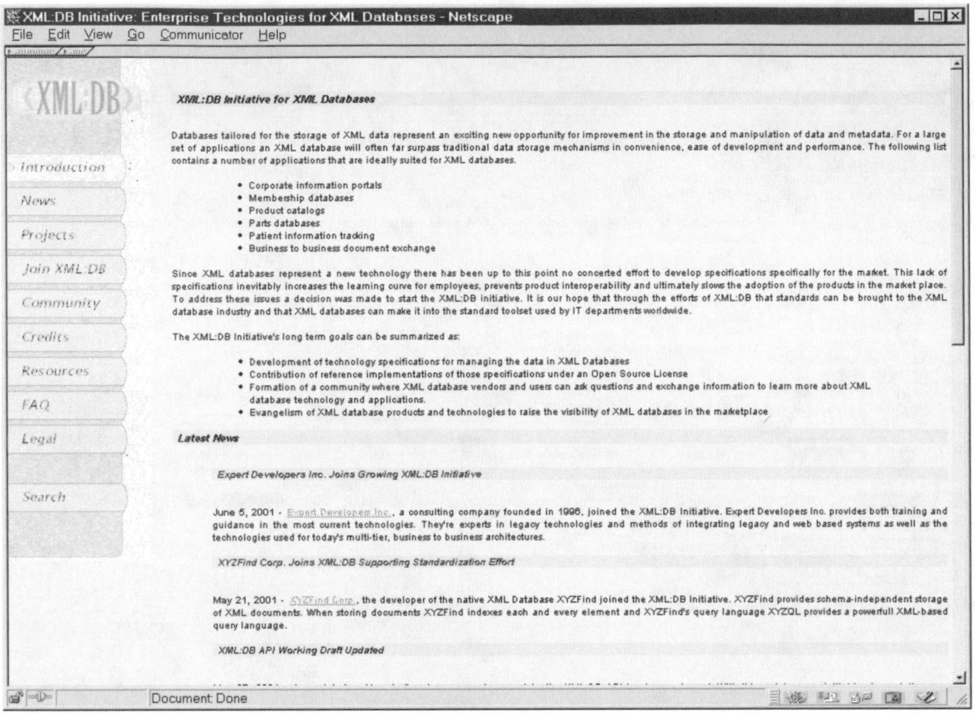

XML:DB Initiative: Enterprise Technologies for XML Databases - Netscape

File Edit View Go Communicator Help

《XML:DB》

Introduction

News

Projects

Join XML:DB

Community

Credits

Resources

FAQ

Legal

Search

XML:DB Initiative for XML Databases

Databases tailored for the storage of XML data represent an exciting new opportunity for improvement in the storage and manipulation of data and metadata. For a large set of applications an XML database will often far surpass traditional data storage mechanisms in convenience, ease of development and performance. The following list contains a number of applications that are ideally suited for XML databases.

- Corporate information portals
- Membership databases
- Product catalogs
- Parts databases
- Patient information tracking
- Business to business document exchange

Since XML databases represent a new technology there has been up to this point no concerted effort to develop specifications specifically for the market. This lack of specifications inevitably increases the learning curve for employees, prevents product interoperability and ultimately slows the adoption of the products in the market place. To address these issues a decision was made to start the XML:DB initiative. It is our hope that through the efforts of XML:DB that standards can be brought to the XML database industry and that XML databases can make it into the standard toolset used by IT departments worldwide.

The XML:DB Initiative's long term goals can be summarized as:

- Development of technology specifications for managing the data in XML Databases
- Contribution of reference implementations of those specifications under an Open Source License
- Formation of a community where XML database vendors and users can ask questions and exchange information to learn more about XML database technology and applications.
- Evangelism of XML database products and technologies to raise the visibility of XML databases in the marketplace

Latest News

Expert Developers Inc. Joins Growing XML:DB Initiative

June 5, 2001 - Expert Developers Inc., a consulting company founded in 1996, joined the XML:DB Initiative. Expert Developers Inc. provides both training and guidance in the most current technologies. They're experts in legacy technologies and methods of integrating legacy and web based systems as well as the technologies used for today's multi-tier, business to business architectures.

XYZFind Corp. Joins XML:DB Supporting Standardization Effort

May 21, 2001 - XYZFind Corp., the developer of the native XML Database XYZFind joined the XML:DB Initiative. XYZFind provides schema-independent storage of XML documents. When storing documents XYZFind indexes each and every element and XYZFind's query language XYZQL provides a powerfull XML-based query language.

XML:DB API Working Draft Updated

Document: Done

FIGURE 11-10. *FinXML Web site, http://www.finxml.org (Copyright 2001, FinXML.org. All rights reserved.)*

XML's Impact on the Internet

HTML is more of a presentation markup language, whereas XML is more suited to the language of e-commerce. XML's inherent advantage over HTML is that data can be surrounded by user-defined tags that can have semantics associated with them. Because this is allowed, the data can easily be stored in databases that back Web sites, retrieved, modified, and sent on to other companies or departments on the Web. In fact, a number of companies working in the XML field are transparently storing XML data in database tables, with DTDs or XML schemas mapping to database schemas. As e-commerce proliferates on the Internet, more and more companies wanting to do business on the Web will thus make use of XML and the seamless storage, retrieval, and modification of XML data in their databases, and the transportation of such data over networks to other companies or departments. Organizations such as the XML:DB initiative for XML Databases will help drive this.

Finally, indirectly or directly, consumers will benefit from this.

The Major Players in the XML Arena

Big corporations are in the business of making money. To the technologists, XML is fun, but to those who realize how e-business applications can be built on top of XML, it is indeed big business. Because the infrastructure of B2B exchanges and marketplaces needs to be built, consulting services, support revenues, and software product sales all translate to billions of dollars in revenues to the companies in the XML arena. While start-ups can and do proliferate, and indeed prosper, in this area, the big companies will be taking most of the business dollars. Hence, it is not surprising to see the resources that companies such as Microsoft, IBM, Sun Microsystems, and Oracle have devoted to XML when you append "XML" to each of the following companies' Web sites, as shown in Figures 11-11 to 11-14.

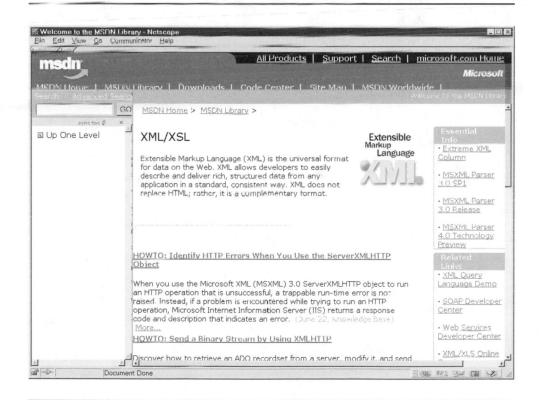

FIGURE 11-11.   *Microsoft's Web site, http://www.microsoft.com/xml (Copyright 2001, Microsoft Corporation. All rights reserved.)*

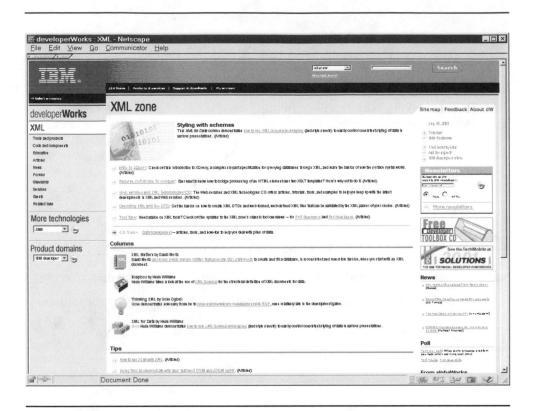

FIGURE 11-12. *IBM's Web site, http://www.ibm.com/xml (Copyright 2001, IBM Corporation. All rights reserved.)*

Upon examination, the resources offered and the news presented by these companies appear surprisingly similar. Who will win in this area, no one really knows, but the trillion-dollar business-to-business arena will be large enough for

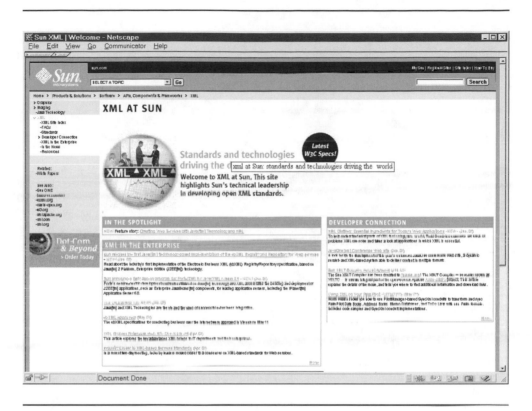

FIGURE 11-13. *Sun Microsystems' Web site, http://www.sun.com/xml (Copyright 2001, Sun Microsystems Corporation. All rights reserved.)*

all those who participate. The underlying winner undoubtedly will be XML and the consumers and businesses that take advantage of the XML-based technologies to reduce costs and facilitate e-commerce on the Internet.

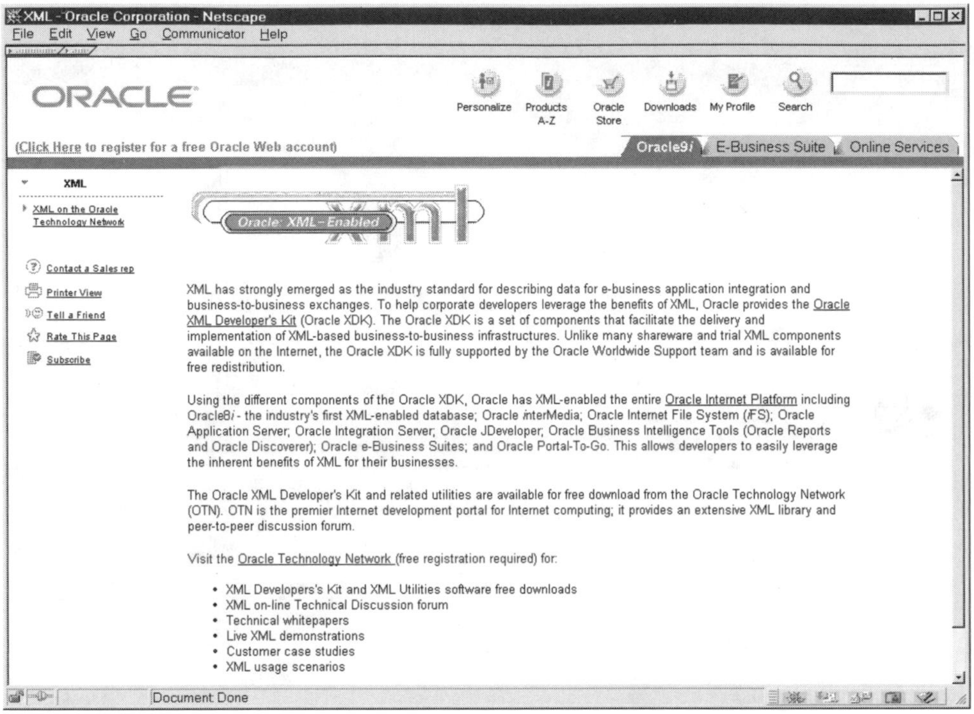

FIGURE 11-14. *Oracle's Web site, http://www.oracle.com/xml (Copyright 2001, Oracle Corporation. All rights reserved.)*

APPENDIX A

W3C XML, DOM, SAX, and XSLT Specifications

The XML Specification

What Is XML?

A software module called an XML parser is used by applications to read XML documents and provide them with access to the documents' content and structure. The XML specification describes the required behavior of an XML parser in terms of how it must read XML data and the information it must provide to the applications using it. However, it does not describe how these applications should interpret the data they have been passed.

Documents

A data object is an XML document if it is *well-formed*, that is, if it satisfies the grammar of a document as defined by the XML specification and if it also meets certain special constraints imposed in different parts of the specification. Each XML document has both a logical and a physical structure. Physically, the document is composed of units called *entities*, which may refer to other entities that are included in the document. A document begins in a "root" or document entity. Logically, the document is composed of declarations, elements, comments, character references, and processing instructions, all of which are indicated in the document by explicit markup. All text that is not mark up constitutes the character data of the document.

Elements

Each XML document contains one or more *elements*, the boundaries of which are either delimited by start tags (for example, **<book>**) and end tags (for example, **</book>**), or, for empty elements, by an empty-element tag (for example, **<book/>**). Each element may also have a set of attributes. Each attribute has a name and a value. For example, **<book isbn="1234-5678-1432-1224"/>** declares a book element with an **isbn** attribute.

Comments

Comments may appear anywhere in a document outside other markup. In addition, comments may appear within the document type definition at places allowed by the grammar. Comments are not part of the document's character data. Comments take the form **<!—** This is a comment **-->**. Note, "--" is not allowed inside the actual comment because it is part of the comment syntax.

Processing Instructions

Processing Instructions are used to provide special instructions to applications. They are not part of the document's character data and are passed through to the application. These begin with a target used to identify the application to which the instruction is directed. The XML Notation mechanism may be used for formal declaration of Processing Instruction targets. Processing Instructions are of the form:

```
<? App This is an instruction ?>
```

The target names **XML** (and its variants) are reserved for standardization. A special processing instruction called the *xml declaration* appears at the beginning of most XML documents. This takes the form **<?xml version=1.0 encoding="ISO-8859-1" standalone="yes"?>**. The version number **1.0** is used to indicate conformance to version 1.0 of the XML specification. The encoding attribute identifies the character set in which the XML document is located. By default, this is **"UTF-8"**. If the **standalone** attribute is **"yes"**, it means an XML parser that does not read an external DTD subset (including external parameter entities referenced from external entities) will produce the same document content as if it had read that subset.

CDATA Sections

```
<![CDATA[<book> No need to escape < and > </book>]]>
```

Document Type Definitions

When an XML document contains a DTD, a validating XML parser (such as any of the various Oracle XML parsers) can be asked to validate the document. A validating parser checks whether the constraints expressed by the DTD are violated in any way. To accomplish this, a validating XML parser reads and processes the entire DTD and all external parsed entities referenced in the document. It also checks on various validity constraints—for example, the name in the document type definition must match the element type of the root element. An XML document that is found by a validating processor to conform to its DTD is said to be *valid.* A DTD contains markup declarations that define the allowed grammar for the use of elements and attributes within the XML document. Four kinds of markup declarations exist: element-type declarations, attribute-list declarations, entity declarations, and notation declarations.

Element-Type Declarations

The following is an example of an element-type declaration:

```
<!ELEMENT book (title, author, publisher, price)>
<!ELEMENT title (#PCDATA)>
<!ELEMENT author (#PCDATA)>
<!ELEMENT publisher (#PCDATA)>
<!ELEMENT price (#PCDATA)*>
```

The previous declaration says a book can have only four children: **title**, **author**, **publisher**, and **price**. Each of these children can have only pure character data content. It also indicates that price need not always be specified (***** denotes 0 or more).

An element-type declaration can also specify content types of **EMPTY**, **ANY**, and **Mixed**. **EMPTY** signifies that the element should not have any children. Note that you should not use this if children are optional (use the * operator instead, as shown previously). **ANY** or **Mixed** signifies that the element can contain character data, optionally interspersed with child elements, that is, anywhere you can put character data where other elements are allowed.

Attribute-List Declarations

String-type attributes can only contain character data values. The following is an example of a string-type attribute-list declaration:

```
<!ATTLIST book isbn CDATA #REQUIRED>
```

The previous declares **isbn** to be a string-type attribute to the *book* element and that every *book* must contain an **isbn** attribute.

Tokenized-type attributes can have one of the following values: **ID**, **IDREF**, **IDREFS**, **ENTITY**, **ENTITIES**, **NMTOKEN**, or **NMTOKENS**. **ID** attribute types are designed for labeling elements in XML documents and are used to declare attributes to be element identifiers. **IDREF** and **IDREFS** are designed to reference elements labeled by **ID** attributes. Elements can have multiple attributes of type **IDREF**, which, in turn, can have fixed or default values. In a valid XML document, every location referenced by an attribute of type **IDREF** or **IDREFS** must be defined by an attribute of type **ID** somewhere in the document. The difference between the **IDREF** and **IDREFS** attribute types is that the attribute of type **IDREFS** can take one or more space-separated name values, which can reference more than one location. The following is an example of an attribute declaration defining ID and IDREF type attributes.

```
<!ATTLIST book isbn ID #REQUIRED>
<!ATTLIST booktitle isbnref IDREF #IMPLIED>
```

This example declares **isbn** as a *book* identifier and **isbnref** as a way to reference *books* that have a certain **isbn**.

The **ENTITY** attribute types allow attribute values to contain references to an existing unparsed entity (declared in the DTD). The following is an example of an attribute-list declaration defining an entity type:

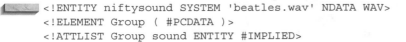

```
<!ENTITY niftysound SYSTEM 'beatles.wav' NDATA WAV>
<!ELEMENT Group ( #PCDATA )>
<!ATTLIST Group sound ENTITY #IMPLIED>
```

This example declares an entity **niftysound** that refers to an external system file called *beatles.wav,* which has an associated **NOTATION** called *WAV.* It also declares an element called **Group** and an optional attribute called **sound**, which can refer to an entity type. So, the following XML would be considered valid:

```
<Group sound="niftysound">The Beatles</Group>
```

The **NMTOKEN** and **NMTOKENS** attribute types allow specification of attributes that can only take name tokens as allowed values. Name tokens have certain additional restrictions on the types of characters allowed other than CDATA.

Enumerated-type attributes can take a list of values provided in the DTD. Two kinds of enumerated attributes exist: **NOTATION** and **Enumeration**. A **NOTATION** attribute identifies a **NOTATION**, declared in the DTD with associated system and/ or public identifiers, to be used in interpreting the element to which the attribute is attached. The following example illustrates an attribute-list declaration that defines a **NOTATION** attribute:

```
<!ATTLIST Group song NOTATION (WAV | AU | RA) #IMPLIED>
```

NOTE
A separate notation declaration must be included in the DTD for each of the notation names WAV, AU, and RA.

An Enumeration attribute has explicitly listed Nametoken values. The following example illustrates an attribute-list declaration that defines an **Enumeration** attribute:

```
<!ATTLIST book genre ( Mystery | Humor | Romance | Children )#REQUIRED>
```

This declares a required attribute called *genre* for the element *book* that has a fixed set of values it can take.

Entities

```
<!ENTITY company "Oracle Corporation">
<!ENTITY soundfile SYSTEM "c:\sounds\beatles.wav">
```

These entities can be referenced inside an XML document using entity references, as follows:

```
<Corporation>&company;</Corporation>
<Group song="soundfile">The Beatles</Group>
```

Parameter entities serve as entities in the DTD. They are valid only within the DTD and may be declared in the DTD by prefixing the entity name with a **%** sign:

```
<!ENTITY % bookchildren "( title, author, publisher, price )">
<!ELEMENT book %bookchildren;>
```

This defines that a *book* element can only have children of the types *title, author, publisher,* and *price.*

Some special predefined general entities are recognized by a XML parser: **amp**, **lt**, **gt**, **apos**, and **quot**. So, for example, **&** can be used to generate the **&** character and serves to escape it when it occurs in character data.

Notations

```
<!NOTATION WAV SYSTEM "c:/musicplayer/playwav.exe">
```

Here, the WAV notation is defined and associated with the **playwav.exe** application.

The DOM Specification

What Is DOM?

DOM is based on an object structure that closely resembles the structure of the documents it models. For instance, consider the following XML document:

```
<booklist>
<book isbn="1234-123456-1234">
    <title>C Programming Language</title>
    <author>Kernighan and Ritchie</author>
    <publisher>IEEE</publisher>
    <price>7.99</price>
  </book>
</booklist>
```

The DOM representation of the previous code is shown in Figure A-1.

In DOM, documents have a logical structure that is similar to a tree, also known as a *structure model.* From Figure A-1, you can see the root element *booklist* serves as the root of the DOM tree, as you would expect. The root element contains one child, *book,* which has four children, *title, author, publisher,* and *price,* and one attribute, *isbn.* The leaf nodes of the tree are simple text string values. The nodes in the DOM tree can be reached by using "tree-walking" methods (this does not

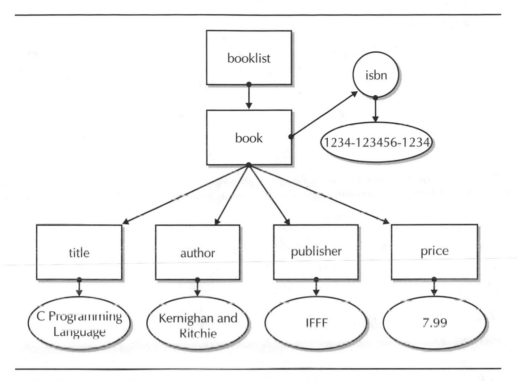

FIGURE A-1. *DOM representation*

include attributes). One important property of DOM structure models is *structural isomorphism:* if any two DOM implementations are used to create a representation of the same document, they create the same structure model. This means implementations are free to choose any data structure (not necessarily a tree) to implement DOM.

DOM Level 2 and Level 3

The DOM Level 3 W3C Working Draft consists of DOM Level 3 CORE, Abstract Schemas and Load/Save, Events, and XPath, further functionality identified by DOM users as useful and necessary for their applications.

A DOM application can use the hasFeature method of the DOMImplementation object to determine whether the module is supported. A DOMImplementation object can be retrieved from a Document using the getImplementation method. The feature strings for all modules in DOM Level 2 are listed in Table A-1.

Module	Feature String
XML	XML
HTML	HTML
Views	Views
StyleSheets	StyleSheets
CSS	CSS
CSS (extended interfaces)	CSS2
Events	Events
User Interface Events (UIEvent interface)	UIEvents
Mouse Events (MouseEvents interface)	MouseEvents
Mutation Events (MutationEvent interface)	MutationEvents
HTML Events	HTMLEvents
Traversal	Traversal
Range	Range

TABLE A-1.   *DOM Level 2 Feature Strings*

NOTE
Strings are case insensitive.

Table A-2 contains all dependencies between modules.

Module	Implies
Views	XML or HTML
StyleSheets	StyleSheets and XML or HTML
CSS	StyleSheets, Views, and XML or HTML
CSS2	CSS, StyleSheets, Views, and XML or HTML

TABLE A-2.   *DOM Level 2 Module Dependencies*

Module	Implies
Events	XML or HTML
UIEvents	Views, Events, and XML or HTML
MouseEvents	UIEvents, Views, Events, and XML or HTML
MutationEvents	Events and XML or HTML
HTMLEvents	Events and XML or HTML

TABLE A-2. *DOM Level 2 Module Dependencies (continued)*

DOM Core

A DOM tree consists of **Node** objects. Different kinds of **Nodes** are used to represent an XML document: **Document, Element, Attr, Text, DocumentFragment, DocumentType, ProcessingInstruction, Comment, CDATASection, EntityReference**, and **Notation**. DOM also defines some other types that represent a list of nodes— **NodeList, NamedNodeMap**—and introduces a **DOMString** type, which is a string of UTF-16 encoded characters. Finally, DOM introduces an exception type **DOMException**, which is raised by the various DOM interfaces if an erroneous operation is performed or if some other error occurred during execution.

Tables A-3 and A-4 describe various DOM types represented by the various Oracle XML Parsers.

DOM Type	Java	PL/SQL
Node	XMLNode	DOMNode
Document	XMLDocument	DOMDocument
Element	XMLElement	DOMElement
Attr	XMLAttr	DOMAttr
Text	XMLText	DOMText
DocumentFragment	XMLDocumentFragment	DOMDocumentFragment
ProcessingInstruction	XMLPI	DOMPI

TABLE A-3. *DOM Types with Corresponding Oracle Types*

DOM Type	Java	PL/SQL
DocumentType	DTD	XMLDTD
EntityReference	XMLEntityReference	DOMEntityReference
Comment	XMLComment	DOMComment
CDATASection	XMLCDATA	DOMCDataSection
NodeList	N/A (private class)	DOMNodeList
NamedNodeMap	N/A (private class)	DOMNamedNodeMap
Notation	XMLNotation	DOMNotation
DOMString	java.lang.String	VARCHAR2
DOMException	N/A (private class)	EXCEPTION

TABLE A-3. *DOM Types with Corresponding Oracle Types* (continued)

DOM Type	C	C++
Node	xmlnode	Node
Document	xmlnode	Document
Element	xmlnode	Element
Attr	xmlnode	Attr
Text	xmlnode	Text
DocumentFragment	xmlnode	DocumentFragment
ProcessingInstruction	xmlnode	ProcessingInstruction
DocumentType	xmlnode	DocumentType
EntityReference	xmlnode	EntityReference
Comment	xmlnode	Comment
CDATASection	xmlnode	CDATA section

TABLE A-4. *DOM Types with Corresponding Oracle Types*

DOM Type	C	C++
NodeList	xmlnodes	NodeList
NamedNodeMap	xmlnodes	NamedNodeMap
Notation	xmlnode	Notation
DOMString	oratext *	DOMString
DOMException	N/A	N/A

TABLE A-4. *DOM Types with Corresponding Oracle Types* (continued)

Node

The attributes **nodeName** and **nodeValue** are included as a mechanism to get at node information without casting down to the specific derived interface. These can be retrieved using the **getNodeName** and **getNodeValue** methods available on a Node object. In cases where no obvious mapping of these attributes occurs for a specific type of Node (for example, an Element node does not have a value of its own), this returns null. Table A-5 summarizes this.

Node Type	nodeName	nodeValue
Document	#document	Null
Element	tag name	Null
Attr	name of attribute	Value of attribute
Text	#text	Content of the text node
DocumentFragment	#document-fragment	Null
ProcessingInstruction	target	Entire content excluding the target
DocumentType	document type name	Null
EntityReference	name of entity referenced	Null
Comment	#comment	Content of the comment
CDATA section	#cdata-section	Content of the CDATA section

TABLE A-5. *Node Types and Attributes*

Note that the specialized interfaces may contain additional and more convenient mechanisms to get and set the relevant information.

Finally, with DOM Level 2, namespace awareness was added for **Node** via the **namespaceURI**, **prefix**, and **localName** attributes.

Document

A **Document** can only have the following types of children: **Element**, **ProcessingInstruction**, **Comment**, and **DocumentType**. Note that only one **Element** child (the root element) and, at most, one **DocumentType** child (the DTD) can exist for a document.

Element

Elements, which represent XML markup tags, are the most frequently encountered objects in XML documents. These provide most of the structure in an XML document. For example, consider

```
<booklist>
  <book isbn="0-04-823188-6">
    <title>The Hobbit</title>
    <author>J.R. R. Tolkien </author>
    <publisher>Unwin Paperbacks </publisher>
    <price>5.79</price>
  </book>
</booklist>
```

When represented using DOM, the top node is a **Document** node containing an **Element** node for **book**, which contains four child **Element** nodes: one each for **title**, **author**, **publisher**, and **price**. Each of these elements contains one **Text** child. Elements may have attributes associated with them. For instance, in the previous example, **booklist** has one attribute, **isbn**, that is represented using an **Attr** object. Methods on the **Element** interface exist to retrieve its attribute (either the **Attr** object representation or its string value) by name.

An **Element** can have the following types of children: **Element**, **Text**, **Comment**, **ProcessingInstruction**, **CDATA section**, or **EntityReference**.

In addition, with DOM Level 2, methods to set/get/remove namespaces with attributes were added.

Attr

An **Attr** represents an attribute in an **Element** object. Its value can be retrieved using the **getValue** method. This value is either an explicitly set value or the default value specified in a DTD. An **Attr** can have two types of children: **Text** or **EntityReference**.

Because **Attr** objects are not actually child nodes of the element they describe, they are not considered part of the DOM tree. Because of this, methods like **getParentNode**, **getPreviousSibling**, and **getNextSibling**, which work as you would expect for most other nodes, return null if they are invoked on an Attr. To navigate among the attributes of an **Element**, you first must retrieve all the attributes of the element (as a **NamedNodeMap**) and then traverse that.

CharacterData

CharacterData extends Node with a set of attributes and methods for accessing character data in the DOM tree. No DOM objects correspond directly to **CharacterData**. However, **Text, Comment**, and **CDATASection** inherit from this.

Text

Text inherits from **CharacterData** and represents the textual content of an **Element** or **Attr**. If no markup is inside an element's content, that is, no other elements, comments, and so forth, the text is contained in a single **Text** object that is the only child of the element. If markup exists, it is parsed into the information items (elements, comments, and so forth) and **Text** nodes that form the list of children of the element.

After parsing an XML document, the Oracle XML parsers "normalize" all text within the document; that is, there will only be one **Text** node for each block of text. Using DOM, you can create adjacent **Text** nodes that represent the contents of a given element without any intervening markup. If you subsequently print this and reparse, however, your text node would get merged with the previous one. You can, if you want, also do this yourself using the **normalize()** method available on the parent **Element** node.

Text nodes always serve as leaves in a DOM tree and do not have any children.

DocumentFragment

DocumentFragment is a lightweight or minimal **Document** object. **DocumentFragment** can represent a portion of an existing document tree or it can be a new fragment that we can insert into a document. When a **DocumentFragment** is inserted into a **Document** (or any other **Node** that may take children), the children of the **DocumentFragment**, not the **DocumentFragment** itself, are inserted into the **Node**. This makes the **DocumentFragment** useful when you want to create nodes that are siblings; the **DocumentFragment** acts as the parent of these nodes, so you can use the standard methods from the Node interface, such as **insertBefore** and **appendChild**.

A **DocumentFragment** can have the following kinds of children: **Element**, **ProcessingInstruction**, **Comment**, **Text**, **CDATASection**, and **EntityReference**.

ProcessingInstruction

A **ProcessingInstruction** object represents a processing instruction, which is used in XML as a way to keep processor-specific information in the text of the document.

DocumentType

The **DocumentType** object provides access to the list of entities and notations that are defined for the document. The **DocumentType** can be retrieved from a **Document** using the **getDoctype** method. If no DTD exists for the **Document**, a null value is returned. Currently, DOM does not allow you to edit **DocumentType** nodes; so if you need to change something in the DTD, the only way is to modify the text and re-parse the XML document.

Notation

Notation represents a notation declared in the DTD. A notation either declares, by name, the format of an unparsed entity or is used for formal declaration of **Processing Instruction** targets. You cannot edit **Notations** using DOM. A **Notation** does not have any parent, and it is retrieved from the **DocumentType**.

Entity

Entity represents an entity, either parsed or unparsed, in an XML document. Note, this models the entity itself, not the entity declaration. You cannot edit **Entity** nodes using DOM. If you want to make changes to the contents of an **Entity**, every related **EntityReference** node in the tree must be replaced by a clone of the **Entity**'s contents, and then the desired changes must be made to each of those clones instead. All the descendants of an **Entity** node are read-only. Important to note is **Entity** nodes do not have any parent and are not a part of the actual DOM tree. Entity nodes can be retrieved only from the **DocumentType**. Entities can have the following kinds of children: **Element**, **ProcessingInstruction**, **Comment**, **Text**, **CDATASection**, and **EntityReference**.

EntityReference

EntityReference is an XML entity reference. The Oracle XML parsers completely expand references to entities while building the DOM tree and, therefore, never create an **EntityReference** object. You can create and insert an **EntityReference** in the DOM tree, however. As with the Entity node, all descendants of the **EntityReference** are read-only and can have the same types of children.

Comment

Comment inherits from **CharacterData** and represents the content of an XML comment, that is, all the characters between the starting **<!—** and ending **-->**.

CDATASection

CDATASections are used to escape blocks of text containing characters that would otherwise be regarded as markup. The only delimiter recognized in a **CDATASection** is the]]> string that ends the **CDATASection**. **CDATASections** cannot be nested. The primary purpose is for including material such as XML fragments, without needing to escape all the delimiters. The **CDATASection** interface inherits from the **CharacterData** interface through the **Text** interface. Adjacent **CDATASections** nodes are not merged by use of the normalize method of the **Element** interface.

NodeList

NodeList represents an ordered collection of nodes. The children of a node can all be retrieved as a **NodeList** using the **getChildNodes** method. These are guaranteed to be in the order in which they were present in the original XML document.

NamedNodeMap

NamedNodeMap represents a collection of nodes that can be accessed by name. Note that **NamedNodeMap** does not inherit from **NodeList**; **NamedNodeMaps** are not maintained in any particular order. Objects contained in an object implementing **NamedNodeMap** may also be accessed by an ordinal index, but this is simply to allow convenient enumeration of the contents of a **NamedNodeMap** and does not imply that DOM specifies an order to these Nodes. As an example, the attributes of an XML element do not have an order; therefore, the **getAttributes** method returns a **NamedNodeMap**, rather than a **NodeList**.

The SAX Specification

What Is SAX?

Simple API for XML (SAX) is a standard interface for event-based XML parsing. A parser that supports SAX, such as the Oracle XML Parser for Java, reports parsing events (such as the start and end of elements) directly to the application through callbacks, and does not usually build an internal tree. The application implements handlers to deal with the different events much like handling events In a graphical user interface.

Using the simple, low-level access to an XML document provided by the SAX API, you can parse documents much larger than your available system memory. You can also construct your own data structures using your callback event handlers. This can be advantageous if you need to represent XML documents in a custom manner for your application to make use of them.

Consider the book-selling example discussed previously:

```
<booklist>
...

  <book isbn="1234-123456-1234">
    <title>C Programming Language</title>
    <author>Kernighan and Ritchie</author>
    <publisher>IEEE</publisher>
    <price>7.99</price>
  </book>
...

  <book isbn="1230-23498-2349879">
    <title>Emperor's New Mind</title>
    <author>Roger Penrose</author>
    <publisher>Oxford Publishing Company</publisher>
    <price>15.99</price>
  </book>
...

</booklist>
```

Assume you needed to locate the book *Emperor's New Mind* to find out its price. Because the number of books being sold could be large (the document could be megabytes in size), constructing and traversing an in-memory parse tree simply to locate this one piece of contextual information would be ineffective. The SAX API would enable you to find it in a single pass using little memory by breaking the structure of this document down into a series of linear events:

```
start document
start element: booklist

...

start element: book
start element: title
character: Emperor's New Mind
end element: title
start element: author
characters: Roger Penrose
end element: author
start element: publisher
characters: Oxford Publishing Company
end element: publisher
start element: price
characters: 15.99
```

```
end element: price
end element: book

...

end element: booklist
end document
```

You can then write a simple SAX application to handle these events. Without having to cache the entire document in memory or secondary storage, you can quickly sift through the document until you find what you are looking for. In this case, you continuously ignore all books whose title is not *Emperor's New Mind*. As soon as this book arrives, you can start paying close attention to the subsequent events to determine its price.

SAX Interfaces and Classes

The SAX API consists of a set of interfaces and classes. Some of these interfaces are implemented by a SAX parser (such as the Oracle XML parser for Java). Others need to be implemented/extended by your application. In addition, with SAX Level 2 the interfaces and methods now have namespace support, along with other functionality such as filters. Consequently, because of the namespace support, some of the interfaces were deprecated and replaced with new ones. SAX interfaces and classes are classified as follows.

Interfaces Implemented by a SAX Parser

Parser   This is the main interface to a SAX parser. The parser enables you to register handlers for callbacks, to set the locale for error reporting, and to start an XML parse. With SAX Level 2, this interface has been replaced by the **XMLReader** interface.

AttributeList   This interface enables you to iterate through an attribute list. With SAX Level 2, this interface has been replaced by the **Attributes** interface.

Locator   This interface enables you to find the current location in the XML source document.

Interfaces Implemented by Applications

DocumentHandler   This is the interface your applications will probably use the most. In many cases, **DocumentHandler** is the only interface you need to implement. With SAX Level 2, this interface has been replaced by the **ContentHandler** interface.

If your application provides an implementation of this interface, it will receive notification of basic document-related events, such as the start and end of an element.

ErrorHandler   If your application needs to use special error handling, then it must provide an implementation of this interface.

DTDHandler   If your application needs to work with notations and unparsed (binary) entities, it must implement this interface to receive notification of **NOTATION** and **ENTITY** declarations in your XML document.

EntityResolver   If your application needs to do redirection of URIs in documents (or other types of custom handling), it must provide an implementation of this interface.

Standard SAX Classes

InputSource   This class contains all the necessary information for a single input source, including a public identifier, a system identifier, a byte stream, and a character stream (as appropriate). Your application must instantiate at least one **InputSource** for the Parser, and the **EntityResolver** may instantiate others.

SAXException   This class represents a general SAX exception.

SAXParseException   This class represents a SAX exception tied to a specific point in an XML source document.

HandlerBase   This class provides default implementations for **DocumentHandler**, **ErrorHandler**, **DTDHandler**, and **EntityResolver**. With SAX Level 2, this interface has been replaced by the **DefaultHandler** interface. Your application can subclass this to simplify handler writing.

Optional Java-Specific Helper Classes

ParserFactory   Your application can use the static methods in this class to load SAX parsers dynamically at run time, based on the class name.

AttributeListImpl   Your application can use this convenience class to make a persistent copy of an **AttributeList**. With SAX Level 2, this interface has been replaced by the **AttributesImpl** interface.

LocatorImpl   Your application can use this convenience class to make a persistent snapshot of a Locator's values at a specific point in the parse.

The XML Namespace Specification

What Is an XML Namespace?

An *XML Namespace* is a collection of names identified by a URI reference that are used in XML documents as element types and attribute names. A namespace is useful when a single XML document contains elements and attributes that are defined for and used by multiple software modules.

A namespace is introduced in an XML document by defining a special namespace prefix and prepending that prefix (followed by a colon) to the names of elements and attributes. Namespace prefixes are attributes that are themselves defined using a special prefix called **xmlns**. For example, consider the following XML document:

```
<doc>
<title>Book List</title>
<author>Oracle XML Team</title>
<booklist>
   <book isbn="1234-5678-1234">
       <title>Oracle XML Handbook</title>
       <author>Oracle XML Team</title>
   </book>
   <book isbn="24345-564478-1344234">
       <title>The C programming language</title>
       <author>Kernighan and Ritchie</title>
   </book>
</booklist>
</doc>
```

In the previous document, two sets of tags have the name **title** and **author**. Clearly, one set refers to the document itself, while the other is specific to the **booklist**. Different actions might need to be taken by a software application that deals with this document depending on the tag. To facilitate this differentiation, you can use a namespace. If you introduce namespaces into the document, it will then look like this:

```
<doc xmlns:document="http://www.osborne.com/document"
     xmlns:books="http://www.osborne.com/books">
<document:title>Book List</document:title>
<document:author>Oracle XML Team</document:title>
<books:booklist>
```

```
<books:book books:isbn="1234-5678-1234">
    <books:title>Oracle XML Handbook</books:title>
    <books:author>Oracle XML Team</books:author>
</books:book>
<books:book books:isbn="24345-564478-1344234">
    <books:title>The C programming language</books:title>
    <books:author>Kernighan and Ritchie</books:author>
</books:book>
</books:booklist>
</doc>
```

Two namespaces having the prefixes **document** and **books** have been introduced in the previous document. These namespaces clearly distinguish between the tags and make it easy for an application familiar with www.osborne.com conventions to process them accordingly.

Another benefit of namespaces is modularity and reusability. Suppose you were writing an application to process book lists and you wanted to process them in the same way as www.osborne.com. You can easily reuse an existing software module that knows how to deal with markup (elements and attributes) in that namespace, within your application.

Namespace Terminology

The XML namespaces specification introduces the terms *Local Name*, *Qualified Name*, *Namespace Prefix*, and *Expanded Name*.

Local Name

This represents the name of the element or attribute without the prefix. In the previous example, **book**, **title**, **author**, **isbn**, and so forth, are considered Local Names.

Qualified Name

This represents the fully prefixed name. In the previous example, **document:title**, **books:book**, and so forth, are considered Local Names.

Namespace Prefix

This represents the namespace prefix declared using the special prefix **xmlns**. The previous example defined two namespace prefixes: **document** and **books**.

Expanded Name

This is the result of applying the namespace defined by the namespace prefix to the Qualified Name. For example, **books:booklist** could be expanded to http:// www.osborne.com/books:booklist. The expanded name is never seen in the XML document itself, but is conceptually important.

Namespace Attributes

Two kinds of namespace attributes exist: prefixed and default. A prefixed namespace attribute is of the form **nsprefix:attr**, where **nsprefix** is the namespace prefix defined previously. Once a prefix has been declared, it can be used to specify a namespace for any elements or attributes in the scope of the element where it was declared. You would, therefore, need to declare global prefixes, that is, prefixes you want to use everywhere in your document, as attributes of the root element.

The default namespace attribute is **xmlns**, which has the effect of specifying a default namespace for the entire scope of an element (including the element itself). This default does not apply to the attributes in the subtree, however. For instance, consider the booklist example:

```
<booklist xmlns="http://www.osborne.com/books>
    <book isbn="1234-5678-1234">
        <title>Oracle XML Handbook</title>
        <author>Oracle XML Team</title>
    </book>
    <book isbn="24345 564478-1344234">
        <title>The C programming language</title>
        <author>Kernighan and Ritchie</title>
    </book>
</booklist>
```

This has the effect of specifying that all the elements under **booklist** (**book**, **title**, **author**) are in the http://www.osborne.com/books Namespace. The attribute **isbn**, however, is not. Default namespaces can be specified at any level of the document and have the effect of overriding previous declarations. Setting **xmlns=""** has the effect of removing the default namespace declaration for a particular document subtree.

Namespaces complicate the determination of attribute uniqueness. For example, consider the following example:

```
<booklist xmlns:dollars="USA" xmlns:pounds="Britain">
    <book dollars:price="7.99" pounds:price="3.99">
        <title>The Code of the Woosters</title>
        <author>P.G. Wodehouse </title>
    </book>
</booklist>
```

The two **price** attributes should be considered different, even though they have the same Local Name, because their Expanded Names are different. The following document would not be considered well formed, however:

```
<booklist xmlns:dollars="USA" xmlns:currency="USA">
    <book dollars:price="7.99" currency:price="3.99">
```

```
        <title>The Code of the Woosters</title>
        <author>P.G. Wodehouse </title>
  </book>
</booklist>
```

Here, even though **dollars:price** and **currency:price** have different Qualified Names, they have the same Expanded Name, which means they are, in fact, the same attribute declared twice on the book element.

The XPath Specification

What Is XPath?

The *XML Path (XPath)* language provides a way to address parts of an XML document and some basic functionality for the manipulation of strings, numbers, and Booleans. Both XSLT and XPointer use it. XPath models an XML document as a tree of nodes. These nodes are of the following types: root nodes, element nodes, text nodes, attribute nodes, namespace nodes, processing instruction nodes, and comment nodes. XPath also defines a way to compute a string-value for each type of node. For some node types, the string-value is part of the node; for other types of node, the string-value is computed from the string-value of descendant nodes. For nodes that have a name, for example, element nodes, XPath models these as an Expanded name—that is, a name/value pair, consisting of a Local Name and a Namespace value.

XPath Expressions

When an XPath expression is evaluated, the result is an object of one of the types: *node-set* (an unordered collection of nodes without duplicates), *Boolean* (true or false), *number* (a floating-point number), or *string* (a sequence of UCS characters). Expression evaluation occurs with respect to a context. XSLT and XPointer specify how the context is determined for XPath expressions that are used in XSLT and XPointer, respectively.

Node-Sets

A *node-set* is typically produced by a location path expression that can be optionally filtered using a predicate expression. Location path expressions are extremely important because they are a powerful means of selecting nodes from an XML document tree. A location path can be specified both as a relative path (from the current context node) or an absolute path (from the root of the tree). They use special axis operators to specify the tree relationship between the nodes selected at various steps in the location path.

Booleans

Boolean objects can have only two values: true and false. These can result either by applying the Boolean function to another object or by evaluating AND, OR, or Equality expressions.

Numbers

A *number* represents a floating-point number. A number can have any double-precision 64-bit format IEEE 754 value. These include a special Not-a-Number (NaN) value, positive and negative infinity, and positive and negative zero. A number object can result by calling either the number function or due to evaluating a numeric expression, that is, an expression that contains one of the numeric operators, for example, +, , *, div, and so forth.

Strings

Strings consist of a sequence of zero or more characters. A single character in XPath thus corresponds to a single Unicode abstract character with a single corresponding Unicode scalar value. A String object usually results from calling the string function on an object.

Functions

XPath introduces a comprehensive library of functions that must be supported by XPath engines. These are classified into the following four groups: Node Set functions, String functions, Boolean functions, and Number functions.

Node Set Functions

The following are functions that operate on node sets:

last　This function returns a number equal to the context size from the expression evaluation context.

position　This function returns a number equal to the context position from the expression evaluation context.

count　The count function takes a node-set argument and returns the number of nodes in it.

id　This function selects elements by their unique ID, that is, the value of the attribute declared in the DTD as type ID.

local-name   This function accepts a node-set argument and returns the local part of the expanded-name of the node in the specified node-set that is first in document order.

namespace-uri   This function accepts a node-set argument and returns the namespace URI of the expanded-name of the node in the specified node-set that is first in document order.

name   This function accepts a node-set argument and returns the string containing the expanded-name of the node in the specified node-set that is first in document order.

String Functions

string   This function accepts an object argument and converts it to a string according to various rules.

concat   This function returns the concatenation of its arguments.

starts-with   This function accepts two argument strings. It returns true if the first argument string starts with the second argument string; otherwise, it returns false.

contains   This function accepts two argument strings. It returns true if the first argument string contains the second argument string; otherwise, it returns false.

substring-before   This function accepts two argument strings. It returns the substring of the first argument string that precedes the first occurrence of the second argument string in the first argument string, or it returns the empty string If the first argument string does not contain the second argument string.

substring-after   This function accepts two argument strings. It returns the substring of the first argument string that follows the first occurrence of the second argument string in the first argument string, or it returns the empty string if the first argument string does not contain the second argument string.

substring   This function accepts a string argument, a number position index, and a length and returns the substring of the first argument starting at the position specified in the second argument with length specified in the third argument. If the third argument is not specified, it returns the substring starting at the position specified in the second argument and continuing to the end of the string.

NOTE
The position of the first character is 1, not 0, as in many other programming languages, such as C or Java.

string-length   This function accepts an argument string and returns the number of characters in the string. If the argument is omitted, it defaults to the context node converted to a string—in other words, the string-value of the context node.

normalize-space   This function accepts an argument string and returns the argument string with white space normalized by stripping leading and trailing white space and replacing sequences of white space characters by a single space. If the argument is omitted, it defaults to the context node converted to a string—in other words, the string-value of the context node.

translate   This function accepts three argument strings and returns the first argument string with occurrences of characters in the second argument string replaced by the character at the corresponding position in the third argument string.

Boolean Functions

boolean   This function accepts an object argument and converts to a Boolean according to various rules.

not   This function returns true if its argument is false and returns false otherwise.

true   This function returns true.

false   This function returns false.

lang   This function accepts an argument string and returns true or false, depending on whether the language of the context node as specified by **xml:lang** attributes is the same as, or is a sublanguage of, the language specified by the argument string.

Number Functions

number   This function converts its object argument to a number according to various rules.

sum   This function accepts a node-set argument and returns the sum, for each node in the argument node-set, of the result of converting the string-values of the node to a number.

floor   This function accepts a number argument and returns the largest (closest to positive infinity) number that is not greater than the argument and is an integer.

ceiling   This function accepts a number argument and returns the smallest (closest to negative infinity) number that is not less than the argument and is an integer.

round   This function accepts a number argument and returns the number that is closest to the argument and is an integer.

XPath Nodes

XPath models an XML document as a tree of nodes of different types. These nodes are ordered by XPath in document order. This order specifies the root node is always the first node. Element nodes are ordered using the order of the occurrence of their start-tag in the XML (after expansion of entities). The element node and its attribute and namespace nodes occur before the children of the element. The namespace and attribute nodes are defined to occur before the attribute nodes.

Root nodes and element nodes have an ordered list of child nodes. Every node other than the root node has exactly one parent, which is either an element node or the root node. A root node or an element node is the parent of each of its child nodes. The descendants of a node are the children of the node and the descendants of the children of the node.

Root Node

The *root node* is the root of the tree. A root node does not occur except as the root of the tree. The *element node* for the document element is a child of the root node. The root node also has as children processing instruction and comment nodes for processing instructions, and comments that occur both in the prolog and after the end of the document element. The string-value of the root node is the concatenation of the string-values of all text node descendants of the root node in document order.

Element Nodes

An *element node* exists for every element in the document. The children of an element node are the element nodes, comment nodes, processing instruction nodes and text nodes for its content. The string-value of an element node is the concatenation of the string-values of all text node descendants of the element node in document order.

Attribute Nodes

Each element node has an associated set of *attribute nodes*. The element is the parent of each of these attribute nodes; however, an attribute node is not a child of its parent element. Note, this is different from DOM, which does not treat the element bearing an attribute as the parent of the attribute. An attribute node has a string-value, which is the normalized value of the attribute.

Namespace Nodes

Each element has an associated set of *namespace nodes*, one for each distinct namespace prefix in scope for the element, including the predefined **xml** prefix and one for the default namespace if one is in scope for the element. The element is the parent of each of these namespace nodes; however, a namespace node is not a child of its parent element. A namespace node has a string-value that is the namespace URI being bound to the namespace prefix.

Processing Instruction Nodes

A *processing instruction node* exists for every processing instruction, except for any processing instruction that occurs within the document type definition. The string-value of a processing instruction node is the part of the processing instruction following the target and any white space. It does not include the terminating **?>**.

Comment Nodes

A *comment node* exists for every comment, except for any comment that occurs within the document type definition. The string-value of a comment is the content of the comment, not including the opening **<!—** or the closing **-->**.

Text Nodes

Character data is grouped into text nodes in a normalized manner. The string-value of a text node is the character data. A text node always has at least one character of data. When a text node that contains a < character is written out as XML, the < character must be escaped by, for example, using **<** or including it in a CDATA section. Characters inside comments, processing instructions, and attribute values do not produce text nodes.

The XSLT Specification

What Is XSLT?

Extensible Stylesheet Transformation Language (XSLT) is used to describe rules for transforming a source tree into a result tree. The transformation is achieved by associating patterns with templates contained within a stylesheet. An XSLT processor matches patterns against elements in the source tree and instantiates associated templates to create various parts of the result tree. While constructing the result tree, the processor might filter and reorder elements from the source tree and add arbitrary structure, as specified by the XSLT transformation. The result tree is separate from the source tree—that is, no nodes are shared between the two, and its structure can be completely different from the structure of the source tree.

XSLT stylesheets are well-formed XML documents that contain elements and attributes in the XSLT namespace (**http://www.w3.org/1999/XSL/Transform**). These elements and attributes are used to provide instructions to an XSLT processor regarding the transformation it needs to effect. A stylesheet may also contain elements and attributes not in the XSLT namespace. XSLT processors typically interpret these as markup to be directly added to the result tree. An exception is the case of extension-elements, which serve as XSLT processor instructions and are in a separate namespace defined using a special mechanism.

XSLT instructions are contained within templates. The result tree is constructed by finding the template rule for the root node and instantiating its template. When a template is instantiated, each instruction within it is executed and replaced by the result tree fragment it creates. These instructions may select and process descendant source elements, which may entail instantiating other templates. It is important to note that elements are processed only when they have been selected by the execution of an instruction. XSLT uses the XPath language to select elements from the source tree and to do conditional processing.

An XSLT processor instantiates templates according to pattern-matching rules. In the process of finding an applicable template rule, more than one template rule may have a pattern that matches a given element. The processor then uses special conflict resolution logic (which uses template priorities) to ensure that the best template rule is applied.

Templates

Templates can be compared to procedures in a structural programming language. Templates contain programming logic expressed in terms of XSLT instructions that process the source tree and change the result tree. In some cases, even a single template can be used to transform your source tree into a result tree. In fact, XSLT has a special mechanism called *Literal Result Element as Stylesheet*, which enables you to embed all your XSLT processing logic in the body of the result document you want to create.

Templates can either be explicitly named or contain a match expression. When the XSLT processor encounters an **xsl:apply-templates** instruction, it attempts to match the nodes that were selected with the most appropriate template (using the match expression). Sometimes, more than one template might match. XSLT specifies a complex set of rules to help resolve this conflict by assigning priorities to various kinds of match expressions (patterns). Additionally, a template may itself specify an explicit priority, and the XSLT processor considers this while determining which template to instantiate.

XSLT Instructions

XSLT comes with a full-fledged set of instructions that enable you to use it almost like a programming language of its own. Conditional statements, variables, parameters, and loops exist, just as you would expect in any programming language. Obviously, XSLT is geared more to do transformations than to write general-purpose programs, but its rich instruction set makes it a powerful tool, indeed.

The various instructions you can use in XSLT, their syntax, and a brief explanation of what they do are described in the next few sections.

<xsl:apply-imports/>

This instruction, when encountered while processing a node within a template, directs the processor also to apply template rules imported into the stylesheet on that node. It has no attributes or content.

<xsl:apply-templates>

```
<xsl:apply-templates select = node-set-expression mode = qname>
          <!-- Content: (xsl:sort | xsl:with-param)* -->
</xsl:apply-templates>
```

This instruction directs the processor to instantiate a template that matches the XPath expression given by the value of the **select** attribute. In the absence of a **select** attribute, the instruction processes all the children of the current node, including text nodes. The optional **mode** attribute can be used to specify the mode of the template to be specified if a conflict occurred. This instruction can also be made to pass parameters to the template being instantiated (using **xsl:with-param**) and change the order of processing the selected nodes (as given by **xsl:sort**).

<xsl:attribute>

```
<xsl:attribute  name = { qname } namespace = { uri-reference }>
          <!-- Content: template -->
</xsl:attribute>
```

This instruction directs the processor to create a new attribute to elements created in the result tree. The name and namespace of the attribute can also be specified. The content of this instruction provides the value of the attribute. Note that processing this content should not result in the creation of any nontext nodes (as an attribute value can only consist of characters).

<xsl:attribute-set>

```
<xsl:attribute-set name = qname use-attribute-sets = qnames>
          <!-- Content: xsl:attribute* -->
</xsl:attribute-set>
```

This instruction can be used to specify a named set of attributes. The content of this instruction consists of a set of **xsl:attribute** instructions that specify the attributes. The attribute **use-attribute-sets** can be used to specify a space-separated list of other attribute-sets, which has the effect of adding **xsl:attribute** instructions contained by those attribute sets to the beginning of the current attribute set's content.

<xsl:call-template>

```
<xsl:call-template name = qname>
          <!-- Content: xsl:with-param* -->
</xsl:call-template>
```

This instruction is used to invoke named templates and, using **xsl:with-param**, can be made to pass in parameters.

<xsl:choose>

```
<xsl:choose>
          <!-- Content: (xsl:when+, xsl:otherwise?) -->
</xsl:choose>
```

This instruction is used to choose one among multiple alternatives. It consists of a sequence of **xsl:when** elements, followed by an optional **xsl:otherwise** element. Each **xsl:when** element has a single attribute, test, which specifies an XPath expression. The content of the **xsl:when** and **xsl:otherwise** elements is a template. When an **xsl:choose** element is processed, each of the **xsl:when** elements is tested in turn, by evaluating the expression and converting the resulting object to a Boolean as if by a call to the XPath Boolean function. The content of the first, and only the first, **xsl:when** element whose test is true is instantiated. If no **xsl:when** is true, the content of the **xsl:otherwise** element is instantiated. If no **xsl:when** element is true and no **xsl:otherwise** element is present, nothing is created.

<xsl:comment>

```
<xsl:comment>
          <!-- Content: template -->
</xsl:comment>
```

This instruction creates a new comment in the result tree.

<xsl:copy>

```
<xsl:copy use-attribute-sets = qnames>
          <!-- Content: template -->
</xsl:copy>
```

This instruction provides an easy way of copying the current node. It creates a copy of the current node but not its attributes or children. If the current node is an element, the value contained in the **use-attribute-sets** attribute can be used to create attributes for it (in the result tree). The content of this instruction is a template for the attributes and children of the created node.

<xsl:copy-of>

```
<xsl:copy-of select = expression />
```

This instruction enables you to copy a set of nodes resulting from evaluating the XPath expression specified by the select attribute to the result tree. If the result of the expression is not a set of nodes, it is converted to a string and copied as a text node.

<xsl:decimal-format>

```
<xsl:decimal-format
        name = qname   decimal-separator = char   grouping-separator = char
        infinity = string   minus-sign = char   NaN = string percent = char
        per-mille = char   zero-digit = char   digit = char
        pattern-separator = char />
```

This instruction declares a decimal-format, which controls the interpretation of a format pattern used by the format-number function. If a name attribute exists, then it declares a named decimal-format; otherwise, it declares the default decimal-format. Its attributes correspond to the methods on the JDK 1.1 DecimalFormatSymbols class. For each get/set method pair, an attribute is defined.

<xsl:element>

```
<xsl:element name = {qname}
              namespace = {uri-reference}
              use-attribute-sets = qnames>
          <!-- Content: template -->
</xsl:element>
```

This instruction creates a new element with the given tag name and namespace in the result tree. The **use-attribute-sets** attribute can be used to specify attributes on the new element. The content specifies the attributes and children of the newly created element.

<xsl:fallback>

```
<xsl:fallback>
          <!-- Content: template -->
  </xsl:fallback>
```

This instruction is executed when an XSLT processor performs fallback for an instruction element. If the instruction element has one or more **xsl:fallback** children, then the content of each of the **xsl:fallback** children is instantiated in sequence.

<xsl:for-each>

```
<xsl:for-each select = node-set-expression>
          <!-- Content: (xsl:sort*, template) -->
</xsl:for-each>
```

The content of this instruction is a template that gets instantiated for each node selected by the XPath expression specified by the select attribute. The order of processing these nodes can be modified by an optional **xsl:sort** instruction.

<xsl:if>

```
<xsl:if test = boolean-expression>
          <!-- Content: template -->
</xsl:if>
```

This instruction has a **test** attribute, which specifies an expression. The expression is evaluated, and the resulting object is converted to a Boolean as if by a call to the Boolean function. If the result is true, then the content template is instantiated; otherwise, nothing is created.

\<xsl:import>

```
<xsl:import href = uri-reference />
```

This instruction is used to import another stylesheet (specified by the value of the **href** attribute). The effect of this is that the templates and definitions contained in the imported stylesheet become visible in the importing stylesheet but have lower priority.

\<xsl:include>

```
<xsl:include href = uri-reference />
```

This instruction is used to include another stylesheet (specified by the value of the **href** attribute). The effect of this is that the templates and definitions contained in the included stylesheet become visible in the including stylesheet and are regarded as if they were defined in the latter.

\<xsl:key>

```
<xsl:key name = qname match = pattern use = expression />
```

This instruction is used to declare keys. The **name** attribute gives the name of the key, while the **use** attribute gives its value. This instruction gives information about the keys of any node that matches the pattern specified in the match attribute.

\<xsl:message>

```
<xsl:message terminate = "yes" | "no">
            <!-- Content: template -->
</xsl:message>
```

This instruction sends a message in a processor-specific way. For example, the Oracle XML Parser for Java simply prints the message to standard out. The content is instantiated to retrieve the value of the message. If the **terminate** attribute has the value yes, then the XSLT processor terminates processing after sending the message. The default value is No.

\<xsl:namespace>

```
<xsl:namespace-alias stylesheet-prefix = prefix | "#default"
                     result-prefix = prefix | "#default" />
```

This instruction declares that the namespace URI bound to the prefix specified by the **stylesheet-prefix** attribute is an alias for the namespace URI bound to the prefix specified by the **result-prefix** attribute. The **stylesheet-prefix** attribute specifies the namespace URI that appears in the stylesheet, and the **result-prefix** attribute specifies the corresponding namespace URI that appears in the result tree.

<xsl:number>

```
<xsl:number level = "single" | "multiple" | "any"
            count = pattern from = pattern
            value = number-expression
            format = { string } lang = { nmtoken }
            letter-value = { "alphabetic" | "traditional" }
            grouping-separator = { char }
            grouping-size = { number } />
```

This instruction is used to insert a formatted number into the result tree. The value of the number is specified by the expression contained by the **value** attribute. The expression is evaluated, and the resulting object is converted to a number, as if by a call to the **number** function. The number is rounded to an integer and then converted to a string using the various attributes specified. After conversion, the resulting string is inserted in the result tree.

```
<xsl:output method = "xml" | "html" | "text" | qname-but-not-ncname
            version = nmtoken
            encoding = string
            omit-xml-declaration = "yes" | "no"
            standalone = "yes" | "no"
            doctype-public = string
            doctype-system = string
            cdata-section-elements = qnames
            indent = "yes" | "no"
            media-type = string />
```

This instruction controls the output of the XSLT processor when it has been asked to output the result as a sequence of bytes rather than as a tree. Specific aspects of the output are controlled by its various attributes:

- **Method**   Identifies the overall method that should be used for outputting the result tree.

- **Version**   Specifies the version of the output method.

- **Indent**   Specifies whether the XSLT processor may add additional white space when outputting the result tree.

- **Encoding**   Specifies the preferred character encoding the XSLT processor should use to encode sequences of characters as sequences of bytes.

- **Media-type**   Specifies the media type (MIME content type) of the data that results from outputting the result tree.

- **Doctype-system**   Specifies the system identifier to be used in the document type definition.

- **Doctype-public**   Specifies the public identifier to be used in the document type definition.

- **Omit-xml-declaration**   Specifies whether the XSLT processor should output an XML declaration.

- **Standalone**   Specifies whether the XSLT processor should output a stand-alone document declaration.

- **Cdata-section-elements**   Specifies a list of the names of elements whose text node children should be output using CDATA sections.

\<xsl:param\>

```
<xsl:param name = qname select = expression>
        <!-- Content: template -->
</xsl:param>
```

This instruction declares a parameter to a template or stylesheet. Its name is given by the **name** attribute. A default value can be specified for this parameter using either the **select** attribute or its content. This value can be overridden when invoking the template or stylesheet.

\<xsl:preserve-space\>

```
<xsl:preserve-space elements = tokens />
```

This instruction specifies the elements in the source tree for which white space needs to be preserved.

\<xsl:processing-instruction\>

```
<xsl:processing-instruction name = {ncname}>
        <!-- Content: template -->
</xsl:processing-instruction>
```

This instruction creates a new Processing Instruction given by the **name** attribute. The target is specified by the content of this instruction.

<xsl:sort>

```
<xsl:sort select = string-expression lang = { nmtoken }
    data-type = {"text" | "number" | qname-but-not-ncname}
    order = {"ascending" | "descending"}
    case-order = {"upper-first" | lower-first"}/>
```

This instruction is used within **xsl:apply-templates** or **xsl:for-each** to specify an order for the nodes being processed. The first **xsl:sort** child specifies the primary sort key, and each subsequent instance, a secondary sort key. The sort key for each instruction is obtained by evaluating the XPath expression contained in the **select** attribute using the nodes being processed. By default, the string value of the node being processed will be used as the sort key. The attributes to this instruction can further modify the sort key:

- **Order** Specifies whether the strings should be sorted in ascending or descending order.

- **Lang** Specifies the language of the sort keys.

- **Data-type** Specifies the data type of the strings (usually either text or number).

- **Case-order** Has the value **upper-first** or **lower-first**; this applies when **data-type="text"** and specifies that uppercase letters should sort before lowercase letters or vice versa, respectively.

<xsl:strip-space>

```
<xsl:strip-space elements = tokens />
```

This instruction specifies the elements in the source tree for which white space should not be preserved.

<xsl:stylesheet>

```
<xsl:stylesheet id = id  extension-element-prefixes = tokens
        exclude-result-prefixes = tokens version = number>
        <!-- Content: (xsl:import*, top-level-elements) -->
</xsl:stylesheet>
```

This instruction represents an XSLT stylesheet. Its contents include templates and other instructions allowed at the top level. The version attribute, which is compulsory, specifies the version of XSLT being used. At press time, only version 1.0 is supported. The attribute **extension-element-prefixes** specifies namespace prefixes for special instructions understood by a processor. The attribute **exclude-result-prefixes** is used to specify namespace prefixes that should not get output to the result tree. This is useful when a stylesheet uses a namespace declaration only for the purposes of addressing the source tree. Specifying the prefix in the **exclude-result-prefixes** attribute avoids superfluous namespace declarations in the result tree.

<xsl:template>

```
<xsl:template  match = pattern  name = qname
               priority = number  mode = qname>
        <!-- Content: (xsl:param*, template) -->
</xsl:template>
```

This instruction specifies a template. The template could be either named using the **name** attribute or instantiated if the match pattern is associated with a particular node by the **xsl:apply-templates** instruction. A mode and priority can also be specified for the template. When a template is instantiated, its content is processed. All parameters are processed first by replacing their default values by any values that were passed in.

<xsl:text>

```
<xsl:text disable-output-escaping = "yes" | "no">
        <!-- Content: #PCDATA -->
</xsl:text>
```

This instruction is used to create a new text node in the result tree. Its content can only be characters. If the **disable-output-escaping** attribute is set to **"yes"**, a processor asked to output a stream of bytes outputs the character as is, rather than trying to represent it using a character reference. For example, the character < would be rendered by a processor as **<** if output escaping is not disabled.

<xsl:transform>

```
<xsl:transform id = id extension-element-prefixes = tokens
        exclude-result-prefixes = tokens  version = number>
        <!-- Content: (xsl:import*, top-level-elements) -->
</xsl:transform>
```

This instruction is a synonym for **xsl:stylesheet** and performs the same function.

<xsl:value-of>

```
<xsl:value-of  select = string-expression
               disable-output-escaping = "yes" | "no" />
```

This instruction evaluates the XPath expression given by the **select** attribute using the current nodes being processed and converts it to a string.

<xsl:variable>

```
<xsl:variable name = qname  select = expression>
          <!-- Content: template -->
 </xsl:variable>
```

This instruction specifies a variable whose name is given by the **name** attribute. Its value can be specified by either the **select** attribute or the content of the instruction. Note that this value cannot be changed in the same element scope.

<xsl:with-param>

```
<xsl:with-param  name = qname  select = expression>
          <!-- Content: template -->
</xsl:with-param>
```

This instruction is used within **xsl:apply-templates** or **xsl:call-template** to override the value of a template parameter given by the **name** attribute. Its value can be specified by either the **select** attribute or the content of the instruction.

XSLT Functions

XSLT specifies some additional functions to those in the XPath library.

document

This function provides a way of referencing data in an XML source besides the main one being referenced. It parses the referenced XML document and returns a set node representing it.

key

This function enables you to retrieve the value of keys declared within the XSLT stylesheet. Keys provide functionality similar to IDs, but have additional functionality, such as allowing multiword values and allowing multiple keys to have the same name.

format-number

This function converts a number to a string using given format strings.

current

This function returns a node-set that has the current node as its only member.

unparsed-entity-uri

This function returns the URI of the unparsed entity with the specified name in the DTD of same document as the context node.

generate-id

This function accepts a node-set argument and returns a string that uniquely identifies the node in the argument node-set that is first in document order.

system-property

This function accepts a name string and returns an object representing the value of the system property identified by the name. If no such system property exists, an empty string is returned.

element-available

This function returns true if its **string** argument is the name of an instruction. If the **name** argument has a namespace URI equal to the XSLT namespace URI, then it refers to an element defined by XSLT. Otherwise, it refers to an extension element. If the namespace URI is null, this function returns false.

function-available

This function returns true if its **string** argument is the name of a function in the function library. If the **name** argument has a non-null namespace URI, then it refers to an extension function; otherwise, it refers to a function defined by XPath or XSLT.

APPENDIX
B

W3C XML Schema Specification

What Is XML Schema?

In February 1999, a W3C Note detailing the requirements of the XML Schema Working Group was created. In this requirements document were an overview, design principles, and the structural and datatype and conformance requirements for the XML Schema language. In the overview, the XML Schema Working Group was chartered to look into a more informative constraint on the XML document than a DTD, namely one that would also, among other things

- Support both primitive and complex datatypes

- Support restrictions or extensions on datatypes

- Be written in XML

For example, the following snippet of a DTD:

```
<!ELEMENT book (title, author, publisher, price)>
<!ELEMENT title (#PCDATA)>
<!ELEMENT author (#PCDATA)>
<!ELEMENT publisher (#PCDATA)>
<!ELEMENT price (#PCDATA)*>
```

could appear in XML Schema format as the following XSD file:

```
<?xml version="1.0"?>
<xsd:schema xmlns:xsd="http://www.w3.org/2001/XMLSchema" xmlns:bk=http://
www.mypublishsite.com/book>
  <xsd:annotation>
    <xsd:documentation xml:lang="en">
    Possible XML Schema equivalent of a DTD shown in Listing 1.
    </xsd:documentation>
  </xsd:annotation>
  <xsd:element name="title" type="xsd:string" minOccurs="1" maxOccurs="1"/>
  <xsd:element name="author" type="xsd:string" minOccurs="1"
   maxOccurs="unbounded"/>
  <xsd:element name="publisher" type="xsd:string" minOccurs="1"
   maxOccurs="unbounded"/>
  <xsd:element name="price" type="xsd:string" minOccurs="0" maxOccurs="*"/>
  <xsd:element name="Book"/>
    <xsd:complexType>
      <xsd:sequence>
        <xsd:element ref="bk:title"/>
        <xsd:element ref="bk:author"/>
        <xsd:element ref="bk:publisher"/>
        <xsd:element ref="bk:price"/>
```

```
      </xsd:sequence>
    </xsd:complexType>
  </xsd:element>
</xsd:schema>
```

As the requirements succinctly put it:

"The purpose of a schema is to define and describe a class of XML documents by using these constructs to constrain and document the meaning, usage, and relationships of their constituent parts: datatypes, elements and their content, attributes and their values, entities and their contents, and notations. Schema constructs may also provide for the specification of implicit information such as default values. Schemas document their own meaning, usage, and function. Thus, the XML Schema language can be used to define, describe, and catalogue XML vocabularies for classes of XML documents."

In addition, the requirements document lists the following usage scenarios for how XML applications would benefit from an XML Schema:

- Publishing and syndication
- Electronic commerce transaction processing
- Supervisory control and data acquisition
- Traditional document authoring/editing governed by schema constraints
- Use schema to help query formulation and optimization
- Open and uniform transfer of data between applications, including databases
- Metadata Interchange

Finally, in addition to listing the design principles, the requirements document lists the structural requirements of what the XML Schema language must define, the datatype requirements of the language, and the conformance requirements.

The XML Schema Working Group then took these requirements and produced a number of working drafts, which culminated in the May 2001 W3C Recommendation for XML Schema. The XML Schema Recommendations consists of three parts: a Primer, Section 0; a Structures section, Section 1; and a Datatypes section, Section 2. The rest of the appendix will go over the Primer in some detail, which in a sense is a short illustration of what can be done with the mechanisms defined in the structures and datatypes sections of the XML Schema specifications.

Introduction

This part of the specifications is simply a very long introduction to XML Schemas, its construction, and usage. In Section 2 of the Primer, it goes over the basic concepts, going into detail about a purchase order schema. As an example of a complex type definition for an address, it shows the following definition:

```
<xsd:complexType name="USAddress">
  <xsd:sequence>
    <xsd:element name="name" type="xsd:string"/>
    <xsd:element name="street" type="xsd:string"/>
    <xsd:element name="city" type="xsd:string"/>
    <xsd:element name="state" type="xsd:string"/>
    <xsd:element name="zip" type="xsd:decimal"/>
  </xsd:sequence>
  <xsd:attribute name="country" type="xsd:NMTOKEN" fixed="US"/>
</xsd:complexType>
```

Important things to note are the XML Schema namespace prefixes even on the built-in datatypes such as string, and how a complex datatype is surrounded by an inner sequence tag. In addition, constraints such as **minOccurs** and **maxOccurs**, whose default values equal 1, could have been put on the name element for number of occurrences, as in the following:

```
<xsd:element name="name" type="xsd:string" minOccurs="1" maxoccurs="2"/>
```

Section 2 of the Primer also lists all the possible simple built-in datatypes for XML Schema, as you can see in Table B-1.

Simple Built-in Datatype	Example (Comments)
string	"this is a string"
normalizedString	"this could be another string" (Newlines, tabs, carriage returns, etc., are translated into spaces)
token	"this could be another string" (Newlines, tabs, carriage returns, etc., are translated into spaces; adjacent spaces are collapsed into 1 space; trailing and leading spaces are removed)

TABLE B-1.   *Simple Built-in Datatypes for XML Schema*

Simple Built-in Datatype	Example (Comments)
byte	-1, 126
unsignedByte	0, 126
base64Binary	GpM7
hexBinary	0fff
integer	-126789, 0, 126789 (integer values only)
positiveInteger	1, 2, 126789 (positive integer values only)
negativeInteger	-126789, -2, –1 (negative integer values only)
nonNegativeInteger	0, 1, 126789
nonPositiveInteger	-126789, -1, 0
int	-1, 0, 2, 126789675
unsigned int	0, 1, 1267896754
long	-1, -2, 0, 12678967543233
unsignedLong	0, 1, 3, 12678967543233
short	-1, -2, -5, 0, 1, 12678
unsignedShort	0, 1, 5, 12678
decimal	-1.2, 0, 1.2, 10000.00
float	-0, 0, 12, INF, NaN 1.0E-2 (32 bit floating point)
double	-0, 0, 13, INF, NaN 1.0E-20 (64 bit floating point)
boolean	true, false, 1, 0
time	21:21:21.000-01:00 (UTC)
dateTime	2001-01-01T121:21:21.000-01:00 (date + time zone + UTC)
duration	P1Y2M3DT10H30M12.0S (year, month, day, hour, minute, second)

TABLE B-1. *Simple Built-in Datatypes for XML Schema* (continued)

Simple Built-in Datatype	Example (Comments)
Date	2001-01-01
gMonth	--01—
gYear	2001
gYearMonth	2001-01
gDay	---31
gMonthDay	--01-01
Name	anyname (XML 1.0 Name)
QName	xsd:anyname (XML Namespace Qualified Name)
NCName	anyname (XML Namespace Qualified Name without the prefix and colon)
anyURI	http://www.oracle.com
language	en-US
ID	(an unique token, XML 1.0 ID attribute)
IDREF	(a token that matches an ID, XML 1.0 IDREF attribute)
IDREFS	(list of IDREF, XML 1.0 IDREFS attribute)
ENTITY	(XML 1.0 ENTITY attribute)
ENTITIES	(XML 1.0 ENTITIES attribute)
NOTATION	(XML 1.0 NOTATION attribute)
NMTOKEN	US, Canada (XML 1.0 NMTOKEN attribute)
NMTOKENS	US UK Canada (XML 1.0 NMTOKENS attribute)

TABLE B-1. *Simple Built-in Datatypes for XML Schema* (continued)

In addition, constraints or "facets" exist for these simple built-in datatypes. For example, the **string, normalizedString, token, base64Binary, hexBinary, Name, Qname, NCName, anyURI, language, ID, IDREFS, ENTITY, ENTITIES, NOTATION, NMTOKEN** and **NMTOKENS** datatypes all can take the following facets: **length, minLength, maxLength, pattern** (this can be a regular expression such as a date format like MM/DD/YYYY), **enumeration, whiteSpace**. The following number-oriented datatypes such as **byte, unsignedByte, integer, positiveInteger, negativeInteger, nonNegativeInteger, nonPositiveInteger, int, unsignedInt, long, unsignedLong, short, unsignedShort, decimal** can all take the following facets: **maxInclusive, maxExclusive, minInclusive, minExclusive, totalDigits, fractionDigits.**

User-defined types—e.g., *<mystates>CA NY MA</mystates>*—such as list types can be referred to via:

```
<xsd:simpleType name="mystates">
  <xsd:list itemType="Juanstates"/>
</xsd:simpleType>
```

Additionally, union types such as *<xsd:union memberTypes="mystates allstate"/ >*, complexTypes from simple types, mixed attributes for complexTypes to indicate data between child elements, anyType such as *type="xsd:anyType"* to indicate that the element could be of any datatype are allowed.

Annotations such as *<xsd:annotation>* are also allowed—they are simply mechanisms to embed documentation in the schema such as:

```
<xsd:annotation>
   <xsd:documentation xml:lang="en">
      hi there
   </xsd:documentation>
</xsd:annotation>
```

Finally, user-defined mechanisms such as an attribute group can be created to have a number of attributes associated with an element. This includes *<xsd:attributeGroup name="BookDelivery">* with a reference like *<xsd:attributeGroup ref="BookDelivery">* within the definition of the **complexType**.

In Section 3, target namespaces, unqualified local names, qualified local names, global vs. local declarations, and undeclared target namespaces are discussed. Sections 4 and 5 of the Primer go over the purchase order schema once again, detailing what can be changed using some of the advanced features.

APPENDIX

C

Other W3C Specifications

Other W3C Specifications

What Is XML Query?

In February 2001, a W3C Note detailing the requirements of the XML Schema Working Group was created. In this requirements document were goals, requirements, and usage scenarios for the W3C XML Query data model, algebra, and query language. Ultimately, according to the group's mission statement, they will "provide flexible query facilities to extract data from real and virtual documents on the Web, therefore finally providing the needed interaction between the Web world and the database world," making the access of collections of XML files similar to the access of databases.

The usage scenarios documented are queries on:

- Human-readable documents
- Data-oriented documents
- Mixed-model documents
- Administrative data
- Filtering streams
- Document Object Model (DOM)
- Native XML repositories and Web servers
- Catalog search
- Multiple syntactic environments

The general requirements of the XML Query Language pertain to:

- Human-readable Query Language syntax
- A declarative XML Query Language
- A protocol-independent XML Query Language
- An XML Query Language supportive of error conditions
- An XML Query Language supportive of updates
- An XML Query Language defined for finite instances

The general requirements of the XML Query Data Model pertain to:

- Reliance on an XML information set

- Datatypes
- Collections of documents and simple/complex values
- Support for references within an XML document and references from one XML document to another
- Schema availability
- Namespace awareness

The general requirements of the XML Query Functionality pertain to:

- Supported operations on all XML Query Data Model datatypes
- Text and element boundaries
- Universal and existential quantifiers
- Hierarchy and sequence
- Combination from different parts or multiple XML documents
- Aggregation of information
- Sorting
- Composition of operations
- NULL values
- Structural preservation
- Structural transformation
- References
- Identity preservation
- Operations on literal data—i.e., XML Query Data Model instances specified with the query
- Operations on names
- Operations on schemas
- Operations on schema PSV infoset
- Extensibility
- Environment information
- Closure

The June 2001 working draft of the XML Query Use Cases details the following scenarios with information about the description, the DTD, sample data, and queries and results:

- **XMP**   Experiences and exemplars
- **Tree**   Queries that preserve hierarchy
- **SEQ**   Queries based on sequence
- **R**   Access to relational data
- **SGML**   Standard Generalized Markup Language
- **Text**   Full-text search
- **NS**   Queries using namespaces
- **Parts**   Recursive Parts Explosion
- **REF**   Queries based on references
- **FNPARM**   Functions and parameters

In the XMP use case scenario, the following are the DTD and sample data:

```
<!ELEMENT bib (book*)>
<!ELEMENT book (title, (author+ | editor+), publisher, price)>
<!ATTLIST book year CDATA #REQUIRED>
<!ELEMENT title (#PCDATA)>
<!ELEMENT editor (last, first, affiliation)>
<!ELEMENT author (last, first)>
<!ELEMENT publisher (#PCDATA)>
<!ELEMENT last (#PCDATA)>
<!ELEMENT first (#PCDATA)>
<!ELEMENT affiliation (#PCDATA)>
<!ELEMENT publisher (#PCDATA)>
<!ELEMENT price (#PCDATA)*>
```

```
<bib>
    <book year="1994">
       <title>TCP/IP Illustrated</title>
       <author><last>Stevens</last><first>W.</first></author>
       <publisher>Addison-Wesley</publisher>
       <price> 65.95</price>
    </book>
    <book year="1992">
       <title>Advanced Programming in the Unix environment</title>
```

```
      <author><last>Stevens</last><first>W.</first></author>
      <publisher>Addison-Wesley</publisher>
      <price> 65.95</price>
   </book>
   <book year="2000">
      <title>Data on the Web</title>
      <author><last>Abiteboul</last><first>Serge</first></author>
      <author><last>Buneman</last><first>Peter</first></author>
      <author><last>Suciu</last><first>Dan</first></author>
      <publisher>Morgan Kaufmann Publishers</publisher>
      <price> 39.95</price>
   </book>
   <book year="1999">
<title>The Economics of Technology and Content for Digital TV</title>
<editor>
         <last>Gerberg</last><first>Darcy</first>
         <affiliation>CITI</affiliation>
      </editor>
      <publisher>Kluwer Academic Publishers</publisher>
      <price>129.95</price>
   </book>
</bib>
```

© 2001, W3C

To find pairs of books that have different titles but the same set of authors, the solution in XQUERY and the expected result would be:

```
<bib>
{
   FOR $book1 IN document("www.bn.com/bib.xml")//book,
       $book2 IN document("www.bn.com/bib.xml")//book
   WHERE $book1/title/text() > $book2/title/text()
   AND bags-are-equal($book1/author, $book2/author)
   RETURN
       <book-pair>
             {$book1/title}
             {$book2/title}
       </book-pair>
}
</bib>
```

```
<bib>
   <book-pair>
      <title>TCP/IP Illustrated</title>
      <title>Advanced Programming in the Unix environment</title>
   </book-pair>
</bib>
```

© 2001, W3C

In the TREE use case scenario, text is mixed with elements, and many elements are optional as specified in a different DTD and sample XML file. To prepare a nested table of contents listing all sections and titles and preserving the original attributes of each <section> element, the solution in XQUERY and the expected result are the following:

```
<toc>
{
    LET $b := document("book1.xml")
    RETURN
            Filter($b//section | $b//section/title
            | $b//section/title/text())
}
</toc>
```

```
<toc>
    <section id="intro" difficulty="easy">
       <title>Introduction</title>
       <section><title>Audience</title></section>
       <section><title>Web Data and the Two Cultures</title>
    </section>
    <section id="syntax" difficulty="medium">
       <title>A Syntax For Data</title>
       <section><title>Base Types</title></section>
       <section><title>Representing Relational Databases</title>
       <section><title>Representing Object Databases</title></section>
</toc>
```

© 2001, W3C

In the SEQ use case scenario, a number of queries based on the sequence in which elements appear in a document are shown, with a different DTD and sample XML file, namely those based on a medical report. To determine which two Instruments should be used first in the Procedure section of Report1, the solution in XQUERY and the expected result are the following:

```
FOR $s IN document("report1.xml")//section[section.title = "Procedure"]
RETURN ($s//instrument) [1 TO 2]
```

```
<instrument>using electrocautery.</instrument>
<instrument>electrocautery</instrument>
```

© 2001, W3C

In the R use case scenario, access to data stored in relational databases, with a possible DTD and sample XML file, is highlighted. To find how many items were auctioned (auction ended) in March 1999, the solution in XQUERY and the expected result are the following:

```
LET $item := document("items.xml")//item_tuple
    [end_date >= date("1999-03-01") AND end_date <= date("1999-03-31")]
RETURN
    <item_count>
    {
        count($item)
    }
    </item_count>
```

```
<item_count>3</item_count>
```

© 2001, W3C

In the SGML use case scenario, the DTD and example document have been translated from SGML to XML, and a number of queries are illustrated. To locate all sections with a title that has "is SGML" in it, the solution in XQUERY and the expected result are the following:

```
<result>
{
    //section[contains(string(.//title), "is SGML")]
}
</result>
```

```
Elements whose start-tags are on lines 51, 60
```

© 2001, W3C

In the TEXT use case scenario, the DTD and example document are based on company profiles and a set of news documents to be searched via queries. To locate all news items where the name "Foobar Corporation" appears in the title, the solution in XQUERY and the expected result are the following:

```
//news_item/title[contains(./text(), "Foobar Corporation")]
```

```
<title>Foobar Corporation releases its new line of Foo products today</title>
<title>Foobar Corporation is suing Gorilla Corporation for patent
infringement</title>
```

© 2001, W3C

In the NS use case scenario, the DTD and example document provide illustrations of a variety of queries on namespace-qualified names. To select the title of each record that is for sale, the solution in XQUERY and the expected result are the following:

```
NAMESPACE music = "http://www.example.org/music/records"
<Q2>
{
  //music:title
}
</Q2>
```

```
<Q2 xmlns:music="http://www.example.org/music/records">
    <music:title>In a Silent Way</music:title>
    <music:title>Think of One … </music:title>
</Q2>
```

The PARTS use case scenario illustrates how a recursive query could be used to construct a structured document of some dept from relational tables stored in a database. In the REF use case scenario, queries based on references are illustrated, with the example DTD and XML file representing a database in which references play a significant role. Finally, the FNPARM use case scenario explores some of the ways that functions can be defined and invoked, with uses of certain datatypes from XML Schema.

What Is XML Protocol?

According to the XML Protocol working group, its goal is to "develop technologies which allow two or more peers to communicate in a distributed environment, using XML as its encapsulation language. Solutions developed by this activity allow a layered architecture on top of an extensible and simple messaging format, which provides robustness, simplicity, reusability and interoperability." What have been developed thus far are the July 2001 XML Protocol Abstract Model working draft and the SOAP V1.2 working draft.

The XML Protocol Abstract Model working draft provides a "framework for XML-based messaging systems, which includes specifying a message envelope format and a method for data serialization, directly mainly, but not exclusively, to RPC applications, and conforming to the usability principles." As part of the architecture, an XMLP Application exists, meaning it is a client or user of the services provided by the XML Protocol Layer. The XML Protocol (XMLP) Application may initiate or respond to one-way or two-way response operations; XML Protocol Handlers are encapsulated within XMLP Applications. In addition, the XMLP Layer is "an abstraction that provides services or operations that transfers packages of XML Protocol Blocks between peer XML Protocol Applications via zero or more XML Protocol

Intermediaries." Some of the XMLP layer primitives include XMLP_UnitData send, receive, status, and forward operations, which are primitive capabilities or services offered by the XMLP layer and are modeled as event sequences crossing the boundaries between XMLP processors and applications.

On the other hand, "SOAP version 1.2 is a lightweight protocol for exchange of information in a decentralized, distributed environment. It is an XML based protocol that consists of four parts, an envelope that defines a framework for describing what is in a message and how to process it, a set of encoding rules for expressing instances of application-defined data types, a convention for representing remote procedure calls and responses and a binding convention for exchanging messages using an underlying protocol. SOAP can potentially be used in combination with a variety of other protocols; however, the only bindings defined describe how to use SOAP in combination with HTTP and the experimental HTTP Extension Framework."

Examples of SOAP message envelopes for a call request and a response follow:

```
POST /StockQuote HTTP/1.1
Host: www.stockquoteserver.com
Content-Type: text/xml; charset="utf-8"
Content-Length: nnnn
SOAPAction: "http://example.org/2001/06/quotes"

<env:Envelope
   xmlns:env="http://www.w3.org/2001/06/soap-envelope">
   <env:Header>
       <t:Transaction
           xmlns:t="http://example.org/2001/06/tx"
           env:encodingStyle="http://www.w3.org/2001/06/soap-encoding"
           env:mustUnderstand="1">
           5
       </t:Transaction>
   </env:Header>
   <env:Body>
       <m:GetLastTradePrice
           env:encodingStyle="http://www.w3.org/2001/06/soap-encoding"
           xmlns:m="http://example.org/2001/06/quotes">
           <m:symbol>ORCL</m:symbol>
       </m:GetLastTradePrice>
   </env:Body>
</env:Envelope>


HTTP/1.1 200 OK
Content-Type: text/xml; charset="utf-8"
Content-Length: nnnn

<env:Envelope
```

```
xmlns:env="http://www.w3.org/2001/06/soap-envelope">
<env:Header>
    <t:Transaction
        xmlns:t="http://example.org/2001/06/tx"
        xmlns:xsi="http://www.w3.org/2001/XMLSchema-instance"
        xmlns:xs=http://www.w3.org/2001/XMLSchema
        xsi:type="xs:int"
        env:encodingStyle="http://www.w3.org/2001/06/soap-encoding"
        env:mustUnderstand="1">
        5
    </t:Transaction>
</env:Header>
<env:Body>
    <m:GetLastTradePriceResponse
        env:encodingStyle="http://www.w3.org/2001/06/soap-encoding"
        xmlns:m="http://example.org/2001/06/quotes">
        <Price>93.5</Price>
    </m:GetLastTradePriceResponse>
</env:Body>
</env:Envelope>
```

GLOSSARY

API   *See* application program interface.

application program interface (API)   A set of public programmatic interfaces that consist of a language and message format to communicate with an operating system or other programmatic environment, such as databases, Web servers, JVMs, and so forth. These messages typically call functions and methods available for application development.

application server   A server designed to host applications and their environments, permitting server applications to run. A typical example is OAS, which is able to host Java, C, C++, and PL/SQL applications in cases in which a remote client controls the interface. *See also* Oracle Application Server.

attribute   A property of an element that consists of a name and a value separated by an equal sign and contained within the start-tags after the element name. In this example, **<Price units='USD'>5</Price>**, *price* is the attribute and *USD* is its value, which must be in single or double quotes. Attributes may reside in the document or DTD. Elements may have many attributes, but their retrieval order is not defined.

BFILES   External binary files that exist outside the database tablespaces residing in the operating system. BFILES are referenced from the database semantics and are also known as *External LOBs*.

Binary Large Object (BLOB)   A Large Object data type whose content consists of binary data. Additionally, this data is considered *raw* because its structure is not recognized by the database.

BLOB   *See* Binary Large Object.

Business-to-Business (B2B)   A term describing the communication between businesses in the selling of goods and services to each other. The software infrastructure to enable this is referred to as an *exchange*.

Business-to-Consumer (B2C)   A term describing the communication between businesses and consumers in the selling of goods and services.

callback   A programmatic technique in which one process starts another and then continues. The second process then calls the first as a result of an action, value, or other event. This technique is used in most programs that have a user interface to allow continuous interaction.

cartridge   A stored program in Java or PL/SQL that adds the necessary functionality for the database to understand and manipulate a new data type. Cartridges interface through the Extensibility Framework within Oracle 8 or 8i. interMedia Text is just such a cartridge, adding support for reading, writing, and searching text documents stored within the database.

CDATA   *See* character data.

CGI   *See* Common Gateway Interface.

character data (CDATA)   Text in a document that should not be parsed is put within a CDATA section. This allows for the inclusion of characters that would otherwise have special functions, such as &, <, >, and so on. CDATA sections can be used in the content of an element or in attributes. The syntax for element content is **<![CDATA[*put the text here*]]>**.

Character Large Object (CLOB)   The LOB data type whose value is composed of character data corresponding to the database character set. A CLOB may be indexed and searched by the interMedia Text search engine.

child element   An element that is wholly contained within another, which is referred to as its *parent element.* For example, **<Parent><Child></Child></Parent>** illustrates a child element nested within its parent element.

Class Generator   A utility that accepts an input file and creates a set of output classes that have corresponding functionality. In the case of the XML Class Generator, the input file is a DTD and the output is a series of classes that can be used to create XML documents conformant with the DTD.

CLASSPATH   The operating system environmental variable that the JVM uses to find the classes it needs to run applications.

client/server   The term used to describe the application architecture in which the actual application runs on the client but accesses data or other external processes on a server across a network.

CLOB   *See* Character Large Object.

command line   The interface method in which the user enters commands at the command interpreter's prompt.

Common Gateway Interface (CGI)   The generic acronym for the programming interfaces enabling Web servers to execute other programs and pass their output to HTML pages, graphics, audio, and video sent to browsers.

Common Object Request Broker API (CORBA)   An Object Management Group standard for communicating between distributed objects across a network. These self-contained software modules can be used by applications running on different platforms or operating systems. CORBA objects and their data formats and functions are defined in the *Interface Definition Language (IDL),* which can be compiled in a variety of languages, including Java, C, C++, Smalltalk, and COBOL.

Common Oracle Runtime Environment (CORE)   The library of functions written in C that provides developers the ability to create code that can be easily ported to virtually any platform and operating system.

CORBA   *See* Common Object Request Broker API.

Database Access Descriptor (DAD)   A DAD is a named set of configuration values used for database access. A DAD specifies information such as the database name or the SQL*Net V2 service name; the ORACLE_HOME directory; and the NLS configuration information, such as language, sort type, and date language.

datagram   A text fragment, which may be in XML format, that is returned to the requester embedded in an HTML page from a SQL query processed by the XSQL Servlet.

DBURITYPE   The Oracle9i datatype used for storing instances of the datatype that permits XPath-based navigation of database schemas.

DOCTYPE   The term used as the tag name designating the DTD or its reference within an XML document. For example, **<!DOCTYPE person SYSTEM "person.dtd">** declares the root element name as *person* and an external DTD as *person.dtd* in
the file system. Internal DTDs are declared within the DOCTYPE declaration.

Document Object Model (DOM)   An in-memory tree-based object representation of an XML document that enables programmatic access to its elements and attributes. The DOM object and its interface is a W3C recommendation.

Document Type Definition (DTD)   A set of rules that define the allowable structure of an XML document. DTDs are text files that derive their format from

SGML and can be included in an XML document either by using the DOCTYPE element or by using an external file through a DOCTYPE reference.

DOM   *See* Document Object Model.

DTD   *See* Document Type Definition.

element   The basic logical unit of an XML document that may serve as a container for other elements, such as children, data, and attributes and their values. Elements are identified by start-tags, **<name>**, and end-tags, **</name>**; or in the case of empty elements, **<name/>**.

empty element   An element without text content or child elements. It may only contain attributes and their values. Empty elements are of the form **<name/>** or **<name></name>** where there is no space between the tags.

Enterprise Java Bean (EJB)   An independent program module that runs within a JVM on the server. CORBA provides the infrastructure for EJBs, and a container layer provides security, transaction support, and other common functions on any supported server.

entity   A string of characters that may represent either another string of characters or special characters that are not part of the document's character set. Entities and the text that is substituted for them by the parser are declared in the DTD.

Extensible Markup Language (XML)   An open standard for describing data developed by the W3C, using a subset of the SGML syntax and designed for Internet use. Version 1.0 is the current standard, having been published as a W3C Recommendation in February 1998.

Extensible Stylesheet Language (XSL)   The language used within stylesheets to transform or render XML documents. There are two W3C recommendations covering XSL stylesheets—XSL Transformations (XSLT) and XSL Formatting Objects (XSLFO).

Extensible Stylesheet Language Formatting Object (XSLFO)   The W3C standard specification that defines an XML vocabulary for specifying formatting semantics.

Extensible Stylesheet Language Transformation (XSLT)   The XSL W3C standard specification that defines a transformation language to convert one XML document into another.

Extract   The Oracle9i SQL operator that retrieves fragments of XML documents stored as XMLTYPE.

Existnode   The Oracle9i SQL operator that returns a TRUE or FALSE based upon the existence of an XPATH within an XMLTYPE.

Functional Index   A database index that, when created, permits the results of known queries to be returned much more quickly.

HASPATH   The Oracle9i SQL operator that is part of Oracle Text and used for querying XMLTYPE datatypes for the existence of a specific XPath.

HTML   *See* Hypertext Markup Language.

HTTP   *See* Hypertext Transport Protocol.

HTTPURITYPE   The Oracle9i datatype used for storing instances of the datatype that permits XPath-based navigation of database schemas in remote databases.

hypertext   The method of creating and publishing text documents in which users can navigate among other documents or graphics by selecting words or phrases designated as hyperlinks.

Hypertext Markup Language (HTML)   The markup language used to create the files sent to Web browsers and that serves as the basis of the World Wide Web. HTML's next version will be called *xHTML* and will be an XML application.

Hypertext Transport Protocol (HTTP)   The protocol used for transporting HTML files across the Internet between Web servers and browsers.

IDE   *See* Integrated Development Environment.

iFS   *See* Internet File System.

INPATH   The Oracle9i SQL operator that is part of Oracle Text and is used for querying XMLTYPE datatypes for searching for specific text within a specific XPath.

instantiate   A term used in object-based languages such as Java and C++ to refer to the creation of an object of a specific class.

Integrated Development Environment (IDE)   A set of programs designed to aid in the development of software run from a single user interface. JDeveloper is an IDE for Java development as it includes an editor, compiler, debugger, syntax checker, help system, and so on, to permit Java software development through a single user interface.

interMedia   The term used to describe the collection of complex data types and their access within Oracle8i. These include text, video, time-series, and spatial data types.

Internet File System (iFS)   The Oracle file system and Java-based development environment that either runs inside the Oracle8i database or on a middle tier and provides a means of creating, storing, and managing multiple types of documents in a single database repository.

Internet Inter-ORB Protocol (IIOP)   The protocol used by CORBA to exchange messages on a TCP/IP network such as the Internet.

Java   A high-level programming language developed and maintained by Sun Microsystems in which applications run in a virtual machine known as a JVM. The JVM is responsible for all interfaces to the operating system. This architecture permits developers to create Java applications and applets that can run on any operating system or platform that has a JVM.

Java Bean   An independent program module that runs within a JVM, typically for creating user interfaces on the client. The server equivalent is called an *Enterprise Java Bean (EJB)*. *See also* Enterprise Java Bean.

Java Database Connectivity (JDBC)   The programming API that enables Java applications to access a database through the SQL language. JDBC drivers are written in Java for platform independence but are specific to each database.

Java Developer's Kit (JDK)   The collection of Java classes, run-time environment, compiler, debugger, and usually source code for a version of Java that makes up a Java development environment. JDKs are designated by versions, and Java 2 is used to designate versions from 1.2 onward.

Java Runtime Environment (JRE)   The collection of compiled classes that make up the Java virtual machine on a platform. JREs are designated by versions, and Java 2 is used to designate versions from 1.2 onward.

Java Server page (JSP)   An extension to the servlet functionality that enables a simple programmatic interface to Web pages. JSPs are HTML pages with special tags and embedded Java code that is executed on the Web or application server providing dynamic functionality to HTML pages. JSPs are actually compiled into servlets when first requested and run in the server's JVM.

Java virtual machine (JVM)   The Java interpreter that converts the compiled Java bytecode into the machine language of the platform and runs it. JVMs can run on a client, in a browser, in a middle tier, on a Web, on an application server such as OAS, or in a database server such as Oracle8*i*.

JDBC   *See* Java Database Connectivity.

JDeveloper   Oracle's Java IDE that enables application, applet, and servlet development and includes an editor, compiler, debugger, syntax checker, help system, and so on. In version 3.1, JDeveloper has been enhanced to support XML-based development by including the Oracle XDK for Java integrated for easy use along with XML support in its editor.

JDK   *See* Java Developer's Kit.

JServer   The Java Virtual Machine that runs within the memory space of the Oracle8*i* database. In Oracle8*i* Release 1, the JVM was Java 1.1 compatible, whereas Release 2 is Java 1.2 compatible.

JVM   *See* Java virtual machine.

LAN   *See* local area network.

Large Object (LOB)   The class of SQL data type that is further divided into *Internal LOBs* and *External LOBs*. Internal LOBs include BLOBs, CLOBS, and NCLOBs, while External LOBs include BFILES. *See also* BFILES, Binary Large Object, Character Large Object, and Non-Character Large Objects.

listener   A separate application process that monitors the input process.

LOB   *See* Large Object.

local area network (LAN)   A computer communication network that serves users within a restricted geographical area. LANs consist of servers, workstations, communications hardware (routers, bridges, network cards, and so on), and a network operating system.

namespace　The term to describe a set of related element names or attributes within an XML document. The namespace syntax and its usage are defined by a W3C Recommendation. For example, the **<xsl:apply-templates/>** element is identified as part of the XSL namespace. Namespaces are declared in the XML document or DTD before they are used by using the attribute syntax **xmlns:xsl="http://www.w3.org/ TR/WD-xsl"**.

NCLOB　*See* Non-Character Large Object.

node　In XML, the term used to denote each addressable entity in the DOM tree.

Non-Character Large Object　The LOB data type whose value is composed of character data corresponding to the database character set.

NOTATION　In XML, the definition of a content type that is not part of those understood by the parser. These types include audio, video, and other multimedia.

n-tier　The designation for a computer communication network architecture that consists of one or more tiers made up of clients and servers. Typically, *two-tier systems* are made up of one client level and one server level. A *three-tier system* utilizes two server tiers, typically a database server as one and a Web or application server along with a client tier.

OAS　*See* Oracle Application Server.

OASIS　*See* Organization for the Advancement of Structured Information.

object-relational　The term to describe a relational database system that can also store and manipulate higher-order data types, such as text documents, audio, video files, and user-defined objects.

Object Request Broker (ORB)　Software that manages message communication between requesting programs on clients and between objects on servers. ORBs pass the action request and its parameters to the object and return the results. Common implementations are CORBA and EJBs. *See also* Common Object Request Broker API and Enterprise Java Bean.

Object View　A tailored presentation of the data contained in one or more object tables or other views. The output of an Object View query is treated as a table. Object Views can be used in most places where a table is used.

OIS　*See* Oracle Integration Server.

Oracle Application Server (OAS)   The Oracle server that integrates all the core services and features required for building, deploying, and managing high-performance, n-tier, transaction-oriented Web applications within an open standards framework.

ORACLE_HOME   The operating system environmental variable that identifies the location of the Oracle database installation for use by applications.

Oracle Integration Server (OIS)   The Oracle server product that serves as the messaging hub for application integration. OIS contains an Oracle8i database with AQ and Oracle Workflow and interfaces to applications using Oracle Message Broker to transport XML-formatted messages between them.

ORB   *See* Object Request Broker.

Organization for the Advancement of Structured Information (OASIS)   An organization of members chartered with promoting public information standards through conferences, seminars, exhibits, and other educational events. XML is a standard that OASIS is actively promoting, as it is doing with SGML.

parent element   An element that surrounds another element, which is referred to as its child element. For example, **<Parent><Child></Child></Parent>** illustrates a parent element wrapping its child element.

Parsed Character Data (PCDATA)   The element content consisting of text that should be parsed but is not part of a tag or nonparsed data.

parser   In XML, a software program that accepts as input an XML document and determines whether it is well formed and, optionally, valid. The Oracle XML parser supports both SAX and DOM interfaces.

PCDATA   *See* Parsed Character Data.

PL/SQL   The Oracle procedural database language that extends SQL to create programs that can be run within the database.

prolog   The opening part of an XML document containing the XML declaration and any DTD or other declarations needed to process the document.

PUBLIC   The term used to specify the location on the Internet of the reference that follows.

renderer   A software processor that outputs a document in a specified format.

result set The output of a SQL query consisting of one or more rows of data.

root element The element that encloses all the other elements in an XML document and is between the optional prolog and epilog. An XML document is only permitted to have one root element.

SAX *See* Simple API for XML.

schema The definition of the structure and data types within a database. It can also be used to refer to an XML document that supports the XML Schema W3C recommendation.

Secure Sockets Layer (SSL) The primary security protocol on the Internet, which utilizes a public key/private key form of encryption between browsers and servers.

Server-Side Include (SSI) The HTML command used to place data or other content into a Web page before sending it to the requesting browser.

servlet A Java application that runs in a server, typically a Web or application server, and performs processing on that server. Servlets are the Java equivalent of CGI scripts.

session The active connection between two tiers.

SGML *See* Structured Generalized Markup Language.

Simple API for XML (SAX) An XML standard interface provided by XML parsers and used by event-based applications.

SQL *See* Structured Query Language.

SSI *See* Server-Side Include.

SSL *See* Secure Sockets Layer.

SOAP *See* Simple Object Access Protocol.

Simple Object Access Protocol A lightweight, XML-based protocol for exchanging information in a decentralized, distributed environment.

Structured Generalized Markup Language (SGML)   An ISO standard for defining the format of a text document, implemented using markup and DTDs.

Structured Query Language (SQL)   The standard language used to access and process data in a relational database.

Stylesheet   In XML, the term used to describe an XML document that consists of XSL processing instructions used by an XSL processor to transform or format an input XML document into an output one.

SYSTEM   The term used to specify the location on the host operating system of the reference that follows.

SYS_XMLAGG   The Oracle9i native SQL function that returns as a single XML document the results of a passed-in SYS_XMLGEN SQL query. This can also be used to instantiate an XMLTYPE.

SYS_XMLGEN   The Oracle9i native SQL function that returns as an XML document the results of a passed-in SQL query. This can also be used to instantiate an XMLTYPE.

tag   A single piece of XML markup that delimits the start or end of an element. Tags start with < and end with >. In XML, there are start-tags (**<name>**), end-tags (**</name>**), and empty tags (**<name/>**).

TCP/IP   *See* Transmission Control Protocol/Internet Protocol.

thread   In programming, a single message or process execution path within an operating system that supports multiple operating systems, such as Windows, UNIX, and Java.

Transmission Control Protocol/Internet Protocol (TCP/IP)   The communications network protocol that consists of the TCP, which controls the transport functions, and IP, which provides the routing mechanism. It is the standard for Internet communications.

TransViewer   The Oracle term used to describe the Oracle XML Java beans included in the XDK for Java. These beans include an XML Source Viewer bean, Tree Viewer bean, DOM Builder bean, Transformer bean, and TransViewer bean.

Uniform Resource Identifier (URI)   The address syntax that is used to create URLs and XPaths.

Uniform Resource Locator (URL)   The address that defines the location and route to a file on the Internet. URLs are used by browsers to navigate the World Wide Web and consist of a protocol prefix, an optional port number, a domain name, directory and subdirectory names, and the filename. For example, http://technet.oracle.com:80/tech/xml/index.htm specifies the location and path a browser will travel to find Oracle Technology Network's XML site on the World Wide Web.

URI   *See* Uniform Resource Identifier.

URL   *See* Uniform Resource Locator.

user interface (UI)   The combination of menus, screens, keyboard commands, mouse clicks, and command language that defines how a user interacts with a software application.

valid   The term used to refer to an XML document when its structure and element content are consistent with that declared in its referenced or included DTD.

W3C   *See* World Wide Web Consortium (W3C).

WAN   *See* wide area network.

Web Request Broker (WRB)   The cartridge within OAS that processes URLs and sends them to the appropriate cartridge.

well formed   The term used to refer to an XML document that conforms to the syntax of the XML version declared in its XML declaration. This includes having a single root element, properly nested tags, and so forth.

wide area network (WAN)   A computer communication network that serves users within a wide geographic area, such as a state or country. WANs consist of servers, workstations, communications hardware (routers, bridges, network cards, and so on), and a network operating system.

Working Group (WG)   The committee within the W3C that is made up of industry members that implement the recommendation process in specific Internet technology areas.

World Wide Web Consortium (W3C)   An international industry consortium started in 1994 to develop standards for the World Wide Web. It is located at **http://www.w3c.org**.

wrapper   The term describing a data structure or software that *wraps around* other data or software, typically to provide a generic or object interface.

XLink   The XML Linking language consisting of the rules governing the use of hyperlinks in XML documents. These rules are being developed by the XML Linking Group under the W3C recommendation process.

XML   *See* Extensible Markup Language.

XML Developer's Kit (XDK)   The set of libraries, components, and utilities that provide software developers with the standards-based functionality to XML enable their applications. In the case of the Oracle XDK for Java, the kit contains an XML parser, an XSLT processor, the XML Class Generator, the TransViewer Java beans, and the XSQL Servlet.

XML query   The W3C's effort to create a standard for the language and syntax to query XML documents.

XML Schema   The W3C's effort to create a standard to express simple data types and complex structures within an XML document.

XPath   The open standard syntax for addressing elements within a document used by XSL and XPointer. XPath is currently a W3C recommendation.

XPointer   The term and W3C recommendation to describe a reference to an XML document fragment. An XPointer can be used at the end of an XPath-formatted URI.

XSL   *See* Extensible Stylesheet Language.

XSLFO   *See* Extensible Stylesheet Language Formatting Object.

XSLT   *See* Extensible Stylesheet Language Transformation.

XSQL   The designation used by the Oracle Servlet providing the ability to produce dynamic XML documents from one or more SQL queries, which optionally transform the document in the server using an XSL stylesheet.

Index

Z

INTERNATIONAL CONTACT INFORMATION

AUSTRALIA
McGraw-Hill Book Company Australia Pty. Ltd.
TEL +61-2-9417-9899
FAX +61-2-9417-5687
http://www.mcgraw-hill.com.au
books-it_sydney@mcgraw-hill.com

CANADA
McGraw-Hill Ryerson Ltd.
TEL +905-430-5000
FAX +905-430-5020
http://www.mcgrawhill.ca

GREECE, MIDDLE EAST,
NORTHERN AFRICA
McGraw-Hill Hellas
TEL +30-1-656-0990-3-4
FAX +30-1-654-5525

MEXICO (Also serving Latin America)
McGraw-Hill Interamericana Editores S.A. de C.V.
TEL +525-117-1583
FAX +525-117-1589
http://www.mcgraw-hill.com.mx
fernando_castellanos@mcgraw-hill.com

SINGAPORE (Serving Asia)
McGraw-Hill Book Company
TEL +65-863-1580
FAX +65-862-3354
http://www.mcgraw-hill.com.sg
mghasia@mcgraw-hill.com

SOUTH AFRICA
McGraw-Hill South Africa
TEL +27-11-622-7512
FAX +27-11-622-9045
robyn_swanepoel@mcgraw-hill.com

UNITED KINGDOM & EUROPE
(Excluding Southern Europe)
McGraw-Hill Education Europe
TEL +44-1-628-502500
FAX +44-1-628-770224
http://www.mcgraw-hill.co.uk
computing_neurope@mcgraw-hill.com

ALL OTHER INQUIRIES Contact:
Osborne/McGraw-Hill
TEL +1-510-549-6600
FAX +1-510-883-7600
http://www.osborne.com
omg_international@mcgraw-hill.com

GET YOUR FREE SUBSCRIPTION
TO ORACLE MAGAZINE

Oracle Magazine is essential gear for today's information technology professionals. Stay informed and increase your productivity with every issue of *Oracle Magazine*. Inside each free bimonthly issue you'll get:

- Up-to-date information on Oracle Database, E-Business Suite applications, Web development, and database technology and business trends
- Third-party news and announcements
- Technical articles on Oracle Products and operating environments
- Development and administration tips
- Real-world customer stories

IF THERE ARE OTHER ORACLE USERS AT YOUR LOCATION WHO WOULD LIKE TO RECEIVE THEIR OWN SUBSCRIPTION TO ORACLE MAGAZINE, PLEASE PHOTOCOPY THIS FORM AND PASS IT ALONG.

Three easy ways to subscribe:

① Web

Visit our Web site at www.oracle.com/oraclemagazine. You'll find a subscription form there, plus much more!

② Fax

Complete the questionnaire on the back of this card and fax the questionnaire side only to +1.847.647.9735.

③ Mail

Complete the questionnaire on the back of this card and mail it to P.O. Box 1263, Skokie, IL 60076-8263

Oracle Publishing

FREE SUBSCRIPTION

signature (required)   date

X

name   title

company   e-mail address

street/p.o. box

city/state/zip or postal code   telephone

country   fax

YOU MUST ANSWER ALL NINE QUESTIONS BELOW.

① WHAT IS THE PRIMARY BUSINESS ACTIVITY OF YOUR FIRM AT THIS LOCATION?
(check one only)

- N 01 Application Service Provider
- N 02 Communications
- N 03 Consulting, Training
- N 04 Data Processing
- N 05 Education
- N 06 Engineering
- N 07 Financial Services
- N 08 Government (federal, local, state, other)
- N 09 Government (military)
- N 10 Health Care
- N 11 Manufacturing (aerospace, defense)
- N 12 Manufacturing (computer hardware)
- N 13 Manufacturing (noncomputer)
- N 14 Research & Development
- N 15 Retailing, Wholesaling, Distribution
- N 16 Software Development
- N 17 Systems Integration, VAR, VAD, OEM
- N 18 Transportation
- N 19 Utilities (electric, gas, sanitation)
- N 98 Other Business and Services

② WHICH OF THE FOLLOWING BEST DESCRIBES YOUR PRIMARY JOB FUNCTION?
(check one only)

Corporate Management/Staff
- N 01 Executive Management (President, Chair, CEO, CFO, Owner, Partner, Principal)
- N 02 Finance/Administrative Management (VP/Director/ Manager/Controller, Purchasing, Administration)
- N 03 Sales/Marketing Management (VP/Director/Manager)
- N 04 Computer Systems/Operations Management (CIO/VP/Director/ Manager MIS, Operations)

IS/IT Staff
- N 05 Systems Development/ Programming Management
- N 06 Systems Development/ Programming Staff
- N 07 Consulting
- N 08 DBA/Systems Administrator
- N 09 Education/Training
- N 10 Technical Support Director/Manager
- N 11 Other Technical Management/Staff
- N 98 Other

③ WHAT IS YOUR CURRENT PRIMARY OPERATING PLATFORM? (select all that apply)

- N 01 Digital Equipment UNIX
- N 02 Digital Equipment VAX VMS
- N 03 HP UNIX
- N 04 IBM AIX
- N 05 IBM UNIX
- N 06 Java
- N 07 Linux
- N 08 Macintosh
- N 09 MS-DOS
- N 10 MVS
- N 11 NetWare
- N 12 Network Computing
- N 13 OpenVMS
- N 14 SCO UNIX
- N 15 Sequent DYNIX/ptx
- N 16 Sun Solaris/SunOS
- N 17 SVR4
- N 18 UnixWare
- N 19 Windows
- N 20 Windows NT
- N 21 Other UNIX
- N 98 Other
- 99 N None of the above

④ DO YOU EVALUATE, SPECIFY, RECOMMEND, OR AUTHORIZE THE PURCHASE OF ANY OF THE FOLLOWING? (check all that apply)

- N 01 Hardware
- N 02 Software
- N 03 Application Development Tools
- N 04 Database Products
- N 05 Internet or Intranet Products
- 99 N None of the above

⑤ IN YOUR JOB, DO YOU USE OR PLAN TO PURCHASE ANY OF THE FOLLOWING PRODUCTS? (check all that apply)

Software
- N 01 Business Graphics
- N 02 CAD/CAE/CAM
- N 03 CASE
- N 04 Communications
- N 05 Database Management
- N 06 File Management
- N 07 Finance
- N 08 Java
- N 09 Materials Resource Planning
- N 10 Multimedia Authoring
- N 11 Networking
- N 12 Office Automation
- N 13 Order Entry/Inventory Control
- N 14 Programming
- N 15 Project Management
- N 16 Scientific and Engineering
- N 17 Spreadsheets
- N 18 Systems Management
- N 19 Workflow

Hardware
- N 20 Macintosh
- N 21 Mainframe
- N 22 Massively Parallel Processing
- N 23 Minicomputer
- N 24 PC
- N 25 Network Computer
- N 26 Symmetric Multiprocessing
- N 27 Workstation

Peripherals
- N 28 Bridges/Routers/Hubs/Gateways
- N 29 CD-ROM Drives
- N 30 Disk Drives/Subsystems
- N 31 Modems
- N 32 Tape Drives/Subsystems
- N 33 Video Boards/Multimedia

Services
- N 34 Application Service Provider
- N 35 Consulting
- N 36 Education/Training
- N 37 Maintenance
- N 38 Online Database Services
- N 39 Support
- N 40 Technology-Based Training
- N 98 Other
- 99 N None of the above

⑥ WHAT ORACLE PRODUCTS ARE IN USE AT YOUR SITE? (check all that apply)

Software
- N 01 Oracle9*i*
- N 02 Oracle9*i* Lite
- N 03 Oracle8
- N 04 Oracle8*i*
- N 05 Oracle8*i* Lite
- N 06 Oracle7
- N 07 Oracle9*i* Application Server
- N 08 Oracle9*i* Application Server Wireless
- N 09 Oracle Data Mart Suites
- N 10 Oracle Internet Commerce Server
- N 11 Oracle inter Media
- N 12 Oracle Lite
- N 13 Oracle Payment Server
- N 14 Oracle Video Server
- N 15 Oracle Rdb

Tools
- N 16 Oracle Darwin
- N 17 Oracle Designer
- N 18 Oracle Developer
- N 19 Oracle Discoverer
- N 20 Oracle Express
- N 21 Oracle JDeveloper
- N 22 Oracle Reports
- N 23 Oracle Portal
- N 24 Oracle Warehouse Builder
- N 25 Oracle Workflow

Oracle E-Business Suite
- N 26 Oracle Advanced Planning/Scheduling
- N 27 Oracle Business Intelligence
- N 28 Oracle E-Commerce
- N 29 Oracle Exchange
- N 30 Oracle Financials
- N 31 Oracle Human Resources
- N 32 Oracle Interaction Center
- N 33 Oracle Internet Procurement
- N 34 Oracle Manufacturing
- N 35 Oracle Marketing
- N 36 Oracle Order Management
- N 37 Oracle Professional Services Automation
- N 38 Oracle Projects
- N 39 Oracle Sales
- N 40 Oracle Service
- N 41 Oracle Small Business Suite
- N 42 Oracle Supply Chain Management
- N 43 Oracle Travel Management
- N 44 Oracle Treasury

Oracle Services
- N 45 Oracle.com Online Services
- N 46 Oracle Consulting
- N 47 Oracle Education
- N 48 Oracle Support
- N 98 Other
- 99 N None of the above

⑦ WHAT OTHER DATABASE PRODUCTS ARE IN USE AT YOUR SITE? (check all that apply)

- N 01 Access
- N 02 Baan
- N 03 dbase
- N 04 Gupta
- N 05 IBM DB2
- N 06 Informix
- N 07 Ingres
- N 98 Other
- N 08 Microsoft Access
- N 09 Microsoft SQL Server
- N 10 PeopleSoft
- N 11 Progress
- N 12 SAP
- N 13 Sybase
- N 14 VSAM
- 99 N None of the above

⑧ DURING THE NEXT 12 MONTHS, HOW MUCH DO YOU ANTICIPATE YOUR ORGANIZATION WILL SPEND ON COMPUTER HARDWARE, SOFTWARE, PERIPHERALS, AND SERVICES FOR YOUR LOCATION? (check only one)

- N 01 Less than $10,000
- N 02 $10,000 to $49,999
- N 03 $50,000 to $99,999
- N 04 $100,000 to $499,999
- N 05 $500,000 to $999,999
- N 06 $1,000,000 and over

⑨ WHAT IS YOUR COMPANY'S YEARLY SALES REVENUE? (please choose one)

- N 01 $500,000,000 and above
- N 02 $100,000,000 to $500,000,000
- N 03 $50,000,000 to $100,000,000
- N 04 $5,000,000 to $50,000,000
- N 05 $1,000,000 to $5,000,000

123101

About the CD-ROM

Inside the back cover you will find the CD-ROM that accompanies *Oracle9i XML Handbook*, by Ben Chang, Mark Scardina, and Stefan Kiritzov. The CD-ROM contains two different types of information:

- The complete production set of Oracle9i XML Developer's Kits for Solaris and Windows NT in a form that can be installed using the included Oracle Universal Installer. These kits include the demos and sample code included in the book.

- The source code, images, and data files for the XML FAQ Case Study described in Chapter 9 is included as an **xdkdemo.tar.gz** archive. This code can be used on Unix and Windows NT.

ORACLE SOFTWARE LICENSE AGREEMENT

YOU SHOULD CAREFULLY READ THE FOLLOWING TERMS AND CONDITIONS BEFORE BREAKING THE SEAL ON THE DISC ENVELOPE. AMONG OTHER THINGS, THIS AGREEMENT LICENSES THE ENCLOSED SOFTWARE TO YOU AND CONTAINS WARRANTY AND LIABILITY DISCLAIMERS. BY USING THE DISC AND/OR INSTALLING THE SOFTWARE, YOU ARE ACCEPTING AND AGREEING TO THE TERMS AND CONDITIONS OF THIS AGREEMENT. IF YOU DO NOT AGREE TO THE TERMS OF THIS AGREEMENT, DO NOT BREAK THE SEAL OR USE THE DISC. YOU SHOULD PROMPTLY RETURN THE PACKAGE UNOPENED.

LICENSE: ORACLE CORPORATION ("ORACLE") GRANTS END USER ("YOU" OR "YOUR") A NON-EXCLUSIVE, NON-TRANSFERABLE DEVELOPMENT ONLY LIMITED USE LICENSE TO USE THE ENCLOSED SOFTWARE AND DOCUMENTATION ("SOFTWARE") SUBJECT TO THE TERMS AND CONDITIONS, INCLUDING USE RESTRICTIONS, SPECIFIED BELOW.

You shall have the right to use the Software (a) only in object code form, (b) for development purposes only in the indicated operating environment for a single developer (one person) on a single computer, (c) solely with the publication with which the Software is included, and (d) solely for Your personal use and as a single user.

You are prohibited from and shall not (a) transfer, sell, sublicense, assign or otherwise convey the Software, (b) timeshare, rent or market the Software, (c) use the Software for or as part of a service bureau, (d) distribute the Software in whole or in part, (e) use the Programs for or as part of any third party training, and/or (f) use the Programs for any other use not expressly permitted by this Agreement. Any attempt to transfer, sell, sublicense, assign, or otherwise convey any of the rights, duties or obligations hereunder is void. You are prohibited from and shall not use the Software for internal data processing operations, processing data of a third party or for any commercial or production use. If You desire to use the Software for any use other than the development use allowed under this Agreement, You must contact Oracle, or an authorized Oracle reseller, to obtain the appropriate licenses. You are prohibited from and shall not cause or permit the reverse engineering, disassembly, decompilation, modification or creation of derivative works based on the Software. You are prohibited from and shall not copy or duplicate the Software except as follows: You may make one copy of the Software in machine readable form solely for back-up purposes. No other copies shall be made without Oracle's prior written consent. You are prohibited from and shall not: (a) remove any product identification, copyright notices, or other notices or proprietary restrictions from the Software, or (b) run any benchmark tests with or of the Software. This Agreement does not authorize You to use any Oracle name, trademark or logo.

COPYRIGHT/OWNERSHIP OF SOFTWARE: The Software is the confidential and proprietary product of Oracle and is protected by copyright and other intellectual property laws. You acquire only the right to use the Software and do not acquire any rights, express or implied, in the Software or media containing the Software other than those specified in this Agreement. Oracle, or its licensor, shall at all times, including but not limited to after termination of this Agreement, retain all rights, title, and interest, including intellectual property rights, in the Software and media.

WARRANTY DISCLAIMER: THE SOFTWARE IS PROVIDED "AS IS" AND ORACLE SPECIFICALLY DISCLAIMS ALL WARRANTIES OF ANY KIND, EITHER EXPRESS OR IMPLIED, INCLUDING, BUT NOT LIMITED TO, THE IMPLIED WARRANTIES OF MERCHANTABILITY, SATISFACTORY QUALITY AND FITNESS FOR A PARTICULAR PURPOSE. ORACLE DOES NOT WARRANT, GUARANTEE OR MAKE ANY REPRESENTATIONS REGARDING THE USE, OR THE RESULTS OF THE USE, OF THE SOFTWARE IN TERMS OF CORRECTNESS, ACCURACY, RELIABILITY, CURRENTNESS, OR OTHERWISE, AND DOES NOT WARRANT THAT THE OPERATION OF THE SOFTWARE WILL BE UNINTERRUPTED OR ERROR FREE. ORACLE EXPRESSLY DISCLAIMS ALL WARRANTIES NOT STATED HEREIN, NO ORAL OR WRITTEN INFORMATION OR ADVICE GIVEN BY ORACLE OR OTHERS SHALL CREATE A WARRANTY OR IN ANY WAY INCREASE THE SCOPE OF THIS LICENSE, AND YOU MAY NOT RELY ON ANY SUCH INFORMATION OR ADVICE.

LIMITATION OF LIABILITY: IN NO EVENT SHALL ORACLE BE LIABLE FOR ANY DIRECT, INDIRECT, INCIDENTAL, SPECIAL, OR CONSEQUENTIAL DAMAGES, OR DAMAGES FOR LOSS OF PROFITS, REVENUE, DATA OR DATA USE, INCURRED BY YOU OR ANY THIRD PARTY, WHETHER IN AN ACTION IN CONTRACT OR TORT, EVEN IF ORACLE HAS BEEN ADVISED OF THE POSSIBILITY OF SUCH DAMAGES. SOME JURISDICTIONS DO NOT ALLOW THE EXCLUSION OF IMPLIED WARRANTIES OR LIMITATION OR

EXCLUSION OF LIABILITY FOR INCIDENTAL OR CONSEQUENTIAL DAMAGES SO THE ABOVE EXCLUSIONS AND LIMITATION MAY NOT APPLY TO YOU.

TERMINATION: You may terminate this license at any time by discontinuing use of and destroying the Software together with any copies in any form. This license will also terminate if You fail to comply with any term or condition of this Agreement. Upon termination of the license, You agree to discontinue use of and destroy the Software together with any copies in any form. The Warranty Disclaimer, Limitation of Liability and Export Administration sections of this Agreement shall survive termination of this Agreement.

NO TECHNICAL SUPPORT: Oracle is not obligated to provide and this Agreement does not entitle You to any updates or upgrades to, or any technical support or phone support for, the Software.

EXPORT ADMINISTRATION: You acknowledge that the Software, including technical data, is subject to United States export control laws, including the United States Export Administration Act and its associated regulations, and may be subject to export or import regulations in other countries. You agree to comply fully with all laws and regulations of the United States and other countries ("Export Laws") to assure that neither the Software, nor any direct products thereof, are (a) exported, directly or indirectly, in violation of Export Laws, either to countries or nationals that are subject to United States export restrictions or to any end user who has been prohibited from participating in the Unites States export transactions by any federal agency of the United States government; or (b) intended to be used for any purposes prohibited by the Export Laws, including, without limitation, nuclear, chemical or biological weapons proliferation. You acknowledge that the Software may include technical data subject to export and re-export restrictions imposed by United States law.

RESTRICTED RIGHTS: The Software is provided with Restricted Rights. Use, duplication, or disclosure of the Software by the United State government is subject to the restrictions set forth in the Rights in Technical Data and Computer Software Clauses in DFARS 252.227-7013(c)(1)(ii) and FAR 52.227-19(c)(2) as applicable. Manufacturer is Oracle Corporation, 500 Oracle Parkway, Redwood City, CA, 94065.

MISCELLANEOUS: This Agreement and all related actions thereto shall be governed by California law. Oracle may audit Your use of the Software. If any provision of this Agreement is held to be invalid or unenforceable, the remaining provisions of this Agreement will remain in full force.

YOU ACKNOWLEDGE THAT YOU HAVE READ THIS AGREEMENT, UNDERSTAND IT, AND AGREE TO BE BOUND BY ITS TERMS AND CONDITIONS. YOU FURTHER AGREE THAT IT IS THE COMPLETE AND EXCLUSIVE STATEMENT OF THE AGREEMENT BETWEEN ORACLE AND YOU.

Oracle is a registered trademark of Oracle Corporation.

MUST REGISTER FOR ORACLE TECHNOLOGY NETWORK

Oracle Technology Network puts you in touch with the online community behind the software that powers the internet. Download the latest development programs and sample code. Engage in discussions with the web's leading technologists. Keep connected with the latest insights and resources you need to stay ahead. Membership is FREE, and so is the latest development software. Before proceeding to use the software, **you must join OTN today at http://www.oracle.com/books/**.